Christian Higher Education
in Canada

McMaster Divinity College Press
McMaster General Studies Series, Volume 12

Christian Higher Education in Canada

Challenges and Opportunities

edited by

STANLEY E. PORTER AND BRUCE G. FAWCETT

PICKWICK *Publications* · Eugene, Oregon

CHRISTIAN HIGHER EDUCATION IN CANADA
Challenges and Opportunities

McMaster General Studies Series, Volume 12
McMaster Divinity College Press

Pickwick Publications
An Imprint of Wipf and Stock Publishers
199 W. 8th Ave., Suite 3
Eugene, OR 97401

McMaster Divinity College Press
1280 Main Street West
Hamilton, ON, Canada L8S 4K1

www.wipfandstock.com

PAPERBACK ISBN: 978-1-7252-8280-3
HARDCOVER ISBN: 978-1-7252-8278-0
EBOOK ISBN: 978-1-7252-8281-0

Cataloguing-in-Publication data:

Names: Porter, Stanley E., editor. | Fawcett, Bruce G., editor.

Title: Christian higher education in Canada : challenges and opportunities / edited by Stanley E. Porter and Bruce G. Fawcett.

Description: Eugene, OR: Pickwick Publications, 2020. | McMaster General Studies Series 12. | Includes bibliographical references and index.

Identifiers: ISBN 978-1-7252-8280-3 (paperback). | ISBN 978-1-7252-8278-0 (hardcover) | ISBN 978-1-7252-8281-0 (ebook).

Subjects: LCSH: Christian universities and colleges. | Christian education.

Classification: LC427 C15 2020 (print). | LC427 (ebook).

Manufactured in the U.S.A.   11/10/20

Contents

Preface

Toronto 2018 Symposium on Christian Higher Education

THE TORONTO 2018 SYMPOSIUM on Christian Higher Education was held October 26–27, 2018, at the Crowne Plaza Toronto Airport hotel. This symposium, the first of its kind in Canada, was planned and hosted by Christian Higher Education Canada (CHEC), an association of 35 Canadian Bible colleges, Christian universities, and theological seminaries. The mission of CHEC is to advance the efficiency and effectiveness of Christian higher education at member schools, including fostering institutional cooperation, and to raise public awareness of the value of Christian higher education in Canada. All member institutions are accredited and degree granting, and would describe themselves as "Christ-centered." These institutions are also affiliates of The Evangelical Fellowship of Canada (EFC).

The idea for a symposium emerged out of a discussion by the Board of Directors of CHEC on ways to highlight the contribution of the Christian higher education movement to the development of Canada during the country's first 150 years since Confederation took place in 1867. The movement itself traces its roots to 1828 and the founding of Horton Academy in Wolfville, Nova Scotia, a Christian educational expression that continues today through CHEC member institution Acadia Divinity College, a Baptist theological seminary affiliated with Acadia University. In the years since 1828 the Christian higher education movement has grown and developed, providing education and a life transforming experience to more than 200,000 Canadians and others who have studied in its institutions.

The goal of the symposium was to provide an opportunity for leaders in the Canadian Christian higher education movement to reflect deeply on its development, current reality, and future possibilities.

After initial discussion by the CHEC Board, a Council of Reference representing the breadth of member institutions was formed to give shape to the symposium. Its members included Dr. Kevin Flatt (Redeemer University College), Dr. Bruce Guenther (ACTS Seminary, Trinity Western University), Dr. David Guretski (EFC), Dr. David Johnson (Providence University College and Theological Seminary), Dr. Stanley Porter (McMaster Divinity College), Dr. Anna Robbins (Acadia Divinity College), and Dr. John Stackhouse (Crandall University).

The final shaping of the program and the leadership of the symposium was provided by a Steering Committee comprising CHEC Executive Director Dr. Justin Cooper, CHEC Board Chair Dr. Bruce Fawcett (Crandall University), CHEC Board member Dr. Aileen Van Ginkel (EFC), and CHEC staff person Nita Stemmler.

The symposium attracted more than 50 attendees, including those who presented 12 parallel-session papers and three plenary talks.

This volume is a collection of the papers and plenary talks, which have been edited in light of participants' feedback, and designed to share the content of the symposium with a wider audience. We trust that it will be helpful to students, faculty, staff, Board members, and supporters of member institutions as well as interested individuals and scholars.

Stanley E. Porter
Bruce G. Fawcett

List of Contributors

Douglas H. Berg, Columbia Bible College, Abbotsford, BC, Canada

Renee Embrée, Acadia Divinity College, Wolfville, NS, Canada

Bruce G. Fawcett, Crandall University, Moncton, NB, Canada

Kevin N. Flatt, Redeemer University College, Ancaster, ON, Canada

Leslie J. Francis, University of Warwick, Coventry, UK

Tracy Freeze, Crandall University, Moncton, NB, Canada

Rick Hiemstra, Evangelical Fellowship of Canada, Toronto, ON, Canada

Elfrieda Lepp-Kaethler, Providence University College and Theological Seminary, Otterburne, MB, Canada

Ted Newell, Crandall University, Moncton, NB, Canada

Stanley E. Porter, McMaster Divinity College, Hamilton, ON, Canada

Nicki Rehn, Coast Mountain College, Terrace, BC, Canada

Adam D. Rudy, McMaster Divinity College, Hamilton, ON, Canada

Catherine Rust-Akinbolaji, Providence University College and Theological Seminary, Otterburne, MB, Canada

Linda Schwartz, Primacorp Ventures, New Westminster, BC, Canada

Victor Shepherd, Wycliffe College, Toronto, ON, Canada

John G. Stackhouse, Jr., Crandall University, Moncton, NB, Canada

Phil C. Zylla, McMaster Divinity College, Hamilton, ON, Canada

Christian Higher Education in Canada

Challenges and Opportunities—An Introduction

STANLEY E. PORTER AND BRUCE G. FAWCETT

THE CHRISTIAN HIGHER EDUCATION movement in Canada has a lengthy and storied history full of tales of various origins and forms of expression. Some of today's institutions of higher education date back to the earliest days of Canada, some of them even before confederation, and even to the beginnings of formalized advanced education within what would become the nation. There are also a variety of other higher education institutions that have arisen since that time, many of them associated with other intellectual and cultural movements that swept across the nation as it developed from a British colony into a member of the commonwealth and matured into the nation as it stands today. As a result, Canadian Christian higher education currently represents a relatively vast and admittedly complex array of institutions. Not only do these institutions have their own histories, often filled with stories of struggle against a variety of odds, but they have their present reality in which they must function. This present situation sits somewhat uncomfortably amidst the more general terrain of higher education itself, even though in many ways they share a common, complex history and origin. The movement of Christian higher education divides its world into three major sectors. These include Bible colleges, universities and university colleges (depending upon the province in which one is located), and seminaries and graduate schools. The sectors are not equal in size or scope, with some obvious imbalances. The largest number of institutions is Bible colleges, but the largest number of students attend universities and university colleges. Sometimes seminaries are embedded within one of the other types of institutions, although many of them are freestanding and relate to their constituencies in varied ways often influenced by denominational connections. All of these institutions, however, are looking to the future. The future, as it always appears, is not necessarily clear and certainly not free of real and potential dangers, even if it holds promise for each of the groups of constituent educational entities. Bible colleges face various tensions related to their status in relation to universities, while some universities and university colleges, besides some tensions with secular universities, also face questions from their constituencies regarding their positions and commitments. Seminaries find themselves in an environment that claims to need an educated professional clergy less than at any time in the last several centuries, so that they are forced to creatively develop new programs and means of delivery. All share similar concerns for retaining the focus of their mission and purpose in a day and age that taxes the increasingly limited financial resources that they have available. All are concerned as postmodern Canada becomes increasingly secular, with the church occupying a place of much less significance and importance within society and in the lives of the country's individuals. All of these factors comprise an exciting and challenging environment for any and all of the major institutional types, and with it the individual members, within Christian Higher Education Canada (CHEC).

This volume is intentionally organized around the tripartite temporal division explicated above, past, present, and future, as a means of both unifying sub-sections within the individual contributions and addressing each of the temporal foci in more detail. As a result, the volume contains essays within each section that, while focused upon an important temporal period, offer their own insights into the full scope of the topic by means of discussing the subject of Christian higher education from the vantage point of one of the three institutional types. Those who have written these essays are all actively involved in the lives of their respective institutions, as researchers or professors or administrators or sometimes a combination of these roles. Sometimes individual essays address specific topics pertinent to one of the particular types of institution, but more times than not essays address subjects that have pertinence for a variety of the institutions involved, along with raising questions regarding the broader field of higher education. Thus, this volume has three main sections, focusing upon the past, present, and future of higher education, and begins with the past in order to move through to the future.

The first section of essays addresses the historical and resulting contemporary context for Canadian Christian higher education. This section consists of four essays that many will find impressively informative because of the quality of their research regarding the past history of the Christian higher education movement. Adam Rudy opens this section with a study of how two student publications at two different educational institutions—McMaster University and Toronto Bible College—treated the second World War. This is an essay in cultural history that explores how the reaction to the war in these publications—both produced in institutions that were at least ostensibly founded on evangelical principles—reflected the contexts of their times. In particular, Rudy examines how these publications, reflective of the general climate of belief in Christendom, supported the British empire, a Christian Canada, and the wider concept of democracy. This democracy was viewed as grounded in a set of Christian ideals. As a result, the war effort became an effort in preservation of what was perceived to be Christian culture and civilization.

Within the context of examining the historical position of Christian higher education, Bruce Fawcett, Tracy Freeze, Leslie Francis, and Renee Embrée perform a social-scientific analysis of the changing religious beliefs of youth within a Baptist denomination in Atlantic Canada from 2002 to 2017. Over the course of this period of time, similar surveys of youth attending a biennial week-long mission and service program provided a guide to the levels of spirituality by means of their self-reporting on such practices as personal prayer, reading of the Bible, baptism, and attendance at Sunday worship services. The general pattern ascertained is that the level of commitment over that time declined among the members of this age-group. All of these results require interpretation, but they are at least suggestive and require explanation. There are a number of possible implications of such a finding, regarding the nature of students who formerly attended Christian undergraduate institutions, whether Bible colleges or universities/university colleges, and those who are now interested in attending such institutions. Since these Christian higher education institutions cannot count on the same level of Christian commitment, at least as indicated by these factors, institutions must adjust to students less well equipped, or at least evidencing their Christian commitment in other ways than previously.

The third essay is an encompassing historical essay by Kevin Flatt that traces the narrative of the secularization of universities within Canada. Many of Canada's well-known universities were founded as Christian institutions but have followed a course of clear and progressive secularization over the last century and more.[1] There are various possible explanations for such secularization, as Flatt outlines, with various degrees of determinism attached. But in this trend, Canadian universities are not alone, as such a trend toward secularization has occurred elsewhere from the Middle Ages to the present, with some nationalistic and local variations across Europe and in North America, as governments and others have exercised more and more direct or indirect control over higher educational institutions. The United States stands out against the more general trend in the strength of numerous Christian colleges that continue to function, but even these institutions are under pressure. Canada has followed a similar pattern of increasing secularization so that by roughly the middle of the last century most provincial universities were thoroughly secularized. Flatt points out the difficulties in reversing such a trend due to the place that education occupies within contemporary culture and how education is a system dominated by cultural elites. This, combined with the decline of the church, does not bode well for Christian higher education unless, as Flatt asserts, drastic steps are taken, but even then he is not optimistic of the outcome.

In the fourth and final essay in this section, Rick Hiemstra provides an essay in some ways similar to the second one, a quantitative study of the situation for evangelical students in contemporary Canada. This essay offers a history of the development of the Christian higher education movement from the perspective of especially the Bible school and Bible college movement, as the vast majority of CHEC institutions were founded during the period of the major rise of Bible colleges in Canada. The academic standards, he notes, were not high, but were not out of the ordinary for Canada of the times, which had a relatively low expectation for educational

1. There is often and continued (although unnecessary for the attentive) confusion over the relationship between McMaster University and McMaster Divinity College. Although they share a common history in Toronto Baptist College, and were a single institution until 1957 (and in that sense shared the story related in Flatt's essay), they at that time separated, so that whatever path the university continued on was not necessarily shared by McMaster Divinity College. McMaster Divinity College today is not a faculty or college of McMaster University and its faculty are employed solely by McMaster Divinity College. McMaster Divinity College retains—and, more importantly, holds to and believes in—the motto, Col 1:17, "In Christ all things hold together." McMaster Divinity College, unlike the secular university next door, is a vibrant evangelical institution.

achievement. The rise of the power, size, and influence of provincial universities throughout the twentieth century, combined with demographic changes after the second World War, led to progressive separation of the universities from the Christian institutions, with more and more students attending the provincial universities. Bible colleges responded, at least in part, by attempting to become accredited or become liberal arts institutions or transform themselves in other ways to become more competitive in the educational marketplace, but they did so at a cost, usually an escalation in cost for the education. CHEC grew out of this attempt to heighten the stature of Christian institutions. A number of factors reveal the challenges that such institutions face as they contemplate the future, as indicated in recent surveys. The students who contemplate such institutions are usually more committed and devout than those in the mainstream, but their numbers seem to be falling, thus presenting a challenge for CHEC institutions.

The second section of essays in this volume focuses more specifically upon the three major sectors of Christian higher education institutions in their contemporary context. Whereas the first section offered a variety of broad overviews and narratives of various specificity on the trends within the sector, these three essays address in particular Bible colleges, then university or university colleges, and finally seminaries. The opening essay of this section, by Douglas Berg, examines one Bible college as a test case for the viability of contemporary Bible college education. After identifying several trends that could hurt Bible colleges, Berg evaluates Columbia Bible College on nine criteria for success. These criteria include: its leadership, vision, self-esteem, institutional narrative, intentionality regarding its purpose, innovative planning, strategic use of finances, student learning, and improved environment. He finds that Columbia is, in fact, fulfilling its mandate regarding these categories and that, on this basis, it has the prospect of success in the future. The implication is that other institutions that perform a similar self-assessment and rise to the occasion may well conclude similarly regarding the future.

The second chapter in this section addresses universities and university colleges. John Stackhouse chronicles what he sees as a renaissance in Christian university education within Canada. He first examines a variety of factors that have influenced the environment in which Christian universities find themselves. These factors include the need for money, the need for leadership, concern for student preparation, and maintenance of the Christian identity of such institutions. The outcome is the current situation, in which there is stress on the institutions, as has recently been indicated by pressures exerted by Universities Canada and the conclusions of several well-known legal wranglings. One must ask questions about the strength and resilience of these institutions. As a result, Stackhouse wishes to offer a defense of Canadian Christian higher education. He argues that we must be advocates for freedom of religion and promote the public benefits of having Christian higher educational institutions within Canadian life. Christian universities occupy an increasingly distinctive place within Canadian culture as promoters of what Stackhouse calls "cultivating shalom," at least in part by retaining classical humanistic values of the university in ways that many secular universities do not. By being universities in this sense, Christian universities are able to create interest in Christianity. Stackhouse does not deny that there are challenges to such a course. These challenges involve remaining clearly focused upon their mission and ensuring that they promote a clear message that is continually enforced and reinforced. He further advocates mutual cooperation and coordination in the use of resources, and concludes by acknowledging that we must follow the leading of Jesus, even if his leading takes us into unknown and unwanted areas. Most of these matters, Stackhouse concludes, are conducted not in the light of recently publicized events, but in the decisions made every day.

The third and final chapter of section two addresses the situation in seminaries. In this paper, Stanley Porter returns to a topic he has addressed before, the numerical wellbeing of seminaries within Canada. Based upon statistics from the Association of Theological Schools (ATS), the major accrediting agency for seminaries in the United States and Canada, Porter examines these statistics in light of his previous research and developments since that time. In earlier research, he predicted that seminary education, if it followed the past trends, would continue to decline to perilously low levels. He admits that he was wrong—the decline did not go as low as he had predicted (although they almost did), but nevertheless the numbers have remained disappointingly low. From a high in enrolment in 2004, enrolment in Canadian seminaries fell to its lowest point in 2015, and from that time has slightly increased. However, the amount of increase, when other factors such as total population of Canada are considered, does not indicate overall growth. If one examines evangelical institutions in relation to the non-evangelical ones, one sees that it is only evangelical protestant institutions that seem to be holding their own in enrolment. As a result of his analysis, Porter looks to the future of seminary education with four considerations. The first is for ATS to embrace Canadian theological education, especially as it differs from that in the US. The second is that Canadian institutions must embrace educational developments with Canadian solutions, rather than simply importing others' proposals. The third is to consider the possibilities and opportunities of consolidation and amalgamation from a position of strength rather than weakness, even to the point of creating institutions of significance in size and resources. Finally, Porter calls all CHEC institutions to support other CHEC institutions in their common cause.

The third and final section of essays turns to the future by identifying various issues and opportunities for Christian higher education institutions. It is rewarding to see that there are five essays in this section, indicating that rather than simply looking at the past or present, members of the Christian higher education community (or at least the authors of this volume) are seeking to identify positive ways forward. The first essay, by Elfrieda Lepp-Kaethler and Catherine Rust-Akinbolaji, addresses the possibilities of creating a hospitable learning environment within the space of higher education. Based upon the notion of hospitality as a central Christian characteristic, as found within Scripture and the Christian tradition, the authors challenge Christian higher education to develop a theology of hospitality so that the stranger is welcomed. In an educational context, this requires the development of hospitable learning communities. The authors use various metaphors to express this welcoming environment, especially that of welcoming a guest to a dinner party and engaging in conversation, along with offering practical guidelines for educators to follow.

In the second essay of this section, Ted Newell looks to the analysis of philosopher and religionist George Parkin Grant, one of Canada's leading figures in higher education, for insight and guidance especially for universities and university colleges. According to Newell's appropriation of Grant, the major problem for Christian higher education institutions in Canada is the major shifts that have occurred within Canadian society that have resulted in radicalized versions of the autonomy of the individual. This is a pervasive shift that has affected most if not all major spheres of life, such as the cultural, political, and legal arenas. The story of Grant's critique of the increasing technologization of Canadian life provides the basis for Newell to make three observations to aid higher education. The first concerns maintaining an orientation to teaching that encompasses the universal scope of knowledge, based upon the English rather than German university model. The second is to shun historicism, which all too easily joins with Grant's critique of technology, and to retain a notion of transcendent time that does not limit the human simply to their time and work between birth and death. The third is to capture and appreciate the power of lament, especially lament over the loss of the good things that have passed, as an encouragement to rethink the present and help to create a possible future.

The third essay, by Nicki Rehn and Linda Schwartz, tries to envision such a future through the kinds of graduates that Christian higher education institutions produce, especially a university or university college in its liberal arts curriculum. Rehn and Schwartz examine in particular the common core curriculum at one such institution, where they were involved in revitalizing such a curriculum to make it more interdisciplinary and flexible, in order to better serve both the institutional needs within the curriculum and the larger institutional purposes. In the course of their involvement, which involved studying how the liberal arts are taught at a variety of similar institutions, Rehn and Schwartz made a number of discoveries. One of these is that members of the teaching faculty are not of the same mind on what is meant by the notion of a Christian liberal arts curriculum. This poses a challenge and opportunity for consistent implementation. A second is that students themselves are not naturally inclined toward interdisciplinarity or integration within the curriculum. Students in that sense are faced with similar challenges as are faculty members. A third discovery is the need to provide optimal sequencing for the curriculum so that students benefit from it. The resulting revised curriculum raises the further question of how one creates educational environments in which faculty and others come to embrace the need for curricular change that has positive effects for students.

Victor Shepherd, in the fourth chapter of this section, addresses the question of how Christian higher educational institutions can keep their charge to be thoroughly Christian. Shepherd identifies a number of signs of an erosion of the Christian mandate as a call to all Christian higher educational institutions to examine themselves in this light. The major sign, for Shepherd, is the shift that can occur within an institution from a culture of belief in the truth to a therapeutic culture. This shift is captured in Thomas Oden's description of a shift from the question of "What *is*?" or "What is *right*?" to "How does it *feel*?" Shepherd identifies three shifts that indicate that such a change is occurring or has occurred. These involve shifts in the meanings of important words, like "guilt," shifts in ideologies, and even shifts in one's view of God. The solution is found in what Shepherd identifies as the catholicity of the church, in which the message is adapted to circumstances but the warnings he identifies above are not adopted. Shepherd also endorses the importance of tradition within the Church. Knowledge of tradition helps to ensure the future by recognizing and appreciating the past.

The final essay in this section addresses the relationships between seminaries and their denominations. This essay, by Phil Zylla, examines the changing situation between seminaries and denominations based upon their both being in defensive postures. They are both struggling with financial issues, numbers of adherents, and the manifold cultural changes in which they find themselves that demand new ways of addressing their constituents. However, once one mines into the nature of seminaries, one realizes that although most of them are in some way denominationally connected, their relationships to their denominations and the wider church vary considerably. Since there is declining support, conflict in churches, and changing patterns of demographics that affect both churches and seminaries, Zylla endorses that seminaries both look to denominations for meaningful relationships and form new relationships with wider constituencies. He thinks that these offer the greatest promise when one considers the trends in seminary education. These trends include the tendency for ministry students to study closer to home, the increased costs of education, and the various ways that churches are now recognizing the credentialing of their ministers. The challenge, according to Zylla, will be to embrace these patterns of change within the resources that are available. Zylla concludes by suggesting that the opportunity is ripe for increased discussion with potential partners so as to develop new models of theological education, while resisting the urge to accept the idea that there are insufficient resources in light of God's abundance.

As one can readily see from this summary of the structure of this volume and its various chapters, this varied collection of essays presents a number of major themes worth further consideration. These themes revolve around the persistent belief in the ultimate will and calling of God upon those involved in Christian higher education, whether this means Bible colleges, universities or university colleges, or seminaries and graduate schools. For as long as God provides the means, there are institutions—filled with committed and dedicated faculty, staff, and administrators—who are determined to do the best they can not just to promote but to cultivate

Christian higher education within the Canadian context that is faithful to their vocational calling, because they believe that it is part of a much larger and higher purpose. A further theme is that Christian higher education has an interesting and significant past. This past intersects at various points with the developments in higher education outside of Christian influence. In many cases, today's institutions of Christian higher education have common historical origins and some parallel developments, while in others, their distinctives are clear from the outset. In any case, Christian higher education is a part of the rich tapestry of Canadian history and thought, a heritage which it can rightly be proud of and build upon. Another theme to consider is that Christian higher education is not immune to the challenges of the contemporary educational and, expanding the scope further, cultural environments. Canadian life is changing, whether in terms of culture, religion, or a host of other factors. Just as the wider scope of Canadian life adjusts to a world that is more interconnected than ever, with economic and ethnographic and religious challenges, so must institutions of Christian higher education adjust to changing realities. Students, faculty, curriculum, finances, church relations are all factors that must be considered. One must also observe the theme that, while definite challenges confront Christian institutions of higher education, and CHEC institutions are certainly not immune to these challenges, there is also room for optimism and encouragement. Christian institutions share the common belief that God has called them to a particular institutional purpose and will, with that calling, provide what is necessary for them, whether that means expansion or retraction or even complete reconceptualization. In that regard, most authors realize that, no matter how optimistic they may be concerning the current situation, Christian higher educational institutions cannot be complacent, but must constantly evaluate themselves and how they relate to their constituencies and other spheres of influence further afield. A final theme of this volume is that there is probably no single and certainly no simple way forward for the diverse institutions that make up Christian higher education. Bible colleges face their own challenges, and even these are varied, but the same can be said of universities and university colleges, as well as of seminaries and graduate schools. This need for individual innovation provides a challenging opportunity for Christian higher education as it looks to its own future within the contemporary Canadian context. We trust that these essays will provide some intellectual content for the ensuing discussion of such opportunities.

Part 1

The Historical and Contemporary Context
for Canadian Christian Higher Education

1

The Protagonist of Justice Against the Forces of the Antichrist

Christian Democracy and the Second World War in The Silhouette and The Recorder

ADAM D. RUDY

THE SECOND WORLD WAR had a profound impact on Western culture. While not everyone living today has a tangible connection to the war, there are still many people alive who do. The war has cast a long shadow over our culture. I myself, for example, grew up with the knowledge that my paternal grandfather had volunteered for active service in the war in 1941. He patiently tolerated my frequent questions about what was, to me, an exceptionally interesting time in history. I grew up in the church, and it was not until I was in graduate school that I discovered, much to my surprise, that the role of Canadian Protestant churches in the Second World War was a subject that had been mostly neglected by historians. Even more so was the subject of the views of students at Christian universities during the war. I thought this was odd given the strong cultural narratives about the war and how they have shaped the national identity of countries like the USA, Britain, and Canada, not to mention the ever-growing library of movies, television shows, video-games, and novels inspired by the war.[1] In light of these, this paper examines the war commentary in

---

1. For example, see Ramsay, "'Call of Duty' and the Cultural Narrative of World War II." In addition, consider some of the Hollywood films of the last two decades, such as

two student newspapers, *The Silhouette* (McMaster University) and *The Recorder* (Toronto Bible College), which represent two different patterns of Canadian evangelicalism and two different educational goals, but which were both dominated by Baptists. This examination supports my contention that the views expressed in these newspapers shared a presupposition of Christendom or Christian civilization. This presupposition was linked with British imperial sentiment, and among other things, entailed a conflation of Christianity and democracy. Through this lens, students at McMaster University (MU) and Toronto Baptist College (TBC) understood the war and articulated their role in it.

Before continuing, it should be noted that the notion of the "presupposition of Christendom" and the term "cultural narrative" were not used by Canadians during or before the war. However, they were acquainted with the idea of Christendom and Christian civilization. My use of these terms, then, is a marker of the historical distance between myself and the time I am writing about. During the interim between then and now, a set of ideas commonly labelled as postmodern (though there is disagreement about what this word really means) has brought into focus narratives, which are, in loose terms, stories that tell us who we are, how we got here, why we are here, and what we are supposed to do about it. Postmodern thought is skeptical of such narratives. These narratives are different than the stories of say, a novel, in that they are not set out in so linear a fashion. These narratives, so the story goes, are imparted to us through popular culture, philosophies, images, advertisements, media, music, and, of course, religion. So, while I argue that the war commentary in these two student newspapers was rooted in a presupposition of Christian civilization, I am also acknowledging that this was the basis of their cultural narrative that formed the lens through which Canadian Christians made sense of the world around them, and consequently admit that the use of this terminology is anachronistic.

Related to this problem of historical distance is the fact that current definitions of evangelicalism are not necessarily applicable to evangelicalism in the 1940s. This is important because MU and TBC were both institutions of Christian higher education that were created by evangelicals. As I have discussed elsewhere, the latter half of the twentieth century saw the

---

Saving Private Ryan, Fury, Dunkirk, Hacksaw Ridge, and shows from the 1960s such as *Hogan's Heroes.* The enduring interest in the war is further evinced by an abundance of documentaries (a recent, excellent example is *World War II in Color*), many focused on Hitler, Nazism, and the Holocaust. Streaming services such as Netflix and Amazon Prime Video have made many of these available to their subscribers.

development of what historians have labelled the "evangelical left," or "post-conservative evangelicalism."[2] These developments began in the late 1940s at Fuller Seminary where some evangelicals began to express discontent with the excesses of Christian fundamentalism.[3] In Canada, these developments were also felt after the Second World War.[4] Neo-orthodoxy was also a powerful movement at the time, represented by figures such as Karl Barth and Emil Brunner, though as this examination demonstrates, it is difficult to determine the extent to which neo-orthodoxy influenced the individuals writing in these two student newspapers. That being said, it is important to acknowledge that the influence of neo-orthodoxy in particular, and perhaps post-conservative evangelicalism to a lesser extent, might be present in some of the primary source material.

David Bebbington's quadrilateral has come to be the classic definition of evangelicalism. It defines evangelicalism as a movement marked by four characteristic emphases: the cross of Christ (crucicentrism), the Bible (biblicism), conversionism, and activism.[5] John G. Stackhouse Jr. defines Canadian evangelicalism similarly. He defines evangelicals as "people who (a) look back to the Protestant Reformation for its emphasis upon the unique authority of Scripture and salvation through faith alone in Christ, (b) display a warm piety in the context of a disciplined moral life, and (c) are concerned about the evangelism of all people."[6] While it is difficult to determine from only these newspapers how the students and faculty of MU and TBC conformed to these criteria, it seems both did to some extent. John McNicol's writing in *The Recorder* demonstrates an emphasis on biblical authority and salvation through Christ, and descriptions of TBC by Stackhouse and Burkinshaw suggest that missions, a combination of conversionism and activism, were a major focus for students who attended TBC. Both MU and TBC had weekly chapel services that students and faculty were expected to attend, and drinking and smoking were not allowed on campus. At the present juncture, it seems that all that can be said with accuracy is that the majority of students at TBC were evangelicals as defined

2. Erickson, *Evangelical Left*, 4. See also my MA thesis, Rudy, "'The Ecumenical Movement, Is it of God?'" 23–25.

3. Marty, "Tensions within Evangelicalism," 173.

4. Rudy, "The Ecumenical Movement," 25. These developments were felt in Canada by the 1960s.

5. Bebbington, *Evangelicalism*, 2–17.

6. Stackhouse, "Mainline, Evangelical, Ecumenical," 15.

by Bebbington and Stackhouse, and a significant number of students at MU were as well. However, because of MU's educational *ethos* one suspects that there were also numerous students there who were nominally evangelical. The *ethos* of TBC, for the most part, tended to preclude those of a nominal faith. The institution's respective origins and goals will be discussed below.

The chapter will be laid out as follows. The next section will outline the origins of the presupposition of Christendom and provide cultural context for the war commentary. The following section will provide a brief history of MU and TBC, respectively. These situate students at MU and TBC within evangelicalism and Canadian Protestantism. Finally, there will be an analysis of the war commentary in *The Silhouette* and *The Recorder*, followed by some concluding remarks.

CANADIAN PROTESTANTS AND "HIS DOMINION"

The Canadian experience of the Second World War can only be explained by the prevailing cultural trends and ideas of the time. The first thing to note is the sheer number of English Canadians who identified with one of four Protestant denominations. The 1921 census measured Canada's total Christian adherence at just over eighty-eight percent of the population.[7] Of this percentage thirty-eight percent identified as Roman Catholic, and fifty percent identified as one of either Methodist, Presbyterian, Anglican, or Baptist.[8]

It is no surprise, in light of the cultural presence of Protestants in Canada, that a predominant narrative of Canadian identity was one of a Christian Canada. Phyllis Airhart notes that the churches were apathetic to Confederation, but after Confederation had been achieved the realities of the new nation began to reshape their outlook.[9] The Western frontier sat waiting for evangelization, and the churches felt they needed to play an important role in forming "His Dominion of Canada."[10] The churches undertook this task with zeal. Indeed, Robert Wright has observed that "the major Protestant denominations—Anglican, Methodist, Presbyterian, and Baptist—had been among the 'corporate' institutions that had shaped the nation in the late nineteenth and early twentieth centuries."[11] The impulse

7. Semple, *The Lord's Dominion*, 182.

8. Semple, *The Lord's Dominion*, 182.

9. Airhart, "Ordering," 98.

10. Airhart, "Ordering," 99. This is also called the "Lord's Dominion."

11. Wright, "Canadian Protestant Tradition," 139.

toward shaping the nation provided the impetus for significant growth in church unity as various sub-groups merged to form national denominations.[12] This common vision, together with the new expressions of unity, laid out the possibility of further realizing the "determination to establish the Kingdom of God in the new country," and so the churches, which were heavily stocked with evangelicals, pursued programs of social reform.[13] Temperance societies, for example, sprang up in a persistent effort to eradicate the alcoholism that plagued the nation. Similarly, the Lord's Day Alliance was established to work toward protecting the sanctity of the Lord's Day.[14]

It is also important to note the influence of the Social Gospel, especially in the development of evangelicalism. Richard Allen argued that this thought movement crested between 1914 and 1928, but its ideas endured in Canadian Protestant circles until at least the 1960s.[15] Crucial for this discussion is the Social Gospel's eschatological assumption that saw the fullness of the kingdom of God on earth as attainable through the Christianization of the social order.[16] This assumption not only legitimized evangelicals' moral reform efforts but also provided the foundation for discussions of reconstructing the world order on a Christian basis after the Second World War.[17]

Canadian evangelicals were also heavily influenced by the imperial sentiments of the day. The British imperialism that was so formative for their worldview was heavily laden with Christian ideals and rhetoric. Canadian historian John S. Moir has argued that Canadians had an enduring sense of loyalty to Britain from the eighteenth century to the 1950s. He argued that Canadian loyalism held a view of life which emphasized things

12. Airhart, "Ordering," 99. For example, the Methodists consolidated into one national group in 1884, and the Presbyterians consolidated into one national group in 1875.

13. Airhart, "Ordering," 99.

14. The Lord's Day Alliance realized success in 1906 when the Lord's Day Act was passed by Federal Parliament. The Temperance movement realized success during the First World War. Using the war effort as their chief argument for the eradication of beverage alcohol, they successfully shaped public opinion to the point that every province except Quebec passed a Prohibition Act by 1919.

15. Allen, *Social Passion*, 15.

16. For an example, see "Report of the Committee on Resolutions," *BCOQ Yearbook 1942–1943*, 157.

17. This does not apply to all evangelicals, for there were many who rejected the Social Gospel. Those who rejected the Social Gospel followed the evangelical tradition of social reform begun by William Wilberforce.

Canadian within a British context.[18] This view was "based on a confidently assumed superiority of British institutions, and an unquestioning belief in the God-given mission—or responsibility—of the British people to share the blessings of the Almighty, with all other peoples."[19] A number of items published in the *Canadian Baptist* can be seen to have been written in such a "British spirit." For example, multiple prayers were published in the denominational newspaper "for our empire" alongside those containing language such as "the Empire's cause" and "the Empire and her Allies."[20]

An example of Canadian loyalism, as late as 1941, can be seen in an article by Rev. J. E. Harris, from Calgary, entitled "My Duty to My Church":

> The best things in our British tradition and our Empire's life are the things that grow out of Christian elements in our past and present. British law and justice, British love of fair-play, British tolerance and liberty, and the strong humanitarian and philanthropic strains in our national life—these are all the products of the Christian faith of Christian Britishers. . . . it is the bounden duty of every Christian citizen to do all in his power to strengthen and deepen such Christian elements in the nation's life. . . . The nation and the Empire need YOUR contribution to its highest life. No one else can take your place. You have a personal responsibility to be a Christian citizen, and side-stepping that responsibility is the thing that has put us where we are today.[21]

This statement demonstrates the imperial framework from which many Canadian Christians viewed the world. Canadian loyalism was one expression of it. The cultural connection between Canada and Britain was so strong that, as John Thompson has argued, in early twentieth-century Canada there was a ubiquitous "Imperial sentiment." He notes a journalist from that time period who described Toronto as "the most ultra-British city on earth . . . Englishmen suffering from a laxity in loyalty should hasten to Toronto, where they can be so impregnated with patriotism that they will want to wear shirt fronts made of the Union jack."[22] Canadians during this time "realized that they were British with a difference. In some respects they thought of themselves as better Britons, living in a land that offered greater

18. Moir, "Loyalism," 73.

19. Moir, "Loyalism," 73.

20. "Praying for the Empire," *Canadian Baptist*, 14 September, 1940, 7.

21. "My Duty to My Church," *Canadian Baptist*, 14 January, 1941, 7.

22. Thompson, "Third British Empire," 88.

economic potential, that avoided the rigid class distinctions of the mother country, and that produced healthier and stronger men and women."[23] Canadian identity was inseparably linked with the British Empire.

Michael Haykin, who has noted that pro-British sentiment was widespread among Canadian Baptists, mentions one piece published by the Ottawa Baptist Association that described the British Empire as "the most truly Christian Empire which ever existed."[24] Gordon L. Heath, who has devoted much study to what he calls "Baptist Imperialism," argues that Baptist imperialism throughout the British Empire/Commonwealth, in both urban and frontier settings, contributed significantly to global and regional identity, as well as a sense of common purpose, during the South African War, 1899–1902.[25] This linkage between Baptist and imperial identities was facilitated by an international network of Baptist newspapers, which itself played a key role in the construction of a worldwide, denominational, evangelical, and imperial identity that transcended regional and national identities. Thus, while the Baptist imperialism in Canada was unique, it was also an expression of a wider phenomenon occurring throughout the British Empire. Indeed, so pervasive was this sentiment that Heath has argued elsewhere that the South African War of 1899–1902 was, for Canadians, a prelude to the First World War in terms of the precedents it set for how Canadians conceived of and talked about war.[26] New research indicates that there were significant continuities between the South African War, the First World War, and the Second World War in terms of Canadian Baptist British imperial sentiment.[27] Therefore, it would seem that Canadian Baptist responses to the Second World War, to put it crudely, had become a tradition, and importantly, shared similarities with other Baptists throughout the empire.

The other key element of Canadian Christian identity was the presupposition of Christendom. For Canadians, the British Empire was synonymous with Christian domains. Church historian John Webster Grant argued that Canadians held a conviction that the institutions and values

---

23. Buckner, "Canada and the Empire," 8.

24. Haykin and Clary, "O God of Battles," 177.

25. See Heath, *The British Nation*, 1–29.

26. Heath, "S.A.W as Prelude," 15–30.

27. See Rudy, "Continuities in Central Canadian Baptist Responses to War, 1899–1945."

of Western society rested on a Christian foundation.[28] Similarly, Michael Gauvreau has argued that in early nineteenth-century Canada, evangelicalism provided a focal point for culture-making that was otherwise lacking in the pluralist context. Thus, "concepts of order, respectability, and the patterns of personal and social behaviour which were to prove most influential in forging the values and institutions of the maturing English Canadian society were provided by evangelicalism."[29] The self-appointed task of evangelicals to provide the nation with moral guidance persisted until the 1960s. Further to this point, for many Canadian Protestants at the time, it seemed as if Christianity and British democracy had become synonymous; this was aided by the "evangelical culture" that had formed in English Canada. Belief in a Christian civilization was built upon the assumption that Christianity was the source of British democratic ideals. As the quote above demonstrated, "[t]he best things of our British tradition and our Empire's life are the things that grow out of Christian elements in our past and present."[30]

The educational enterprise of Canadian Protestants was no stranger to any of the sentiments mentioned above. Sandra Beardsall has argued that the mainline denominations adopted the tasks of guarding and instilling cultural and moral values for the nation and that undergraduate education was essential to that task.[31] Similarly, Catherine Gidney, in her study of the Protestant university establishment in the twentieth century, argued that the Canadian university was perceived as a moral community; this would apply equally to TBC.[32] Indeed, a common belief among the leaders of Canadian universities in the first half of the twentieth century was the conviction that Christianity was the glue that held Western civilization together.[33] The evangelicalism that dominated the denominational colleges was the

28. Grant, *Canadian Era*, 213. Grant also argues that this presupposition was one of the foundations of the success enjoyed by ecumenical efforts in Canada. For more on Canadian British Imperialism, see Heath, *The British Nation*.

29. Gauvreau, "Protestantism Transformed," 50.

30. "My Duty to My Church," *Canadian Baptist*, 15 January, 1941, 11. For more examples see "The Spiritual Foundations of Democracy," *Canadian Baptist*, 2 February, 1939, 7; "Where Democracy was Born," *Canadian Baptist*, 2 February, 1939, 11; "Spiritual Freedom from Constraints of Earthly Authority," *Canadian Baptist*, 30 March, 1939, 8; "Baptist Democracy in a World of Dictators," *Canadian Baptist*, 13 April, 1939, 5.

31. Beardsall, "School/Church Relationship," 49.

32. Gidney, *Long Eclipse*, 3.

33. Gidney, *Long Eclipse*, 10.

special home of these sentiments, and Mark Noll tells of the impact of this: "the effect from uniting these two—strong proprietary denominations with strong liberal evangelicalism—was immense. The combination preserved social and political goals in tandem, it pushed belief and practice toward moderation, and it kept relatively traditional Christian perspectives alive at all levels of Canadian university life."[34] Higher education, then, together with the church, passed on this Protestant, imperial, moral narrative.

A BRIEF HISTORY OF MCMASTER UNIVERSITY AND TORONTO BIBLE COLLEGE

There is one important commonality between MU and TBC that must be emphasized before proceeding any further, and this is that the student populations at both schools were dominated by Baptists. Stackhouse points out that, despite being a small group relative to other mainline denominations, Baptists "continued to support TBC, with both the Baptist Convention and the separated Fellowship Baptist churches sending the largest contingents of students to TBC throughout the century."[35] Noting a similar trend at MU, Mark Steinacher shows that, from 1890–1929, Baptist students made up the majority of the student body at MU.[36] Even in subsequent years as other students from other denominations increased their numbers as a proportion of the student body, Baptists remained a majority. The common Baptist ground is important not only for understanding the following examination, but also Canadian Baptists more generally. Given the Baptist overlap between the institutions, views in *The Silhouette* and *The Recorder* will be compared to views expressed in the Baptist Convention of Ontario and Quebec's (BCOQ) denominational paper the *Canadian Baptist* to highlight certain points of comparison.

McMaster University was the fruit of a prolonged effort by Baptists in Ontario to establish a university chartered by the province where they could not only train their own ministers but also offer a liberal arts education for Baptists not called to the pastorate. As such, the history of MU until the 1950s is closely linked with the history of the BCOQ. Over the course of the nineteenth century, as some historians have suggested, Baptists in Canada not only grew in their respectability but even became a part of what

---

34. Noll, "Learning from Canada," 49.
35. Stackhouse, "Canadian Evangelicalism," 69.
36. Steinacher, "Sheep Not of this Fold," 274.

Grant has labelled the "unofficial Protestant establishment" that wielded significant social influence.[37] This shift was manifested in the establishment of a Baptist newspaper, various Baptist institutes of learning, and successful work to bring unity to the fragmented Baptist scene, resulting in regional Conventions/Unions and Associations being organized across the country.

McMaster University, George Rawlyk suggests, was born out of this impulse.[38] Initially established in Toronto by the generous endowment of Baptist Senator William McMaster's last will and testament, the university received a charter in 1887. The school belonged to the BCOQ and was not merely for the training of clergy but sought to offer a liberal arts education that would bring about "human progress."[39] Historian D.C. Masters notes that "McMaster University began with a comparatively liberal charter. Professors must be members of an evangelical church, but not necessarily Baptists."[40] Thus were planted the seeds for evangelical diversity.[41]

Trouble arose out of a series of controversies surrounding what was often called modernist theology (also known as theological liberalism) and fundamentalism that polarized Canadian evangelicals. This polarized climate erupted into controversy twice in MU's history. The first controversy in 1908–1909 has been called the "Matthews Controversy." This centered around the person of Professor Isaac G. Matthews who was accused of holding modernist views. Matthews was a graduate of the University of Chicago, which was a locus for theological liberalism at the time.[42] George Rawlyk has argued that the response of MU's university senate to this controversy was important in two ways. First, it endorsed the role of Christian higher education in bringing about human progress, and second, it ratified their belief that an accommodation was possible between the evangelical consensus and the new scholarship behind modernism.[43] Rawlyk also ob-

---

37. Grant, "The Churches," 359. For example, see Rawlyk, "Christian Higher Education"; and Steinacher, "Sheep Not of This Fold."

38. Rawlyk, "McMaster," 32.

39. Rawlyk, "McMaster," 44.

40. Masters, *Protestant Colleges*, 117.

41. This diversity was a reflection of the BCOQ. The Convention was far more theologically diverse than McMaster's identity would indicate. The Convention had a sizeable conservative contingent who likely went to TBC if they pursued Christian higher education at all. For a detailed treatment of the character of the BCOQ, see Rudy, "The Ecumenical Movement, Is it of God?"

42. Pinnock, "Modernist Impulse," 198.

43. Rawlyk, "McMaster," 44.

serves that the chancellors of MU were increasingly less conservative over time, which seemed to parallel a trend toward secularization. A second episode of controversy occurred in the 1920s when Rev. T. T. Shields accused Professor L. H. Marshall of holding modernist views. A statement that had been issued by the university senate in 1909 had affirmed that "McMaster stands for freedom, for progress, for investigation. It must welcome truth from whatever quarter, and never be guilty of binding the spirit of free enquiry."[44] This continued to be their principle as the university expressed satisfaction with Marshall's views in the 1920s.[45] Ultimately, this culminated in Shields and his followers leaving the BCOQ.[46]

McMaster University's response to the Second World War had precedent in the First World War. Not only did a large number of MU students enlist and see combat in The Great War, but there were significant similarities between the war commentary in the *McMaster Monthly* (the predecessor of *The Silhouette*) in the First World War and the commentary in *The Silhouette* in the Second World War.[47] However, the war commentary in *The Silhouette* lacked much of the zeal that characterized war commentary in the *McMaster Monthly*. So, while there were thematic similarities in terms of expressions of imperial loyalty, the war as a just cause, and the defense of Christian democracy, the commentary on the Second World War was more subdued and lacked the zealous and at times jingoistic rhetoric that was prominent in the Great War.

The origins of TBC also lie in the ethos of late nineteenth-century evangelicalism. While the denominational colleges, such as MU, arose out of a mainline Protestant ethos, TBC arose out of transdenominational evangelicalism of a different hue.[48] The Bible college movement had two primary purposes, Burkinshaw argues: teaching the Bible as truth rather than as an academic subject and training Christians for practical living and ministry.[49] The December 1914 edition of *The Recorder* stated that

44. Rawlyk, "McMaster," 43.

45. Pinnock, "Modernist Impulse," 201.

46. Rawlyk, "McMaster," 51. This event has been referred to by many as "the Schism of 1927." Initially, thirty churches left the convention with Shields, but by the end of the year the number had climbed to seventy-seven. This event shaped all subsequent Baptist activities in Canada.

47. For example, see *McMaster Monthly*, February 1915, 187–88; *McMaster Monthly*, February 1918, 204; *McMaster Monthly*, November 1918, 71, 81.

48. Stackhouse, *Canadian Evangelicalism*, 54.

49. Burkinshaw, "Evangelical Colleges," 373.

"the Bible College exists for this one purpose, that the Scriptures may be studied, known, understood, and obeyed—that their light and truth may be translated into human lives and thus be carried into the near and distant places, where men 'sit in darkness and the shadow of death.'"[50] Burkinshaw suggests that "conservative biblical doctrines appealed to many Canadians, especially those living in the Prairies, and in a period when many evangelicals had lost confidence in, for example, the theological departments of Brandon, Acadia, and McMaster, large numbers saw Bible schools as trustworthy in terms of traditional evangelical doctrines and emphases."[51] Thus, a school like TBC appealed to a different evangelical constituency. Remarkably, the college had both fundamentalist and modernist teachers at various times and yet managed to avoid controversy and division.[52]

According to TBC Principal John McNicol, who led the school for the first half of the twentieth century, the Bible college's own purpose was to be the "handmaid to the churches."[53] This meant that the school did not align itself with one particular denomination. In fact, both students and faculty hailed from all mainline Protestant denominations as well as smaller groups.[54] The school's identity as the handmaid of the churches "was epitomized by its theological centrism," which entailed a rejection of both fundamentalism and modernism and focused on training laypeople (a focus that purposely avoided overlap with seminaries).[55] It would seem that the goals which guided TBC, indeed the entire Bible college movement, stood the test of time as they continue to exist in Canada, though not necessarily in the form in which they began.[56]

TBC's response to the Second World War, similar to MU, also had precedent in the First World War. In fact, while the First World War commentary in *The Recorder* is also characterized by more zeal than the Second World War, there is a striking resemblance between *The Recorder*'s

---

50. "Twenty-First Session," *The Recorder*, December 1914, 1.

51. Burkinshaw, "Evangelical Colleges," 373.

52. Stackhouse, *Canadian Evangelicalism*, 56–57.

53. Cited in Stackhouse, *Canadian Evangelicalism*, 61.

54. Stackhouse, *Canadian Evangelicalism*, 61.

55. Stackhouse, *Canadian Evangelicalism*, 63–4.

56. In 1968, TBC merged with the London College of Bible and Missions (LCBM began in 1935) to form Ontario Bible College (OBC). Today OBC lives on in the form of Tyndale University College.

commentary on both wars.[57] This is perhaps due to the fact that McNicol, who wrote a great deal in *The Recorder*, was principal of TBC during the First World War as well.

This brief history of the origins of MU and TBC, though lacking in many regards, establishes that the two schools shared an evangelical heritage, both had a multidenominational student body, both were dominated by Baptists, and both had supported the Empire's cause in the First World War without hesitation and, indeed, without much questioning of what the Christian's relationship to war should be. The two schools differed in that MU was formed as a liberal arts college that sought to form the whole person and prepare them for citizenship in a Christian nation (and also included the seminary for the BCOQ), while TBC was a Bible college that emphasized reading the Bible with many students becoming missionaries after their time at TBC. Another difference is that MU sustained two explosive controversies over charges that modernism was being taught at the seminary. TBC, likely due to McNicol's wise leadership, avoided such controversy while maintaining a faculty that included professors of both modernist and fundamentalist orientations.

THE WAR IN THE SILHOUETTE

The pre-war editions of *The Silhouette* indicate a marked divergence from popular opinion regarding the possibility of war and the so-called "imperial connection." An editorial from early 1939 discussed whether Canadian neutrality was possible in the event of a war. The writer[58] claimed that "the question of the possibility of Canada's neutrality in any future European wars is at present occupying more space in our college newspapers than any other single problem."[59] The writer of the editorial noted that the college newspapers "without exception . . . lean towards isolation for Canada."[60] On the other hand, "the regular daily newspapers—the English speaking

57. For example, see "The Year of the Great War," *The Recorder*, March 1915, 1; "Are You Doing Your Bit?" *The Recorder*, March 1916, 1.

58. Most articles in *The Silhouette* did not include the name of the writer. Each edition contained a list of the editors, but since there were at least four at any given time, it is impossible to identify who exactly wrote which piece.

59. "Is Neutrality Possible?" *The Silhouette*, 24 February, 1939, 2.

60. "Is Neutrality Possible?" *The Silhouette*, 24 February, 1939, 2.

ones at any rate—are in favour of strengthening the British ties, or at least maintaining them."[61]

The latter view was also the dominant view of the denominational press, which the editorial admitted: "the church would probably not oppose any intervention in an imperialistic war, and would more likely support it, linking democracy with Christianity."[62] Making it clear that this view was not representative of the student body, the writer declared that "we ourselves are not in sympathy with the imperialistic attitude that Canada's frontier is found wherever the Union Jack flies," suggesting instead that Canada strengthen its ties with the United States.[63] As these statements suggest, prior to the war, Canada's young people did not seem to be as en- amoured with Canadian-British imperialism as their parents' generation had been.

Another aspect of the pre-war outlook exhibited in *The Silhouette* was the desire for peace. Charles Johnston, in his history of MU, noted that the peace movement attracted a respectable following.[64] One editorial dis- cussed the matter quite frankly. In response to Hitler's march into Prague, many were reminded, the writer noted, "that might is right." Admitting that the League of Nations had been a failure, the writer suggested that the only "way of maintaining peace at the present time, other than a strong alli- ance of the democratic powers which seems far from possible at the pres- ent time, is the way being pursued by Chamberlain—that is by a policy of concession."[65] But even by this method, the writer confessed, the future was bleak: "looking forward, it is true that further concessions might have to be made if a world war is to be avoided . . . [but] there is a point at which conditions become intolerable, we grant."[66] The hope for peace, together with the belief that Canada should not involve itself in an imperial war, seemed to characterize the pre-war outlook of MU students.

The results of a questionnaire conducted among university students across the country were printed in *The Silhouette*. The results only partially reflected the editor's sentiments. In response to the question, "are you in favour of military action to check the expansion of the totalitarian states,"

61. "Is Neutrality Possible?" *The Silhouette*, 24 February, 1939, 2.

62. "Is Neutrality Possible?" *The Silhouette*, 24 February, 1939, 2.

63. "Is Neutrality Possible?" *The Silhouette*, 24 February, 1939, 2.

64. Johnston, *McMaster University*, 75.

65. "Is Peace Possible?" *The Silhouette*, 17 March, 1939, 2.

66. "Is Peace Possible?" *The Silhouette*, 17 March, 1939, 2.

52.4 percent answered "yes."[67] In response to the question, "if England becomes involved in a war should Canada enter the war," 64.7 percent answered "yes."[68] An article from the same edition discussed the questionnaire results. The writer focused on the percentages that were opposed to Canada involving itself in England's war and commented that "we ourselves are very glad that so large a percentage opposed entry of Canada into an English war."[69] What the author did not mention, however, was that 64 percent of MU students who were surveyed, and over 70 percent of the students in Eastern Canada who participated in the survey, responded affirmatively to the question, "if England becomes involved in a war, should Canada enter the war?"[70] The writer also worried about MU's involvement in the war, "that McMaster's corridors and lecture halls should be prostituted into barracks service is unthinkable. We cannot imagine the faculty of any Christian university condoning war to such an extent."[71] It seems that the writer was unwilling to countenance the prospect of war, concluding that "it is all very well to talk about fighting for the glory of the empire, but the question takes on a very different aspect when you realize that the actual fighting involves killing with your own hands people who have done you no harm and whom you do not even know."[72]

The outbreak of the Second World War was not unexpected. The first edition of *The Silhouette* in the autumn of 1939 was printed just under a month after Canada had declared war on Germany. It was notably subdued about the war. The front page included an article about the revival of the Canadian Officers Training Corps (COTC), and the second page bore an editorial that did not exceed half a column. The tone of the editorial was resigned: "Canada is at war. Probably you have heard about it."[73] The negative view of war portrayed in previous editorials arguing for a policy of isolationism underlay this editorial as well. The writer was critical: "now, no one in Canada can reasonably believe that war can solve the ills of the economic and social world. Nor can democracy be saved by war. For the purposes of prosecuting this campaign the very principles of democracy for which it is

---

67. "War Questionnaire Results," *The Silhouette*, 31 March, 1939, 3.

68. "War Questionnaire Results," *The Silhouette*, 31 March, 1939, 3.

69. "Mainly About War," *The Silhouette*, 31 March, 1939, 2.

70. "Mainly About War," *The Silhouette*, 31 March, 1939, 2.

71. "Mainly About War," *The Silhouette*, 31 March, 1939, 2.

72. "Mainly About War," *The Silhouette*, 31 March, 1939, 2.

73. "About the War," *The Silhouette*, 31 March, 1939, 2.

fighting have to be scrapped, with an inevitable setback as a consequence."[74] The author went on to register a complaint about the "imperial connection" too. He wrote, "the British empire has seen fit to register its active disapproval of Germany's international tactics. Canada has thrown in her lot with the Empire, and no matter what our attitude may be toward the idea of war, it behooves us as citizens of the Dominion to lend our entire and unreserved support to Canada in her time of need."[75] While the author begrudgingly admitted, despite his disagreement with the reasons for Canada joining the war, that Canada's citizens had a responsibility to help out, he also argued for humane treatment of the vanquished foes: "this with the hope and prayer that the victors (as it appears most likely the Allies shall be) will deal with the conquered nation so humanely and so rationally as to obviate the very causes of this militaristic socialism against which we are fighting."[76]

An editorial from January 1941 attacked the notion of progress that had dominated Canadian's outlook up until the First World War. He observed "that the war-weary generation that has sprung from the ruins of one world-conflict can create a *Blitzkrieg*, and the horrors of total war would seem to refute the whole idea of evolution toward greater things in human affairs."[77] The editorial went on, however, to describe democracy in terms very similar to those used in the Protestant newspapers, conflating Christianity with democracy: "if there is any good to come from this war, this must be it, this must be the lesson that democracy will have to learn from our quarrel with the dictatorships, as the protagonist of justice and the principle of Christian love—that the ideal state is not to be remote Utopia . . . the Golden Age must be present."[78]

The Silhouette constantly described the changes wrought by the war on campus life, of which mandatory military training was only one

74. "About the War," *The Silhouette*, 6 October, 1939, 2.

75. "About the War," *The Silhouette*, 6 October, 1939, 2.

76. "About the War," *The Silhouette*, 6 October, 1939, 2.

77. "Where Are We Going?" *The Silhouette*, 31 January, 1941, 2.

78. "Where Are We Going?" *The Silhouette*, 31 January, 1941, 2. An example of the Protestant press can be seen in the *Canadian Baptist*, the BCOQ newspaper. It carried articles entitled "The Spiritual Foundations of Democracy"; another article declared "I like to think that democracy was born in the Garden of Gethsemane in that hour when the Master cried, 'Father' . . . In that hour the complete surrender of self-will and self-interest for the good of humanity was achieved" (see "Where Democracy Was Born," *Canadian Baptist*, 2 February, 1939, 11).

aspect.[79] Numerous male students enlisted in the armed forces, the demand for trained nurses resulted in a collaboration between MU and Hamilton General Hospital School of Nursing, and a huge demand for physicists and chemists resulted in a sharp increase in science students, along with important defense related research carried out by faculty members, to name only a few of the changes.[80]

The war was felt on the university campus in ways that few others felt it, likely due to the general age group of male students who were the likeliest to enlist. Take, for example, the COTC unit at MU. The COTC came to symbolize MU's contribution to the war effort. An editorial from mid-way through the war stated that "when the war first came to McMaster in the form of a COTC unit, there was at the start an undercurrent of resentment among a generation who had been bred in an environment of Agnes McPhailian disarmament, brotherly love, and expression of the individual. We think this feeling has almost passed away."[81] The editor noted that the establishment of the COTC had produced a "certain military *esprit de corps* which, given time, would build a pride and tradition."[82] The pride in MU's military effort carried over to MU graduates who enlisted and fought in the war. A front-page article, for example, told the stories of two MU graduates who fought at Dieppe. One of them, Captain Matchett, former coach of MU's rifle team, was killed there. Soon after this, every edition of *The Silhouette* bore a small column entitled "The Honour Roll" that listed every MU graduate killed in the war. Despite the pride that was taken in MU's contributions to the war effort, there was also serious discussion about what the world would, or should, look like after war.

The theme of postwar construction became commonplace in *The Silhouette* about mid-way through the war. One editorial argued that it was absolutely crucial that Canadians avoid a hateful attitude toward the Germans or punishing them even worse than they had been punished by the Treaty of Versailles. The writer stated, "we cannot in short hate them, then or now. We recall the injunction 'love your enemies.' That word love connotes for us overt action. We recognize that such action is impossible

79. Johnston (*McMaster University*, 89) notes that initially thirty days of military training was required of males twenty-one years of age and older. Soon, however, legislation was passed that increased the allotment to four months and lowered the age to eighteen.

80. Johnston, *McMaster University*, 89–114.

81. "McMaster Military," *The Silhouette*, 21 March, 1941, 2.

82. "McMaster Military," *The Silhouette*, 21 March, 1941, 2.

until we have won the war, but we point out that its possibility rests on our not hating now."[83] The goal, of course, was to establish a lasting peace, which is why the editor was so worried about a hateful attitude, for he saw that it was precisely that sort of attitude that had helped spark the war in the first place. Indeed, even as many on the Allied side began to think of peace part way through the war, there were concerns that this was too late. "We have not begun to gird our minds for the enormous tasks before us. If we are to meet the crisis of the peace successfully we must begin now to think of the basis on which a peace worthy of the name is possible," argued the editor.[84] And while the student paper had only occasionally recommended Christian ideals as a remedy for international ailments, it seems that the writers believed that Christianity was crucial for the reconstruction of a Christian civilization, one that would not be shattered by war. A corollary to this belief was the idea that Christendom had perverted its purposes and aligned itself with gross capitalistic gain. The editor wrote,

> Our problem resolves itself into decided [sic] whether or not in our attempt to gain the whole world economically we have lost our own souls. Certainly we have to face the bitter fact that we have not even succeeded in our economic goal. Our vaunted resources of pre-war days have vanished like the mists of the morning. We are threadbare, well-nigh destitute materially. May this not be a sign and a symbol of our moral and spiritual condition?[85]

For this editor, the only cure for this problem was Christianity. He argued that "our task is that we must orient our lives according to eternal purposes and not ephemeral ends . . . we must in short, seek to know the will of God and do it."[86]

The following year, a meeting was organized by a student group that presented four viewpoints on post-war reconstruction: historical, scientific, arts and education, and theology. The student who posited the historical viewpoint echoed the sentiments of *The Silhouette*'s editor. He argued that "the absence of revenge is essential in formulating the next peace treaty," and that "in ideal post-war internationalism there will need to be a spiritual force behind a world loyalty. There is only slight hope of spiritual unity after

83. "On Hating the Enemy," *The Silhouette*, 9 October, 1942, 2.
84. "Thinking Toward Peace," *The Silhouette*, 16 October, 1942, 2.
85. "Thinking Toward Peace," *The Silhouette*, 16 October, 1942, 2.
86. "Thinking Toward Peace," *The Silhouette*, 16 October, 1942, 2.

the war and Christianity is that hope."[87] For this speaker sacrifice was the key. The historical presenter declared that "Christians must sacrifice much of their present dogma and simplify their ideals to a few axioms which all the world can accept."[88] The theological presenter noted that sacrifice, a theme in each viewpoint, was essential to the Christian message. He argued that

> the church must preach the doctrine of sacrifice . . . it has been the message of the Christian Church that sacrifice is the foundation of life . . . the mature conception of the Christian faith is the realization that the cross speaks of the principle of sacrifice for all men . . . Sacrifice in the Christian sense is a willing acceptance of itself as a principle of action. In reconstructing a new world, men must realize this and put personal interests aside . . . In reconstructing our new world . . . Christianity must be taught.[89]

Christianity, then, was a crucial element in reconstructing the world once the war had been won. Indeed, though some editors were critical of Christianity's relationship with the British Empire, Christianity continued to inform their conception of Canadian and British democracy. Below, an examination of *The Recorder* indicates similar assumptions.

THE WAR IN THE RECORDER

In stark contrast to *The Silhouette*, *The Recorder* did not even mention the outbreak of the war. Indeed, the war was directly mentioned only a handful of times in the published quarterly from that period. A veiled description of world events may have been what Principal McNicol was attempting in his article "If Isaiah Were Alive Today," which graced the front page of the March 1939 issue of *The Recorder*. In this article he drew parallels between the world in Isaiah's day and his own world. Isaiah would "recognize the spirit of that haughty pagan power at work again in those states that put their trust in force and frightfulness. He would find the Kingdom of God confronted with the same kind of attack that was made upon Judah and

---

87. "Four Viewpoints at M.C.U. On Post-War Reconstruction," *The Silhouette*, 26 February, 1943, 2.

88. "Four Viewpoints at M.C.U. On Post-War Reconstruction," *The Silhouette*, 26 February, 1943, 2.

89. "Four Viewpoints at M.C.U. On Post-War Reconstruction," *The Silhouette*, 26 February, 1943, 2.

Jerusalem in his time."[90] McNicol's concern in the article is to answer the question of how Isaiah "would meet the state of things if he were alive today."[91] In this effort, his answer consisted of two points. His first point was to remind his readers of God's sovereignty over the earth and human affairs: "He is the sovereign Lord of the universe . . . All nations before Him are nothing. He uses them for His own purposes in the course of world history, raising up one nation for the chastisement and judgement of another nation, and then overturning it for its own transgressions when His work with it is done . . . It is His Kingdom that is finally to be established in the world."[92]

McNicol's second point, very much related to the first, was that God's rule in the world was through the same powers and principles as in Isaiah's day. McNicol stated that "the fundamental forces of the world are not military and economic, but moral and spiritual. It is not upon their might, armament, nor upon their economic policies, nor upon their international alliances that the future of the nations depends, but upon their relation to the Moral Governor of the world."[93] In the midst of these realities, McNicol advised, Isaiah gives the same message as in his day, "that the way of peace and safety in the midst of conditions like these is to return to God and rely upon Him."[94]

McNicol's comments regarding international affairs in this article indicate a rather different view than the one exhibited in *The Silhouette*. The most obvious difference is how McNicol used a biblical text to understand world events in his day. Biblical texts were rarely quoted in *The Silhouette*. McNicol provided a spiritual explanation of the war that emphasized not only God's interventions in human affairs but also the primacy of the moral and spiritual realms in world events, though they might be hidden by such things as military or economic strength.

McNicol further developed his spiritual explanation for the war in later issues of *The Recorder*. In the December 1940 issue, McNicol took on the fundamentalist practice of viewing war "as a sign of the Lord's Second Coming."[95] McNicol provided the example of a fundamentalist rumor that

90. "If Isaiah Were Alive Today," *The Recorder*, March 1939, 1.
91. "If Isaiah Were Alive Today," *The Recorder*, March 1939, 1.
92. "If Isaiah Were Alive Today," *The Recorder*, March 1939, 1.
93. "If Isaiah Were Alive Today," *The Recorder*, March 1939, 2.
94. "If Isaiah Were Alive Today," *The Recorder*, March 1939, 2.
95. "Prophecy in War Time," *The Recorder*, December 1940, 1.

spread after the First World War that believed that the League of Nations was the revival of the Roman Empire. Around the same time, he noted, a document known as the "Protocols of the Elders of Zion" prophesied the coming of a Jewish Antichrist and claimed to reveal a deep Jewish plot to bring about a world-wide revolution.[96] Many who claimed to be Christian, McNicol believed, fell under the sway of these so-called prophecies.

This description of a biblical prophecy's misinterpretation led McNicol to declare that "any theory of prophetic interpretation which leads good people astray like this and unwittingly plays into the hands of the foes of God, must have gone off the track somewhere."[97] Instead of following such a road, he proposed that Christians were in a very real struggle against the Antichrist. McNicol wrote,

> This is the witness we should bear today. It is no time for "prophetic" pessimism. The Christian who is truly loyal to his Lord will not stand aloof from the world in its woe and leave it to Antichrist. That is to turn one's back on the foe. Our business is to bring the powers of the spiritual world into the field and "turn the battle to the gate . . . The best tonic for these days is the Book of Revelation . . . [in it] We are shown the spiritual conflict that lies behind all world history, the real conflict with Antichrist, behind the present war."[98]

McNicol concluded by stating that,

> The war has to be fought with worldly weapons, but it will not be won by them alone. As citizens, it is our duty to give the state all the material help we can, but as Christians we have a still further duty. It is ours to seek to have the spiritual forces brought into play against the forces of Antichrist. When the heart of the nation turns to God in penitence and humility, in prayer and faith, then we may expect the powers of that unseen world where Christ is enthroned to be released for the final victory.[99]

The key idea to note in this statement is that of national repentance and its connection with "the final victory." In this piece McNicol articulated both a framework for a Christian understanding of the war and the role of the Christian in such a war. This understanding of the war made certain

96. "Prophecy in War Time," *The Recorder*, December 1940, 1–2.

97. "Prophecy in War Time," *The Recorder*, December 1940, 2.

98. "Prophecy in War Time," *The Recorder*, December 1940, 2.

99. "Prophecy in War Time," *The Recorder*, December 1940, 3.

assumptions about Canada being a Christian nation and the relationship between a Christian Canada (and by extension the British Empire) and a sovereign God. Indeed, McNicol apparently believed in a Canadian corporate identity before God, much like Israel's relationship with Yahweh in the Old Testament. Thus, the status of a nation before God became an important element in his spiritual explanation of the war.

Associated with the relationship between God and a nation, in this case Canada, was the timeworn evangelical emphasis on morality. Grant points out that "the declared social aim of the evangelicals was to make Christian principles the foundation of Canadian life. They conceived of this aim chiefly in moral rather than political terms."[100] In *The Recorder* morality was linked with spiritual realities. This idea, which was widespread among Canadian evangelicals in the first half of the twentieth century, was often presented in the context of spiritual warfare but became an important way for linking one's Christian responsibility as a Canadian Christian with the war effort. The front page of *The Recorder* in September 1941 elucidated this notion:

> In the midst of these strenuous days we need to watch lest we lose our sense of proportion. When such tremendous energy is being put forth all around us to build up the physical forces required to carry on the war, we are in danger of forgetting that the spiritual forces have to be built up too. As citizens we have our contribution to make to the one. As Christians it is our duty and our responsibility to maintain and build up the other. And the other is by far the most important; for if the war were won without a revival of the spiritual it would be lost in the end.
>
> It is encouraging to notice that this is realized by many of our leaders throughout the Empire, and especially by many of our leaders in the Church. As a matter of fact, the war has brought into grim prominence the problem of leadership. It was the failure to recognize that the fundamental forces in this world of God's are moral and spiritual, not economic and political, that has brought the present disaster upon the human race. It is the special business of the Christian Church to magnify these forces in proclaiming the Gospel of Jesus Christ. In view of all this the function which the Bible College fulfills as the handmaid of the churches becomes increasingly important. While it goes on with the work of training young men and women for doing the will of God in the world, the

100. Grant, *Canadian Era*, 80.

> College must continue its ministry of bearing witness to the reality
> of the spiritual.[101]

In this statement not only were Christians being called to build up the
nation's spiritual forces, but the moral and spiritual failure of the nation
was considered to be the cause of the war. The tying of TBC's identity with
"bearing witness to the reality of the spiritual" meant that TBC too, was
perceived as a moral community for the handing down of a certain Christian Canadian narrative.

A corollary to this perspective was the need for national days of prayer
and repentance. These were considered crucial to an Allied victory. For example, the *Canadian Baptist* printed numerous prayers for "the Empire's
Cause" and "the Empire and her Allies."[102] *The Recorder* registered a similar
view: "Nationally we are all guilty of the moral stupor and spiritual palsy
that allowed the present storm of judgement to gather and break upon the
world. For this there ought to be corporate and national repentance."[103]

Yet another corollary to this view was the linkage of Christianity with
democracy. The front page of *The Recorder*, in September 1942, declared:

> The war has come upon us as a Divine judgement upon national
> policies which ignored the moral and spiritual order of this world
> of God's. Wars are waged on earth but they are won in heaven. ....
> Those who have power with God are nearer the source of victory
> than those whose power is only with men. While we fight for the
> cause of democracy, we should seek to make democracy worth
> fighting for. A democracy that ignores the principles of the Kingdom of God cannot safely be entrusted with victory.[104]

The final sentence in the above quote implies a belief that democracy
cannot function without Christianity. As discussed above, this notion was
deeply rooted in the Christian British imperialism that produced the narrative of "His Dominion" and sought the creation of a morally perfect society
that would herald Christ's kingdom on earth.

Unfortunately, compared to *The Silhouette*, *The Recorder* does not
include much discussion on the subject of postwar reconstruction. In the
Annual Principal's Report of 1943 the postwar world is connected with

101. "The Forty-Eighth Session," *The Recorder*, September 1941, 1.

102. "Praying for the Empire," *Canadian Baptist*, 14 September, 1940, 7.

103. "Prayer in Wartime," *The Recorder*, December, 1941, 1.

104. "The Task of the Bible College," *The Recorder*, September 1942, 1.

TBC's identity: "In view of the work which the College will be called upon to do after the close of the war, it will be well to keep in mind the special contribution which it has been making to the Christian cause, and the unique place which it occupies in Canadian church life." McNicol went on to elucidate the unique role of TBC in Canada, highlighting its interdenominational composition and its emphasis on "the historic faith of the whole Christian Church" that "magnifies the essential reality that lies at the heart of Christianity."[105] These will become crucial, McNicol noted, because "it is evident to all thoughtful observers that the churches will have a greater need than ever for just this kind of service when the war is over. It is not difficult to see that if Christianity is to prosper in the future and if the Gospel is to make headway in the world, a much larger share of Christian work and witness must be undertaken by trained laymen and laywomen."[106] Beyond this, *The Recorder* does not discuss the postwar world further.

CONCLUSION: CHALLENGES AND OPPORTUNITIES

I have argued that the war commentary in *The Silhouette* and *The Recorder* was rooted in a presupposition of Christendom, which was a key aspect of the framework from which Canadian Protestants understood the world around them. Other aspects of this framework included the British empire and their loyalty to it, and the importance of Canada being Christian (Protestant), morally upright, and, of course, democratic. The concept of Christian civilization that was so fundamental to the Canadian Protestant outlook of the Second World War was interwoven with notions of Christian democracy, the belief that democracy was rooted in Christian ideals, and that one could not survive without the other. When it came down to it, from their perspective this meant that the war was fought in order to defend Christian civilization.

This conclusion reveals several challenges and opportunities for Christians living in the post-Christian Western societies of the twenty-first century. The first challenge is that we have to decide whether the Canadian Protestant view of the Second World War (and the First) as a just cause, fought to defend Christian civilization, was actually a just cause and a legitimate reason for a Christian to support a war. Today the war is often understood as a just cause to defend freedom, but is it appropriate for us to

---

105. "The Principal's Report," *The Recorder*, June 1943, 5.
106. "The Principal's Report," *The Recorder*, June 1943, 5.

hold this stance when it is divorced from its religious dimensions? A second related challenge is that for right or wrong, our spiritual and physical ancestors went to war to defend Christian civilization, but in the absence of the presupposition of Christendom today, how do we justify going to war? Should Christians even be involved in wars to defend current Western values?

Third, understanding that the Second World War was fought, at least in the view of many Canadian Protestants, in defense of Christian civilization and by extension the British empire challenges the common narratives about the war that we encounter in popular culture. Rarely do we conceive of the war as the result of clashing imperial programs, or in defense of Christian civilization. Rather, the war is often explained as a struggle between the champions of freedom and the evil, genocidal Nazis, thus divorcing the conflict, to some extent, from its religious dimensions. Thus, we have an opportunity to question the narratives about the war, and war in general, that one encounters today.

Finally, wars typically take the greatest toll on the 18–30 age group. This means that Christian higher education has a major responsibility in equipping its students to grapple with the questions surrounding the relationship between church and culture and the role of the Church in war. This does not necessarily mean encouraging students to enlist or not, but rather educating them well so that they can think for themselves on the matter and articulate a position that is true to their faith. War has been and always will be a contentious and complex subject for Christians, and so it is critical that we continue to learn from history about how Christians in other places and times have, or have not, reconciled their faith with war.

BIBLIOGRAPHY

Airhart, Phyllis D. "Ordering A New Nation and Reordering Protestantism." In *The Canadian Protestant Experience 1760–1990*, edited by George A. Rawlyk, 98–138. Montreal and Kingston: McGill-Queen's University Press, 1990.

Allen, Richard. *The Social Passion: Religion and Social Reform in Canada, 1914–1928.* Toronto: University of Toronto Press, 1973.

Beardsall, Sandra. "The Church/Theological School Relationship in Canada: A Reflection on Historical and Recent Trends." *Theological Education* 44 (2008) 43–64.

Bebbington, David. *Evangelicalism in Modern Britain: A History from the 1730s to the 1980s.* London: Routledge, 1989.

Buckner, Phillip. "Canada and the British Empire." In *Canada and the British Empire*, edited by Phillip Buckner, 1–21. The Oxford History of the British Empire Companion Series. New York: Oxford University Press, 2008.

Burkinshaw, Robert K. "Evangelical Bible Colleges in Twentieth-Century Canada." In *Aspects of the Canadian Evangelical Experience*, edited by George A. Rawlyk, 369–86. Montreal and Kingston: McGill-Queen's University Press, 1997.

Erickson, Millard. *The Evangelical Left: Encountering Post-Conservative Evangelical Theology*. Grand Rapids: Baker, 1997.

Faulkner, Charles Thompson Sinclair. "'Christian Civilization': The Churches and Canada's War Effort, 1939–1942." PhD diss., University of Chicago, 1975.

Gauvreau, Michael. "Protestantism Transformed: Personal Piety and the Evangelical Social Vision, 1815–1867." In *The Canadian Protestant Experience 1760–1990*, edited by George A. Rawlyk, 48–97. Montreal and Kingston: McGill-Queen's University Press, 1990.

Gidney, Catherine. *A Long Eclipse: The Liberal Protestant Establishment and the Canadian University, 1920–1970*. McGill-Queen's Studies in the History of Religion 2. Montreal and Kingston: McGill-Queen's University Press, 2004.

Grant, John Webster. *The Church in the Canadian Era: A History of the Christian Church in Canada*. 3 vols. Vancouver: Regent College Publishing, 1988.

———. "The Churches in Canadian Space and Time." *Mid-Stream* 22 (1983) 354–62.

Handy, Robert T. "Trends in Canadian and American Theological Education, 1880–1990." *Theological Education* 18 (1982) 175–218.

Haykin, Michael, and Ian Hugh Clary. "'O God of Battles': The Canadian Baptist Experience of the Great War." In *Canadian Churches and the First World War*, edited by Gordon L. Heath, 170–96. McMaster General Series 4. Eugene, OR: Pickwick, 2014.

Heath, Gordon L. *The British Nation is Our Nation: The BACSANZ Baptist Press and the South African War, 1899–1902*. Studies in Baptist History and Thought. Bletchley, UK: Paternoster, 2017.

———. "The South African War as Prelude to the First World War." In *Canadian Churches and the First World War*, edited by Gordon L. Heath, 15–33. McMaster General Series 4. Eugene, OR: Pickwick, 2014.

Johnston, Charles M. *McMaster University: The Early Years in Hamilton, 1930–1957*. Toronto: University of Toronto Press, 1981.

Marty, Martin E. "Tensions Within Contemporary Evangelicalism: A Critical Appraisal." In *The Evangelicals*, edited by David F. Wells and John D. Woodbridge, 170–88. Nashville, TN: Abingdon, 1975.

Masters, D. C. *Protestant Church Colleges in Canada: A History*. Studies in the History of Higher Education in Canada. Toronto: University of Toronto Press, 1966.

Moir, John S. "Loyalism and the Canadian Churches." In *Christianity in Canada: Historical Essays by John S. Moir*, edited by Paul Laverdure, 71–81. Yorkton, SK: Redeemer's Voice, 2002.

Noll, Mark A. "Learning from Canada: Canadian Religious History and the Future of Theological Education in North America." *Theological Education* 50 (2015) 33–52.

Pinnock, Clark H. "The Modernist Impulse at McMaster University, 1887–1927." In *Baptists in Canada: Search for Identity Amidst Diversity*, edited by Jarold K. Zeman, 193–208. Burlington, ON: Welch, 1980.

Ramsay, Debra. "Brutal Games: 'Call of Duty' and the Cultural Narrative of World War II." *Cinema Journal* 54 (2015) 94–113.

Rawlyk, G. A. "A. L. McCrimmon, H. P. Whidden, T. T. Shields, Christian Higher Education, and McMaster University." In *Canadian Baptists and Christian Higher*

Education, edited by G. A. Rawlyk, 31–62. Kingston and Montreal: McGill-Queen's University Press, 1988.

Rudy, Adam D. "Continuities in Central Canadian Baptist Responses to War, 1899–1945." *McMaster Journal of Theology and Ministry* 20 (2018–2019) 3–41.

———. "'The Ecumenical Movement, is it of God?': Central Canadian Baptist Identity and Ecumenism in the 1960s." MA thesis, McMaster Divinity College, 2017.

Semple, Neil. *The Lord's Dominion: The History of Canadian Methodism.* McGill-Queen's Studies in the History of Religion 1. Montreal and Kingston: McGill-Queen's University Press, 1996.

Stackhouse, John G., Jr. *Canadian Evangelicalism in the Twentieth Century: An Introduction to Its Character.* Toronto: University of Toronto Press, 1993.

———. "Mainline, Evangelical, Ecumenical: Terms, Stereotypes, and Realities in Canada." *Touchstone* 13 (1995) 14–23.

Steinacher, Mark C. "'Sheep Not of This Fold': Case Studies of Non-Baptist Student Populations at McMaster University 1890–1929." In *Baptists and Public Life in Canada*, edited by Gordon L. Heath and Paul R. Wilson, 263–303. McMaster General Series 2; Canadian Baptist Historical Society Series 1. Eugene, OR: Pickwick, 2012.

Thompson, John Herd. "Canada and 'Third British Empire,' 1901–1939." In *Canada and the British Empire*, edited by Phillip Buckner, 87–107. The Oxford History of the British Empire Companion Series. New York: Oxford University Press, 2008.

Wright, Robert. "The Canadian Protestant Tradition 1914–1945." In *The Canadian Protestant Experience 1760–1990*, edited by George A. Rawlyk, 139–97. Montreal and Kingston: McGill-Queen's University Press, 1990.

2

The Changing Religious Profile of "Committed" Baptist Youth in Atlantic Canada 2002–2017

Implications for Christian Higher Education in Canada

BRUCE G. FAWCETT, TRACY FREEZE, LESLIE J. FRANCIS, AND RENEE EMBRÉE

THE SECULARIZATION OF CANADIAN YOUTH

SECULARIZATION HAS BEEN THE topic of both research and debate for several decades. Generally thought of as the decline in the importance and influence of religion in modern society, Dobbelaere[1] further differentiated secularization into three components: societal, organizational, and individual. Dobbelaere referred to societal secularization as the decline in the influence of the church on society and organizational secularization as the decline in the influence of society on the church. However, it is the third component that is the focus of much research in the sociology of religion—individual secularization. Individual secularization encompasses the individual's decline in church involvement, other religious practices, and religious belief. Examining this component of secularization, researchers have noted the sweeping decline in religious attendance, affiliation,

1. See Dobbelaere, "Secularization—A Multidimensional Concept," 1; Dobbelaere, *Secularization*, 24–25.

40

and belief in Northwest Europe.[2] Though the United States was long seen as a counterargument to secularization theory, examining trends in the United States, Voas and Chaves[3] refuted the counterargument claims and reported that decline is indeed occurring, albeit slowly. In Canada, the decline in institutionalized religion, ongoing since the 1950s, has been well documented.[4] For instance, Bibby[5] reported that religious identification declined from 91% in 1975 to 85% in 2005; weekly church attendance declined from 31% in 1975 to 25% in 2005; and belief declined from 61% in 1975 to 49% in 2005.

Stark, along with a number of collaborators,[6] offered one of the first challenges to secularization. Utilizing a market analogy to explain the decline (and possible incline) of religiousness, Stark suggested that religion provides a service for which there will always be a market. Among other things, religion helps individuals find purpose as well as meaning for life and life events. Though other entities may enter the market and take some of the market share that once belonged to organized religion, Stark also notes that this loss in market share could motivate change in the church. If the church changes its ways of thinking and practice, it can regain some of the market share. Continuing to use the market analogy and applying a costs/benefits analysis, Stark further noted that people tend to value things that cost more because that which has a greater cost also has a greater reward. When faiths and their organizations demand more of their adherents, there is more opportunity for reward and this, in turn, earns the organizations more loyalty. Far from the doom and gloom of a continuing decline in religion that secularization theory offers, Stark notes that there will always be a market for religion.

Influenced by Stark, Bibby, once a proponent of secularization, claimed that "there is something of a renaissance of organized religion in Canada."[7] Utilizing data from three different data sets, Bibby[8] noted three different trends. Though Roman Catholics both inside and outside Quebec had

---

2. Voas and Crockett, "Religion in Britain," 11–28.

3. Voas and Chaves, "Is the United States," 1517–56.

4. Bowen, *Christians in a Secular World*, 3–22.

5. Bibby, *Beyond the Gods*, 5, 17.

6. See Stark and Bainbridge, *The Future of Religion*, 39; Stark and Iannaccone, "Supply-Side Reinterpretation," 230–52; Stark and Finke, *Acts of Faith*, 193–217.

7. Bibby, *Restless Gods*, 90.

8. Bibby, *Restless Gods*, 73.

experienced precipitous drops in weekly attendance from 1957 to 2000, the drop in weekly attendance for mainline Protestants had tapered off by the 1990s and plateaued in 2000. Further, according to Bibby[9] the weekly attendance of conservative Protestants had begun to increase by the 1990s, reaching higher levels in 2000 than was noted in 1957. It is this increase in the weekly attendance of conservative Protestants that compelled Bibby to propose the revitalization theory. According to this theory, declines are not necessarily continuous, such that if those that identify with religion have needs and interests (a market) that are met by their religious organization (after innovation/change), revitalization will occur. Bibby's current theory, however, is not revitalization but polarization.[10]

To Bibby, polarization theory can be visualized on a continuum with committed pro-religious individuals on one end and committed non-religious individuals on the other end. Between the two ends of the continuum are "The Religious Middle" who are neither embracing nor rejecting religion.[11] Bibby proposed this theory after analysing a number of datasets, including the Project Teen Canada data on youth. According to this data, youth reported weekly attendance in 1984 (23%) at similar rates as in 2008 (21%). On the other hand, monthly attendance (21%) and attending hardly ever (28%) decreased (12% and 20%, respectively). Finally, participants reporting that they never attended church rose from 28% to 47%.

Leading Canadian researchers in the sociology of religion, however, disagree with Bibby. For example, in a reanalysis of the data, Reimer found little support for polarization theory.[12] Instead, the data are clearly indicating secularization of religion in Canada. In an examination of conservative Protestants, Reimer stated that "there is evidence that their growth has plateaued, and may be declining."[13] Compared to earlier reports on evangelical Protestants that suggested that evangelicals may not be subject to the forces of secularization and that they continued to remain strong in their attendance,[14] this is discouraging. Bibby noted that one of the reasons evangelical Protestants were remaining strong is because of their ability

9. Bibby, *Beyond the Gods*, 37.

10. Bibby, *Beyond the Gods*, 34–61.

11. Bibby, *Beyond the Gods*.

12. Reimer, "Conservative Protestants," 187–208.

13. Reimer, "Conservative Protestants," 187–208.

14. Bowen, *Christians in a Secular World*, 50.

to retain their youth. However, recent evidence indicates that this may no longer be the case.

At first glance the data are promising. Penner, Harder, Anderson, Désorcy, and Hiemstra[15] conducted the Church and Faith Study of Young Adults and found that in terms of religious identification, evangelical Protestants retained their youth better than either mainline Protestants or Roman Catholics (63.1%, 34.4%, and 46.9%, respectively). Religious attendance also indicated better retention for evangelical Protestants as 38.8% of young adult evangelical Protestants reported attending church services, compared to that of mainline Protestants (11.8%) or Roman Catholics (9.2%). However, evangelical Protestants in Canada are still losing 36.9% of their youth as measured by identification and 61.2% of their youth as measured by weekly church attendance. It is important to note that the majority of the unretained youth are not switching to other world religions but to the "no religion" category.[16]

This loss is not because churches have not focused on children and youth. Reimer, Wilkinson, and Penner suggested that church leaders are aware of the importance of youth retention to the church. Indeed, the inability to retain the children and youth of the church would mean the death of many congregations. This importance is evidenced in the number of programs, youth pastors, and denominational units dedicated to children and youth ministry. Reimer et al., in their sample of churches from across Canada, reported that 98% had programs for children and approximately 75% had programs for youth. Through interviews and quantitative data, they concluded that, beyond parental religiosity, experiencing God through mission trips and Christian camps and mentoring by adult members of the congregation (e.g., youth leaders) were the most important factors in youth retention.

The retention of youth into adulthood is also influenced by emerging adulthood.[17] Coined by Arnett,[18] *emerging adulthood* refers to young adults between the ages of approximately 18 and 25 and is characterized by the feeling that one is neither a youth nor an adult. According to Hiemstra et al.,[19] the achievement of adulthood is thought to be delayed because of the

---

15. Penner et al., *Hemorrhaging Faith*.
16. Reimer and Wilkinson, *A Culture of Faith*, 158.
17. Hiemstra et al., *Renegotiating Faith*, 10.
18. Arnett, "Emerging Adulthood," 469–80.
19. Hiemstra et al., *Renegotiating Faith*, 10.

longer period spent obtaining an education. They suggested one notable consequence of this delay: the life stages that often see an increase in religiousness (e.g., marriage and children) are also delayed. Further, emerging adulthood is not conducive to church attendance and following God.[20]

Hiemstra et al.[21] conducted a large mixed-methods study on 18 to 28 year olds that attended church at least monthly as a teen and found that emerging adulthood is a time of disconnection. First, young adults move away from home for education or work and may not connect with a church in their new community and/or become involved in the life of that church. Second, drawing from prominent psychological theorist Erik Erikson, Hiemstra et al. noted that this is a time of identity development where the emerging adults explore different roles and decide on their own values and beliefs. Part of the reason for identity exploration is differentiation—the need to set oneself apart from parents and siblings. Originally thought by Erikson to occur during adolescence and achieved by 18, a commitment to an identity in this generation may not be achieved until much later. This, of course, leaves plenty of opportunity for emerging adults who once identified as Christians and who attended church regularly as teens to choose identities decidedly non-religious as adults. Hiemstra et al.[22] suggest that some ways that churches may help youth and emerging adults include providing mentors to help navigate this time period and helping youth make connections with a church in their new community.

Against this broader background, the focus of this chapter will now turn to research conducted among Baptist youth in Atlantic Canada.

PREVIOUS RESEARCH ON BAPTIST YOUTH IN ATLANTIC CANADA

Tidal Impact is a weeklong mission and service event for young people between 12 and 18 years of age which includes children's ministry, ministries of social concern, large worship gatherings, and fun events. The event is held in two locations simultaneously every second summer, generally alternating between the provinces of New Brunswick and Nova Scotia as host locations. Tidal Impact, which is Canada's largest youth mission and service event, is planned by the staff of the Canadian Baptists of Atlantic

---

20. Smith and Snell, *Souls in Transition*, 75–76.

21. Hiemstra et al., *Renegotiating Faith*, 21.

22. Hiemstra et al., *Renegotiating Faith*, 16–21.

Canada in partnership with local church leaders in the host locations.[23] A comprehensive history of Tidal Impact can be found in Fawcett.[24]

Data reported in this study were collected during Tidal Impact events held in 2002, 2006, 2009, and 2017. Tidal Impact 2002 was hosted by churches located in Moncton and Saint John, New Brunswick. The event was attended by approximately 1,100 young people (12 to 18 years of age) and youth leaders. The survey was completed by 557 young people. Tidal Impact 2006 was hosted by churches located in Halifax and the Annapolis Valley, Nova Scotia. The event was attended by 1,185 young people (12 to 18 years of age) and youth leaders. The survey was completed by 663 young people. Tidal Impact 2009 was hosted by churches located in Moncton and Saint John, New Brunswick. The event was attended by 815 young people (12 to 18 years of age) and youth leaders. The survey was completed by 519 young people.

A significant research tradition exists related to the young people and leaders who have attended Tidal Impact. A study by Fawcett, Francis, and Robbins published in *The Journal of Youth Ministry* used the Adolescent Form of the Francis Psychological Type Scales (FPTSA) to explore the psychological type preferences of young people who attended Tidal Impact.[25] A study by Fawcett and Francis[26] published in the *Journal of Youth and Theology* explored the relationship between baptismal status and spiritual practices among young people who attended Tidal Impact. Fawcett, Francis, and Robbins reported in *Pastoral Psychology* on a study conducted among young people attending Tidal Impact who completed a trial 80-item form of the FPTSA designed for use among adolescents.[27] The scale properties of the new instrument commended the 40-item Adolescent form of the FPTSA for future use.

A study by Fawcett, Francis, and Robbins published in *Research in the Social Scientific Study of Religion* invited young people attending Tidal Impact to imagine themselves serving as ordained ministers and to rate their approach to ministry on the revised Payne Index of Ministry Styles (an instrument based on Jungian psychological type theory).[28] Based on

23. Fawcett et al., *Mission Tour*, 189–200.

24. Fawcett, *Recruiting Clergy*, 5–24.

25. Fawcett et al., "Psychological Type Profile," 25–38.

26. Fawcett and Francis, "Relationship between Baptismal Status," 10–21.

27. Fawcett et al., "Scale Properties," 201–16.

28. Fawcett et al., "Imagining Themselves," 264–85.

the data reported, the recommendation was made that religious vocations among young people should be fostered by encouraging them to recognize that there is room within ministry for different personality types to bring different gifts and to exercise different ministry styles.

In the journal *Religions*, Francis, Fawcett, Robbins, and Stairs explored the properties of the New Indices of Religious Orientation Revised (NIROR) among young people who attended Tidal Impact.[29] A study by Francis, Fawcett, Linkletter, Robbins, and Stairs published in the *International Journal of Christianity and Education* reported on research conducted among youth leaders at Tidal Impact regarding their psychological type preferences.[30] A somewhat similar study by Fawcett, Francis, Linkletter, Robbins, and Stairs published in *Pastoral Psychology* utilized the Francis Psychological Type Scales for Adolescents to extend previous studies in psychological type by exploring whether male and female young people who attended Tidal Impact preferred to use feeling over thinking when making decisions.[31]

Studies conducted on Canadian Baptist young people attending other Christian youth events explored their attitudes toward alcohol[32] published in *Journal of Youth Ministry*, sexuality[33] published in *Journal of Youth Ministry*, and music copyright theft[34] published in *Journal of Research on Christian Education*.

In addition to the data presented in previously published articles, data were also collected in previous studies of young people attending Tidal Impact to measure the extent of their Christian commitment by asking about the frequency of their spiritual practices. The intention was to be able to compile a profile to assess the increasing or decreasing level of Christian commitment of these young people over a period of time.

29. Francis et al., "New Indices," 56.
30. Francis et al., "Psychological Type Profile," 220–33.
31. Fawcett et al., "Assessing the Reliability," 213–23.
32. Fawcett et al., "Religiosity and Alcohol," 45–63.
33. Francis et al., "Sexual Attitudes," 7–24.
34. Fawcett et al., "Religiosity and Music," 153–64.

TRAJECTORY OF CANADIAN BAPTISTS
IN ATLANTIC CANADA

Virtually all measurable indicators suggest the Canadian Baptists of At-lantic Canada (CBAC), the eastern-most regional grouping of Canadian Baptists, is a denomination experiencing a slow decline in a geographic region where the size of the population has remained relatively stable in re-cent decades. One marker of the decline of the CBAC is the denomination's annual budget. Whereas in 1987 the total operating budget of the CBAC stood at $3,274,300,[35] by 2017, in spite of 30 years of inflation, the bud-get stood at only $2,469,366.[36] Similarly, another marker of decline is the number of churches who hold membership in the CBAC. Whereas in 1986 the denomination reported 560 member churches,[37] by 2017 CBAC publi-cations regularly spoke of "about 450 member churches" in spite of the fact that no significant schisms took place causing churches to withdraw from membership. Attendance at the annual denominational assembly could be considered another indicator of health. Whereas in 1986 paid registra-tion was 993,[38] by 2018 the CBAC was reporting that only 760 individuals had registered to attend.[39] Worship attendance is another key indicator of health. The fact that member churches are not required to report annual statistics to the denominational office makes a precise comparison diffi-cult; however, the consensus of denominational staff is that overall wor-ship attendance has been in decline for decades, though a small number of churches are experiencing growth in weekend worship attendance.

If the overall portrait suggests a decline in the health of the CBAC, to further understand the context of this study it would be prudent to exam-ine the state of health of the denomination's work with young people. The CBAC sponsors two major youth events: an annual spring weekend youth conference called Springforth, and the biennial weeklong Tidal Impact youth mission and service event. According to the CBAC's Director of Youth and Family Ministries, in recent years Springforth attendance has been in decline. Whereas in 2015 there were 1,425 young people and leaders who attended Springforth, by 2017 the number had shrunk to 1,196. Similarly, Tidal Impact attendance shrank from 1,100 in 2002 to 743 in 2017. The

35. Thompson, *Yearbook*, 151.

36. Canadian Baptists of Atlantic Canada, *Book of Business*, 25.

37. Thompson, *Yearbook*, S–157.

38. Thompson, *Yearbook*, S–157

39. Myers, email communication.

CBAC also monitors the number of paid youth ministers. Whereas in 1999 there were 74 churches who employed youth pastors,[40] by 2017 that number had dropped to 62, and according to the CBAC's Director of Youth and Family Ministries, a larger proportion of youth pastors was now serving in a part-time capacity. Again, the fact that annual statistical reports are not required by the CBAC makes charting the number of local church youth groups and the number of young people attending these groups difficult. However, the observation of the Director of Youth and Family Ministries is that both the number of groups and the number of young people in attendance is shrinking. The overall denominational context and the context of its ministry with young people is one of shrinking influence and input into the life of Eastern Canada.

RESEARCH QUESTION, METHOD, AND RESULTS

Against this background, the aim of the present study is to explore whether the spiritual practices of committed Canadian Baptist young people in Atlantic Canada have changed in the 2002–2017 period and, if so, to identify some implications for evangelical Christian universities, Bible colleges, and seminaries who typically recruit students from among young people who attend church-sponsored events like Tidal Impact.

Procedure

All the young people (12 to 18 years of age) attending Tidal Impact 2017 were invited to complete a detailed survey following their participation in afternoon "Dive Deeper" workshops, which focused on engaging and training the participants in Christian spiritual disciplines. Once the workshops were complete, the participants were gathered together and seated in a church sanctuary. The nature of the voluntary survey was then explained, and the young people were given assurances of confidentiality and anonymity. The questionnaires were then handed out. From the 549 young people registered for the event, a total of 329 questionnaires were returned wholly or partially completed, making a response rate of 60%.

The data gathered from these 329 questionnaires completed in 2017 are compared below with the data gathered from 557 completed questionnaires in 2002, 663 completed questionnaires in 2006, and 519 completed questionnaires in 2009.

40. Fawcett, "Effective Youth Ministry," 12–17.

Instrument

During Tidal Impact 2017 the young people were invited to complete a survey entitled "Today's Youth Speak: Discipleship Pathways." This 18-page questionnaire was developed by Leslie Francis, Bruce Fawcett, Tracy Freeze, and Renee Embrée. In addition to demographic questions and questions concerning personal spiritual practices, the survey also contained the Francis Scale of Attitude Toward Christianity, The Francis Measure of Family Influence, and the New Indices of Religious Orientation Junior.

Participants

Tidal Impact 2017 took place in two locations simultaneously and was attended by young people and youth leaders from 71 churches. Of the 329 young people who completed the questionnaire, 113 were based in Bridgewater, Nova Scotia and 216 were based in Halifax, Nova Scotia. Of the young people who completed a questionnaire, 36% were male and 63% were female.

Of the young people, 59% were 12 to 14 years of age and 41% were 15 to 18 years of age. In terms of real numbers, 58 were 12 years of age or younger, 59 were 13 years of age, 78 were 14 years of age, 54 were 15 years of age, 35 were 16 years of age, 33 were 17 years of age, and 14 were 18 years of age.

In terms of home province, 58% were from New Brunswick, 40% were from Nova Scotia, 2% were from Newfoundland and Labrador, and 1% were from Prince Edward Island. Only 1% of the respondents identified another Canadian province as their home province. In terms of their home environment, 57% of the young people indicated that they lived in a rural area or village, 40% indicated that they did not live in a village or rural area, and the remaining 3% did not supply an answer.

In terms of their mother tongue, 92% identified English and 3% identified French. Approximately 4% identified another language as their mother tongue. Regarding ethnic group, 82% indicated "White/Caucasian," 5% indicated "Native American, First Nations or Indigenous," 4% indicated "African descent," 2% indicated "East Asian/Asian American," 1% indicated "Biracial/multiracial," 2% indicated "Other," and less than 1% indicated "Middle Eastern/Arab American."

In terms of the school program in which they were enrolled, 53% indicated English, 21% indicated early French immersion, 20% indicated late French immersion, 5% indicated French, and 2% indicated "other." In terms of the grades they earned in school, 72% indicated that they earned an "A" average, 19% indicated a "B" average, 6% indicated a "C" average, and 2% responded that they earned a "D" average. Only one student said that their average grade was an "F."

Descriptive Profile

Table 1: Gender of Participants, Percentage by Year

Gender of Participants	2002	2006	2009	2017
Male	35	37	36	37
Female	65	63	64	63

Table 1 shows that over the time period in which the four surveys were taken at Tidal Impact the male to female breakdown remained largely similar, with the percentage of males falling in the 35–37% range, and the percentage of females falling in the 63–65% range.

Table 2: Age of Participants, Percentage by Year

Age of Participants	2002	2006	2009	2017
12 and under	9	13	14	18
13	18	19	20	18
14	22	20	23	24
15	21	23	16	16
16	16	13	14	11
17	9	9	9	10
18	7	2	4	4

Table 2 shows that the percentage of young people reporting that they were age 12 and under doubled during the time period studied from 9% to 18%. The percentage of respondents aged 15 declined over time from 21% in 2002 to 16% in 2017. Similarly, the percentage of respondents aged 16 declined from 16% to 11%. The age of those attending Tidal Impact over the years is generally lower with those reporting that they were age 14 and under growing from 49% in 2002, to 52% in 2006, to 57% in 2009, and to 60% in 2017.

Table 3: Home Province, Percentage by Year

Home Province	2002	2006	2009	2017
New Brunswick	59	47	64	58
Nova Scotia	27	43	24	40
Prince Edward Island	3	5	6	1
Other	11	5	7	1

Table 3 shows that the province of origin for the young people who attend Tidal Impact seems to be greatly influenced by the province where the event was held. This observation makes sense given that the event operates on a model whereby Tidal Impact teams are hosted by local churches who typically would have groups who participate in the event. While in each of the surveys the number of respondents from New Brunswick was larger than the number of respondents from any other province, the percentage of respondents from New Brunswick was greatest in 2002 (59%) and 2009 (64%) when the event was held in New Brunswick.

Table 4: Church Location, Percentage by Year

Church Location	2002	2006	2009	2017
City/Suburb/Town	76	69	75	41
Village/Rural	23	32	25	59

Table 4 shows that, generally, most survey participants (69–75%) indicated that their church was located in a city, suburb, or town. However, in 2017 that dynamic changed and the majority (59%) indicated that their church was located in a village or rural area. This development may be in part explained by the fact that the vast majority of host churches in 2017 were located in the villages or rural areas located on Nova Scotia's South Shore, in the Annapolis Valley, or in other regions outside of the Halifax Regional Municipality.

Table 5: Average Grade, Percentage by Year

Average Grade	2002	2006	2009	2017
A	66	67	65	72
B	24	25	26	19
C	7	7	8	6
D	2	1	0	2
F	0	0	1	0

Table 5 shows that those attracted to Tidal Impact tend to be academically-able students, with anywhere between 65% and 72% reporting that they earned an "A" average in school. It may be that the training program required by some of the youth groups in order to be invited to attend Tidal Impact shaped the appeal of the event to favour those who are academic achievers. It may also be that local church youth groups from which a Tidal Impact team would be recruited tend generally to attract those who tend to be academic high achievers.

Table 6: Denominational Affiliation, Percentage by Year

Denominational Affiliation	2002	2006	2009	2017
Baptist	95	97	94	96
Other	5	3	6	4

Table 6 shows that the vast majority of the young people who attend Tidal Impact are affiliated with Baptist congregations, most of whom are located in Atlantic Canada (see Table 3) and who hold membership in the Canadian Baptists of Atlantic Canada denomination.

Religious Profile

Table 7: Sunday Worship Attendance, Percentage by Year

Sunday Worship Attendance	2002	2006	2009	2017
Every week	89	83	80	73
Once per month	4	6	6	9
Once in a while	8	8	12	16
Never	1	3	2	2

Table 7 shows that the percentage of young people who reported attending Sunday morning worship "every week" declined steadily over the time of the study from 89% to 73%. Correspondingly, the percentage of young people who reported attending Sunday morning worship "once a month" or "once in a while" increased.

Table 8: Private Prayer, Percentage by Year

Private Prayer	2002	2006	2009	2017
Daily	66	54	52	45
Weekly	19	22	25	26
Monthly	4	4	4	9
Occasionally	9	19	14	17
Never	1	2	4	3

Table 8 shows that the percentage of young people who reported engaging in private prayer on a daily basis declined steadily from 66% to 45% over the time of the study. Correspondingly, the percentage of young people who reported praying privately on a weekly or monthly basis increased. The percentage of young people who reported praying "occasionally" or "never" showed no clear trend of increase or decrease over the period of the study.

Table 9: Personal Bible Reading, Percentage by Year

Personal Bible Reading	2002	2006	2009	2017
Daily	21	15	14	9
Weekly	29	26	25	23
Monthly	15	14	15	19
Occasionally	28	37	37	36
Never	7	8	10	13

Table 9 shows that the percentage of young people who reported reading the Bible on a daily basis declined from 21% to 9% over the period of the study, and the percentage who reported reading the Bible on a weekly basis declined from 29% to 23%. The percentage reporting reading the Bible "monthly," "occasionally," or "never" was higher in 2017 than 2002.

Table 10: Baptism, Percentage by Year

Baptism	2002	2006	2009	2017
Baby	24	20	23	23
Child	32	28	25	29
Teen	36	33	31	22
Adult	1	1	0	0
Never	18	30	29	32

Table 10 shows that generally the percentage of young people who reported being baptised as a baby or as a child remained steady during the time period studied. However, the percentage of young people who reported being baptised as a teen decreased from 36% in 2002 to 22% in 2017. Correspondingly, the percentage of young people who reported never having been baptised increased from 18% to 32% over the time period studied.

Table 11: Father Attend Worship? Percentage by Year

Father Attend Worship?	2002	2006	2009	2017
Every week	62	60	61	58
Once per month	7	5	4	6
Once in a while	22	12	14	14
Never	15	22	22	21

Table 11 shows that the young people reported that the percentage of their fathers who attended worship weekly declined from 62% in 2002 to 58% in 2017. The percentage of fathers attending monthly changed little over time, whereas the percentage of those who never attended worship increased from 15% to 21% over the time period studied.

Table 12: Mother Attend Worship? Percentage by Year

Mother Attend Worship?	2002	2006	2009	2017
Every week	75	73	71	69
Once per month	4	5	5	7
Once in a while	13	9	11	14
Never	8	13	13	10

Table 12 shows that the young people reported that the percentage of their mothers who attended worship weekly declined steadily from 75% in 2002 to 69% in 2017. The percentage of mothers attending "monthly," "once in a while," or "never" increased marginally over the time period studied.

Table 13: Attend Same Church as Youth Group? Percentage by Year

Attend Same Church	2002	2006	2009	2017
Yes	89	90	N/A	95
No	11	10	N/A	5

Table 13 shows that the percentage of young people who reported attending worship in the same church they attended youth group increased from 89% in 2002 to 95% in 2017.

DISCUSSION AND CONCLUSION

Overall, data gathered at the same event over a 15-year period indicate a progressively weaker level of Christian commitment on the part of the young people as measured by engagement of the young people with basic spiritual practices such as Sunday worship attendance, baptism, Bible reading, and private prayer. As a result of this overall observation the following practical suggestions are offered for consideration.

Oftentimes in the Canadian environment, the senior leadership of a Christian university, Bible college, or seminary emerges from vocational roles in a local church or denomination. In many cases these previous roles would likely have involved working with young people. It may be fair to conclude that such individuals progressed to new higher education leadership roles based on their record of successful ministry with young people, a record which was likely rooted in their clear and accurate understanding of the young people they served. A challenge with this dynamic can be that the intuitive sense possessed by these leaders about how to shape an attractive academic and co-curricular experience can, over time, be increasingly negatively influenced by an understanding of a previous generation of young people rather than the current generation. For the health of the ministry of these educational institutions, perhaps the longer one has been away from "ministry in the trenches" with young people, the more attention the leadership of these institutions needs to pay to the changing identity, practices, and priorities of the intended audience of their higher education ministry.

It may be that organizations that provide support to Christian universities, Bible colleges, and seminaries such as Christian Higher Education Canada could have a role in assisting these institutions by providing professional development programs that enhance the understanding of prospective students by senior administrators, thus contributing to greater institutional effectiveness in student recruitment and service.

Historically (as evidenced by the 2002 study results) it may have been fair to conclude that many incoming students to Christian universities, Bible colleges, and seminaries had generally integrated basic Christian disciplines into their daily or weekly lives. It now appears that institutions of Christian higher education in Canada may have to give consideration to developing strategies to highlight the importance, and foster the development, of basic Christian piety. Modelling by faculty and staff, intentionally-designed institutional programs and initiatives, and encouragement of leadership by the students themselves may all be needed to help Christian higher education institutions produce graduates who are equipped to live a life that includes what most denominations have historically identified as basic indications of Christian piety.

Historically, a central strategy for spiritual formation at a Christian university, Bible college, or seminary has been to conduct regular chapel services that provide an opportunity for students to augment their private piety with public worship and celebration. While a well-designed and led chapel experience may still be important to a school's identity and a key part of the desired student experience, the weakening level of Christian commitment among the pool of prospective students suggests that a much more comprehensive strategy for spiritual formation ought to be embraced. Formation that results from intentional integration of faith with the formal curriculum, co-curricular initiatives such as small group Bible studies and worship experiences in campus housing, opportunities for large group common service experiences, the screening of films followed by a panel discussion, and opportunities for spiritual retreat, all led by a staff and faculty championing a dream for spiritual formation, can enable Christian young people and others to grow in their understanding and mature in their relationship with God. Far from leading with a student recruitment message that focuses on protecting Christian young people from the "evils of the wider society," such an emphasis allows Christian educational institutions to speak of unparalleled opportunities for growth and maturation in a young person's Christian commitment.

The polarization hypothesis by Ozorak suggests that there is a tendency for less religious adolescents to further shift away from religion.[41] This is thought to occur not only when they attend secondary school, but also across their lifespan. For more religious adolescents, the tendency is opposite. These adolescents become more religious as they attend secondary school and more religious across their lifespan. Some studies support this theory. Hunsberger conducted a cross-sectional study with senior citizen participants.[42] Those participants who reported higher levels of religiosity noted gradual increases of religiosity since their childhood. On the other hand, less religious seniors reported that they became gradually less religious over their lifespan. The implication is that these less committed Christian adolescents are at risk of becoming even less committed as time passes. Spiritual formation initiatives within Christian higher education should be planned with attention given towards those most at risk.

Part of the challenge of this study may be how Christian commitment is measured. In this study, it is defined by factors such as church attendance, prayer, and Bible reading. Though religiosity (measured by practices like church attendance, prayer and Bible reading) seems to be declining, spirituality (measured by constructs like experience of the divine, emotion, transcendence, meaning, purpose, etc.) may be stable.[43] Oman and Thoresen suggest that the explicit teaching of religious practice and disciplines may not be as effective as connection with a spiritual model/mentor.[44] Perhaps in designing their spiritual transformation initiatives, Christian institutions of higher education ought to give consideration to a significant initiative focusing on mentoring.[45]

The observable decline in the frequency of personal Bible reading and worship attendance in the population examined in this study suggests that there is likely now a much lower level of Bible knowledge possessed by those studying at Christian universities, Bible colleges, and seminaries than in the past. This reality raises the question of whether Christian institutions of higher education ought to revisit their basic core courses in biblical content to determine whether the historical assumptions of prior knowledge apply any more to the students the institutions are attracting. Is the content

41. Ozorak, "Social and Cognitive Influence," 448–63.

42. Hunsberger, "Religion, Age," 615–20.

43. Levenson et al., "Religious Development," 183–97.

44. Oman and Thoresen, "How Does one Learn," 39–54.

45. Hiemstra et al., *Renegotiating Faith*.

of the foundational courses accessible and engaging enough for those who enrol in Canadian Christian higher educational institutions?

It is not unusual within Christian higher education institutions to find degree programs, certificate programs, or elective courses that seek to equip students to minister effectively to young people. Given the changing depth of Christian piety among some young people in this series of surveys, as a service to the church and to young people themselves, Christian universities, Bible colleges, and seminaries would be wise to alert students to these trends and equip them with skills and knowledge to help reverse this trend.

It may be wise to consider additional studies of young people attending similar Christian events over a period of time that explore trends in their level of Christian commitment. This would allow researchers to arrive at greater clarity on the extent to which Tidal Impact participants are similar or different when compared with young people who attend events in other parts of Canada or events that are sponsored by other denominations or parachurch ministries.

In addition, it would be wise when studying young people who attend Tidal Impact or other similar events to add additional measures of Christian commitment. This study primarily explored the more private and personal side of a young person's Christian commitment. Might it be possible that today's young people are more concerned with joint action, care, and community than they are with a more private practice of spiritual disciplines as shown in studies such as Growing Young?[46] The greater the understanding of the audience for Christian higher education, the more likely it is that the institutions are able to shape a student recruitment message that appeals to Christian young people and to achieve their goal of seeing students transformed in Christ, ready to serve in various capacities throughout our world.

Finally, in order to develop effective spiritual formation programming and initiatives within the context of Christian higher education, future research should consider focusing on identifying the risk factors associated with less commitment to traditional religious practices. Focus on those risk factors that can be changed (e.g., the absence of a spiritual mentoring program) may be especially salutary.

46. "Growing Young," https:fulleryouthinstitute.org/growingyoung.

BIBLIOGRAPHY

Arnett, Jeffrey Jensen. "Emerging Adulthood: A Theory of Development from the Late Teens Through the Twenties." *American Psychologist* 55 (2000) 469–80.

Bibby, Reginald W. *Beyond the Gods and Back*. Lethbridge: Project Canada, 2011.

———. *Restless Churches: How Canada's Churches can Contribute to the Emerging Religious Renaissance*. Ottawa: Novalis, 2004.

———. *Restless Gods: The Renaissance of Religion in Canada*. Toronto: Stoddart, 2002.

Bowen, K. *Christians in a Secular World: The Canadian Experience*. Montreal: McGill-Queen's University Press, 2004.

Canadian Baptists of Atlantic Canada. *Book of Business* for Annual Assembly. Saint John, NB: Canadian Baptists of Atlantic Canada, 2017.

Dobbelaere, Karel. "Secularization—A Multidimensional Concept." *Current Sociology* 29.2 (1981) 1.

———. *Secularization: An Analysis at Three Levels*. Bern: Peter Lang, 2002.

Fawcett, Bruce G. "Effective Youth Ministry in Atlantic Canada." *Atlantic Baptist* (Summer 2000) 12–17.

———. *Recruiting Clergy for Canadian Baptist Churches*. New York: Mellen, 2006.

Fawcett, Bruce G., and L. J. Francis. "The Relationship between Baptismal Status and Spiritual Practices among Committed Baptist Youth." *Journal of Youth and Theology* 8.2 (2009) 10–21.

Fawcett, Bruce G., L. J. Francis, and M. Robbins. "Imagining Themselves as Ministers: How Religiously Committed Baptist Youth Respond to the Revised Payne Index of Ministry Styles (PIMS2)." *Research in the Social Scientific Study of Religion* 22 (2011) 264–85.

———. "Psychological Type Profile of Religiously Committed Male and Female Canadian Baptist Youth: A Study among Participants at Tidal Impact." *The Journal of Youth Ministry* 8.1 (2009) 25–38.

———. "The Scale Properties of the Adolescent Form of the Francis Psychological Type Scales (FPTSA) Among Canadian Baptist Youth." *Pastoral Psychology* 60 (2011) 201–16.

Fawcett, Bruce G., M. McDonald, and R. Nylen. *Mission Tour*. Saint John, NB: Convention of Atlantic Baptist Churches, 2005.

Fawcett, Bruce G., L. J. Francis, and Jody Linkletter. "Religiosity and Alcohol Avoidance: A Study among Canadian Baptist Youth." *Journal of Youth Ministry* 11 (2013) 45–63.

Fawcett, Bruce G., L. J. Francis, Amanda Henderson, M. Robbins, and Jody Linkletter. "Religiosity and Music Copyright Theft: A Study among Canadian Baptist Youth." *Journal of Research in Christian Education* 22 (2013) 153–64.

Fawcett, Bruce G., L. J. Francis, Jody Linkletter, M. Robbins, and Dale Stairs. "Assessing the Reliability and Utility of the Francis Psychological Type Scales for Adolescents (FPTSA) among Canadian Baptist Youth." *Pastoral Psychology* 66 (2017) 213–23.

Francis, L. J., Bruce G. Fawcett, Jody Linkletter, M. Robbins, and Dale Stairs. "Psychological Type Profile of Canadian Baptist Youth Leaders: Implications for Christian Education." *International Journal of Christianity and Education* 20 (2016) 220–33.

Francis, L. J., Bruce G. Fawcett, and Jody Linkletter. "The Sexual Attitudes of Religiously Committed Canadian Youth within the Convention of Atlantic Baptist Churches." *Journal of Youth and Theology* 12 (2013) 7–24.

Francis, L. J., Bruce G. Fawcett, M. Robbins, and Dale Stairs. "The New Indices of Religious Orientation Revised (NIROR): A Study among Canadian Adolescents Attending a Baptist Youth Mission and Service Event." *Religions* 7.5 (2016) 56.

"Growing Young," https:fulleryouthinstitute.org/growingyoung.

Hiemstra, Rick, Lorianne Dueck, and Matthew Blackaby. *Renegotiating Faith: The Delay in Young Adulthood Identity Formation and What it Means to the Church.* Toronto, ON: The Evangelical Fellowship of Canada, 2018, https:p2c.com/renegotiating-faith/.

Hunsberger, B. "Religion, Age, Life Satisfaction, and Perceived Sources of Satisfaction: A Study of Older Persons." *Journal of Gerontology* 40 (1985) 615–20.

Levenson, M. R., C. M. Aldwin, and H. Igarashi. "Religious Development from Adolescence to Middle Adulthood." In *Handbook of the Psychology of Religion and Spirituality*, edited by R. Paloutzian and C. Park, 183–97. 2nd ed. New York: Guilford, 2014.

Oman, D., and C. E. Thoresen. "How Does one Learn to be Spiritual? The Neglected Role of Spiritual Modeling in Health." In *Spirit, Science and Health: How the Spiritual Mind Fuels Physical Wellness*, edited by T. G. Plante and C. E. Thoresen, 39–54. Westport, CT: Praeger, 2007.

Ozorak, E. W. "Social and Cognitive Influences on the Development of Religious Beliefs and Commitment in Adolescence." *Journal for the Scientific Study of Religion* 28 (1989) 448–63.

Penner, James, Rachael Harder, Erika Anderson, Bruno Désorcy, and Rick Hiemstra. *Hemorrhaging Faith: Why & When Canadian Young Adults Are Leaving, Staying & Returning to the Church.* Toronto, ON: The Evangelical Fellowship of Canada Youth & Young Adult Ministry Roundtable, 2012.

Reimer, Sam. "Conservative Protestants and Religious Polarization in Canada." *Studies in Religion/Sciences Religieuses* 46 (2017) 187–208.

Reimer, Sam, and Michael Wilkinson. *A Culture of Faith: Evangelical Congregations in Canada.* Montreal: McGill-Queen's University Press, 2015.

Reimer, Samuel Harold, and Michael Wilkinson, with James Penner. *A Culture of Faith: Evangelical Congregations in Canada.* Montreal: McGill-Queen's University Press, 2015.

Smith, Christian, and Patricia Snell. *Souls in Transition: The Religious and Spiritual Lives of Emerging Adults.* Oxford: Oxford University Press, 2009.

Stark, Rodney, and William Sims Bainbridge. *The Future of Religion: Secularization, Revival and Cult Formation.* Berkeley: University of California Press, 1985.

Stark, Rodney, and Roger Finke. *Acts of Faith: Explaining the Human Side of Religion.* Berkeley: University of California Press, 2000.

Stark, Rodney, and Laurence R. Iannaccone. "A Supply-Side Reinterpretation of the 'Secularization' of Europe." *Journal for the Scientific Study of Religion* 33 (1994) 230–52.

Thompson, E. *Yearbook of the United Baptist Convention of the Atlantic Provinces.* Saint John, NB: United Baptist Convention of the Atlantic Provinces, 1987.

Voas, David, and Alasdair Crockett. "Religion in Britain: Neither Believing nor Belonging." *Sociology* 39 (2005) 11–28.

Voas, David, and Mark Chaves. "Is the United States a Counterexample to the Secularization Thesis?" *American Journal of Sociology* 121 (2016) 1517–56.

3

Navigating Secularization

Implications of the History of Secularization
for Christian Higher Education in Canada

KEVIN N. FLATT

THE MOTTO OF MCMASTER University, adopted in 1888 and still seen in its official coat of arms, is ΤΑ ΠΑΝΤΑ ΕΝ ΧΡΙΣΤΩΙ ΣΥΝΕΣΤΗΚΕΝ, "in Christ all things hold together."[1] A faculty member once pointed this out to me while I was a graduate student there, though the conversation turned to other things and I did not learn her purpose in drawing it to my attention. Now, it should be obvious to anyone who has spent much time at McMaster University that few of its faculty or students today would affirm that all things hold together in Christ.[2] Most of them would probably find that assertion unintelligible, embarrassing, or even offensive. From their point of view, it is perhaps just as well that this vestigial reminder of the university's Christian origins is safely hidden away behind the veil of *koine* Greek.

---

1. Colossians 1:17. See https://www.mcmaster.ca/coat/motto.htm.

2. For clarity, McMaster Divinity College, which as Toronto Baptist College was the founding institution of McMaster University and shares the same motto, formally separated from McMaster University in 1957 and is not a faculty or college of the university, and its faculty are not a part of the university. McMaster Divinity College has thus not followed the mainstream secularization trajectory described here, but belongs to the different story of CHEC institutions noted below.

I begin with this anecdote not, I hope, to pick on my *alma mater*, but as a concrete instance of something all of us know to be true about many universities in Canada and, indeed, throughout the Western world: they were founded as Christian institutions, but they are not Christian institutions anymore. While traces of their heritage still exist, like McMaster's motto, they exist only as symbolic vestiges of a long-dead institutional history. In Canada, this observation is true of nearly every publicly-funded university established before the 1950s. We could say much the same of the great universities of the United States, Britain, France, Germany, and other Western countries.

Most of the member institutions of Christian Higher Education Canada (CHEC) were founded against this backdrop, as a self-conscious "Plan B" for Christian higher education. Their founders established them as a conservative Protestant alternative, first, to the increasingly liberalized and secularized theological and biblical training available in mainstream institutions, and then later as an alternative to secular university education in other disciplines. A first wave of mostly Bible college foundings concentrated in the 1920s, 1930s, and 1940s was followed by a second wave of foundings from the 1960s through the 1990s, which included several liberal arts colleges or universities. These institutions were founded, not because there were no educational options available, but because the educational options on offer, from a conservative Protestant perspective, simply were not good enough. "Plan A"—the great Christian universities of the past—had failed with respect to their Christian mission. Hence a "Plan B" was necessary. At great expense and with great difficulty, our forebears established, maintained, and grew these institutions in what must have seemed to outsiders like pigheaded defiance of the obvious direction of higher educational progress.[3]

Such efforts reflected, at least implicitly, a judgment that secularization in higher education was real, but neither desirable nor inevitable. The character of secularization, therefore, is a topic closely bound up with the past and the future of Christian higher education in Canada, and with CHEC specifically. The founders were working with some concept of secularization, whether they articulated it or not. "Plan B" was part of their response to secularization. In the case of most of our institutions, the founding generation has now retired or passed away, and Canadian society

---

3. The early history of several of these Canadian institutions of Christian higher education is recounted in Stackhouse, *Canadian Evangelicalism*.

has continued to become more secular (in a variety of senses) in the de-cades since they did their work. To the extent we continue to pursue "Plan B," however, we share in some of their understanding of secularization and how to respond to it.

But what is secularization? How do we imagine it and explain it? How does it operate in the realm of higher education specifically? The answers to such questions have implications that go beyond the immediate concerns of our founders and speak directly to how we think of our mission and role today, including the long-term visions and institutional strategies we pursue.

In what follows, I first survey the major scholarly schools of thought concerning the nature and causes of secularization, identifying the best thinking emerging out of at least half a century of debate on these matters. I then draw on the most promising insights to give a thumbnail sketch of the history of the secularization of universities across five Western countries: Germany, France, Britain, the United States, and Canada. Finally, I draw out the sobering implications of this history for institutions of Christian higher education in Canada today, concluding by suggesting three strategic priorities that will need to be pursued if "Plan B" is to have even a chance of success.

SECULARIZATION: THREE SCHOOLS OF THOUGHT

The Classical Secularization Paradigm

Claims of a decline in religion and attempts to explain said decline in terms of a larger historical process go back at least as far as the work of the found-ing figures of the social sciences like Auguste Comte (1798–1857), Émile Durkheim (1858–1917), and Max Weber (1864–1920).[4] The basic truth of the thesis that modernization caused secularization, and that religion was in decline in some sense, was almost universally assumed by nineteenth- and twentieth-century sociological thinkers.[5] Thinkers in the 1960s and 1970s provided the most extensive theoretical formulations of the idea that modernization leads to secularization. Sociologists like Peter Berger, Richard Fenn, Thomas Luckmann, and Bryan Wilson published theories

---

4. See, for example, Comte, *Auguste Comte and Positivism*; Durkheim, *The Divi-sion of Labor*; Weber, "Religious Rejections"; Weber, *Economy and Society*.

5. Casanova, *Public Religions*, 17.

articulating and explaining the secularization process.[6] Although they differed on many points, they fit into a shared "secularization paradigm" based on the belief that a general process of social development was reducing the role of religion in modern society.[7] Some versions of the paradigm allowed for the persistence and continuing importance of religion in some form, but most versions expected that religious beliefs, practices, institutions, or social influences would continue to decline in importance as modernization progressed. This dim prognosis for religion was, if anything, sharpened in the accounts offered in the following decades by theorists like Karel Dobbelaere, Bryan Wilson, and Steve Bruce.[8] In their account of "the orthodox model" of secularization, for example, Roy Wallis and Steve Bruce point to general processes of modernization which work together to undermine the institutional power of the churches, the "plausibility of any single overarching moral and religious system," and the ability of religion to offer satisfying explanations of the world.[9] Bruce's later restatement of the classical paradigm likewise portrays widespread decline in the importance of religion as an irreversible long-term trend in nearly all Western countries, one that is likely both to continue in the future and to be replicated in other societies as they modernize.[10]

The classical secularization paradigm seemed plausible to most Western scholars for most of the twentieth century, perhaps in part because most of them lived in Western European countries whose rates of religious belief and participation were in decline and themselves tended to belong to an unusually secular subculture of intellectuals.[11] Yet as the twentieth century wore on, a growing chorus of voices pointed to problems with the classical paradigm. For one thing, outside of Western Europe and a few other Western countries like Canada, there was not much evidence of religious decline. American sociologists demonstrated that levels of church membership in the United States, a modernized society if there ever was one,

6. Berger, *Sacred Canopy*; Fenn, *Toward a Theory*; Luckmann, *Invisible Religion*; Wilson, *Religion in Secular Society*.

7. Tschannen, "Secularization Paradigm," 395–415. See also Gorski, "Historicizing," 140–42.

8. E.g., Dobbelaere, *Secularization*; Wilson, *Religion in Sociological Perspective*; Bruce, *Secularization*.

9. Wallis and Bruce, "Secularization," 8–9, 13, 14.

10. Bruce, *Secularization*, 4, 23, 24–26, 54–56, 59.

11. Berger, "Desecularization," 10–11.

had actually been steadily increasing for two hundred years.[12] In most parts of the world, religion seemed to be as vibrant as ever, and more politically active all the time, as the phenomena of the Moral Majority in the United States and the Islamic Revolution in Iran seemed to suggest. Sociologists demonstrated that, even in nineteenth-century Britain, urbanization had been positively correlated with church attendance and that most of the decline in churchgoing had been quite recent and rapid, not at all the gradual long-term trend one might expect from the classical paradigm.[13] Several scholars also mounted brilliant critiques of the theoretical assumptions and conclusions embedded in the paradigm.[14]

The Religious Economies School

The second major approach to understanding secularization, the religious economies, "supply-side," or rational choice school, emerged in the 1980s and 1990s as an explicit challenge to the classical paradigm. Led by the pugnacious American sociologist Rodney Stark and his associates, the supply-siders rejected the classical paradigm's claim of a general long-term decline in religion. Instead of theorizing a long-term decline in *demand* for religion caused by modernization, the religious economies school pointed to differences in religious *supply* to explain the high levels of religious belief and practice in the United States, on the one hand, and the low levels in most Western European countries, on the other.[15] Stark and his colleagues proposed that churches be thought of as religious "firms" that offer religious products and compete with one another for religious "customers." Where a competitive free market existed, as in the pluralistic, no-establishment United States, a huge variety of religious firms could compete, satisfying a wide range of religious wants and weeding out lazy or otherwise ineffective competitors. In such a situation, passionate, high-commitment, strict, and otherworldly churches would thrive. In contrast, where the religious market was dominated by one or a few established or semi-established churches propped up by government subsidies, compulsory tithes, or cultural inertia, as in much of Europe, the religious products on offer would be

12. Finke and Stark, *Churching of America*.

13. Brown, "Revisionist Approach"; Brown, *Death of Christian Britain*.

14. E.g., Smith, "Introduction," 12–25; Casanova, *Public Religions*, 17–39.

15. For key works from this school, see Finke and Stark, *Churching of America*; Stark and Iannaccone, "Supply-Side Reinterpretation"; Stark, "Secularization, R.I.P."; Stark and Finke, *Acts of Faith*.

comparatively few and of poor quality, thus explaining the lack of participation on the part of the masses. Stark pushed the point further and argued that European societies had probably never been all that religious in the first place: evidence from before the modern era suggested that religious indifference and low church participation had always been widespread under the monopolistic conditions of European Christendom.[16] By imaging a fictional past of religious vitality, secularization theorists were seeing decline where none existed. Instead of trying to perpetuate the failed secularization paradigm, Stark proposed, sociologists should concentrate on explaining religious *change*, which could go in either direction depending on market conditions.

By proposing a clear explanatory model that could account for an impressive array of historical and contemporary evidence, the religious economies school put the classical paradigm on the defensive.[17] But it too was subject to criticisms, both empirical disputes about the interpretation of the statistics and theoretical critiques. One serious criticism was that the model did not properly account for changing conceptions of religiosity across centuries and cultures. In medieval European Christianity, for example, church attendance may have been a relatively unimportant index of piety compared to involvement in pilgrimages or ceremonies of blessing.[18] Moreover, the religious economies approach had much to say about individual religious belief and behaviour and the dynamics affecting churches, but it had nothing to say about the secularization of other institutions (e.g., the state) or cultural domains (e.g., art). Finally, the underlying anthropology of the model—human beings as utility-maximizing actors who rationally calculate the costs and benefits of religious participation—seemed to critics to be an insufficient account of the reality of observed human behaviour.[19]

Historicist Approaches

Despite their many differences, the classical secularization paradigm and the religious economies school were alike in that both sought to explain

16. Stark, "Secularization, R.I.P.," 255–60; see also Bruce's response, "Christianity in Britain, R.I.P."

17. See, e.g., Bruce, "Christianity in Britain, R.I.P.," and Bruce, *Secularization*, 141–56.

18. Gorski, "Historicizing," 144–49; Bruce, "Christianity in Britain, R.I.P.," 193–94.

19. For a sympathetic critique, see Smith, *American Evangelicalism*, 118–19. For a more hostile example, see Bruce, "Christianity in Britain, R.I.P.," 192–93.

secularization or religious vitality in terms of general social dynamics that were in principle universally applicable. Several alternative approaches have emerged more recently, however, which instead stress the ways in which the secularization of Western societies was the product of specific, unique historical events that could and did unfold differently in different places at different times. Although this group is more diverse, disciplinarily and theoretically, than the religious economies school, Samuel Nelson and Philip Gorski describe it as a third school of thought following a "contingent and historicist approach."[20] Historicist accounts of secularization bring secularization theory closer to the work of historians who seek to document and understand the specific events of particular times and places, but without giving up on the idea that there are broader patterns at work that affect multiple societies over longer periods of time.

David Martin, for example, the pioneer of this school, argues that there is not one trajectory of secularization, but at least four to six different patterns of secularization just within the West, each reflecting important historical differences between different major cultural regions. Thus he identifies a French (or Latin) pattern of secularization, an Anglo-Saxon pattern, a Lutheran pattern, and so on.[21] The work of José Casanova likewise stresses that although there may be some common elements of modernization across societies, we should think in terms of "multiple modernities" that relate religion to society in different ways.[22] A shrinking in the institutional role of churches due to the increasing complexity and differentiation of society, for example, need not lead to the privatization of religious faith or a decline in religious observance.[23] Gorski and Nelson argue in their works that claims about secularization or the lack thereof need to be better grounded in historical realities, which are more complex than assumed by the other two schools, and tend not to follow long-term linear patterns.[24] In this they resemble the historians who document sudden shifts

---

20. Nelson and Gorski, "Conditions of Religious Belonging," 4. The three-school categorization used here is derived from Nelson and Gorski, though my third category may be broader than theirs.

21. Martin, *General Theory*, 5–8. See also Martin, *On Secularization*.

22. Casanova, "Rethinking Secularization," 13–14.

23. Casanova, *Public Religions*.

24. Gorski, "Historicizing"; Nelson and Gorski, "Conditions of Religious Belonging."

and reversals, such as the work of Callum Brown and Hugh McLeod on the recent and rapid decline of churchgoing in the 1960s.[25]

Some work in this group of approaches also calls into question deeper assumptions of the classical paradigm. Canadian philosopher Charles Taylor, for example, narrates secularization not as a "subtraction story," where religion gradually fades from the picture and secular society is what is left, but rather as what might be called a construction story: the ways of thinking about humans and the world that made a secular age possible had to be imagined and developed and made plausible first.[26] "The secular" is an achievement in its own right, not just the absence of a something called religion. Anthropologist Talal Asad makes a similar point, calling for an "anthropology of secularism."[27] In a complementary vein, Christian Smith forcefully demonstrates that, in the case of American public life at least, secularization

> was not an abstract, natural, and inevitable by-product of some evolutionary modernization process. Rather, it was the achievement of intentional agents, influenced by particular ideologies and interests, seeking to enhance their own status and authority by actively displacing the competing status and authority of religious actors.[28]

Secularization, he argues, was a revolution. In general, Smith calls for a way of thinking of secularization that emphasizes human agency and multiple historical possibilities and that pays attention to individuals and ideologies as well as the structural and material factors so beloved of classical secularization theory.[29]

Though the religious economies school was the first to seriously challenge the secularization paradigm that had dominated social science for more than a century, the historicist school has continued the job with more broadly plausible assumptions and a richer array of historical and contemporary evidence. It is probably fair to say that the classical paradigm has

25. Brown, *Death of Christian Britain*; McLeod, *Religious Crisis*.

26. Taylor, *Secular Age*, e.g. 22, 26–28, 572.

27. Asad, *Formations*, 21–66. Peter Berger puts it this way: "The difficult-to-understand phenomenon is not Iranian mullahs but American university professors." Berger, "Desecularization," 2.

28. Smith, "Secularizing American Higher Education," 105. See also the other essays in this volume.

29. Smith, "Introduction," 24.

been dethroned, at least among specialists in the study of religion, though it continues to have capable advocates.[30] As may already be obvious, my own view is that while the classical paradigm and the religious economies model do a good job of explaining some aspects of the changing place of religion in Western societies, the historicist school on the whole employs a better understanding of human nature, the dynamics of human society, and the complexities of human history, and therefore produces more plausible accounts of secularization.

As we have seen, the classical secularization paradigm portrays secularization as the marginalization or decline in religion's institutional power and/or social relevance as the result of a long-term developmental process of modernization, while the religious economies school explains low levels of religious participation in terms of uncompetitive religious markets. Drawing on the best work in the historicist school, we might instead imagine secularization this way: secularization was a series of historical developments in Western countries over several centuries that replaced Christendom with a new secular order. The defining characteristic of the secular order is that it attempts to ground our common institutions, practices, and beliefs in purely human terms without reference to God, who is treated (usually implicitly) as nonexistent, irrelevant, or unwelcome in our common life. Since the eighteenth century, the secular order has become hegemonic over most domains of social life in all Western countries, though at different times and speeds in different places—sometimes through revolutionary upheaval, sometimes through more gradual change. This process was neither automatic, inevitable, nor natural, in the sense of being a simple by-product of socio-economic development or scientific progress, or a stage in social evolution. Instead, secularization was brought about through the exercise of power in conflict, competition, and control whereby advocates of the secular order and their allies were able to overturn or marginalize older Christian forms of order and meaning—sometimes through intentional strategies, sometimes as a result of unintended consequences.[31] Likewise, once established, the secular order is maintained by various forms of cultural, economic, and political power. To bring us back to our main purpose in this chapter, the secular university plays an

30. Notably Steve Bruce, but also others; e.g., Norris and Inglehart, *Sacred and Secular.*

31. An emphasis on interests, agency, and conflict can still allow for unintended results to play a key role in secularization, as both Taylor, *Secular Age*, and Gregory, *Unintended Reformation*, demonstrate.

important role in the maintenance of the secular order, by elaborating and preserving its basic assumptions and transmitting them to the next generation of intellectuals, cultural authorities, professionals, and rulers. But how did this role come about? From a historicist perspective, what is the place of the university in the history of secularization?

THE HISTORY OF THE SECULARIZATION OF UNIVERSITIES

Let us begin with some general observations about the overall historical picture, before delving into different patterns of university secularization in different parts of the Western world.

General Features

First, early universities from the High Middle Ages until the time of the Reformation tended to be fairly autonomous institutions, thanks to their papal or royal charters, their largely self-governing structure as basically guilds of professors or students, their relatively low costs, and church and state authorities' high regard for the prestige and usefulness of university learning. Medieval universities themselves decided what would be taught and by whom.[32] When left to their own devices, as they typically were in the Middle Ages under these conditions, universities tended to be quite conservative. They saw their role primarily as the preservation, extension, and transmission of the established way of thinking and a set body of knowledge. This basically conservative orientation continued well into the early modern period for reasons that will be discussed below.[33] In fact, surprising though it is to twenty-first-century Westerners who have learned to think of universities as incubators of innovation, experimentation, and radicalism, nearly every major paradigm shift or wave of intellectual innovation that took place in the Western world between the fourteenth and the nineteenth century came from outside the university world. The Reformation, as an "affair of universities,"[34] was the conspicuous exception to the rule, but Renaissance humanism, the Scientific Revolution, and the Enlightenment all began outside the universities—typically among innovators who enjoyed sufficient leisure time due to the patronage of rulers or notables—and at

32. Gieysztor, "Management and Resources," 133–35; Nardi, "Relations with Authority"; Rudy, *Universities of Europe*, 21–26, 29–30, 34–35, 38.

33. E.g., Brockliss, "Curricula," 617.

34. Rudy, *Universities of Europe*, 58.

first had only tenuous and indirect connections to the university world.[35] The default historical social role of the Western university has been to re-inforce, flesh out, and replicate the regnant ways of looking at the world.

Second, since at least the end of the Middle Ages, the story of the university has been one of increasing government regulation, funding, and control. The period of confessionalization that followed the Reformation led temporal and ecclesiastical authorities to collaborate in tightening the regulation of universities, which became important assets in the ideological conflicts between Catholics, Lutherans, and the Reformed.[36] State building and absolutism in the seventeenth and eighteenth centuries further extend-ed the reach of the ruler into the university in several countries, especially in central Europe, and the French Revolution and its aftershocks dramatically deepened this trend.[37] The expansion of scientific and technical research and education in the nineteenth century was both driven by state objectives and required ever-increasing reliance on state funding to pay for the neces-sary laboratories and equipment.[38] In the twentieth century the turn to mass enrollment as an instrument of governments' scientific and economic policies further solidified these trends. The long-term trajectory in every major Western country into at least the twentieth century was thus towards less institutional autonomy for universities and greater state control.

Third, at some point between the eighteenth and the twentieth century in most countries, the professorial class used the increasing specialization, technical complexity, and professionalization of knowledge to enhance its own independence and prestige, especially relative to rival knowledge authorities like the clergy. The notions of academic freedom, scholarly societies, tenure, self-governance, and faculty control over the curriculum emerged to guarantee the independence of this class from most outside constraints or responsibilities. Such independence was often attenuated by the watchful eye of the state, especially where political matters were

35. On Renaissance humanism, see Rudy, *Universities of Europe*, 40–46; Rüegg, "Rise of Humanism," 449–57; on the Scientific Revolution and the Enlightenment, see Rüegg, "Themes," in *Universities in Early Modern Europe*, 14, 20–22, 38; Frijhoff, "Patterns," 44–45; Porter, "Scientific Revolution," 533; Hammerstein, "The Enlightenment," 631; Rudy, *Universities of Europe*, 78–80, 84, 97; and Anderson, *European Universities*, 17–18.

36. Rudy, *Universities of Europe*, 63–73.

37. Anderson, *European Universities*, 20–21, 40–45.

38. E.g., Gerbod, "Relations with Authority," 111–12, 120; Rudy, *Universities of Europe*, 126–29.

concerned, and it made progress only where faculty were able to convince allies with wealth or political power that professionalization was in the interests of scientific progress and therefore provided economic or military benefits. Nevertheless, a symbiotic relationship developed between professional scholars and the state, intentionally furthering the interests of both at the expense of other groups that might have a stake in university education, such as churches and local university administrations.[39] Now to specifics.

National Variations

Of the major Western European countries, the secularization of universities seems to have taken place first in the German states, especially Brandenburg-Prussia. The ruling house of this north German state, the Hohenzollerns, held to the Reformed faith, but the established church was Lutheran. This juxtaposition made the dynasty nervous about the power of the Lutheran clergy, and from the reign of Frederick III (r. 1688–1713), the Hohenzollerns encouraged the growth of Pietism, a spiritual revival movement that downplayed the authority of the clergy. The University of Halle, founded in 1694 under Pietist auspices and with royal blessing, was, according to one prominent historian of European universities, "intended to break with Lutheran orthodoxy and teach religion in the interests of the state."[40] Frederick the Great (r. 1740–1786), however, rejected the Calvinism of his forefathers and befriended Enlightenment thinkers such as Voltaire. Under his influence, Halle was transformed into a center of rationalism in opposition to religious orthodoxy. Early in his reign, for example, Frederick reinstated the Enlightenment rationalist professor Christian Wolff, who had lost his post at Halle in 1723 for his determinist views, and allowed him to rise to the position of chancellor.[41] The idea that faculty should be free to advocate their ideas without religious tests or constraints, subject only to the judgment of their academic peers, became a hallmark of Halle, and was imitated by other universities in northern and central Europe, including the prominent University of Berlin (founded 1809).[42] By the early nineteenth century in several German states, intellectuals of a rationalist, deist, or Enlightenment bent enjoyed wide latitude in pursuing ideas counter to

39. Anderson, *European Universities*, 20, 24, 58–63, 104; Hammerstein, "The Enlightenment," 634–5; Rudy, *Universities of Europe*, 89–93, 103.

40. Anderson, *European Universities*, 24. See also Rudy, *Universities of Europe*, 89–91.

41. Rudy, *Universities of Europe*, 93.

42. Rudy, *Universities of Europe*, 94–97, 103.

religious orthodoxy and in criticizing the religious establishment. The German model was the earliest example of the alliance between the professoriate and the state, whereby rulers who hoped to benefit from the advance of knowledge granted scholars a great deal of autonomy in their writing and teaching, typically with the proviso that they stop short of outright atheism, stick to their subjects of expertise, and refrain from criticizing the government. Broadly speaking it reflected the characteristic preexisting Lutheran pattern in which religion and intellectual and creative pursuits were sponsored by the state because they were thought to serve the state's interests. In the Prussian legal code of 1794, for example, universities were defined as state institutions, giving rise to a long-lasting bias in German thinking against private or religious universities.

The secularization of German universities thus developed from within the country, rather than through the influence of foreign universities. Nor was it the result of a sudden, revolutionary break with religion, but rather a more gradual growth of unorthodox and rationalist religious views with the backing of political power.[43] In this way an academic elite committed to Enlightenment ideals and resistant to religious orthodoxy became a self-governing and self-perpetuating class that could dictate what was taught and whose ideas were favored in the university system. Although such a system was not hostile to religion *per se*, the kind of religion it fostered was of a liberal and heterodox variety refashioned to conform to Enlightenment critiques of dogmatism and revelation. Within a few generations, even theology and biblical research in German universities proceeded from Enlightenment presuppositions; Friedrich Schleiermacher, of course, was one of the leading figures in the founding generation at the University of Berlin. Moreover, because German universities were highly regarded in several other countries, especially in the later nineteenth century when the research-intensive approach made Germany a leader in scientific discovery, German scholarship and the German university became a powerful secularizing model imitated in other lands.[44]

Things happened quite differently in France. Here, while the eighteenth-century Enlightenment was flourishing in the *salons*, the universities maintained such a strict commitment to Catholic orthodoxy that historians have tended to accuse them of stagnation.[45] The sudden and

---

43. Anderson, *European Universities*, 26, 37, 58–64.

44. Anderson, *European Universities*, 3, 63–64, 109–10.

45. Rudy, *Universities of Europe*, 84; Frijhoff, "Patterns," 58; Hammerstein, "The

violent overthrow of the *ancien régime* in the French Revolution, however, also extended to the universities. The revolutionaries abolished the entire medieval university system, even the ancient University of Paris, and began creating a fully secular system of education at all levels under tight state control—a policy largely continued under Napoleon, who allowed some religious education in his system but only as an instrument of state policy and without any church involvement or clerical influence.[46] There were openings again to church involvement at various points in the nineteenth century, but intensifying conflict between conservative Catholics and secularist liberals over education were eventually resolved in favour of the latter.[47] Compared to the German experience, secularization in France proceeded much more as a sudden imposition by the state on the universities, creating a new, largely secular intelligentsia existentially opposed to any reintroduction of church influence in education. This more conflictual, revolutionary type of secularization, involving a protracted winner-takes-all culture war between a conservative clerical party and a secular anticlerical party, exemplifies what David Martin calls a French or Latin pattern of secularization that was replicated in some other predominantly Catholic countries of southern Europe and Latin America.[48]

The British pattern was different yet again, though with more similarities to the German pattern than the French one. British universities enjoyed much greater autonomy than their continental counterparts throughout the nineteenth century and well into the twentieth. In England, where Oxford and Cambridge were really the only two universities to speak of until well into the nineteenth century, the universities were not only overwhelmingly Christian but still closely tied to the established church. The Scottish universities, though more intellectually open than their English counterparts to moderate Enlightenment ideas, likewise required faculty and students to subscribe to the Westminster Confession.[49] Both active state involvement and secularization came relatively late to Britain, not playing a significant

Enlightenment," 125–28; Anderson, *European Universities*, 5, 17–18, 39–40.

46. Rüegg, "Themes," in *Universities in the Nineteenth and Early Twentieth Centuries*, 3; Anderson, *European Universities*, 40–45.

47. Anderson, *European Universities*, 75, 81, 84, 97–101, 181–82; Rudy, *Universities of Europe*, 113–14.

48. Martin, *General Theory*, 6–7, 16–20.

49. Bebbington, "Secularization," 259–60.

role until the second half of the nineteenth century.[50] According to David Bebbington, the challenge to the religious university establishment came not primarily from rationalists allied with state patrons, as in Germany, nor from revolutionary secularists backed by government force, as in France, but from nonconformist Protestants and political liberals who opposed the exclusion from the university system of those who did not belong to the established churches. Through political connections, they were successful in convincing the government to intervene and remove religious tests from both the English and the Scottish universities between 1853 and 1889.[51] In contrast to the French case, considerable elements of Christian symbolism and significant ties to the churches remained in the older universities, especially Oxford and Cambridge. These changes nevertheless opened the door to a gradual secularization of the universities alongside the decline of religious belief and adherence more generally in the country in the twentieth century. Unfortunately, Bebbington's account does not devote much attention to the nature and rise of secular ideologies among British professors, though there are hints they may have played a significant role. For example, he mentions in passing that by the mid-twentieth century ideologies like logical positivism and "scientism" had undercut the intellectual plausibility of traditional religion, though he does not say how they rose to prominence in British universities.[52]

This brings us to the American case. The situation in early nineteenth-century America resembled Britain in that higher education was deeply and explicitly Christian, except that other than a few universities tied to the established church, these schools were mostly small colleges aligned with a variety of Protestant denominations. Evangelical Protestantism dominated higher education, not only in the denominationally affiliated colleges but even in the state colleges, many of which in 1890 still required chapel attendance.[53] But according to George Marsden, after 1870 or so traditional Protestantism was displaced as the dominant force by a "broadly liberal Protestantism" allied with "a growing ideological secularism."[54] These two

---

50. Anderson, *European Universities*, 35, 94; Hammerstein, "Relations with Authority," 137.

51. Bebbington, "Secularization," 264–65.

52. Bebbington, "Secularization," 271.

53. Marsden, *Soul of the American University*, 4; Marsden, "Soul of the American University," 11.

54. Marsden, "Soul of the American University," 21.

camps worked together to marginalize traditional Protestantism, writes Marsden, "and within only about fifty years they effected a remarkable revolution that eliminated most traditional views from respectable academia."[55] In Marsden's account, secularists became more influential after World War I and by the 1960s had successfully ousted their liberal Protestant allies, leaving the leading American universities dominated by "a more aggressive pluralistic secularism" from the 1960s onward.[56]

Increasing money and influence from wealthy progressive benefactors and governments played a role in these developments, but just as important was the turn to faculty specialization and professionalization on the German model.[57] In particular, in 1915 a small scholarly elite based at the leading universities and connected to the newly formed scholarly associations formed the American Association of University Professors (AAUP) in order to oppose religious control over faculty and replace local church and community authorities with a national self-governing academic profession as the dominant influence in higher education.[58] As Christian Smith has demonstrated in the case of American sociology, many of these leading intellectuals were personally deeply hostile to evangelical Christianity, or any kind of orthodox religion for that matter, and sought to reproduce in the United States the German university model they experienced in graduate school (nearly ten thousand American students went to graduate school in Germany between 1815 and 1914). Their conscious aim was the marginalization of religion in the academy, especially any religiously-based competition to their emerging discipline and scholarly associations.[59] A secularist intelligentsia was thus able to create a kind of colony of the German system west of the Atlantic, in which the professorial class made itself immune from outside control or criticism, especially from the churches, established its own leading members as the highest academic authority, and secured a monopoly of government support in the name of science, progress, and religious neutrality.

55. Marsden, "Soul of the American University," 22.

56. Marsden, "Soul of the American University," 21.

57. Marsden, "Soul of the American University," 15, 20, 28.

58. Marsden, *Soul of the American University*, 302–8; Smith, "Secularizing American Higher Education," 103.

59. Smith, "Secularizing American Higher Education," 102, 111–53; Smith, "Introduction," 56.

An important difference between the British and the American case was the continuing presence in the United States of a large network of conservative Christian colleges, at first mostly evangelical Protestant but increasingly also Catholic, alongside the secularizing or secularized mainstream universities. These Christian colleges drew on the strength of popular Christianity in the United States, which continued unabated through most of the twentieth century at levels of belief and practice far exceeding most other Western countries. Some of these colleges, like Notre Dame (1842), Wheaton (1860), and Calvin (1876), were founded before or during the early stages of university secularization, while many others such as Biola (1908), Dordt (1955), Thomas Aquinas (1971), and Boyce (1998) sprang up during the twentieth century.[60] These schools provided some counterweight to the dominant secular model, certainly more of a counterweight than existed in Britain, France, or Germany. But the independent Christian college sector stood at a major financial disadvantage to the state universities and lacked the prestige and resources of the older and better endowed private universities. Most Christian believers in the United States continued to attend secular colleges and universities for their postsecondary education. By Marsden's reckoning, at the beginning of the 1990s the combined enrollment of all evangelical colleges in the US amounted to "about the same as that of two state universities."[61]

The Christian colleges were also susceptible to powerful secularizing influences, in many cases following the same secularizing path already trodden by their older siblings.[62] Across denominational lines, Protestant and Catholic colleges passed from robust Christian faith connected to particular churches or traditions, through an intermediate stage of a vaguer, more liberal Christianity, to a final stage where the only real connection to their founding aims and ethos was historical and symbolic. In his systematic study of seventeen originally Christian colleges, most of which had reached that final stage, James Tunstead Burtchaell identified certain common elements in their stories. Among these were the failure of churches to serve as an adequate primary funder or to play a competent governance role, the increasing regulatory interference of governmental or quasi-governmental

---

60. Burtchaell (*Dying of the Light*, 743–45) provides a list by founding date of Protestant colleges that were members of the Coalition [later Council] of Christian Colleges and Universities in 1996.

61. Marsden, "Soul of the American University," 10.

62. The preeminent guide to this phenomenon is Burtchaell, *Dying of the Light*.

bodies including accrediting agencies, the ability of a single liberalizing president to uncouple an institution from its past, and the prevalence of a pietistic approach to faith that favors experience and emotion over doctrinal orthodoxy and the intellectual implications of faith.[63]

A particularly important element identified by Burtchaell was the growing orientation of the faculty and administrators toward the larger professional academic guild, with its guiding values and attitudes, rather than toward the church or the religious tradition of their institution.[64] As Burtchaell states, "The faculty transferred their primary loyalties from their college to their disciplines and their guild, and were thereby antagonistic to any competing norms of professional excellence related to the church."[65] Given what we have already seen regarding the origins and character of the academic guild in Germany and the mainstream American universities, what followed can hardly be surprising. In the face of increasing resistance, faith questions became less important in hiring decisions and were eventually dispensed with; religious tests or confessional subscriptions for faculty were either made formalities, loosened, or limited to certain parts of the faculty, before finally being dropped altogether. The original guiding values of fidelity and distinctiveness thus gave way to the contrary values of openness, broadmindedness, and non-sectarianism.[66] Due to the powerful cultural influences of the leading secular universities and elite reaches of the academic guild, in just a couple of generations such colleges reenacted what took two centuries in Germany and half a century in the older American universities.[67]

---

63. Burtchaell, *Dying of the Light*, 823–28, 837–47.

64. Burtchaell, *Dying of the Light*, 828–37.

65. Burtchaell, *Dying of the Light*, 837.

66. Burtchaell, *Dying of the Light*, 829–31.

67. Just how widespread or advanced such tendencies are among independent Christian colleges *in general* in the early twenty-first century United States is a difficult question to answer with confidence. In its closing chapter, Ringenberg's *The Christian College* paints a more mixed picture of the overall situation than do Burtchaell's vignettes, noting evidence of continuing fidelity especially among some evangelical colleges, while also acknowledging cultural and legal pressures toward secularization consistent with the trends identified by Burthchaell. Schmalzbauer and Mahoney, *The Resilience of Religion*, 55–94, affirms the general secularization trend but points to evidence of a renewed emphasis on the role of religion in things like new mission statements and discussions about faith and learning at some Christian colleges. Yet much of this evidence does not go beyond institutional aspirations, while the book also provides evidence that faculty at many Christian colleges are uneasy or divided about the limitations on academic

The final national example is Canada.[68] It is worth mentioning in passing that the secularization of the universities in Quebec during the Quiet Revolution of the 1960s resembled the French pattern, with the important difference that the Catholic church largely acquiesced in its displacement from education both because of prior intellectual sympathies in its ranks and because of the disorienting and pacifying effects of Vatican II.[69] Given that nearly all private religious institutions of higher education in Canada are Protestant and English-speaking, the situation in English Canada is more relevant to our purposes. Although there is less historical research to draw on, it is clear enough that English-Canadian universities followed something like the American pattern of secularization. The landscape of university education in Canada in the nineteenth century more closely resembled the American one, with its young colleges linked to a variety of evangelical Protestant denominations, than the British one, with its very small and very old university sector dominated by two established churches. Later, moving through the nineteenth century and into the twentieth, the Canadian mainstream followed much the same path as the American mainstream.

George Rawlyk, focusing on McMaster University but applying his conclusions more broadly to Canadian higher education as a whole, tells a story much like Marsden's. After an initial conservative Protestant phase, McMaster's leaders and faculty shifted to downplaying doctrinal requirements and resisting denominational authorities who wanted to enforce religious orthodoxy. Then, from the 1920s, the university's leaders allied themselves with progressive businessmen and then the provincial government to dismantle what remained of the founding convictions of the institution and cut its ties to the Baptist Convention.[70] Discussing the country as a whole, Rawlyk claims that "[b]y the 1920s virtually every Canadian Protestant institution of higher education had evolved in the McMaster manner (most of them, however, had moved at a far more accelerated rate) . . . Moreover, by the 1920s all the mainline Protestant seminaries had abandoned the nineteenth-century conservative evangelical consensus

---

freedom suggested by the role of religion on campus and in faculty hiring.

68. Fernhout ("Quest for Identity and Place") provides a good overview of the history and recent situation of Christian higher education in Canada.

69. On the religious and educational dimensions of the Quiet Revolution, see Baum, "Catholicism and Secularization in Quebec"; Gauvreau, *Catholic Origins*; and Seljak, "Why the Quiet Revolution was 'Quiet.'"

70. Rawlyk, "Protestant Colleges," 283–98.

and replaced it with an accommodating liberalism."[71] For several decades the major universities across English Canada continued to possess a kind of diffuse liberal Protestant ethos, seen mostly in ceremonial elements like opening chapels and in the moral regulation of students. Yet by the 1960s even this liberal Protestant shadow establishment had collapsed.[72]

Overall, then, the story of the secularization of Canadian universities parallels the American one: a traditionalist Protestant beginning, followed by a transitional phase of liberal Protestantism allied with progressive elements and opposed to the imposition of religious orthodoxy, ending with a completely secular system from the 1960s onward.[73] There is one important difference between the American and Canadian situations, however, which is that the Canadian independent religious sector in higher education is much smaller, much younger, and less easily accommodated into the overall landscape than in the United States. Taken as a whole, then, although it has followed a very similar trajectory, Canadian higher education is today more monolithically secular than American higher education.

IMPLICATIONS FOR CHRISTIAN HIGHER EDUCATION IN CANADA

The foregoing narrative portrays the history of secularization of universities, not as a byproduct of social evolution, nor as a result of a lack of competition among religious firms, but as the result of particular historical developments involving power, interests, conflict, and the dynamics of cultural influence. Assuming this way of thinking about secularization is correct, what are the implications for Christian higher education in Canada today?

First, on a general level, it needs to be recognized that most university education in the Western world functions as part of a powerful system of cultural hegemony. Western universities are the beating heart of what Casanova calls "the knowledge regime of secularism,"[74] and the creators and sustainers of what Berger describes as follows:

71. Rawlyk, "Protestant Colleges," 298.

72. Gidney, *A Long Eclipse*.

73. The public school system in Ontario at the elementary and secondary levels seems to have followed a similar path, but about 20–30 years later. Gidney and Millar, "Christian Recessional."

74. Casanova, "Rethinking Secularization," 15.

There exists an international subculture composed of people with Western-type higher education, especially in the humanities and social sciences, that is indeed secularized. This subculture is the principal "carrier" of progressive, Enlightened beliefs and values. While its members are relatively thin on the ground, they are very influential, as they control the institutions that provide the "official" definitions of reality, notably the educational system, the media of mass communication, and the higher reaches of the legal system . . ..[75]

As has been noted, the secular university was created by, and is maintained by, a symbiotic relationship between, on the one hand, an international, self-governing academic guild dedicated to secular perspectives and resistant to any outside claimants to socially legitimate knowledge, and on the other, the state—now itself almost entirely run by graduates of the secular university system. The state provides the financial resources and regulates the system in such a way as to maintain its current features, partly in the belief that it generates substantial technological, economic, and military benefits and advances the government's social policies.[76] Although it may seem odd to put it this way, given the deserved reputation of this system for radical ideological leanings, the role of Western universities within the secular order is still at its base a conservative one. They maintain the dominance of the secular order by providing its intellectual justification, further working out its implications, and duly inducting its most capable children into the rituals and doctrines of the secular age, thereby ensuring that the population at large shares, at least to some degree, a secular outlook. Their function is, in fact, not much different from the function of medieval and early modern universities with respect to Christendom.

Furthermore, intellectual influence within the secular university system moves almost exclusively from center to periphery, that is, from small personal networks of elite scholars at the world's leading research universities, through the top journals and scholarly societies, to their colleagues in the broader public university systems, and ultimately trickling all the way down to marginal institutions like private Christian colleges in North America, where professors demonstrate their academic *bona fides* by dutifully replicating the thought patterns of Michel Foucault, Judith Butler, and

75. Berger, "Desecularization," 10.

76. As a hypothesis, it could further be suggested that the major tensions within the system today have to do with the relationships between these elements, especially between faculty autonomy and the state's expectation of "value for money."

Edward Said.[77] It needs to be stressed that this dynamic is not a "bug," but a "feature," of the system. The German model, where aspiring scholars are trained in a form of graduate education that prizes above all the ability to make one's ideas acceptable to more senior academics, where there is a definite hierarchy of institutions such that newly minted PhDs will only be hired by institutions less prestigious than the ones that trained them, and where one's ability to advance within the profession depends almost entirely on the approval of one's peers in publishing and the tenure review process, more or less guarantees this outcome.[78] And this system, remember, was established precisely to insulate faculty from the demands of ecclesiastical authorities and the constraints of religious orthodoxy.[79]

In such an environment, the natural tendency of a Christian university in Canada or anywhere in the Western world will be to assimilate into the larger secular system.[80] If one is sitting in a canoe in a moving river, deciding *not* to paddle against the current is to choose a direction. To remain meaningfully committed over the long term to a tradition of Christian orthodoxy, a Christian university will have to paddle very hard against contrary cultural currents that are powerful indeed.

Three Vectors of Secularization

How do those currents operate? The foregoing analysis suggests three main points of entry for secularizing influences in the typical Christian university. The first, of course, is pressure from the state, particularly through strings attached to public funding, but also through accreditation and quality assurance mechanisms, faculty grants, student loans, and other avenues.

A second point of entry is the faculty, whose role in secularization is comparatively subtle.[81] Their graduate training, as well as the require-

---

77. My analysis in this section follows the understanding of intellectual and cultural influence proposed for philosophy by Collins, *Sociology of Philosophies*, and in a more general form by Hunter, *To Change the World*, 32–78. Foucault, Butler, and Said are mentioned here simply as examples of influential elite theoreticians.

78. On the "caste system" in academia, see Burris, "The Academic Caste System."

79. Cf. Cavanaugh, "Sailing under True Colors," 36–38.

80. Note that this chapter is not making empirical claims about the actual state of Christian higher education in Canada at the time of writing but is rather arguing that there are well established secularizing patterns that will tend to have a certain kind of effect on the sector over time.

81. "In the past century, the professionalization of the faculty by discipline . . . and the long-term effect of prevailing faculty recruitment practices have probably contributed

ments of maintaining their status in their disciplines through publications, involvement in scholarly associations, and so on, almost inevitably orient them to secular standards. In such conditions the requirements of Christian fidelity may become professionally embarrassing. Given the influence faculty typically have in hiring, coupled with the challenge of finding faculty who both believe in the school's religious tradition and possess the right qualifications,[82] a school's strict fidelity to a particular confessional standard easily gives way to an increasingly broad and accommodating approach. Once some faculty are hired who no longer really conform to the faith commitments of the school, administrators are in a difficult bind: either acquiesce quietly in looser *de facto* standards, or undertake unpalatable, impractical, and probably unpopular measures to constrain or remove them. The decision practically makes itself. The new, looser standard (often tacit rather than explicit), however, inevitably excludes some potential new hires and in time suffers the same fate as the original strict standard. The Apostles' Creed contains fewer culturally implausible propositions than the Westminster Confession. Yet it still contains culturally implausible propositions (to put it mildly), and someone will eventually object to them. If the faculty unionize at some point, these trends are likely to be accelerated.

A third potential vector of secularization is the erosion of the supporting faith community that provides a Christian university with donations and tuition-paying students. Churches face liberalizing and secularizing pressures as well, even if these are not as intense or institutionally ingrained as they are for the universities. Decline in membership or commitment levels in the supporting churches spells trouble for the enrollment and donor support of the university. A lack of interest in or commitment to the distinctiveness of the faith tradition on the part of the church will likewise tend to weaken the orthodoxy of the university through the influence of governance structures and donors.

These are, it bears repeating, formidable forces for secularization. If there is to be any chance of maintaining faithful Christian institutions of higher education in such a context—in other words, if "Plan B" is to have even a hope of success—university leaders must face them and counter

more to the distancing of church colleges and universities from their churches than any other single factor. The long-term relationship of schools to a church or other societal group with a distinctive mission will depend more on getting key faculty members than on any other factor" (Meyer, *Realizing Our Intentions*, 90).

82. Meyer (*Realizing Our Intentions*, 149–72) incisively critiques the counterproductive tendencies in this regard of traditional faculty hiring practices.

them effectively. Here I am particularly aware that I am getting further away from my own area of expertise and trespassing on the territory of administrators who know more about these matters than I do. Nevertheless, if the foregoing historical and sociological analysis is correct, it suggests three strategic priorities.

Three Strategic Priorities

The first strategic priority, simply put, is to maintain maximum autonomy from the state. Public funding, of course, needs to be viewed critically and accepted only under particular guarantees. A heavy reliance on public funding for operating costs is almost certainly a bad idea, because in such a case a university will have almost no choice but to comply if the state later imposes new requirements for that funding that undermine the university's religious identity. Given the paucity of public funding available to most Christian universities in Canada, other regulatory requirements related to accreditation or student loans are a more present danger. The development of an alternative accreditation network for Christian liberal arts colleges and universities in North America, apart from those already in place for biblical and theological education, if done well, could serve as a counterweight to secularizing pressures from the mainstream accreditation bodies and as a fallback position if those pressures intensify in the future. Trying to avoid state financing and control while offering degrees that compete with publicly funded universities, of course, puts Christian university administrators in an almost impossible position. Nevertheless, it seems to be the only viable option.

The second strategic priority, and probably the most difficult one to carry out, is to have professors who are deeply and authentically committed to the religious basis of their Christian university. The challenge here is to strengthen faculty members' "vertical" ties and obligations of faithful transmission of the university's Christian tradition across generations to the point that they are stronger than the "horizontal" ties that link them to their secular colleagues for models and validation. The cultivation of what Christian Smith would call "sacred umbrellas," including local plausibility structures of worship, prayer, fellowship, and mutual encouragement, is certainly part of the answer.[83] But successfully implementing this strategy would also require radically countercultural approaches to faculty hiring,

---

83. Smith, *American Evangelicalism*, 106.

formation, and retention that would put the greatest stress on factors like personal understanding of, and commitment to, the school's religious tradition, rather than the conventional measures of academic success.[84] It would also require that faculty members be held accountable *by someone other than their fellow faculty members* for a faithful appropriation of the school's religious tradition. All of this would court the high cultural costs of exclusion—the exclusion of potential faculty members who are sympathetic to, but not really aligned with, the institution's faith basis and the exclusion of faculty members who turn their backs on that basis—as well as difficult dilemmas about where and how to draw the lines. Where a looser approach is already established, the internal political costs may simply be too high to implement such an approach without provoking an institutional crisis. In terms of strengthening vertical ties relative to horizontal ones, the building of faithful Christian doctoral programs may be an additional important long-term strategic priority, though it is obviously beyond the reach of nearly all individual Christian universities.

Finally, although it lies largely outside the control of universities, there are some things Christian universities can do to cultivate a strong and secularization-resistant support community. To the extent that they can train faithful teachers, pastors, youth leaders, and engaged lay professionals who are sent back to the support community, Christian universities can counter, rather than further, secularizing tendencies—indeed, this is one of the main reasons these universities were founded in the first place. They can also strengthen the "sacred umbrella" of the wider support community through public events and programs that invest some of the university's cultural capital (small though it may be in the eyes of faculty accustomed to looking to the larger research institutions) in commending the founding tradition anew to its own constituency. Finally, as a kind of insurance against creeping secularization of the main sponsoring denomination or denominations, the Christian university should cultivate ties—where possible and appropriate—with neighbouring denominations that possess higher levels of commitment and greater theological conservatism (i.e., secularization-resistance).[85] I am here assuming that one of

84. See Meyer (*Realizing Our Intentions*, 149–72) for practical suggestions on implementing some countercultural approaches.

85. For an exploration of the links between theological conservatism and secularization resistance in contemporary mainline Protestant churches in Canada, see Haskell, Flatt, and Burgoyne, "Theology Matters," and Flatt, Haskell, and Burgoyne, "Secularization and Attribution."

the dynamics of the relatively free market for religion in North America is a continuously ongoing process by which older denominations achieve social respectability, liberalize, and decline, while newer, stricter, and more theologically conservative denominations arise to take their place.[86] In the event of serious erosion of the primary support community, the university may be able to still carry out the founding mission—though possibly on a smaller scale—with the support of such groups. This tactic will less often be a legitimate option for schools supported by a single denomination than for schools with an interdenominational basis of support.

CONCLUSION

Three decades ago, George Rawlyk observed that "Christian higher education in Canada . . . may be entering the first phase of an extended renaissance."[87] Despite my admiration for Rawlyk and the fact that I *want* him to be right, I see less cause for optimism. James Davidson Hunter rightly argues that American evangelicals perpetually overestimate their ability to shape the dominant culture rather than be shaped by it,[88] and the same is probably true to some extent of Canadian evangelicals. The cultural, political, and economic pressures arrayed against Christian higher education in Canada, and indeed throughout the Western world, are immense. Were we the gambling sort, the safe bet would be that over the next two generations or so most of the members of CHEC will follow the same script that has played out so many times before: the liberalization of the faculty, the watering down of doctrinal tests, becoming increasingly beholden to the guild and the state, and finally, the same end reached by McMaster University with its forgotten motto.[89] Then again, the people who founded the institutions that make up CHEC were not thinking primarily about the odds. They probably were not thinking much about human obstacles at all,

86. There is ample evidence for such a process throughout American and Canadian history; see for example Finke and Stark, *Churching of America*, and Burkinshaw, *Pilgrims in Lotus Land*.

87. Rawlyk, "Protestant Colleges," 299. Around the same time, John Stackhouse, though also recognizing the successes of evangelical higher education, sounded a more cautious note (*Canadian Evangelicalism*, 203–4).

88. Hunter, *To Change the World*, 6–47.

89. Of course, this trajectory assumes that the state system would welcome a sufficiently liberalized Christian university with open arms; if not, the death of the institution is the alternative outcome, since few students would be willing to pay extra for what can be had at the public universities for less money.

which was their glory and may yet be their undoing. If we can revive the fiery against-the-odds faith of our forebears, while marrying it to a sober strategic assessment of our situation and the steps that are necessary to navigate it, then—and only then—will "Plan B" have a chance of success.

BIBLIOGRAPHY

Anderson, R. D. *European Universities from the Enlightenment to 1914.* Oxford: Oxford University Press, 2004.

Asad, Talal. *Formations of the Secular: Christianity, Islam, Modernity.* Stanford, CA: Stanford University Press, 2003.

Baum, Gregory. "Catholicism and Secularization in Quebec." *Cross Currents* 36 (1986–1987) 436–58.

Bebbington, David. "The Secularization of British Universities since the Mid-Nineteenth Century." In *The Secularization of the Academy,* edited by George M. Marsden and Bradley J. Longfield, 259–77. Oxford: Oxford University Press, 1992.

Berger, Peter L. "The Desecularization of the World: A Global Overview." In *The Desecularization of the World: Resurgent Religion and World Politics,* edited by Peter L. Berger, 1–18. Grand Rapids: Eerdmans, 1999.

———. *The Sacred Canopy.* Garden City, NY: Anchor Doubleday, 1967.

Brockliss, Laurence. "Curricula." In *Universities in Early Modern Europe (1500–1800),* edited by Hilde de Ridder-Symoens, 565–620. A History of the University in Europe 2. Cambridge: Cambridge University Press, 1996.

Brown, Callum G. *The Death of Christian Britain: Understanding Secularisation 1800–2000.* London: Routledge, 2001.

———. "A Revisionist Approach to Religious Change." In *Religion and Modernization: Sociologists and Historians Debate the Secularization Thesis,* edited by Steve Bruce, 31–58. Oxford: Clarendon, 1992.

Bruce, Steve. "Christianity in Britain, R.I.P." *Sociology of Religion* 62 (2001) 191–203.

———. *Secularization: In Defence of an Unfashionable Theory.* Oxford: Oxford University Press, 2011.

Burkinshaw, Robert K. *Pilgrims in Lotus Land: Conservative Protestantism in British Columbia, 1917–1981.* Montreal: McGill-Queen's University Press, 1995.

Burris, Val. "The Academic Caste System: Prestige Hierarchies in PhD Exchange Networks." *American Sociological Review* 69 (April 2004) 239–64.

Casanova, José. *Public Religions in the Modern World.* Chicago: University of Chicago Press, 1994.

———. "Rethinking Secularization: A Global Comparative Perspective." *The Hedgehog Review* 8 (2006) 7–22.

Cavanaugh, William. "Sailing under True Colors: Academic Freedom and the Ecclesially Based University." In *Conflicting Allegiances: The Church-Based University in a Liberal Democratic Society,* edited by Michael L. Budde and John Wright, 31–52. Grand Rapids: Brazos, 2004.

Collins, Randall. *The Sociology of Philosophies: A Global Theory of Intellectual Change.* Cambridge, MA: The Belknap Press of Harvard University Press, 1998.

Comte, Auguste. *Auguste Comte and Positivism: The Essential Writings,* edited by Gertrud Lenzer. New York: Harper & Row, 1975.

Dobbelaere, Karel. *Secularization: An Analysis at Three Levels*. Brussels: Peter Lang, 2002.

Durkheim, Émile. *The Division of Labor in Society*. Translated by George Simpson. 1869. Reprint, New York: The Free Press of Glencoe, Illinois, 1933.

Fenn, Richard. *Toward a Theory of Secularization*. Storrs, CT: Society for the Scientific Study of Religion, 1978.

Fernhout, Harry. "A Quest for Identity and Place: Christian University Education in Canada." In *Christian Higher Education: A Global Reconnaissance*, edited by Joel Carpenter et al., 230–56. Grand Rapids: Eerdmans, 2014.

Flatt, Kevin N., David Millard Haskell, and Stephanie Burgoyne. "Secularization and Attribution: How Mainline Protestant Clergy and Congregants Explain Church Growth and Decline." *Sociology of Religion: A Quarterly Review* 79 (2018) 78–107.

Finke, Roger, and Rodney Stark. *The Churching of America, 1776–2005: Winners and Losers in Our Religious Economy*. 2nd ed. New Brunswick, NJ: Rutgers University Press, 2005.

Frijhoff, Willem. "Patterns." In *Universities in Early Modern Europe (1500–1800)*, edited by Hilde de Ridder-Symoens, 43–113. A History of the University in Europe 2. Cambridge: Cambridge University Press, 1996.

Gauvreau, Michael. *The Catholic Origins of Quebec's Quiet Revolution, 1931–1970*. Montreal: McGill-Queen's University Press, 2005.

Gerbod, Paul. "Relations with Authority." In *Universities in the Nineteenth and Early Twentieth Centuries*, edited by Walter Rüegg, 83–100. A History of the University in Europe 3. Cambridge: Cambridge University Press, 2004.

Gidney, Catherine. *A Long Eclipse: The Liberal Protestant Establishment and the Canadian University, 1920–1970*. Montreal: McGill-Queen's University Press, 2004.

Gidney, R. D., and W. P. J. Millar. "The Christian Recessional in Ontario's Public Schools." In *Religion and Public Life in Canada: Historical and Comparative Perspectives*, edited by Marguerite Van Die, 275–92. Toronto: University of Toronto Press, 2001.

Gieysztor, Aleksander. "Management and Resources." In *Universities in the Middle Ages*, edited by Hilde de Ridder-Symoens, 108–43. A History of the University in Europe 1. Cambridge: Cambridge University Press, 1992.

Gorski, Philip S. "Historicizing the Secularization Debate: Church, State, and Society in Late Medieval and Early Modern Europe, ca. 1300 to 1700." *American Sociological Review* 65 (2000) 138–67.

Gregory, Brad S. *The Unintended Reformation: How a Religious Revolution Secularized Society*. Cambridge, MA: The Belknap Press of Harvard University Press, 2012.

Hammerstein, Notker. "The Enlightenment." In *Universities in Early Modern Europe (1500–1800)*, edited by Hilde de Ridder-Symoens, 621–40. A History of the University in Europe 2. Cambridge: Cambridge University Press, 1996.

———. "Relations with Authority." In *Universities in Early Modern Europe (1500–1800)*, edited by Hilde de Ridder-Symoens, 114–54. A History of the University in Europe 2. Cambridge: Cambridge University Press, 1996.

Haskell, David Millard, Kevin N. Flatt, and Stephanie Burgoyne. "Theology Matters: Comparing the Traits of Growing and Declining Mainline Protestant Church Attendees and Clergy." *Review of Religious Research* 58 (2016) 515–41.

Hunter, James Davison. *To Change the World: The Irony, Tragedy, and Possibility of Christianity in the Late Modern World*. Oxford: Oxford University Press, 2010.

Luckmann, Thomas. *The Invisible Religion: The Problem of Religion in Modern Society*. New York: Macmillan, 1967.

Marsden, George M. "The Soul of the American University: An Historical Overview." In *The Secularization of the Academy*, edited by George M. Marsden and Bradley J. Longfield, 9–45. Oxford: Oxford University Press, 1992.

———. *The Soul of the American University: From Protestant Establishment to Established Nonbelief.* Oxford: Oxford University Press, 1994.

Martin, David. *A General Theory of Secularization.* Oxford: Blackwell, 1978.

———. *On Secularization: Towards a Revised General Theory.* Farnham, UK: Ashgate, 2005.

McLeod, Hugh. *The Religious Crisis of the 1960s.* Oxford: Oxford University Press, 2007.

Meyer, Albert J. *Realizing Our Intentions: A Guide for Churches and Colleges with Distinctive Missions.* Abilene, TX: Abilene Christian University Press, 2009.

Nardi, Paolo. "Relations with Authority." In *Universities in the Middle Ages*, edited by Hilde de Ridder-Symoens, 77–107. A History of the University in Europe 1. Cambridge: Cambridge University Press, 1992.

Nelson, Samuel, and Philip S. Gorski. "Conditions of Religious Belonging: Confessionalization, De-parochialization, and the Euro-American Divergence." *International Sociology* 29 (2014) 3–21.

Norris, Pippa, and Ronald Inglehart. *Sacred and Secular: Religion and Politics Worldwide.* 2nd ed. Cambridge: Cambridge University Press, 2011.

Porter, Roy. "The Scientific Revolution and Universities." In *Universities in Early Modern Europe (1500–1800)*, edited by Hilde de Ridder-Symoens, 531–64. A History of the University in Europe 2. Cambridge: Cambridge University Press, 1996.

Rawlyk, George A. "Protestant Colleges in Canada: Past and Future." In *The Secularization of the Academy*, edited by George M. Marsden and Bradley J. Longfield, 278–302. Oxford: Oxford University Press, 1992.

Ringenberg, William C. *The Christian College: A History of Protestant Higher Education in America.* 2nd ed. Grand Rapids: Baker Academic, 2006.

Rudy, Willis. *The Universities of Europe, 1100–1914: A History.* London: Associated University Presses, 1984.

Rüegg, Walter. "The Rise of Humanism." In *Universities in the Middle Ages*, edited by Hilde de Ridder-Symoens, 442–68. A History of the University in Europe 1. Cambridge: Cambridge University Press, 1992.

———. "Themes." In *Universities in Early Modern Europe (1500–1800)*, edited by Hilde de Ridder-Symoens, 3–42. A History of the University in Europe 2. Cambridge: Cambridge University Press, 1996.

———. "Themes." In *Universities in the Nineteenth and Early Twentieth Centuries*, edited by Walter Rüegg, 3–32. A History of the University in Europe 3. Cambridge: Cambridge University Press, 2004.

Schmalzbauer, John, and Kathleen A. Mahoney. *The Resilience of Religion in American Higher Education.* Waco, TX: Baylor University Press, 2018.

Seljak, David. "Why the Quiet Revolution was 'Quiet': The Catholic Church's Reaction to the Secularization of Nationalism in Quebec after 1960." *CCHA Historical Studies* 62 (1996) 109–24.

Smith, Christian. "Introduction: Rethinking the Secularization of American Public Life." In *The Secular Revolution: Power, Interests, and Conflict in the Secularization of American Public Life*, edited by Christian Smith, 1–96. Berkeley: University of California Press, 2003.

————. "Secularizing American Higher Education: The Case of Early American Sociology." In *The Secular Revolution: Power, Interests, and Conflict in the Secularization of American Public Life*, edited by Christian Smith, 97–159. Berkeley: University of California Press, 2003.

Stackhouse, John G., Jr. *Canadian Evangelicalism in the Twentieth Century: An Introduction to Its Character*. Toronto: University of Toronto Press, 1993.

Stark, Rodney. "Secularization, R.I.P." *Sociology of Religion* 60 (1999) 249–73.

Stark, Rodney, and Roger Finke. *Acts of Faith: Explaining the Human Side of Religion*. Berkeley: University of California Press, 2000.

Stark, Rodney, and Laurence Iannaconne. "A Supply-Side Reinterpretation of the 'Secularization' of Europe." *Journal for the Scientific Study of Religion* 33 (1994) 230–52.

Taylor, Charles. *A Secular Age*. Cambridge, MA: The Belknap Press of Harvard University Press, 2007.

Tschannen, Olivier. "The Secularization Paradigm: A Systematization." *Journal for the Scientific Study of Religion* 30 (1991) 395–415.

Wallis, Roy, and Steve Bruce. "Secularization: The Orthodox Model." In *Religion and Modernization: Sociologists and Historians Debate the Secularization Thesis*, edited by Steve Bruce, 8–30. Oxford: Clarendon, 1992.

Weber, Max. *Economy and Society*. 2 vols. Edited by Guenther Roth and Claus Wittich. Berkeley: University of California Press, 1968.

————. "Religious Rejections of the World and their Directions." In *From Max Weber: Essays in Sociology*, edited and translated by H. H. Gerth and C. Wright Mills, 323–59. Oxford: Oxford University Press, 1946.

Wilson, Bryan. *Religion in Secular Society: A Sociological Comment*. London: C. A. Watts, 1966.

————. *Religion in Sociological Perspective*. Oxford: Oxford University Press, 1982.

4

Competition for Character Education

What Emerging Adulthood Means for Christian Higher Education in Canada

Rick Hiemstra[1]

INTRODUCTION

CHRISTIAN HIGHER EDUCATION CANADA (CHEC) students are more likely to maintain their teenage religious affiliation, more likely to attend religious services as young adults, and more likely to hold orthodox Christian views than other young adults from Christian backgrounds. These data and others are good news for CHEC institutions and their constituencies.

Although CHEC students have such positive outcomes, the long-term trend in CHEC enrolment is one of decline. In this chapter, I will argue that increased government support for other forms of post-secondary education, the consequences of responding to that competition, and the growth of a new life stage called *emerging adulthood*, along with other factors, have created a challenging environment for CHEC institutions seeking to recruit young adult students. I will also present select data from the 2018 Young Adult Transition Research (YATR) that compare religious engagement outcomes for CHEC students with other young adults who had either

1. This chapter is a condensed version of Hiemstra, "Competition for Character Education," the second report arising from the YATR research.

a Christian religious affiliation or non-nominal religious engagement as teens.

It is necessary to define how I am using the term *Christian Higher Education Movement* (CHEM). By CHEM I mean *evangelical, English-speaking*, Bible schools, Bible institutes, Bible colleges, Christian liberal arts colleges, seminaries, and graduate schools. CHEC institutions form an *accredited* subset of the CHEM. The "movement" language is borrowed from the term "Bible college movement" (BCM) used by historian Robert Burkinshaw to describe the early phase of CHEM beginning in 1885.[2]

I would like to qualify my use of the terms *evangelical* and *English-speaking* in describing CHEM here. It would be anachronistic to include Mennonite Bible schools and institutes from the late 1800s and early 1990s as part of an *evangelical* movement. In the intervening years, however, many Mennonites (but not all) have come to be associated with the wider evangelical movement through participation in organizations like The Evangelical Fellowship of Canada. I am attaching the adjective *evangelical* to the term CHEM in this introduction as a way to signal a shared theological and/or cultural disjunction with established mainline and Catholic churches. I have chosen to drop the adjective *evangelical* when I use the term CHEM in the body of this report as a recognition of these problems and not to overemphasize the role of strictly evangelical traditions.

The term *English-speaking* could be problematic because it excludes other language groups (significantly French and various indigenous languages), and it is sometimes anachronistic. I am limiting the term CHEM in this chapter to conform to the composition of CHEC, an association of English-speaking schools on which the dataset to be analyzed is based. CHEM also includes many schools that historically operated exclusively in another language. For example, in the late 1880s and early 1900s there were many exclusively German-speaking Mennonite schools. I have chosen to include the adjective *English-speaking* in this introduction to indicate the focus of this chapter, but I have chosen not to use it as part of CHEM as a recognition of the problems associated with conceiving of CHEM as an exclusively English-speaking enterprise. See the excellent work of Bruce Guenther for a more nuanced account of this CHEM history.[3]

---

2. Burkinshaw, "Evangelical Bible Colleges in Twentieth-Century Canada," 367.

3. Guenther, "Slithering Down the Plank of Intellectualism?"; Guenther, "The Origin of the Bible School Movement in Western Canada."

Anything that I write in this report about the history of the BCM or the CHEM in Canada will necessarily be an over-simplification of a rich and complex story. The works of historians such as Bruce Guenther, John G. Stackhouse Jr., and Robert Burkinshaw should be consulted for more nuanced accounts.[4]

The idea of *emerging adulthood* is the interpretive framework for the YATR study.[5] Psychologist Erik Erikson proposed the idea of the *emerging individual* in the late 1960s which psychologist Jeffrey Arnett then developed into the idea of the *emerging adult* in 2000.[6] Emerging adulthood is a break or moratorium in psychosocial development that is characterized by a "delay of adult commitments" and identity formation.[7] Emerging adults have not yet formed a persistent adult identity, and significantly for a discussion on higher education, they have not yet made enduring decisions about "occupation, romantic relationships, and *religious* or political beliefs" (emphasis added).[8]

THE CHRISTIAN HIGHER EDUCATION MOVEMENT

According to historian Bruce Guenther a *Bible school* was founded in 1885, the first of at least 340 Canadian CHEM institutions.[9] Many of these 340 institutions have since merged with other schools or closed. Of the current 34 CHEC institutions, 26 were founded between 1920 and 1950, and none were founded after 1990.[10]

According to historian Robert Burkinshaw, the early BCM had "twin purposes" of "teaching the Bible as truth rather than an academic subject,

---

4. See, for example, Guenther, "The Origin of the Bible School Movement in Western Canada"; Burkinshaw, "Evangelical Bible Colleges in Twentieth-Century Canada"; Stackhouse, *Canadian Evangelicalism in the Twentieth Century*.

5. Hiemstra et al., "Renegotiating Faith," 16–20.

6. Erikson, *Identity*, 159; Arnett, "Emerging Adulthood."

7. Erikson, *Identity*, 128, 156.

8. Sokol, "Identity Development throughout the Lifetime," 5.

9. Hiebert et al., *Character with Competence Education*, 1.

10. ACTS Seminaries is a consortium of four seminaries. For the purpose of this statistic the consortium was treated as a single institution and its founding date was taken to be 1985 the year the consortium was formed. McMaster Divinity College and Acadia Divinity College were founded prior to the 1882 start of the CHEM in Canada but stood outside the movement's associative structures until they joined CHEC in 2005 and 2013 respectively.

and training for practical Christian living and ministry."[11] Bible schools sprang up to serve conservative evangelical communities that felt either abandoned by the established seminaries or shut out of other forms of higher education by money or class. In many cases, CHEM schools were also founded to pass on the cultural heritage of minority religious communities to their children.

In the early movement, the training was not typically at the academic level of a "full collegiate or theological course of study" but nevertheless was sufficient to prepare students to take on responsible roles within their respective churches.[12]

Historian John G. Stackhouse Jr., writing about the Toronto Bible Training School, a precursor of Tyndale University College and Seminary, states:

> Admission standards were academically low, if spiritually high: 'Candidates for admission to the full course of study must be recommended by their Pastors, Churches, or other responsible persons as possessing an approved Christian character, and giving promise of usefulness in the Lord's service.'[13]

While the seminaries of the day concentrated on training clergy, Burkinshaw writes that Bible schools

> displayed a great deal of flexibility by accepting students not usually admitted to theological colleges. While many schools encouraged students to consider entering full-time ministry, such a vocational goal was not a criterion of admission, and thousands of individuals planning on lay vocations enrolled.[14]

These "thousands of students" could afford Bible schools because of "very low or, in some cases, non-existent tuition fees," which were made possible because of relatively modest facilities and "the availability of faculty willing to work for very low stipends."[15] Many of these early faculty did not have advanced training themselves, and most early Bible schools

---

11. Burkinshaw, "Evangelical Bible Colleges in Twentieth-Century Canada," 373.

12. Stackhouse, *Canadian Evangelicalism in the Twentieth Century*, 55.

13. Stackhouse, *Canadian Evangelicalism in the Twentieth Century*, 55–56.

14. Burkinshaw, "Evangelical Bible Colleges in Twentieth-Century Canada," 374–75.

15. Burkinshaw, "Evangelical Bible Colleges in Twentieth-Century Canada," 375.

or institutes operated in an academic zone above high school but below university or college.[16]

In the early CHEM, students often returned to serve in the churches that sent them or to be part of the sending church's missionary ministry. Burkinshaw writes about the high esteem in which Bible colleges and their students were held in the evangelical community:

> The Bible school's practical, ministry-oriented approach was also well received, as can be seen in the regular reports in institutional publications of the extent of students' activities in various ministries. This included detailed statistics of the number of evangelistic tracts distributed, of homes and hospital beds visited, of street sermons preached, and of Sunday school and mid-week Bible classes taught. The statistics most proudly presented by many schools, however, were those indicating the number of graduates entering some kind of full-time ministry, whether on the foreign mission field or at home.[17]

Earning a Bible college degree conferred status in the evangelical community, and the institutions themselves were generally held in high regard by the evangelical community.

COMPETITION FOR STUDENTS PRE-WWII

When the CHEM began in the late nineteenth century, high school graduation was rare, and post-secondary education was generally reserved for Canada's elites. In his history of higher education in Canada, Glen Jones writes that, prior to the Second World War, university in Canada was for "the children of the politicas [sic]," and "served as a finishing school[s] for their daughters and prepared their sons for admission to the liberal professions."[18]

High school graduation, usually an admission requirement for university, was rare even in the 1930s when only "about 15 per cent of Canadian students graduated from high school. This figure did not rise above 25 percent until several years after the end of the Second World War and just reached 50 per cent by 1960."[19] Burkinshaw writes that Bible colleges were "open, at least until the 1960s, to students without high-school

16. Guenther, "Slithering Down the Plank of Intellectualism?" 198.

17. Burkinshaw, "Evangelical Bible Colleges in Twentieth-Century Canada," 374.

18. Jones, "An Introduction to Higher Education in Canada," 8.

19. Burkinshaw, "Evangelical Bible Colleges in Twentieth-Century Canada," 374.

graduation. Entry standards thus were low, but they reflected the realities of the educational context in Canada."[20]

Although Bible colleges served a primarily evangelical Christian market, prior to the 1951 Massey Commission report, they were generally not competing with other kinds of higher education institutions for evangelical students. One reason for this lack of competition was the relative scarcity of competing higher education institutions. In 1901, for example, there were only 18 degree granting institutions in the entire country.[21] By comparison, Universities Canada currently lists 98 member institutions, and Colleges and Institutes Canada lists 129 member institutions.[22]

Some of the changes in higher education were prompted by disputes among denominational colleges associated with Ontario universities. In its 1906 report, the Ontario Royal Commission on the University of Toronto, also known as the Flavelle Commission, made recommendations on, among other things, "the relations between the said University of Toronto and the several Colleges affiliated or federated therewith."[23] Andrew Boggs documents how quarrels between these colleges caused headaches for politicians and led to the defunding of denominational schools in Ontario.[24] Jones notes how these Ontario disputes affected the establishment of universities in the Western provinces:

> Recognizing the importance of higher education for the development of these new jurisdictions [the western provinces], and *attempting to avoid the denominational disputes that had emerged in the east,* each of the new western provinces decided to create a single 'provincial' university with a monopoly over the authority to grant degrees (emphasis added).[25]

The monopoly power initially granted to these Western provincial universities was, in part, an attempt to head off the kind of denominational

20. Burkinshaw, "Evangelical Bible Colleges in Twentieth-Century Canada," 374.

21. Clark, "100 Years of Education," 4.

22. Universities Canada Members, https://www.univcan.ca/universities/member-universities/, and Colleges and Institutes Canada Members, https://www.collegesinstitutes.ca/our-members/member-directory/, accessed September 27, 2018.

23. Ontario. The Royal Commission on the University of Toronto, "The Report of The Royal Commission on the University of Toronto," iv.

24. Boggs, "Ontario's Royal Commission on the University of Toronto, 1905–1906."

25. Jones, "An Introduction to Higher Education in Canada," 8. See also Boggs, "Ontario's Royal Commission on the University of Toronto, 1905–1906."

college disputes that had been witnessed in Ontario and precluded the establishment of denominational universities with independent degree granting power.

The 1928–1929 Royal Commission on Radio Broadcasting, otherwise known as the Aird Commission, also dealt with religious conflict—this time dealing with religious radio programming—and formed part of the back drop for the 1949–1951 Massey Commission.

Historian Mark McGowan writes about "the new religious interest in radio" in the late 1920s stating that "religiously inspired radio programming emerged as a new weapon with which one religious group could bludgeon another."[26] In response to this conflict, the Aird Commission recommended regulations for religious broadcasting to prohibit statements of a controversial nature or one religion making an attack on another religion's leaders or doctrine.[27] Religious radio broadcasting licences were phased out after 1932, a few years after the release of the Aird Commission report, and none were granted again until 1983.[28]

Denominational college squabbles and radio broadcast squabbles had marked religion as a divisive force in society and inclined governments to non-sectarian or secular governmental solutions. We see this in the establishment of secular provincial universities in the Western provinces, and we see this in the recommendations of the Massey Commission that dramatically expanded funding for public post-secondary education.

The CHEM did not have significant competition from public post-secondary institutions prior to the 1950s because universities were for the elite. This was about to change.

COMPETITION FOR STUDENTS POST-WWII

In the post-WWII years, several factors started to change the higher education landscape. First, returning veterans were given an opportunity to have their university education funded by the federal government. Second, Canada was moving from an agrarian to an urban society. Third, the report of the Royal Commission on National Development in the Arts, Letters and Sciences, otherwise known as the report of the Massey Commission, radically reshaped the government's relationship with higher education.

26. McGowan, "The People's University of the Air," 6.

27. Canada. Royal Commission on Radio Broadcasting, "Report of the Royal Commission on Radio Broadcasting," 13.

28. Faassen, "A Fine Balance," 304–5.

After WWII, the veterans benefit program "provided qualified return-ing soldiers with the option of receiving a free university education; tuition fees and basic living costs would be paid for by the federal government."[29] Thirty-five thousand veterans enrolled in the first year of the program, ef-fectively doubling university enrolment.

The post-war period was a significant period of urbanization for a country whose population had been predominantly rural. Canada's urban population grew from 6,252,416 in 1941 to 16,410,785 by 1971, or 162%. By comparison, Canada's rural population declined from 5,254,239 in 1941 to 5,157,520 in 1971, or 2%.[30] Where previously agricultural skills acquired on the farm might have been sufficient, now new skills were needed for the jobs opening up in the towns and cities.

The cohort of veterans entering university almost doubled the num-ber of undergraduate students between 1940 and 1945, from 34,817 to 61,861. Even so, at that time undergraduates comprised a very small 0.5% of the population.[31] More dramatic increases came in the 1950s when in-creases in enrolment also drove up the share of the population enrolled in university.

By 2015, 2.82% of the population was enrolled full-time in a university undergraduate program. Total enrolment in all Canadian post-secondary higher education institutions in 2015–2016 was 2,034,957 or 5.7% of the population.[32] In 2016, CHEC total enrolment was 16,100, or less than one percent of total post-secondary enrolment.

The 1951 Massey Commission, more formally known as the Royal Commission on National Development in the Arts, Letters and Sciences recommended that the federal government provide direct grants to uni-versities based on provincial population.[33] The federal government acted

29. Jones, "An Introduction to Higher Education in Canada," 10.

30. Canadian census.

31. "Table W430–455, Full-Time University Undergraduate Enrolment, by Field of Specialization and Sex, Canada, Selected Years, 1861 to 1975"; "Censuses of Canada 1665 to 1871: Estimated Population of Canada, 1605 to Present."

32. Statistics Canada Government of Canada, "Postsecondary Enrolments, by Reg-istration Status, Institution Type, Sex and Student Status."

33. Jones, "An Introduction to Higher Education in Canada," 17; Canada. Royal Commission on National Development in the Arts, Letters and Sciences, "Report of the Royal Commission on National Development in the Arts, Letters and Sciences, 1949–1951."

swiftly extending new and ongoing grants beginning with the 1951–1952 academic year.[34]

In 1974, government expenditures on all post-secondary education were $3.8 billion compared to just $134.9 million in 1950.[35] By 2013–2014, post-secondary education in Canada was a $35.1 billion industry with $17.2 billion, or 48.9%, coming directly from different levels of government and $8.7 billion or 24.7% coming from tuition and fees.[36]

In recent decades, post-secondary education has become a normative experience for Canadians, and particularly younger ones. In 1911, only 1.3% of 20- to 24-year-olds were full-time students, a number that only rose to 18.6% by 1981.[37] In 2015–2016, however, almost one in three (32.4%) Canadians age 20- to 24-year-olds were full-time students, and another 6.3% were part-time students.[38] In 1981, the normative experience for 20- to 24-year-olds was work, not school. In 1981, 72.5% of 20- to 24-year-olds were part of the labor force (working or being available for work), and 85.1% of these were employed.[39]

Following the release of the 1951 Massey Commission report, the post-secondary education market in Canada expanded dramatically with the infusion of government funds. This new funding began to reshape the post-secondary education landscape.

THE MASSEY COMMISSION

The Massey Commission was called in 1949 in the wake of World War II and at the onset of the Cold War. In Canadian society there were fears about American economic and cultural influence. As well, those concerned about totalitarian regimes' use of propaganda and cultural institutions during World War II were advocating for the government to support art and

---

34. Clark, "100 Years of Education," 6.

35. Statistics Canada, "Historical Statistics of Canada: Section W: Education."

36. Statistics Canada, "Historical Statistics of Canada: Section W: Education."; "Federal Spending on Postsecondary Education" Includes operating and capital expenditures of institutions, federal and provincial departmental expenditures and student aid.

37. Canadian Census.

38. Statistics Canada Government of Canada, "Postsecondary Enrolments, by Program Type, Credential Type, Age Groups, Registration Status and Sex."

39. 1981 Canadian census.

culture as a way to protect democracy. There were lingering anxieties "about the return of economic depression; and a reconfigured world order."[40]

The Massey Commission consciously understood education as an instrument for the development of morals and cultural taste. The Massey Commission report states:

> Education is the progressive development of the individual in all his faculties, physical and intellectual, aesthetic and moral. As a result of the disciplined growth of the entire personality, the educated man shows a balanced development of all his powers; he has fully realized his human possibilities.[41]

The Commission argued for a central role for the federal and provincial governments in "formal education," which it defined as "schools and universities." It also argued for a government interest in "general non-academic education through books, periodicals, radio, films, museums, art galleries, lectures and study groups," on the basis that "these are instruments of education," and when they are "used by the school, they are a part of formal education."[42] In this way, the Commission articulated a superintending role for "schools and universities" over the vehicles of culture. In fact, the Massey Commission envisioned the government as the guarantor of the "intellectual and moral purpose" of society and its "conception of the common good," and saw the education system as its instrument.[43] This articulation of education as the superintending instrument of culture placed public education institutions in a position to influence what Erikson called the "ideal prototypes of the day."[44]

Although much of the literature about the mid-twentieth century expansion of higher education in Canada focuses on program and enrolment growth, the Massey Commission report reminds us of the moral purpose the government sought in education. Although the report tips its hat to the place of Christianity in the nation, the reality was that the Flavelle, Aird,

---

40. Stewart and Kallman, "Massey Commission"; Druick, "International Cultural Relations as a Factor in Postwar Canadian Cultural Policy."

41. Canada. Royal Commission on National Development in the Arts, Letters and Sciences, "Massey Commission," Part 1, Chapter 1, The Mandate.

42. Canada. Royal Commission on National Development in the Arts, Letters and Sciences, "Massey Commission," Part 1, Chapter 1, The Mandate.

43. Canada. Royal Commission on National Development in the Arts, Letters and Sciences, Part 1, Chapter 1, The Mandate.

44. Erikson, *Identity*, 128.

and Massey Commissions all saw religion as a political and social problem to be managed rather than seeing religion as the guarantor of public morals.

Facing threats such as Communism and American cultural domination, the government of Canada decided that the character formation of the nation was too important to leave in the hands of churches or Christian ministries such as Bible colleges. The investment in education was an investment in the character development of the nation, and, as such, it directly competed with the CHEM.

ACCESS TO GOVERNMENT FUNDING

Post-Massey Commission government funding has not been as accessible for CHEM institutions as for secular institutions. Using 2012 Charitable Information Return (T3010) data, the total revenue of CHEC's 36 full members was $264,987,823. Of that total revenue, 8.3% came directly from different levels of government.[45] By comparison, secular higher education institutions received 48.9% of their revenue from government sources in 2013–2014.[46] Only 20 of the 36 CHEC institutions reported receiving government money of any kind.

Charitable Information Returns (CIR) do not record tuition revenues; however, these are most likely reflected in "Total revenue from sale of goods and services" (line number 4640). In 2012, 30 of the 36 CHEC members reported line 4640 values that averaged 45.7% of total revenues. Assuming line 4640 data substantially represents tuition and fee revenue, CHEC institutions on average generate almost twice as much of their budget (45.7% in 2012) from tuition and fees compared to secular universities (24.7% in 2013–2014).[47]

CIR and Parliamentary Budget Officer reports on education come from different datasets, and there are likely discrepancies in budget line item definitions, so some caution should be exercised in drawing conclusions about CHEC institutions and government funding. Even allowing for these discrepancies, it is clear that CHEC institutions are at a funding disadvantage compared with secular higher education institutions.

---

45. 2012 Charitable Information Returns (T3010).
46. "Federal Spending on Postsecondary Education."
47. "Federal Spending on Postsecondary Education."

THE MOVE TO LIBERAL ARTS AND ACCREDITATION

In the early decades of the CHEM, institutions were primarily Bible schools or Bible institutes. These had "typically offered a Bible-centred, intensely practical, lay-oriented program of post-secondary theological training," and they "operated in a zone between the upper years of secondary education and the undergraduate years of post-secondary education."[48] Bible colleges, however, came to be "accredited, conferred degrees, and possessed curricula including significantly more liberal arts or general education courses alongside course offerings in religious studies."[49]

In the 1960's evangelical liberal arts colleges started to be founded in Canada. These were founded in response to demand for a broader education than what was on offer at Bible schools, institutes, and colleges and in response to different philosophies of education.[50] These liberal arts colleges were founded in either the tradition of American liberal arts (i.e., Trinity Western University [1962]) or Reformed liberal arts (i.e., the Institute for Christian Studies [1967], The King's University College [1979], and Redeemer University College [1982]).

Justin Cooper explains that the move to liberal arts models also came out of a growing conviction that "the public university education and character formation was a brand of secularism that was undermining Christianity, not complementary. Hence the move to compete for this ground."[51]

Some of the CHEM institutions were founded as liberal arts colleges while others began to transition to become liberal arts colleges. These transitions can be seen in CHEC institution name changes. More than three-quarters (76%) of current CHEC institutions have changed their names since their founding.[52] There have been three principal kinds of name changes. First, some signalled an improvement in academic standards by upgrading their institution type. An institute, for example, might become a college, or a college might become a university. Second, some institutions moved to drop references to the Bible from their names. Third, some

---

48. Guenther, "Slithering Down the Plank of Intellectualism?" 198.

49. Guenther, "Slithering Down the Plank of Intellectualism?" 199.

50. See, for example, the reasons given for the founding of Trinity Western College in Hanson, *On the Raw Edge of Faith*, 29.

51. Email correspondence from November 16, 2018.

52. CHEC affiliate member ACTS Seminaries in British Columbia, which is itself a partnership of four denominational seminaries, is not included in this name change analysis.

institutions moved to drop or soften references to a denominational affiliation.

1. Eighteen out of thirty-three (55%) CHEC institutions upgraded their institution type since their founding, and twelve of these did so since 2000.

2. Twenty-one out of thirty-three (64%) CHEC institutions at one time had a reference to the Bible in their name. Fourteen of these twenty-one have since dropped the references to the Bible, and ten of these did so since 2000.

3. Thirteen out of thirty-three (39%) CHEC institutions had a reference in their name to a denominational tradition. Ten of these thirteen have since dropped or softened their names' denominational references, and six of these have done so since 2000.

A name is often the first opportunity a school has to create an impression on a prospective student. For example, a student may reasonably conclude that she will find a curricular emphasis on the Bible at a school that describes itself as a Bible college. Whatever reasons a particular CHEC institution may have had for changing its name, it is clear that name changes as a whole, especially in the last two decades, have sought to present CHEC institutions as more academically rigorous and less tied to denominational traditions or a Bible focus.

Guenther identifies two impulses behind the CHEM drive for accreditation beginning in the 1960s:

- A perceived link between higher education and the technological and economic growth of the country;

- Student and parent demands for "more recognition in the form of degrees and transferable credit for the time and money spent at Bible schools."[53]

When the Canadian CHEM initially sought accreditation, it looked south to the Accrediting Association of Bible Colleges (AABC, now known as the Association of Biblical Higher Education), which was founded in 1947 during the annual meeting of the National Association of Evangelicals

---

53. Guenther, "Slithering Down the Plank of Intellectualism?" 199.

(NAE), as an association of denominations, Christian ministries, and churches in the United States.[54]

Guenther argues that rather than providing the sought after "respectability and recognition for their schools among public universities in Canada," AABC accreditation may have further isolated CHEM schools. While AABC accreditation facilitated transfer credits between other member institutions, it did not facilitate transfer to the wider Canadian post-secondary education system.[55] Moreover, at a time when the Massey Commission was addressing a perceived American cultural threat through education, it positioned evangelical institutions within the orbit of the threat.

THE FORMATION OF CHRISTIAN HIGHER EDUCATION CANADA

CHEM also responded to increased competition from secular institutions by forming cooperative, associative structures for professional development, enrolment, and marketing. CHEC was formed in 2005 as the union of three other CHEM associative structures: The Association of Canadian Bible Colleges, the Christian Higher Education Enrollment Association, and the Christian Higher Education Roundtable. CHEC's mission is "to advance the efficiency and effectiveness of Christian higher education at member schools, including fostering institutional cooperation, and to raise public awareness of the value of Christian higher education in Canada."[56]

CHEC is an association of accredited schools. There are, however, other non-accredited evangelical Christian post-secondary schools or training institutions. These include discipleship training schools such as Capernwray or Youth With A Mission (YWAM), Bible schools hosted in large evangelical congregations, and seminars offered by ministry organizations such as the Canadian Council of Christian Charities and the Willow Creek Global Leadership Summit.[57] In addition, many global mission sending agencies, such as WEC International–Canada and denominational agencies, do at least some of the missionary training that might previously have

54. Guenther, "Slithering Down the Plank of Intellectualism?" 208.

55. Guenther, "Slithering Down the Plank of Intellectualism?" 210.

56. Guenther, "Slithering Down the Plank of Intellectualism?" 210.

57. See, for example, http://capernwrayquebec.ca/, https://www.ywamcanada.org/, https://willingdon.org/willingdon-school-of-the-bible, https://www.lifecentre.org/connect/training/, https://www.cccc.org/member_resources, https://www.willowcreek.com/events/leadership/.

been offered through Christian higher education (CHE) institutions.[58] Competency-based education is another CHE model that is gaining traction in North America.[59] Finally, there are non-accredited Bible colleges and Bible schools. All these non-accredited models share a greater focus on practical Christian ministry training and discipleship than is possible at a liberal arts school. The scope and scale of these non-accredited CHEM options in Canada is not well understood. In many cases, these alternatives have arisen to fill a market that was underserved as accredited CHEM schools moved toward liberal arts models. Some CHEC institutions moved toward liberal arts models both out of philosophical convictions about education and in order to compete with secular higher education institutions. They formed associative structures that helped them work cooperatively in areas such as recruitment and marketing.

Although young adults are often encouraged to choose a post-secondary program that corresponds to a career choice, many do not know what career they want to pursue. Young adults often choose a post-secondary program that they believe will maximize their options for their future career decisions. Liberal arts programs, and university programs more generally, are perceived as offering more career options than a curriculum that focuses on the Bible or ministry training.

THE 2007 IPSOS REID CHEC MARKETING STUDY

Ipsos Reid conducted a marketing study for CHEC in 2007 and identified six market segments or "mindsets": Evangelical Enthusiasts, Cultural Christians, Private Believers, Church & State, Deeply Disinterested, and Ambivalent Agnostics.[60] Close to 17 in 20 of the high school prospects and 16 in 20 CHEC students were Evangelical Enthusiasts, and about a tenth of each of these segments were Cultural Christians.

Evangelical Enthusiasts and Cultural Christians were both described as very committed Christians with "very strong beliefs" or "solid doctrinal beliefs/values." Moreover, Evangelical Enthusiasts have high levels of church attendance, hold to strong views that church and religion have a role to play in Canadian society, have very favorable views of CHE institutions,

---

58. See, for example, https://wec-canada.org/index.php/training/ and https://www.cmacan.org/education/#additional.

59. Long, "Credit for What You Know and Do." In 2012, Northwest Baptist Seminary launched the first ATS-accredited competency-based MDiv program.

60. Grenville, "Christian Post-Secondary Education in Canada," 20.

and believe that CHE institutions offer opportunities for personal and spiritual growth not available outside of CHE institutions.[61]

The Ipsos study concluded that 80% of the "captive" CHEC market came from Evangelical Enthusiasts and Cultural Christians, and that 44% of the "probably attend" and 48% of the "might attend" growth markets came from these two market segments as well.[62] When CHEC students were asked for the main reason they decided to attend a CHEC institution, the top two responses were "Faith-based education" (38%) and "Christian oriented/focused (education)" (27%). In fact, of the 14 responses listed, only 5 did not have an explicit link to the Christian faith.[63] The study found that CHEC schools scored more poorly on perceptions of course selection, accreditation, job placement record, and location. These factors, however, were usually not cited as important factors in school selection for students who actually chose CHEC institutions.

Significantly, accreditation was not a top factor in school choice for high school students or 18- to 24-year-olds, the demographic groups that typically make up the undergraduate market.[64] Rather, for all respondents, the top six factors affecting school choice ranked by importance were: Reputation, Teachers/Instructors, Education/Learning Environment, Program/Curriculum, Location, and Cost.[65]

Strong Christian commitment and a prior belief in the value of CHE are what defined actual and potential CHEC markets in 2007. These strong belief and community commitments are consistent with having achieved the Eriksonian "virtue of fidelity" and having formed an adult identity, that is, having moved past emerging adulthood. In fact, Grenville notes that 81% of CHEC students describe their faith commitment *prior* to attending a CHEC institution as either "very strong" (39%) or "somewhat strong" (42%).[66] Strong religious commitments are inconsistent with emerging adulthood.

The study identified some key challenges for the CHE market:

- Many self-identified Christians would not consider attending a CHE institution.

61. Grenville, "Christian Post-Secondary Education in Canada," 14–15.
62. Grenville, "Christian Post-Secondary Education in Canada," 24.
63. Grenville, "Christian Post-Secondary Education in Canada," 33.
64. Grenville, "Christian Post-Secondary Education in Canada," 34.
65. Grenville, "Christian Post-Secondary Education in Canada," 37.
66. Grenville, "Christian Post-Secondary Education in Canada," 34.

- Two key target audiences—high school prospects and 18- to 24-year-old prospects—are less inclined than others to attend CHEC institutions.

- CHE more generally, and its institutions more specifically, are generally unknown in Canada among the key target audiences and segments.

- In three of the four Christian segments, there are specific challenges tied to perceptions of Christian post-secondary education, personal faith commitment, and the competitive context of higher education in Canada.[67]

These key challenges are with the "non-captive," self-identified Christians who are also not among the religiously "very committed." A commitment to the Christian faith is implicit in choosing to attend a CHE institution. This implicit faith commitment may be the specific challenge tied to "personal faith commitment" in the fourth bullet of the above list of challenges for the CHE market. Emerging adults, by definition, have not yet made an adult, enduring, faith commitment.

ADMISSIONS AND OPENNESS

CHEC institutions have a variety of admission practices: open, selective, or faith-based admissions. In an unpublished discussion paper, CHEC Executive Director Justin Cooper outlines these three approaches:

- Open—Students from any background: Students are admitted from all faith backgrounds or no faith background (atheist or agnostic). Explicit support for the faith-based academic mission of the institution may be required. This can be paired with a comprehensive, aspirational, voluntary or ethical approach to community standards (comprehensive/mandatory standards may be the least compatible).

- Selective—Mission-related selection: Students are asked to submit a pastor's recommendation and often an essay about their desire to study at a Christian university; those without a pastor's recommendation are usually interviewed. Students with a suitable recommendation and essay, as well as searching agnostics and those from other world religions with a positive interview (interest in the mission), are admitted; committed atheists and adherents of other world religions

---

67. Grenville, "Christian Post-Secondary Education in Canada," 68.

are not admitted. Those admitted also commit to the community standards of the institution.

- Faith-Based ("Closed")—Only Christian students are admitted: Students are asked to submit a faith statement or sign the institution's statement of faith as part of the admission process; it may include a commitment to the institution's faith-based community standards or may take the faith statement to include a commitment to moral and lifestyle standards.[68]

Open admissions are the newest form of admission practice for CHEC schools and are usually practiced by liberal arts institutions that are trying to broaden their appeal beyond the Christian community. The openness of the admission practice with respect to religion means that there is no impediment to admission for those who do not share the Christian faith or are uncertain about their faith commitments.

The understanding that enrolling in a CHEC institution might imply or require some kind of Christian faith commitment can be seen in the arguments advanced by the law societies in the *Law Society of British Columbia v. Trinity Western University* and *Trinity Western University v. Law Society of Upper Canada* cases.[69] At the time, although Trinity Western practiced open admissions and did not require a declaration of faith, it required students to sign a Community Covenant that represented a commitment to a Christian code of conduct. The law societies argued the Community Covenant would nevertheless constitute a barrier to participation in a law school for LGBTQ students. CHEC institutions implement open admission policies in order to remove religious impediments to admission; however, emerging adults, who typically have not made faith commitments, may still consider these institutions to be closed due to the Christian provenance and character of the institution.

COMPARISON OF THE CHEC AND MAIN DATASETS

The YATR study's young adult survey was screened by polling firm MARU/Matchbox with two samples resulting in two datasets. Respondents for both samples were 18- to 28-year-olds who had a Christian religious affiliation

---

68. Cooper, "Approaches to Admissions & Community Standards," 1.

69. Law Society of British Columbia v. Trinity Western University, No. 37318 (Supreme Court of Canada June 15, 2018); Trinity Western University v. Law Society of Upper Canada, No. 37209 (Supreme Court of Canada June 15, 2018).

as a teen and who attended religious services at least monthly at some point during their teen years. The first dataset, which we will call the Main dataset and on which the *Renegotiating Faith* report is based, was screened with a representative national sample of 1,998 young adults who met the screening criteria. The second dataset, which we will call the CHEC dataset, was screened with a population of 773 current or former CHEC students who met the screening criteria. Twenty-six of the current 34 CHEC institutions participated in the study.[70] Apart from a modified survey introduction, one additional question dealing with consent and two additional questions dealing with CHEC respondents' status as CHEC students, the CHEC and Main sample surveys were identical. In this section we will compare the CHEC and Main responses to select questions. Space limitations preclude a comprehensive comparison of the two datasets. The presented points of comparison highlight the different religious engagement profiles of respondents from the two samples.

Youth Group

There was little difference in how CHEC and Main sample respondents viewed the focus of their home church youth groups. Almost nine in ten (87%) of CHEC sample respondents agreed that "Learning about Jesus, the Christian faith and how to live out the Christian faith was the focus of the church youth group I attended as a teenager," compared to eight in ten (80%) of those from the Main sample.[71] There was a significant difference, however, in how often CHEC respondents attended their church youth group as a teen. CHEC respondents were almost twice as likely (55%) as Main sample respondents (28%) to say they attended youth group weekly as a teen (see Table 1 below).

---

70. For more on the methodology, see Hiemstra, "Competition for Character Education," 80–83; Hiemstra, Dueck, and Blackaby, "Renegotiating Faith," 175–82.

71. For those whose average youth group attendance as a teen was more often than "never."

Table 1: "During your teenage years (age 14 to 17), on average, how often did you attend a church youth group?," CHEC and Main samples, percent

Frequency	CHEC	Main
At least weekly	55	28
1–3 times a month	29	37
Less than monthly	16	34

Columns may not add to 100 because of rounding.

Connections with a New Church

Five in six (83%) CHEC respondents who moved out of their parents' home connected with a new local church after moving out, compared to just over one third (35%) of Main sample respondents.

The *Renegotiating Faith* report found a strong correlation between having a home church mentor and making connections to new local congregations after moving out of the parental home.[72] Main sample respondents were more than twice as likely to connect with a new local church if they had a home church mentor a teen (53%) than if they did not (20%) (see Table 2 below). Main sample respondents were also almost three times as likely to make this connection (68%) if someone from their home church made a connection or introduction for them with a new local church than if no one from their home church made a connection for them (23%).

For CHEC respondents, however, the presence or absence of a teen home church mentor is not correlated with the same dramatic differences in connection rates. Seventeen in twenty (85%) CHEC respondents who had a teen home church mentor connected with a new local church after moving out of their parents' home compared to about sixteen in twenty (79%) of those who did not have a home church mentor. Nine in ten (92%) CHEC respondents who had home church help connecting to a new church went on to connect with another local church compared to eight in ten (81%) who did not have this home church help.

72. Hiemstra, Dueck, and Blackaby, "Renegotiating Faith," 131–42.

Table 2: Young adults who made connections with a new local church[a], CHEC and Main samples, percent

	CHEC	Main
Home Church Connection		
Yes	92	68
No	81	23
Had a home church mentor		
Yes	85	53
No	79	20

[a] For those who had moved out of their parents' home. "Home Church Connection" means someone from the young adult's home church tried to make a connection for them to either a new local church/parish or a Christian campus group. "Mentor" means they had a local church/ parish mentor as a teen.

Connections with a Christian Campus Group

We asked both CHEC and Main sample respondents about their connections with Christian campus groups. Christian campus groups will mean something quite different on a secular college or university campus than on a CHEC campus. On secular campuses it usually means groups like InterVarsity Christian Fellowship, Power to Change—Students, Navigators or a chaplaincy, whereas CHEC schools themselves may organize Christian campus groups.

CHEC respondents were more likely to connect with Christian campus groups than Main respondents. Although CHEC respondents connected with local churches at similar rates irrespective of the presence of mentors in their lives, the presence of teen, home church mentors in the lives of CHEC students was correlated with different rates of connection with Christian campus groups, as was having someone from one's home church make a connection with a Christian campus group (see Table 3. below).

Main sample respondents were four times (66%) as likely to connect with a Christian campus group if someone from their home church made a connection than if no connection was made for them (16%). By comparison, four in five (80%) CHEC respondents connected with a Christian campus group with the help of an introduction and just 56% made the connection without the benefit of an introduction.

Main sample respondents were more than three times as likely (48%) to connect with a Christian campus group if they had a home church mentor than if they did not (13%). Similarly, CHEC respondents were more likely to connect with a Christian campus group (63%) having had a home church mentor than not having had one (54%).

Table 3: Young adults who made connections with a Christian[a] campus group, CHEC and Main samples, percent

	CHEC	Main
Home Church Connection		
Yes	80	66
No	56	16
Had a home church mentor		
Yes	63	48
No	54	13

[a] Catholic or Orthodox or other Christian.

[b] For those who had gone on to post-secondary education.

"Home Church Connection" means someone from the young adult's home church tried to make a connection for them to either a new local church/parish or a Christian campus group. "Mentor" means they had a local church/parish mentor as a teen.

We asked those who had not connected with a Christian campus group why they did not make the connection. Respondents were presented with lists of explanations that were drawn from our earlier interviews with young adults (see listed explanations in Table 4 below).

Table 4: Explanations for not connecting with a Christian[a] campus group[b],
CHEC and Main samples, percent

Explanations	CHEC	Main
Not aware of any	43	19
Not enough time	40	33
Not interested	35	50
Do not know anyone there	31	23
Doctrinal conflict[c]	6	12
Not comfortable around religious people	5	14
Hate groups[d]	3	9

[a] Catholic or Orthodox or other Christian.

[b] For those who had attended university or college and made a connection.

[c] Did not feel my religious views would be welcome / Doctrinal conflict.

[d] Do not want to be associated with groups that promote hate.

Columns may not add to 100 because of rounding.

Timing of Connections

The first month after a transition such as starting university or college is critical for making connections with new local churches and Christian campus groups. Almost four-fifths of both CHEC respondents (79%) and Main sample respondents (78%) who connected with a new local church after having moved out of their parents' home did so within four weeks of moving out (see Table 5 below). Similarly, majorities of both CHEC (88%) and Main (74%) sample respondents who connected to a Christian campus group did so within four weeks of starting their post-secondary program.

Table 5: How long before connecting with new local church or Christian campus group, CHEC and Main samples, percent

	Connected with a new local church[a]		Connected with a Christian[b] campus group[c]	
	CHEC	Main	CHEC	Main
Within the first two weeks	57	42	67	37
Within the first month	25	36	21	37
Within the first four months	8	11	7	16
Within the first year	7	4	3	6
Longer than a year	3	7	2	4

[a] For those who had moved out of their parents' home and connected with a different (local church/parish).

[b] Catholic or Orthodox or other Christian.

[c] For those who had attended university or college and made a connection.

Columns may not add to 100 because of rounding.

Change in Religious Affiliation

Only 3% of CHEC respondents reported an Atheist, Agnostic, Spiritual or None (AASN) religious affiliation as a young adult compared to one third (33%) of Main sample respondents (see Table 6 and Table 7 below).

Table 6: Religious affiliation change, teen to young adult, CHEC sample, counts

		Teen Affiliation							
		Catholic	Mainline	Evang.	Orth.	OWR	AASN	Other	Total
	Catholic	11	0	1	0	0	0	0	12
	Mainline	0	48	11	0	0	0	0	59
Young adult Affiliation	Evang.	7	19	635	0	0	2	1	664
	Orth.	0	0	2	0	0	0	0	2
	OWR	0	0	0	0	0	0	0	0
	AASN	2	2	12	0	0	4	0	20
	Other	1	2	6	0	0	0	0	9
	Total	21	71	667	0	0	6	1	766

"AASN" is Atheist, Agnostic, Spiritual or None. "OWR" is Other World Religions. "Orth" is Orthodox Christian.

Table 7: Religious affiliation change, teen to young adult, Main sample, counts

| | | Teen Affiliation | | | | | | | |
		Catholic	Mainline	Evang.	Orth.	OWR	AASN	Other	Total
Young adult Affiliation	Catholic	460	2	9	0	0	0	3	474
	Mainline	10	184	14	0	0	0	0	208
	Evang.	14	13	434	1	0	0	1	463
	Orth.	2	0	2	9	0	0	0	13
	OWR	47	17	26	2	30	0	4	126
	AASN	297	127	167	7	6	42	14	660
	Other	10	5	23	1	0	2	15	56
	Total	840	348	675	20	36	44	37	2,000

"AASN" is Atheist, Agnostic, Spiritual or None. "OWR" is Other World Religions. "Orth" is Orthodox Christian.

Change in Religious Service Attendance

We asked respondents how often, on average, they had attended religious services both as a teen and in the last twelve months. For each question they could choose one of the following five ordered categories: At least weekly, two to three times a month, once a month or so, once or a few times a year, or never.

As teens, four-fifths (81%) of CHEC respondents attended religious services at least weekly compared to just 38% of Main sample respondents (see Table 8 below).

Table 8: Teen and young adult attendance, CHEC and Main samples, percent

| | CHEC | | Main | |
Attendance	Teen	YA	Teen	YA
At least weekly	81	76	38	24
2–3 times a month	13	17	24	17
Once a month or so	3	4	18	15
Once or a few times a year	3	3	17	24
Never	0	1	4	20

YA is Young Adult.

Columns may not add to 100 because of rounding.

The changes from one frequency category to the next are not directly comparable in magnitude or in personal significance. Nevertheless, we can get a measure of religious service attendance change by measuring the category movement along this ordered scale from their teen to young adult responses. For example, if a young adult's attendance in the last twelve months was "Once a month or so" and their teen attendance was at "At least weekly," we would say that their attendance was down two categories.

Nearly three-quarters (74%) of CHEC respondents continued attending religious services as young adults at the same frequency they had when they were teens (see Table 10 below). Only 17% of CHEC respondents' teen religious service attendance fell while 10% increased their religious service attendance. Where CHEC respondents' teen-to-young-adult attendance fell, it was usually down just one attendance category. By comparison, only about half (49%) of Main sample respondents continued to attend religious services at the same frequency they did as a teen, almost the same share (45%) reduced their religious service attendance, and a small minority (6%) increased their religious service attendance.

Table 9: Attendance category change from teen to young adult, CHEC and Main samples, percent

Attendance Category Change	CHEC	Main
Down 4	0	5
Down 3	1	10
Down 2	2	11
Down 1	14	16
No Change	74	53
Up 1	6	4
Up 2	2	1
Up 3	2	0
Up 4	0	0

Columns may not add to 100 because of rounding.

Christian Doctrinal Specifics

We asked respondents three Christian doctrine questions drawn from Andrew Grenville's Christian Evangelical Scale (CES).[73] The CES has been

73. Grenville, "Development of the Christian Evangelicalism Scale."

used in Canadian polling to identify evangelical Christians since the early 1990s.

The first two questions deal with Christology. In the first instance, respondents were asked for their agreement with "In my view, Jesus Christ was not the divine Son of God." Most CHEC respondents (94%) disagreed with the statement compared to just over half (57%) of Main sample respondents (see Table 10 below). It is important to remember that, to qualify for the study, respondents had to be Christian affiliates as a teen.

Table 10: "In my view, Jesus Christ was not the divine Son of God," CHEC and Main samples, percent

Agreement	CHEC	Main
Strongly agree	2	12
Moderately agree	1	10
Moderately disagree	2	14
Strongly disagree	92	43
Don't know	2	15
Not Applicable	2	6

The second question dealing with Christology (and soteriology) asked for their agreement with the statement, "I believe that through the life, death and resurrection of Jesus, God provided the way for the forgiveness of sins." Almost all CHEC respondents (97%) agreed compared to just three-fifths (61%) from the Main sample (see Table 11 below).

Table 11: "I believe that through the life, death and resurrection of Jesus, God provided the way for the forgiveness of my sins." CHEC and Main samples, percent

Agreement	CHEC	Main
Strongly agree	95	41
Moderately agree	2	20
Moderately disagree	0	12
Strongly disagree	1	15
Don't know	1	9
Not Applicable	1	3

The third CES question asked for the level of agreement with the statement, "I believe the Bible to be the Word of God and is reliable and trustworthy." Almost all CHEC respondents (97%) agreed with the statement compared to just 58% of Main sample respondents (see Table 12 below).

Table 12: "I believe the Bible to be the Word of God and is reliable and trustworthy," CHEC and Main samples, percent

Agreement	CHEC	Main
Strongly agree	90	33
Moderately agree	7	25
Moderately disagree	1	15
Strongly disagree	1	17
Don't know	0	8
Not Applicable	0	3

CONCLUSION

The CHEM in Canada began at a time when there was little competition for students from secular or non-Evangelical higher education institutions. Following the 1951 Massey Commission report, massive new government spending on post-secondary education created a secular college and university system that offered new and significant competition to CHEM schools. The CHEM responded to this competition in some cases by pursuing accreditation, by establishing schools based on liberal arts models, or by transitioning existing institutions to become liberal arts institutions. In many cases, the costs associated with these changes meant that CHE institutions that were once affordable came to be seen as more expensive compared with secular schools that enjoyed heavy government subsidies. Accreditation also tended to limit CHEM schools' responsiveness to the needs of their constituencies. As the CHEM focus, particularly among CHEC schools, has moved away from practical ministry training, new unaccredited schools and ministries have begun to fill the education and training space vacated by CHEC schools.

Post-secondary education, most of which happens in the secular system, is now the normative experience for Canadian young adults. Over time, the intentional character-forming mission of the secular system has reshaped the culture's understanding of the good citizen away from the vision of the CHEM, making recruitment more difficult. As post-secondary education has become a normative path for Canadian young adults so has a new life stage called Emerging Adulthood, which is characterized by delays in identity and faith formation.

CHE is typically chosen by young adults who already have strong faith commitments and are well integrated into their Christian communities. Emerging adults are less likely to choose a school where there is either an implicit or explicit faith commitment associated with attending. This study does not prove emerging adults are taking a pass on CHE, but along with CHEC's own 2007 Ipsos study, it shows that young adults who choose CHE tend to be more committed to the Christian faith than Main sample respondents.

BIBLIOGRAPHY

Arnett, Jeffrey Jensen. "Emerging Adulthood: A Theory of Development from the Late Teens Through the Twenties." *American Psychologist* 55 (2000) 469–80.

———. *Emerging Adulthood: The Winding Road from the Late Teens Through the Twenties*. 2nd ed. Oxford: Oxford University Press, 2015.

Boggs, Andrew Michael. "Ontario's Royal Commission on the University of Toronto, 1905–1906: Political and Historical Factors that Influenced the Final Report of the Flavelle Commission." MA thesis, University of Toronto, 2007.

Burkinshaw, Robert T. "Evangelical Bible Colleges in Twentieth-Century Canada." In *Aspects of the Canadian Evangelical Experience*, edited by George A. Rawlyk, 369–84. Montreal: McGill-Queen's University Press, 1997.

Canadian Royal Commission on National Development in the Arts, Letters and Sciences. "Report of the Royal Commission on National Development in the Arts, Letters and Sciences, 1949–1951." Edmond Cloutier, Printer to the King's Most Excellent Majesty, 1951. No pages. Online: https://www.collectionscanada.gc.ca/massey/index-e.html.

Canadian Royal Commission on Radio Broadcasting. "Report of the Royal Commission on Radio Broadcasting." F. A. Acland, Printer to the King's Most Excellent Majesty, 1929. No pages. Online: http://publications.gc.ca/collections/collection_2014/bcp-pco/CP32–104-1929-eng.pdf.

"Censuses of Canada 1665 to 1871: Estimated Population of Canada, 1605 to Present." No pages. Online: https://www150.statcan.gc.ca/n1/pub/98–187-x/4151287-eng.htm.

Clark, Warren. "100 Years of Education." *Canadian Social Trends* 59 (2000) 3–6.

Cooper, Justin. "Approaches to Admissions & Community Standards: An Overview (A Discussion Paper)." Unpublished, September 2018.

Druick, Zoë. "International Cultural Relations as a Factor in Postwar Canadian Cultural Policy: The Relevance of UNESCO for the Massey Commission." *Canadian Journal of Communication* 31 (2006) 177–95. Online: https://doi.org/10.22230/cjc.2006v31n1a1742.

Erikson, Erik H. *Identity: Youth and Crisis*. New York: Norton, 1968.

Faassen, Mark. "A Fine Balance: The Regulation of Canadian Religious Broadcasting." *Queen's Law Journal* 37 (2011) 303–37.

"Federal Spending on Postsecondary Education." Office of the Parliamentary Budget Officer, May 5, 2016. No pages. Online: http://www.pbo-dpb.gc.ca/web/default/files/Documents/Reports/2016/PSE/PSE_EN.pdf.

Government of Canada, Statistics Canada. "Postsecondary Enrolments, by Program Type, Credential Type, Age Groups, Registration Status and Sex." May 30, 2018. No pages. Online: https://www150.statcan.gc.ca/t1/tbl1/en/tv.action?pid=3710001501.

————. "Postsecondary Enrolments, by Registration Status, Institution Type, Sex and Student Status." June 12, 2018. No pages. Online: https://www150.statcan.gc.ca/t1/tbl1/en/tv.action?pid=3710001801.

Grenville, Andrew. "Christian Post-Secondary Education in Canada: Defining the Market." Paper presented at the CHEC Annual General Meeting, Calgary, Alberta, October 19, 2007.

————. "Development of the Christian Evangelicalism Scale: Working Draft." Unpublished, February 1995.

Guenther, Bruce L. "Slithering Down the Plank of Intellectualism? The Canadian Conference of Christian Educators and the Impulse towards Accreditation among Canadian Bible Schools during the 1960s." *Historical Studies in Education / Revue d'histoire de l'éducation* 16 (2004) 197–228.

————. "The Origin of the Bible School Movement in Western Canada: Towards an Ethnic Interpretation." *Historical Papers: Canadian Society of Church History* (1993) 135–73.

Hanson, Calvin B. *On the Raw Edge of Faith: The Miracle of Trinity Western College.* Langley, BC: Trinity Western University, 1977.

Hiebert, Al, et al. *Character with Competence Education: The Bible College Movement in Canada.* Steinbach, MB: Association of Canadian Bible Colleges, 2005.

Hiemstra, Rick. "Competition for Character Education: What Emerging Adulthood Means for Christian Higher Education in Canada." *Faith Today Publications* (2018) 1–83. Online: https://p2c.com/renegotiating-faith/#resources.

Hiemstra, Rick, et al. "Renegotiating Faith: The Delay in Young Adult Identity Formation and What It Means for the Church in Canada." *Faith Today Publications* (2018) 1–177. Online: www.RenegotiatingFaith.ca.

"Historical Statistics of Canada: Section W: Education." Statistics Canada. No pages. Online: https://www150.statcan.gc.ca/n1/pub/11-516-x/sectionw/4147445-eng.htm.

Jones, Glen A. "An Introduction to Higher Education in Canada." In *Higher Education across Nations*, edited by K. M. Joshi and Saee Paivani, 1:1–38. Delhi: B. R. Publishing, 2014.

Law Society of British Columbia v. Trinity Western University, No. 37318 (Supreme Court of Canada June 15, 2018).

Long, Charla. "Credit for What You Know and Do, Not for Time in Class: The Rise of Competency-Based Education." *In Trust Magazine* (Summer 2016). No pages. Online: http://www.intrust.org/Magazine/Issues/Summer-2016/Credit-for-what-you-know-and-do-not-for-time-in-class.

McGowan, Mark G. "The People's University of the Air: St. Francis Xavier University Extension, Social Christianity, and the Creation of CJFX." *Acadiensis* 41 (May 1,

2012). No pages. Online: https://journals.lib.unb.ca/index.php/Acadiensis/article/view/19072.

Ontario. The Royal Commission on the University of Toronto. "The Report of The Royal Commission on the University of Toronto." The Legislative Assembly of Ontario, 1906. No pages. Online: https://ia600501.us.archive.org/31/items/uoftcommissionooonta/uoftcommissionooonta.pdf.

Rawlyk, George A. *Is Jesus Your Personal Saviour? In Search of Canadian Evangelicalism in the 1990s.* Montreal: McGill-Queen's University Press, 1996.

Sokol, Justin T. "Identity Development Throughout the Lifetime: An Examination of Eriksonian Theory." *Graduate Journal of Counseling Psychology* 1 (Spring 2009). No pages. Online: http://epublications.marquette.edu/cgi/viewcontent.cgi?article=1030&context=gjcp.

Stackhouse, John G., Jr. *Canadian Evangelicalism in the Twentieth Century: An Introduction to Its Character.* Toronto: University of Toronto Press, 1993.

Stewart, J. D. M., and Helmut Kallman. "Massey Commission." *The Canadian Encyclopedia* (February 7, 2006). No pages. Online: https://www.thecanadianencyclopedia.ca/en/article/massey-commission-emc.

"Table W430–455, Full-Time University Undergraduate Enrolment, by Field of Specialization and Sex, Canada, Selected Years, 1861 to 1975." Statistics Canada. No pages. Online: https://www150.statcan.gc.ca/n1/pub/11–516-x/sectionw/W439_455-eng.csv.

Trinity Western University v. Law Society of Upper Canada, No. 37209 (Supreme Court of Canada June 15, 2018).

Part 2

Canadian Bible Colleges,
Christian Universities,
and Seminaries Today

5

Can Bible Colleges Thrive?

A Case Study of Columbia Bible College

Douglas H. Berg

INTRODUCTION

THERE ARE MANY OPTIONS for post-secondary students within the continuum of Christian higher education in Canada. On one end of the continuum are the church or mission-based internship programs, and on the other end of the continuum are the provincially-approved Christian universities. In between are experiential discipleship schools, unaccredited Bible schools, and degree-granting accredited Bible colleges.

With all these options, is it possible for Bible colleges[1] in Canada to thrive? Stanley Porter does not think so. He asserts that "there are many good things about Bible colleges and what they provide. However, I believe that there is little to no future for the Bible college movement as currently known. They will need to reinvent themselves as something significantly different if they hope to survive."[2] There is a common assumption that a Bible college should follow the example of others[3] and move toward some

---

1. For the purposes of this chapter, a Bible college is a school accredited either institutionally or programmatically with the Association for Biblical Higher Education (ABHE).

2. Porter, "Theological Education in the Twenty-First Century," 43.

3. There are currently eighteen member schools in Canada listed with ABHE.

type of university status to remain viable. But is it possible for Bible colleges to thrive within the current Canadian context?

The purpose of this chapter is to answer this question using Columbia Bible College as a case study, making use of the extensive research performed by the higher education consultant firm Credo. In their work with private colleges and universities, Credo has established nine indicators of thriving for a private college.[4] Applying Credo's framework as an evaluation tool for Columbia Bible College provides a helpful model for others to follow, as Columbia's unique setting and challenges illuminate key themes and issues faced by other Bible colleges.

Located in Abbotsford, British Columbia, Columbia Bible College is owned by two denominational partners, is progressive in its programming, but has not changed its name or its identity as a Bible college. Contrary to prevailing assumptions about the viability of Bible colleges, Columbia is not moving down the path toward seeking university status. Further, Columbia has recently had its accreditation with the Association for Biblical Higher Education (ABHE) renewed for another ten years, as well as having significant dialogue with the Advanced Ministry of Education for the Province of British Columbia in regard to its certificates, diplomas, and degrees. Several diplomas are recognized by the province. Columbia has also recently signed agreements securing 60 units of block transfer credit with the University of the Fraser Valley (UFV) and Trinity Western University (TWU) for students completing Columbia's Diploma in General Studies.

The academic accountability that Columbia has achieved in the last years (i.e., accreditation, provincial recognition) and its initiatives (recruitment, marketing, programming, transferability), along with its proximity to a provincial and Christian university and one of its denominational seminaries, place Columbia in a unique position to be used as a case study for the ability of Bible college education in Canada to thrive. This chapter applies Credo's Thriving Framework, meant broadly for private college and universities, to a specific Canadian Bible college, exposing critical questions and areas of focus that Bible colleges should consider as they assess their own health and make decisions about their future within the Canadian educational landscape.

Of these eighteen schools, only five have retained "Bible" in their name. Eleven of the schools have the term "college," two have "university college," and two schools only use the term "university" in their name.

4. Soliday and Mann, *Surviving to Thriving*.

COUNTERPOINTS TO THRIVING BIBLE COLLEGES

Before this chapter moves to an analysis of Columbia Bible College, I will first interact with three studies that show the difficulty for Bible colleges to thrive in Canada. First is the matter of the pull towards a liberal arts curriculum to make a Bible college education more attractive to students and parents. The history of Mennonite Brethren Bible College (MBBC) helps us to visualize the power of this pull.[5] Dueck recounts the tensions within the denomination of affirming a vision for the college. There was vision for having the college prepare students with a "higher calling" to ministry as well as for graduate ministry training in Winnipeg, but there was also the pull toward the inclusion of liberal arts and a connection to a university. "The Canadian Conference ultimately failed to come up with a vision for its primary educational program which the majority of Canadian Mennonite Brethren could rally around."[6] The resolution of these tensions was the establishment of Canadian Mennonite University (CMU) in 2000 as a regional post-secondary institution within the Canadian Mennonite Brethren. Dueck concludes,

> Only after the demise of MBBC and its successor, Concord College, did a clear vision for a university emerge with the founding of CMU in 2000. Although CMU could claim some degree of continuity with the original vision of MBBC, it adopted a focus that was more in keeping with a liberal arts identity, an option that had been resisted by many in the Mennonite Brethren community for much of the college's history.[7]

The emergence of Canadian Mennonite University illustrates the pull away from the identity of a Bible college towards the liberal arts identity. Is it possible for a Bible college to resist that pull and still thrive in Canada?

Another difficulty to consider in having a thriving Bible college is the perception of students, their parents, and their churches regarding the purpose of post-secondary education. The Barna Group's "What's Next for Biblical Higher Education" report[8] provides a number of insights and predictors related to Bible college viability. Even though the data is from the United States, this chapter assumes that the data would be applicable to

5. Dueck, "Mennonite Brethren Bible College."
6. Dueck, "Mennonite Brethren Bible College," 40.
7. Dueck, "Mennonite Brethren Bible College," 56.
8. Barna Group, "What's Next for Biblical Higher Education."

the Canadian environment as well. The Barna Group's survey data demonstrates that primary reasons for attending college are to prepare for a
specific career and to increase financial opportunities. What is surprising is
that the differences between evangelicals and the general population of the
United States are "negligible, nonexistent or counterintuitive."[9]

> In lockstep with all U.S. adults, only 7 percent of self-identified
> Christians say college is for encouraging spiritual growth, and just
> 14 percent say it's for developing moral character. Unexpectedly,
> those with no faith—a category that includes atheists, agnostics
> and "nones"—are statistically tied with self-identified Christians
> in saying that spiritual growth is the purpose of college.[10]

When parents of prospective students were surveyed by the Barna
Group, "with few exceptions, Christian colleges and universities receive
higher marks than Bible colleges in the strength categories and lower marks
in the weakness categories, suggesting that parents tend to see these schools
as stronger in general."[11]

The Barna Group, however, sees much potential in the perceptions of
potential employers to call a Bible college graduate for an interview just as
much as other candidates (68%).[12] "The nature and structure of work will
continue to undergo rapid change, and Barna researchers predict the 'soft
skills' of effective leadership and communication, and the maturity necessary to work successfully as part of a team, will be in ever-high demand."[13]

Another insight that the Barna Group highlights is that the Bible
college should play to its strength and offer non-professional programs in
partnership with denominational churches to provide "richer, more comprehensive, biblical training."[14]

This data does not support the thriving of Bible colleges. Adults, in
general, equate post-secondary education with career development and
individual financial enhancement. Many do not believe that a key purpose
of post-secondary education should be faith formation. Bible colleges rank
lower in public credibility than Christian colleges and universities. If Bible
college graduates have some of the soft skills that employers are looking for,

9. Barna Group, "What's Next for Biblical Higher Education."
10. Barna Group, "What's Next for Biblical Higher Education," 10.
11. Barna Group, "What's Next for Biblical Higher Education," 30.
12. Barna Group, "What's Next for Biblical Higher Education," 33.
13. Barna Group, "What's Next for Biblical Higher Education," 33–34.
14. Barna Group, "What's Next for Biblical Higher Education," 37.

does that really justify spending four years in a Bible college? And further, non-formal education could be offered by a variety of sources, not just a Bible college. Based on this data, Bible colleges have an uphill battle in order to thrive.

In his article "The Disappearing Middle Class in Christian Higher Education,"[15] Cone makes some pertinent points regarding the viability of Bible colleges. Cone divides Bible colleges into three categories: the Economic Lower Class (ELC), the Economic Middle Class (EMC), and the Economic Upper Class (EUC). The ELC consists of unaccredited Bible schools that are more resistant to market fluctuations because they have lower administrative and infrastructure costs. Further, they have been more mission and ministry focused than other colleges, and his estimate is that the "annual cost for operating a credible unaccredited institution can be less than half of those for an accredited school."[16]

Cone defines schools in the EUC as "hitting the 350-student threshold, sustaining revenue above 2%, reinvesting for future growth, developing alternate significant sources of funding, and employing efficient cost structures. Schools that are able to achieve these markers are best positioned to sustain. Institutions in this sector are growing largely through strategic institutional growth initiatives and partnerships, and a broadening of academic offerings."[17]

Cone argues that the EMC Bible colleges face "the greatest challenges and even extinction."[18] One of these challenges is cost in relation to ELC schools. EMC Bible colleges "are providing an education that costs roughly twice that of the ELC institutions, but the difference in perceived value and quality is often not substantial enough to offset the increased cost. So prospective students are not choosing the EMC as they once did. The major difference between the two sectors is simply accreditation (and all that implies), and for ministry training, accreditation seems to offer little value."[19]

The picture painted by Cone for EMC schools is bleak. He states that this category of Bible colleges will disappear if they do not move up (EUC) or down (ELC). These are the two choices according to Cone: "Will they back away from the accreditation, facilities, and personnel commitments

15. Cone, "The Disappearing Middle Class in Christian Higher Education."
16. Cone, "The Disappearing Middle Class in Christian Higher Education."
17. Cone, "The Disappearing Middle Class in Christian Higher Education."
18. Cone, "The Disappearing Middle Class in Christian Higher Education."
19. Cone, "The Disappearing Middle Class in Christian Higher Education."

that the middle class demands and move into a niche in the economic lower class, or will they strive to move from the middle class into the upper echelon?"[20]

However, Cone warns that EMC schools with hopes of moving into the EUC "are in a global economy of higher education and must look beyond provincial market-share models. In pursuing this more aggressive stance, these institutions must also realize that they must be all the more diligent to pursue mission fulfillment, and to avoid sacrificing mission integrity on the altar of sustainability."[21]

Cone is describing the difficult journey for accredited Bible colleges to thrive who are below his criteria for the EUC. If the school is not able to attain the standards of the EUC, his solution is for the institution to abandon accreditation and become an unaccredited Bible school, or cease to exist. An example of an institution caught in this tension is Bethany College in Hepburn, Saskatchewan that closed its doors in 2015.

So, even in light of these counterpoints to the thriving of Bible colleges, is it possible for Bible colleges in Canada to thrive despite what they are going up against? Columbia Bible College will now be the focus for the rest of the chapter, with me asking pertinent questions about whether this is a thriving institution. Even though the landscape is bleak, can a Canadian Bible college thrive?

CASE STUDY: COLUMBIA BIBLE COLLEGE
AND THE CREDO FRAMEWORK

What are the signs of a thriving institution? Credo, a partner of ABHE, has sought to define what thriving means for private colleges and universities.[22] After conducting a thorough investigation, consultant Joanne Soliday[23] and researcher Rick Mann[24] proposed a Thriving Framework that includes nine elements.

Individuals may take a survey, constructed by Credo, regarding their particular college. The survey goes through all the various factors mentioned in the nine categories of thriving in *Surviving to Thriving*, and rates

20. Cone, "The Disappearing Middle Class in Christian Higher Education."
21. Cone, "The Disappearing Middle Class in Christian Higher Education."
22. Soliday and Mann, *Surviving to Thriving.*
23. "Explore the Thriving Framework" — Credo | Higher Education Consulting."
24. Soliday and Mann, *Surviving to Thriving*, vii.

them on whether or not the college is thriving in the category. One receives a percentage-of-urgency score regarding a particular category and an overall percentage-of-urgency regarding the institution. The higher the percentage of urgency, the more necessary to take corrective action. The lower the percentage of urgency, the less concern regarding that particular category. The writer took this survey in regard to Columbia Bible College, and the scores will be reported below.

In what follows, Columbia Bible College will be evaluated in light of each of the nine Credo elements. Columbia Bible College was chosen for the case study because of its uniqueness in the following ways. First, it has had stable enrolment for the past several years.[25] Second, it is free of debt. Third, it has interacted with government agencies in defining its programs. It is the only Bible college in British Columbia certified with the Private Training Institutions Branch (PTIB) of the Advanced Ministry of Education (AVED). Fourth, it recently was approved for full, ten-year accreditation with the ABHE. Fifth, it is geographically close to a Christian university and, therefore, it intentionally does not offer similar programs. Sixth, it recently negotiated block transfer agreements with both the University of the Fraser Valley and Trinity Western University. It seems to be a thriving institution. Whether this is in fact so will be determined through careful application of Credo's framework to Columbia's situation, making use of College documents, established operating practices, personal interviews, and reports.

I was the Academic Dean of Columbia for seven years (2010–2017) and thus have inside knowledge of some items, as well as access to current data through the permission of the president. I admit to a positive bias toward Columbia, which I trust will not impede an objectivity regarding the evaluation of the nine categories. The subjectivity of this study is acknowledged given the fact that it is primarily my perception of the college that is reflected.

Thriving Category 1: Courageous and Collaborative Leadership

The first element of a thriving college in the Credo framework is a Courageous and Collaborative Leadership, defined as "the courage of strong leaders to stay," as well as the ability of the president "to balance people and

---

25. Enrolment figures: 2012—414, 2013—419, 2014—405, 2015—406, 2016—418, 2017—426, 2018—419.

tasks in decision-making."[26] Courageous and Collaborative Leadership is to reside in the president, the leadership team, and the board of trustees.

To succeed in the critical role of leading a thriving college, a Bible college president must navigate the tension between collaboration, which leads to inefficient decision-making when taken to its extreme, and courage, which may lead to authoritarian decision-making. Somewhere between the two is the healthy balance that takes time to consult even as it moves projects forward. By all accounts, Columbia's president is a courageous and collaborative leader. A previous faculty member and program director, the president was appointed in 2012. His most recent review highlights the level of trust placed in him by the constituency and employees in the leadership of the Bible college, as well as his ability to move initiatives ahead.

Credo states that the staying power of the president determines whether a college will thrive. *Surviving to Thriving* names four phases that a president moves through in staying at an institution. Phase one, operation; phase two, campus leadership development; phase three, external relations; and phase four, partnerships and significance.[27] The president of Columbia understands the operation, has developed a stable leadership team, and has worked well in external relations. The next matter is a major building project, which is being undertaken. Leadership effectiveness, at this point of Columbia's development, needs the staying power of the current president.

Recently the Best Christian Workplace data highlighted that the faculty thought that the Lead Team of Columbia did not collaborate enough with vested stakeholders (i.e., faculty) in decisions. The result was a clarification of the roles of the Lead Team, Academic Committee, Faculty Council, and the Faculty Executive. An Advisory Group to the Lead Team was created, and the need for communication between the Lead Team and Faculty Council was highlighted. One result was an increase in the score of the Best Christian Workplace data to the point that Columbia was named a Best Christian Workplace for 2017.

Another important aspect of institutional leadership is the Board of Directors. In Columbia's case, this Board is made up of representatives from the two supporting constituencies, the British Columbia Conference of Mennonite Brethren Churches and the Mennonite Church of British Columbia, who are elected at the Annual General Meeting of Columbia.

26. "Courageous & Collaborative Leadership," https://www.credohighered.com/about/our-methodology.

27. Soliday and Mann, *Surviving to Thriving*, 18–21.

The Board also has the capacity to appoint other members to the Board of Directors in areas of deficit (e.g., areas where the Columbia Board of Directors needs more expertise). In the past years Board capacity has been built through orientation and the evaluation of individual board meetings. Professional development of Board members should be considered by the college to increase Board leadership capacity.

In my opinion, below are the thriving elements in Courageous and Collaborative Leadership that are especially strong at Columbia. The Recommendations for Thriving are elements within Courageous and Collaborative Leadership that need strengthening. This pattern will follow in each category of the Thriving Framework.

Thriving Elements:

- Excellent courageous and collaborative President
- Results of the Best Christian Workplace data

Recommendations for Thriving:

- Support the staying power of the current president
- Continued development of Board capacity

This category was given a 16 percent urgency score.[28]

Thriving Category 2: Vision

The second category in the Thriving Framework is Vision. According to Credo, thriving institutions keep three clear guides at the center of all initiatives: "A mission statement (what you do), a set of core values (why you do what you do), and a vision statement (where you are going)."[29]

In recent years, Columbia has worked at all three of these statements. The college has articulated a focused mission statement: "to equip men and women for a life of discipleship, ministry and leadership in service to the church and community."[30] The identity statement, which follows the mission statement, makes it clear that Columbia educates students in a post-secondary accredited Bible college from an Anabaptist perspective. Further, a cross-department team recently created a widely-adopted Columbia Graduate Attributes document. This document is a common vision for the

28. "Thriving Framework Diagnostic Tool Results."

29. "Vision," https://www.credohighered.com/about/our-methodology.

30. "About Columbia—Columbia Bible College."

college community, and it is the college's hope that every student will grow significantly in each of the attributes.[31] The president, together with a task force, created nine values for the college that have Board approval. These values are promoted on the college website as well as on campus posters. Columbia, in recent years, has consistently produced vision documents to state where the college is moving in the next years. The current vision statement is valid until 2020. The summarized vision statement is as follows:

> By God's grace, Columbia Bible College will be a thriving, Christ-centered post-secondary institution, embodying and promoting God's kingdom vision of transformation for the church and world as reflected in Scripture, and developing Christ-followers who are maturing spiritually, academically, and ethically—inspired and able to positively impact their careers, churches, and communities.[32]

In addition, Columbia has worked intentionally at defining its identity within the landscape of Christian higher education in Canada as a Bible college. It is not moving toward a university college model, but it has obtained transferability with secular and Christian universities. It is certified with Private Training Institutions Branch (PTIB) and offers diplomas recognized by the Ministry of Advanced Education, Skills and Training (AVED), both with the province of British Columbia. It has negotiated a college graduate advanced placement agreement with the Associated Canadian Theological Schools (ACTS) at TWU, as well as partnering with a program offered in a church in North Vancouver.

Thriving Elements:

- Columbia has a mission, values, and vision statement.
- The formation of Columbia Graduate Attributes.
- Identity definition as a Bible college within the context of Christian higher education in Canada

This category was given an 11 percent urgency score.[33]

---

31. "About Columbia—Columbia Bible College."

32. "Columbia Vision 2020." The vision's short form: "Christ-centered, Kingdom-focused, World-impacting."

33. "Thriving Framework Diagnostic Tool Results."

Thriving Category 3: Institutional Self-Esteem

The "true driver of success" at thriving colleges, Credo observes, is institutional self-esteem, "that feeling that shows up on college campuses as excitement and motivation."[34] They identify seven building blocks that contribute to institutional self-esteem.[35] Each will be examined in turn, along with relevant examples from Columbia Bible College.

KNOW YOUR STUDENT

One building block is to gear institutional instruction toward the students who are present, not the students who are not present.[36] The Bible college might be tempted to gear its teaching to students who are more academically gifted than those who presently attend, or to teach to students from the past who no longer exist in the present college. Columbia undertakes a number of initiatives to stay connected to the needs of current students. A recent faculty workshop provided insights into the characteristics of Generation Z, the next generation of students entering college. After noticing more students with academic difficulties, Columbia recently increased personnel resources devoted to academic support and is re-evaluating the credit load required by its discipleship certificate program.

HIGHLIGHT STORIES OF SUCCESS[37]

Columbia works hard to build esteem by highlighting "success stories." The marketing and communications team issues frequent invitations to staff and faculty to submit stories about students and alumni, which are gathered in a digital story bank. These stories are then included in blog posts, social media posts, videos, and college reports and magazines. Verbal stories are also celebrated: at all-staff meetings, for example, time is often devoted to sharing highlights from the year.

SHARING OUTCOME STORIES

What are the results that the college is producing? What are the graduation rates? What are graduates involved in? People are concerned about their

34. "Institutional Self-Esteem," https://www.credohighered.com/about/our
-methodology.

35. Soliday and Mann, *Surviving to Thriving*, 51.

36. Soliday and Mann, *Surviving to Thriving*, 52.

37. Soliday and Mann, *Surviving to Thriving*, 52–53.

return on investment.[38] This building block is similar to the one above and covered there. In addition, program directors track the placement of graduates in their program, and the results can be found on Columbia's website.

RETENTION RATES

Do individuals want to come to the college, and do enrolled students want to stay? Colleges who thrive are as concerned about their retention and graduation numbers as they are about the first-time enrolees.[39] The retention percentages at Columbia have been a challenge, reported at 51% for the 2017 year. More energy and focus at Columbia are put into the recruitment of students than the retention of students. The area of retention will need a more coordinated effort within the Columbia environment to reap appropriate results in this area.

"THRIVING COLLEGES ARE VISIBLY REINVESTING IN PEOPLE, PLACES AND PROGRAMS."[40]

The Thriving Framework notes that self-esteem is boosted "when it is clear that money is being spent in the places that make the most difference according to careful, collaborative strategic planning."[41] Careful budgeting in recent years has provided more funds for strategic initiatives, as have creative approaches to reallocating existing personnel in developing new programs.

THERE IS CELEBRATION WITHIN THRIVING COLLEGES OF ACCOMPLISHMENTS.

Along with Credo, Columbia is aware that "appreciation is essential, and the culture is built around it."[42] The president seeks to celebrate success. Examples include celebratory events after receiving full accreditation from ABHE or balancing the budget. Appreciation is also given to different employees at the periodic All-Team meetings.

38. Soliday and Mann, *Surviving to Thriving*, 53–54.
39. Soliday and Mann, *Surviving to Thriving*, 54–55.
40. Soliday and Mann, *Surviving to Thriving*, 55.
41. Soliday and Mann, *Surviving to Thriving*, 55.
42. Soliday and Mann, *Surviving to Thriving*, 56.

ENGAGEMENT

This building block highlights the engagement of employees and the Board in the operation of the college. A weekly communication keeps faculty, staff, and Board members engaged in the goings on at the college. There is an expectation for faculty and staff to be in-attendance at certain college events. For Credo, engagement also includes parents and donors, who "are clearly informed and excited about what they see and hear through a strategic communications plan. It means that donors are being cared for at the best levels of stewardship, and their numbers are increasing."[43] At Columbia, a strategic plan is not in place to communicate with parents or donors.

Thriving Elements:

- The intentional effort to understand students
- The dissemination of stories of success
- The funding of strategic initiatives
- The emphasis on celebratory events
- The internal communication that fosters engagement

Recommendations for Thriving:

- Increased collaboration on retention
- Strategic communication to parents, alumni, and donors

This category was given a 26 percent urgency score.[44]

Thriving Category 4: Institutional Story

This category of the Thriving Framework emphasizes the importance of the right communication that connects with the appropriate segments of your constituency. In order to do this communication, market research is necessary, and the marketing area needs to be organized for success. The marketing department of thriving institutions develops the value proposition and brand of the school, and it prioritizes the recruitment and retention of students.[45]

Market research continues to be developed at the college. Several years ago, marketing moved from an external provider to internal college staff.

43. Soliday and Mann, *Surviving to Thriving*, 57.

44. "Institutional Story," https://www.credohighered.com/about/our-methodology.

45. "Thriving Framework Diagnostic Tool Results."

The department has grown, and in the opinion of the author is organized for success. Market research is part of launching new programs at Columbia. There is an incoming student questionnaire on what is important to students, as well as focus groups giving feedback for all degree programs. This research is supporting relevant and compelling communication regarding the distinctives of a Bible college education to a niche market.

The market research enables Columbia to communicate the value proposition of the college. The value proposition is the outcomes students receive for the investment made. What students are looking for is a biblical foundation, discernment to decide next steps, and a Christ-centered community. Columbia has one of the highest tuition rates for Bible colleges in Canada. It is incumbent on the institution to have a clearly defined value proposition for students.

The Thriving Framework also emphasizes the brand of the college. What is the perception of people when they hear Columbia Bible College? The brand is the total of what the college communicates, but it is also what people experience through being exposed to the college as a visitor, student, alumnus, constituency member, and donor. What the college is trying to portray, and what is actually experienced should be congruent. Columbia has produced a document that defines the brand of Columbia. So far it is only an internal document for the marketing and communication department and needs further distribution. The Graduates Attributes document was used as a foundation for an Employees Attributes document. This document further defines the brand of what Columbia desires to communicate to all those who come in contact with the college. An advisory group to the Lead Team, including the Communication and Marketing Manager, speaks into the development of strategic initiatives at the college. This connection allows for consistency of communication to various constituencies of the school.

Thriving Elements:

- The building of strong market research
- Compelling communication in alignment with that research

Recommendations for Thriving:

- The increased internal dissemination of the value proposition and brand of Columbia

The category was given a 51 percent urgency score.[46] Many of the questions in the survey in this category deal with the brand of the college. Because the brand is not widely known in the institution, it led to a higher urgency score.

Thriving Category 5: Habit of Reflection and Intentionality

This element emphasizes that thriving institutions collect relevant data regarding the fulfillment of the strategy of the college, reflect on the significance of the data, and use it intentionally to make decisions based on the data. The interpretation of the data and the metrics produced contribute to the continual improvement of the institution.[47]

Prior to and during the self-study process for ABHE accreditation, Columbia refined its Assessment Framework document. This comprehensive document includes all data that will be gathered, who is responsible for gathering and interpreting the data, and the cycle when the data is gathered, including time of year. The data gathered includes both student academic outcomes as well as administrative departments. Program directors analyze program academic data annually. The ABHE conditions for accreditation are also evaluated annually by college administrators. Columbia is working on assessment both with internal measures, such as the Spiritual Life Indicator, and with external surveys that compare Columbia to other institutions, such as the Noel Levitz Student Satisfaction Indicator.

The college has sought to reduce the number of strategic initiatives in order to be more aware of the data and make decisions based on the data. Columbia recently introduced *The Discipline of Execution*[48] framework wherein a strategic goal would be formulated with lead and lag measures. The lag measures, such as retention percentages, are predicted to a certain extent through lead measures, such as number of visits with the program director or other ways retention percentages could be increased. The strategy of the college is to be included in the annual personnel Ministry Action Plans. The goal is for personnel to remain accountable to these metrics in the fulfillment of a strategic initiative.

---

46. "Thriving Framework Diagnostic Tool Results."

47. "Habit of Reflection and Intentionality," https://www.credohighered.com/about/our-methodology.

48. McChesney et al., "The 4 Disciplines of Execution: Achieving Your Wildly Important Goals."

Thriving Elements:

- Progress in the area of assessment for both academic programs and administrative areas
- The limiting of strategic initiatives

Recommendations for Thriving:

- The clarification of key areas to measure in fulfillment of strategic initiatives
- The continued implementation of the four disciplines of execution framework

This category was given a 54 percent urgency score.[49] The sense of urgency score is higher because Credo suggests a full-time position for institutional research and a "centralized process by which data is collected, reviewed, and shared."[50] Columbia continues to grow in this category.

Thriving Category 6: Culture of Planning and Innovation

This thriving element highlights the generation of innovative initiatives that will be the most significant for the future thriving of the college. The leadership of the college completes each initiative with efficiency and collaboration including transparent communication about the process. The Credo framework limits these initiatives to four or five.[51]

Columbia continues to implement a helpful planning cycle with the description of annual strategic initiatives. These strategic initiatives are to fulfill the mission and vision of the college. The college has reduced the number of strategic initiatives that are tackled each year to two or three, lower than the number suggested by Credo. It was found that the more initiatives implemented in any given year was in proportion to a decrease in the fulfillment of the initiatives. This finding was congruent with the suggestion of the Execution Framework with only naming one or two initiatives per year.[52]

---

49. "Thriving Framework Diagnostic Tool Results."

50. "Thriving Framework Diagnostic Tool Results," 84–85.

51. "Culture of Planning and Innovation," https://www.credohighered.com/about/our-methodology.

52. McChesney et al., "The 4 Disciplines of Execution: Achieving Your Wildly Important Goals."

The planning of the budget has been stretched out to five years. The Columbia Vision document also moves out five years. It would be appropriate if the strategic initiative planning would also be stretched out past one year to give advance notice on the funding of strategic initiatives. It would seem helpful to continue to coordinate the Columbia Vision, budget, and strategic initiative planning.

After attendance at a Global Leadership Summit, the Lead Team went through *The Other Side of Innovation*[53] to increase the college's understanding of innovation and its implementation. A procedure was approved to enable innovative ideas to come from any level within the college. An example of innovation at the college is the implementation of a Health Care program. It has taken some time to launch the program, but it is innovative as far as a traditional Bible college curriculum is concerned.

Thriving Elements:

- A culture of planning in the college

Recommendations for Thriving:

- Coordinate the Columbia Vision process, budget development, and the planning of strategic initiatives

This category was given a 21 percent urgency score.[54]

Thriving Category 7: Net Revenue and Strategic Finance

Credo names several items that need to be looked at in this category: 3–5 percent in reserve each year to reinvest in programs, faculty, and facilities; debt below fifty percent of operating revenue; an endowment greater than annual budget; a Composite Financial Index (CFI) score greater than 3, and annually generating new income as well as reducing costs.[55] The academic efficiency of the curriculum is also included in this category.[56]

Columbia Bible College budgets conservatively and creates the annual budget on realistic enrolment and fund-raising goals. Thus, in the last several years the college has met or exceeded its budget. Over the past three

53. Govindarajan and Trimble, *The Other Side of Innovation.*

54. "Thriving Framework Diagnostic Tool Results."

55. Soliday and Mann, *Surviving to Thriving*, 105.

56. "Net Revenue and Strategic Finance," https://www.credohighered.com/about/our-methodology.

years, Columbia has provided either cost-of-living or experience increments for personnel in the budget, but not both. In 2018, they are budgeting for both increments in their operating budget. Columbia does not have
an operating or a capital deficit. Realistic budgets, along with the policy that
capital expenditures will not go into debt, have protected the college from
financial problems.

In recent years, Columbia has also increased the margin, in the positive, between revenue and expenses. Over the past five years, net operating
revenues have averaged 3.1 percent, with a high of 4.9 percent in 2017. The
college, however, does not meet the need for 3 to 5 percent in reserve each
year to reinvest in new programs, new faculty, and new facilities. In 2012
the College implemented a board-mandated capital reserve equivalent to
2.5 percent of operating revenues. This internally restricted reserve is intended for the maintenance and repair of facilities. There is also a separate
reserve set aside each year for the maintenance of the gymnasium. Columbia has not always been able to establish the full capital reserve in the annual operating budget, but through prudent financial management has met
or exceeded target allocations at fiscal year-end.

Columbia has an endowment that it has sought to grow in recent
years, but it is less than its annual budget. Endowment interest has funded
some student scholarships. The college received a major gift to host the
Metzger Collection of artifacts. This gift was similar to an endowment in
that it is funding the creation and maintenance of the Metzger Collection
for ten years.

The 2018 Composite Financial Index score for Columbia is 3.08.

Composite Financial Index (CFI)

Ratio	Ratio Value	Strength Factor	Weighting Factor	Score
Primary Reserve	0.41	0.133	55%	1.70
Net Operating Revenues	3.17%	1%	15%	0.68
Return on Net Assets	4.67%	2%	30%	0.70
Viability[57]	N/A	N/A	0%	0

CFI 3.08

57. Columbia has no long-term debt; therefore, the viability ratio is not used in the
CFI calculation.

The three ratios included in this score include: primary reserve ratio (expendable net assets/total expenses), net operating revenues ratio (operating surplus or deficit/operating revenues), and return on net assets ratio (change in net assets/beginning net assets). Columbia has no long-term debt, therefore, the Viability Ratio is not used in the CFI calculation.

Fundraising is enjoying a period of stability at Columbia with a president that embraces the fundraising role, is appreciated in the constituency, and is an effective director of development as an alumnus and director of one of Columbia's academic programs. There is intentionality in growing the donor base, but more focus will be required to make fundraising a system at Columbia that is not based on personality. "Thriving colleges have implemented a system to be sure that there is continuity in relationships and proposals. The system is not dependent upon a person."[58]

Columbia is a college funded primarily by tuition, constituency donations, and individual or corporate donations. Auxiliary revenue, through rental of the campus and catering, have brought in some revenue, but it is not substantial enough to be viewed as another revenue stream. Other ideas have been floated, but at the time of writing there is not an alternate revenue stream for the college.

Credo suggests that academic efficiency is an area for evaluation in the budget. Several years ago, Columbia increased the core requirements for its diplomas and degrees thus increasing academic efficiency. Work has been done on the cost of a course at Columbia as well as a program audit done in 2015 on the revenue and expense of each program in the college. The emphasis on core programming has allowed Columbia to add new programs, increasing the enrolment in core courses that then subsidize courses with low enrolment. Columbia will need to be more tenacious in reducing the number of low-enrolment courses.

Thriving Elements:

- Balanced budgets and no debt
- CFI above 3
- Review of academic efficiency

Recommendations for Thriving:

- Creation of a new revenue stream

---

58. Soliday and Mann, *Surviving to Thriving*, 113.

- Increased donor growth

This category was given a 42 percent urgency score.[59]

Thriving Category 8: Student Learning and Success

According to the Thriving Framework, a thriving college takes students from where they are to their highest potential. It is the mandate of the college to find out about the students they have and to teach well those students.[60] The author of the Credo Framework states that this category is the most important for a thriving college.

> Spend your time understanding them, plan for them, and be courageous enough to change because of them. It is one of the most energizing times to be an educator . . . You will need to make difficult decisions, but if you keep students at the center of, and as the motivation for, everything you do, then you will always be walking the right path.[61]

Soliday states that "student learning and success is at the center of everything we believe in."[62]

As stated under Institutional Self Esteem, the college has sought to understand the next generation of students coming to the college. Teachers in the Bible college must adapt their andragogy to the students who are entering. The college must assist in this adjustment, but the teacher also needs to continue to change. Teachers teach people to learn. Part of teaching is learning about the people in order to teach in the most effective way.

Columbia Bible College has defined what teaching well means within its context. It has produced a Missions Alignment document that includes a Theology of Teaching Statement. All teaching is to align with the mission, vision, and values of the college. Further, Columbia hosted an ABHE workshop on teaching in Bible colleges. Teaching well includes understanding the context in which one is teaching, a Bible college.

"An integrated, respectful, and proactive relationship between academic affairs and student affairs is crucial for today's students to learn and

---

59. "Thriving Framework Diagnostic Tool Results."

60. "Student Learning and Success," https://www.credohighered.com/about/our-methodology.

61. Soliday and Mann, *Surviving to Thriving*, 164–65.

62. Soliday and Mann, *Surviving to Thriving*, 130.

thrive."[63] Student development must move students toward engagement and learning through the residential and on-campus activities. The significance of chapels, commuter services, residential activities, and student leadership all contribute to student success. The Student Life department at Columbia is very intentional about developing students' spiritual life toward maturity in Christ. They provide excellent leadership development training for all student leaders, as well as intentional focus regarding community development and student life culture on campus.

Student success at Columbia includes the value proposition to parents and students. "The success of our students and the service to them must be invaluable."[64] Employers are looking for certain types of people with certain characteristics and skills that can fit into many occupations. The Graduate Attributes document has addressed this matter and further implementation of this document is needed in the programs and courses of the college.

Student success also means support for at-risk students. Columbia has implemented an Academic Support department. The demand is exceeding the number of hours available. Also, in the Student Life area, the number of counsellors needed to be increased due to the demand for services. Columbia is seeking to meet the need in both these areas.

An area that needs further development at Columbia is the area of life/career coaching. The fourth-year degree students take a course in which this matter is incorporated, and there has been some assistance for second year students. However, a coordinated systematic approach to the matter has not been implemented yet for second year students.

Thriving Elements:

- Professional development for teaching faculty that highlights the characteristics of present students
- An increase in academic and counselling support for students
- A culture of teaching and learning at the college
- Collaboration between Student Life and Academics in the area of leadership development

Recommendations for Thriving:

---

63. Soliday and Mann, *Surviving to Thriving,* 138.

64. Soliday and Mann, *Surviving to Thriving,* 140.

- Discussion of content and andragogy that specifically targets the generation entering the college with reference to the college mission, values, vision, and theology of teaching statement
- Implementation of the Graduate Attributes document into the programs and courses of the college
- The need for career/life coaching as part of student success

This category received a 50 percent urgency score.[65]

Thriving Category 9: Transformative Environments

This thriving category emphasizes a campus environment that is attractive, well-kept, and high-tech. However, that is only the base from which to develop. The campus should be a place that aligns space with mission, vision, values, learning facilitation, and dialogue.[66] Soliday believes that this area is critical as to whether a college may thrive. "It is usually possible to change direction on most things and improve them, but the big issue will be the campus itself. If the deferred maintenance is high and the campus is not appealing, the opportunity to turn things around is bleak."[67] In addition, thriving colleges are always improving the campus, even if it is a small project.[68]

Columbia has a well-kept and attractive campus. Technology continues to improve in the classroom as well as with the WiFi throughout the campus. A new residence was added recently, and the college continually updates facilities with little deferred maintenance. In the near future, however, one of the residences will need either major renovation to the infrastructure or to be replaced. The dining hall has become the preferred place for students to dialogue with faculty around tables. Students have meeting rooms in the library as well as the student lounge. Columbia is planning a new Learning Centre with faculty consultation and research into other facilities in regard to teaching and learning facilitation.

Thriving Elements:

- The attractive and well-kept campus of Columbia Bible College

---

65. "Thriving Framework Diagnostic Tool Results."
66. "Thriving Framework Diagnostic Tool Results."
67. Soliday and Mann, *Surviving to Thriving*, 148.
68. Soliday and Mann, *Surviving to Thriving*, 151.

- Plenty of meeting places for collaborative learning as well as building community

Recommendations for Thriving:

- The addition of the new Learning Center in alignment with the mission, vision, values, and teaching methodology of the college
- A plan for the renovation or replacement of the Columbia Hall residence

This category was given a 28 percent urgency score.[69]

CONCLUSION

Is it possible for a Bible college to thrive in Canada? These nine categories produced an institutional urgency score of 33%, which suggests that the author perceives a moderate level of urgency for Columbia Bible College across all nine categories of the Thriving Framework.[70] This means "a need for examination of the concerns at hand, and action to correct course before the concerns become highly urgent."[71]

Columbia has thriving elements in each of the nine categories. In summary:

1. Courageous and Collaborative Leadership: The president demonstrates these qualities, and the category has evidence through the Best Christian Workplace results.
2. Vision: The college intentionally develops vision statements that have board approval and wide distribution. The addition of a Graduate Attributes document also gives clarity to college direction.
3. Institutional Self-Esteem: This category is difficult to objectify, but in terms of the seven builders, Columbia is strong in communicating stories of success and internal engagement. The other builders are dealt with in other categories.
4. Institutional Story: The internal marketing and communication department is doing an excellent job of telling the story of Columbia.

---

69. "Thriving Framework Diagnostic Tool Results."
70. "Explore the Thriving Framework® — Credo | Higher Education Consulting."
71. "Explore the Thriving Framework® — Credo | Higher Education Consulting."

5. Habit of Reflection and Intentionality: The Assessment Framework document that outlines what will be assessed, by when, and by whom, gives evidence of thriving in this category.

6. Culture of Planning and Innovation: Columbia continues to have a strong culture of planning. Reducing the number of annual strategic initiatives and implementing the execution framework are further indications of thriving.

7. Net Revenue and Strategic Finance: Columbia has a CFI number above 3.0 with no operational or capital debt.

8. Student Learning and Success: The teaching andragogy, academic support, and student life program are in support of student learning at Columbia.

9. Transformative Environments: The attractive campus at Columbia has many spaces for dialogue.

In conclusion, I suggest three areas in which Columbia needs to pay particular attention in order to decrease the urgency score. I address the top three urgency categories, Habit of Reflection and Intentionality (54 percent), Student Learning and Success (50 percent), and finally Institutional Story (51 percent). It is not that Columbia does not have resources and direction in each of these categories, but further enhancement is suggested in each category.

First, the Habit of Reflection and Intentionality emphasizes reflection on the data produced through assessment and research, as well as the intentionality of decisions based on the data. I encourage the Bible college to enhance the resources necessary to gather the data it needs and to efficiently analyze the data, prayerfully reflect on that data, make strategic decisions, and then intentionally implement the decisions. I affirm the continued implementation of the Execution Framework. In accreditation language, it is continuing to move the Bible college from a culture of conversation to a culture of evidence. In other words, decisions are to be based on researched data.

Second, in the category of Student Learning and Success, Columbia needs to excel in the transformative education of its students. It is not that Columbia does not thrive in this category, but with the many options of Christian post-secondary education, the Bible college cannot afford to lapse in this area. Student transformation is the primary indicator of the quality of the school. The primary agenda of Columbia is to teach toward discipleship, ministry, and leadership, in alignment with the mission of the college. The Bible college should be the best place for the serious study of the Bible for personal life transformation. The role of the Bible college is discipleship more than scholarship. Given the Anabaptist heritage of Columbia, it needs to be a Great Commission school emphasizing teaching toward obedience.

A third suggestion is to have sufficient resources to tell the Institutional Story. Again, it is not that Columbia does not do a good job in this area, but as times change, the Bible college needs to do an exceptional job of communicating the value proposition and brand of the Bible college. The value proposition of the school needs to be very clear for churches, parents, and students to see the benefits of the Bible college program in comparison to other Christian and provincial academic programs. Communicating the credibility of the Bible college is critical for thriving.

I hope that this analysis of Columbia Bible College will be of benefit to other Bible colleges seeking to thrive in the current educational environment. It is hoped that by analyzing various categories in the case of Columbia Bible College, other Bible colleges will be able to analyze their situation and identify areas that, through the grace of God and His empowerment, will be strengthened to move the school toward a thriving framework rather than a surviving modality.

BIBLIOGRAPHY

"About Columbia—Columbia Bible College." No pages. Online: https://www.columbiabc.edu/about/columbia?section=mission-statement.

Barna Group. "What's Next for Biblical Higher Education," 2017. No pages. Online: https://www.barna.com/product/biblical-higher-education/.

"Columbia Vision 2020." No pages. Online: https://www.columbiabc.edu/file/Columbia-Vision-2020.pdf.

Cone, Christopher. "The Disappearing Middle Class in Christian Higher Education," 2017. No pages. Online: http://www.drcone.com/2017/03/13/disappearing-middle-class-christian-higher-education/.

Dueck, Abe J. "Mennonite Brethren Bible College: Competing Visions for Mennonite Brethren Education in Canada." *Direction* 46 (2017): 40–56. No pages. Online: http://www.directionjournal.org/46/1/mennonite-brethren-bible-college.html.

"Explore the Thriving Framework® — Credo | Higher Education Consulting." No pages. Online: https://www.credohighered.com/about/our-methodology.

Govindarajan, Vijay, and Chris Trimble. *The Other Side of Innovation: Solving the Execution Challenge.* Boston: Harvard Business School Publications, 2010.

McChesney, Chris, et al. *The 4 Disciplines of Execution: Achieving Your Wildly Important Goals.* New York: Free Press, 2012.

Porter, Stanley E. "Theological Education in the Twenty-First Century." *Toronto Journal of Theology* 25 (2009) 41–53. Online: https://doi.org/10.3138/tjt.25.suppl_1.41.

Soliday, Joanne, and Rick Mann. *Surviving to Thriving: A Planning Framework for Leaders of Private College & Universities*. Whitsett, NC: Credo Press, 2013.

"Thriving Framework Diagnostic Tool Results," n.d.

6

The Renaissance of Christian University Education in Canada

JOHN G. STACKHOUSE, JR.

INTRODUCTION

IN THE LAST FEW years, a certain Christian university near the west coast of Canada has been in the news, as you likely are aware. Meanwhile, near Canada's east coast, another university has been making its own news, as you likely are not aware—unless you, like me, work at Crandall University in Moncton, New Brunswick.[1]

Item 1: Crandall University's faculty, administration, and board approved a new policy dispensing with sabbaticals. Sabbaticals have been replaced by what are now called research leaves, on the basis of "6 + 1": six terms or years of full-time work in teaching, research, and other service to be followed by a half-year or year, respectively, of full-time research at full pay.

Item 2: This enlightened policy—that replaced an elaborate and under-funded policy that essentially meant that no one ever took a sabbatical—allowed Dr. Sam Reimer, professor of sociology, to take up the Alan Richardson Fellowship at the University of Durham in aid of his current research program. It also allowed Dr. Keith Bodner, professor of biblical

1. I am grateful for the critical reading of an earlier version of this article by David Barnard, Keith Bodner, Bruce Guenther, Allyson Jule, Patricia Janzen Loewen, Ted Newell, and Sam Reimer.

studies, to write his ninth (or is it tenth? eleventh?) book on the Old Testament for Oxford University Press.

Item 3: This same Christian university's most recent faculty hires include Dr. Keith Grant in history and Dr. Adam Stewart in sociology, both of whom held the so-called gold-plated SSHRC doctoral grants, the Bombardier Fellowships, and both of whom have already published their first books along with a sheaf of articles. Not incidentally, these top-drawer junior scholars were hired only at the end of rather persistent searches.

Item 4: Kira Smith, a first-year student who, within months of matriculating, took over the editorship of the student newspaper at Crandall, told me that she forewent her acceptance at McGill in order to attend Crandall because, in her words, she wanted a strongly Christian university education.

Item 5: Carol Marshall, a thirty-year-old single mother of two returning to school after a decade away, testified at a year-end chapel service that, mainly through the courses she had been required to take in religious studies and through the chapel program itself, she had come to faith and now declared herself a Christian.[2]

I mention these items not because Crandall University is unique in any of these respects, but because I am strongly inclined to think that it is not. Behind the headlines of court cases and new schools and large donations, similar stories, I am confident, are being told at the likes of Tyndale, Providence, Canadian Mennonite, King's, yes, and Trinity Western. Likewise, I expect there are similar good news items to share from the Bible college world as well.

After virtually disappearing by the 1960s, there has been, in fact, a renaissance of Christian university education in Canada. Whether that rebirth will result in the maturation of these institutions into lasting, influential, and faithful schools depends on, at least in part, there being many more such stories as the ones I have mentioned. And the efflorescence of such stories will depend on the considerations upon which this chapter will now focus.

LEARNING FROM THE PAST

My first scholarly love is history, and scanning the heritage of Christian higher education in Canada is instructive. Nonetheless, a short chapter,

---

2. I have changed the student's name in the interest of her privacy.

whose burden is primarily hortatory rather than historical, can only point to resources and select a few key reflections.[3]

In terms of sources, then, I note that a new account of Christian higher education in Canada awaits its historian. A full generation and more has elapsed since Donald Masters wrote his history of *Protestant Church Colleges in Canada* (1966), and while the literature on education in Canada since then has exploded, no synthetic account of Christian higher education has yet emerged.[4] Indeed, beyond Tim Callaway's interesting dissertation-cum-book about Prairie Bible Institute, no academic book-length study of any Bible college or university in Canada has been published, with few chapters or articles emerging, either, since my own work on several of them published now a quarter-century ago.[5]

Still, reading what there is, and judiciously comparing Canadian sources with American counterparts, yields a few key conclusions. I focus on American, rather than British or Australasian, histories because the situations in the two North American countries in regard to Christian higher education are, in my judgment, much more similar to each other than they are to those of other countries in the Anglosphere. Here, then, are four key observations from a survey of these sources.[6]

---

3. I note that "Christian" in this language-game means "evangelical Protestantism." It does not include Roman Catholic or Orthodox Christianity, nor does it include liberal forms of Protestantism. This use of "Christian" can appear chauvinistic, but in this respect, evangelicals are doing only what Catholics and Orthodox do—namely, view their version of Christianity as normative. Since the time of the Pietists, the evangelical movement has regarded its concerns as generically Christian, not the peculiarities of a party. So when an evangelical statesman of the previous generation sets out his understanding of the gospel in a distinctively evangelical register, he does not entitle it "Basic Evangelicalism," but "Basic Christianity" (Stott, *Basic Christianity*). This is the understanding of the institution sponsoring this conference volume—Christian Higher Education Canada—and so I defer to their usage in this essay.

4. Masters, *Protestant Church Colleges in Canada*.

5. Stackhouse (*Canadian Evangelicalism in the Twentieth Century*) discusses *inter alia* the history of Tyndale University, Prairie Bible Institute, Trinity Western University, and Regent College. See also Callaway, *Training Disciplined Soldiers for Christ*; Fawcett and Ryder, eds., *Faith and Education*; Fernhout, "Quest for Identity and Place"; Hiebert et al., *Character with Competence Education*; and the invaluable bibliography maintained by the Centre for Research on Canadian Evangelicalism.

6. Chief among these American sources would be Ringenberg, *The Christian College*.

Money

Higher education is expensive, and for everyone concerned. It is so expensive, in fact, that even very rich people generally cannot, or at least do not, attempt to fund it by themselves. To my knowledge, no college or university in Canada nor any major school in the United States was funded entirely by a single major donor.[7] Even entire Canadian denominations have found higher education so expensive that, one by one, they all ceded their schools to provincial governments a generation or more ago, and the new crop of schools generally have struggled financially in our own time.[8]

Financial wisdom is thus imperative in university life, and professors and administrators with stars in their eyes must be careful to be grounded in the facts of life—namely, that finding funds is hard work, not guaranteed, and much more difficult to do in the wake of any sort of failure. This observation is not meant to imply that dollar signs should replace those stars. But it is to say that the tension between the ideal and the real is best faced by everyone, rather than letting situations devolve into one group appointing themselves the defenders of principle while the other defends practicality with equal fervency. This situation guarantees an eventual stalemate that too often produces strong-man action by a senior leader who simply cuts the Gordian knot of balanced governance and due process by mere fiat. We must keep remembering that we are in this together, helping each other in the constant tension between principle and practicality.

A second observation is that there seems never to be enough money to do all that Christian educators want to do. While one might just smile ruefully and hope for more tomorrow, one practical implication of this fact of life is that money, or the lack of it, always threatens to drive decisions: whom to hire, whom to admit, whom to lead, what to do, and how to do it. New ventures can be excitedly created by faculty members and administrators, but they have to be paid for—and that means getting trustees and donors on board. Even current activities, if a school has a proper process of

7. One thinks of the Stanfords's support of their eponymous university and the Rockefellers' support of the University of Chicago as possible exceptions, but neither school could survive even on the largesse of those generous benefactors.

8. It is difficult to predict the future on this score in terms of large-scale demographics. Studies that show decline in the giving of evangelicals to charities, such as Christian universities, also show that the sheer number of evangelicals in Canada continues to increase, at pace with the population. So there should be more prospective students and donors in the future. See Reimer and Wilkinson, *A Culture of Faith*; and Clarke and Macdonald, *Leaving Christianity*.

rolling evaluation, must keep justifying their budgets. In such a situation, in which everyone is conscious of financial pressure, it is tempting, always and everywhere, to focus overmuch on finances—on what is most likely to attract and retain funding, rather than on what is most likely to maintain or even advance the university's mission. Indeed, it is easy under stress to prioritize institutional survival (and our jobs) over any serious consideration of mission—whether the institution is actually still performing a function worth all these efforts and dollars.

A third related observation of the history of Christian higher education in North America is that large fortunes and big academic visions are never combined in the same person. In the providence of God (a Christian historian might want to say to a reader), the gifts of being able to make a large amount of money and of being able to create a broad, bold, and practical scheme for higher education seem never to coinhere in the same individual. Cooperation and, yes, compromise thus are built into the enterprise of Christian higher education. Leadership, where resources and vision most effectually meet, thus matters a very great deal.

Leadership

Yes, leadership can be made too much of. Studies have shown that wildly overpaid CEOs do not affect the welfare of their companies nearly as much as desperate directors and stockholders hope they can. But the history of Christian higher education in Canada indicates that few institutions rise higher than the quality of their leadership. Moreover, leaders clearly constrain and even curse their institutions with their weaknesses. Leadership matters.[9]

Two corollary principles also emerge. The former is that leaders cannot effect significant and lasting change alone. Even giants such as Queen's University principal George Munro Grant and Trinity College's John Strachan could get done what they did only by convincing others—others with money, yes, and with administrative, political, and intellectual ability—to agree, and agree enthusiastically, with their agenda. The most benign of dictators cannot get much positive work done on his or her own, and such autocrats ignore or resist the involvement of others at the peril of their institutions. Without capable leaders, however, not much positive happens.

---

9. For a recent introduction to the debate over the importance of CEOs, see Chamorro-Premuzic, "Are CEOs Overhyped and Overpaid?"

Alas, the latter principle of this pair is that leaders can wreak significant and lasting havoc on their own, whether through badly conceived or badly executed initiatives, or even just neglect of, or incompetence in, their duties. There is no way to assess what historians call counterfactuals, the "what would have happened if . . . " scenarios, but aware readers will hardly doubt that department heads, deans, and presidents can stifle and even destroy ideas, initiatives, and individuals by failing to do their jobs properly. Even if, as I say, they lack the power on their own to make good things happen, they have the power on their own—as key links in a symbiotic ecology—to make bad things happen and to keep good things from happening. Positively and negatively, then, leadership matters.

In the recent renaissance of Christian higher education in Canada, third, leadership has generally not been characterized by charismatic presidents. What I mean by this (I rush to make clear) is not that these presidents have been un-gifted! Instead, I mean that very few brought to their presidencies a major platform or profile.[10] They were not, so to speak, stars somewhere else who brought significant personal clout to the role. Instead, each has brought the network that helped get him or her the job and then had to work hard to connect with the broader networks necessary to run and fund an enterprise on this scale. Canadian Christian higher education, that is, has not yet developed a culture of high-profile leaders—which is, as I observed twenty-five years ago, a pattern typical of Canadian evangelicalism in general.

This pattern means that Canadian university leaders cannot throw their weight around or, alternately, blaze brave new trails, but must instead become consummate tenders of the grass roots, keepers of the flame of institutional heritage, and only cautious innovators careful not to run ahead of very broad support. This situation, if I read it correctly, entails that startling creativity and big steps forward will be rare, but so should costly gambles and silly fads.

Finally, successful academic leaders combine vision with a degree of personal charm, savvy, patience, realism, cooperativeness, integrity, and respect for others—as do, one might note, good leaders generally. What

10. One thinks of Brian Stiller as the exception to the rule. Stiller had a national reputation as the head of the Evangelical Fellowship of Canada before taking over the deeply troubled Ontario Bible College and Theological Seminary, later renamed Tyndale University. Only later observers, of course, will be able to judge properly the effects of his presidency on that institution, but the record shows that it was about to go under when he took over, and instead it survives to this day.

is "academic" about it is the distinctively academic mission of the institution, with the means of administration actually quite generic except in ways appropriate to the furtherance of that mission, such as, for instance, the vexed questions of faculty governance and academic freedom, to the latter of which we will turn presently. (Shared governance is a complex enough question that I must leave it for another time.) Academic leadership is thus simply another mode of politics, or of what Peter Drucker would call "management"—again, as qualified, *mutatis mutandis*, per the particular mission of the institution.

Plus Ça Change . . .

A look back over the previous century of Christian higher education reveals what to some will be surprising parallels to situations they might otherwise have thought were peculiar to our own time. Professors complain about the low level of university preparation evident in first-year students. They also decry the lack of serious intellectual interest among a majority of older students who seem instead to be focused on the apparently incoherent double goals of enjoying the maximum amount of irresponsible fun at college while also somehow undergoing job training that will guarantee them lucrative and meaningful employment directly upon graduation.[11]

As Catherine Gidney demonstrates, chaplains and administrators were bemoaning the decline in both piety and sheer Bible knowledge in successive classes of Canadian university students at least as early as the 1940s. Indeed, the president of the University of Toronto in the early 1950s challenged the universities themselves to remedy this problem:

> I believe that we have gone too far along the road of secularizing institutions of higher learning. There is a gap in liberal education: it has been caused by the policy, which is all too prevalent in

11. These latter two goals were not incongruous, of course, for many decades at the likes of Harvard, Yale, and Princeton, which served as finishing schools and networking opportunities for the scions of aristocrats and the upper middle class on the American eastern seaboard. It was against such a paradigm that the University of Chicago defined itself, in fact, in its formative decades, as unabashedly "intellectualist" (Boyer, *The University of Chicago*, 220). The history of this once-Baptist university is replete with examples along each of these lines, which illustrates that the pressing issues of today are, in most cases, perennial issues on most campuses.

For Canadian examples, see the following: Jones, ed., *Higher Education in Canada*; Beach et al., eds., *Higher Education in Canada*; and Fisher et al., *The Development of Postsecondary Education Systems in Canada*.

universities throughout the English-speaking world, of evading, ignoring, or even opposing, the teaching of religion. . . . It is impossible to claim that we are fulfilling adequately our duty if we are contributing to, or even if we are tolerating, religious illiteracy.[12]

Teaching versus research, lectures versus seminars, board governance versus faculty governance, growing endowment versus facing current needs, staff salaries versus new buildings, residential versus commuter campuses, job training versus truth-seeking and character-shaping, and the proper roles of intercollegiate athletics and fraternities and sororities—these topics of current debate go back a century or more. And what also goes back a century or more is concern about the Christian character of the university: What is it, what should it be, and how ought it to be properly fostered?

Christian Character

As has been detailed in Canada by Masters and Gidney, but also strikingly in the United States by James Burtchaell and George Marsden, the Christian character of a university does not generally collapse in a revolution, but erodes step by step.[13]

Indeed, there seems to be a general pattern to these steps. Chapel, once daily and mandatory, becomes less frequent and then elective. Soon, it is just another option in the co-curriculum. The student body, once assumed to be, or even required to be, confessing Christians, becomes variegated by those from outside the founding tradition of the school and eventually by those outside Christianity itself. Likewise, the faculty, administration, and governing board becomes steadily less homogenous religiously, even as class, ethnicity, regionalism, or some other social dynamic emerges as a unifying principle. The curriculum, once understood to be Christian from top to bottom, becomes segmented into "Christian" or "religious" studies versus the "real" curriculum and then finally loses all Christian distinctiveness in both content and pedagogy. To be sure, as Masters's history makes clear, a curriculum being thoroughly Christian does not necessarily mean it

12. Sidney Smith, University of Toronto Archives, Hart House Records, A73–0050, Box 55, File 29, Annual Report, B'nai B'rith Hillel Foundation, University of Toronto, 1953–54; quoted in Gidney, *A Long Eclipse*, 125. Gidney quotes Christian missioners at Queen's and Western universities remarking on "the illiteracy of most students in Biblical knowledge" in 1942 (University of British Columbia Archives, President's Office, General Correspondence, Roll 68, "Report of University Christian Missions"; quoted on 73).

13. Burtchaell, *The Dying of the Light*; Marsden, *The Soul of the American University*.

is full of courses in biblical and theological studies: many Canadian Christian universities of a previous generation assumed church and family were providing that dimension of education, while the new group understand otherwise.

The last features to change, it seems, are the constitutive documents and public pronouncements of the university. The slogans on the university seals—as Christian as most of them have been in Canada—eventually shorten to innocuous logos, as historian Gerald Bowler notes. The University of Saskatchewan had a very simple coat of arms: three wheat sheaves and an open book whose pages displayed the motto "Deo et Patriae" — "For God and Country." Now those pages are blank. The University of Manitoba's arms were jam-packed with religious imagery: St John the Evangelist and his eagle, St. George's cross, and a book with a quotation in Latin from the Old Testament: "To these children God gave knowledge." It now features only a buffalo, a crown, a maple leaf and another book—empty, of course. Under the shield, where a motto should be, is a banner with the inspiring phrase: "Est. 1877." The University of Alberta's motto is "Quaecumque Vera," referencing St Paul's advice to the church at Philippi to think on "Whatsoever things are true . . . " but its website now shows only a shield and a stylized landscape. God's first words in the Bible, "Let there be light," is the motto, in Hebrew, of the University of Victoria, which now gives us only three birds and, yes, another empty book.[14]

Likewise, as Catherine Gidney shows, evangelical language still permeated Canadian universities well into the middle of the last century, but the influence of Christian values and categories has long since ebbed from the policies and aspirations of those schools, with (liberal) Christianity increasingly a mere echo of the rising chorus of post-Christendom values of pluralism, liberty, and tolerance that soon break forth like a storm across the cultural landscape in the 1960s.[15]

What, then, about those constitutive documents? They have been in the news recently—statements of faith that constrain academic freedom

---

14. Gerald Q. Bowler on Facebook: https://www.facebook.com/gerry.bowler.18. For good measure, Gidney mentions McMaster University's "In Christ All Things Consist" and the University of King's College's "For God, for Law, for King, and for Country" (Gidney, *A Long Eclipse*, 13).

15. Kevin Flatt notes the same sustained use of evangelical terminology by those increasingly out of sympathy with evangelical convictions in the history of the United Church—a history importantly germane, of course, to the history of Canadian culture and thus of Canadian universities: Flatt, *After Evangelicalism*.

and community covenants that warrant scrutiny by the highest court in the land. Let's consider them as we take on the broader question of Christian higher education in Canada today and tomorrow.

TODAY AND TOMORROW

It will surprise no reader that Christian higher education in Canada is under significant stress today and likely will be tomorrow. The key metrics of enrolment and finances have not generally been encouraging. Declining enrolments have been the recent trend in more than half of the universities. Financial shortfalls have meant slowdowns in development, failure to raise salaries even according to cost-of-living indices, and increasing debt in institutions across the country.

Meanwhile, fundamental questions of institutional identity and autonomy have been raised recently on two fronts. Universities Canada, formerly the Association of Universities and Colleges of Canada, decided in 2016, after years of debate, to maintain its insistence that member schools not discriminate on any of the terms of current human rights language and, according to their 2011 statement on academic freedom, continue to guarantee complete academic freedom for faculty members. According to qualifications in these and other documents, however, Universities Canada might be understood as allowing religious schools to apply a doctrinal test if such a theological stance was a bona fide requirement of the job according to the express mission of the school. So can a doctrinal test be applied at the point of hiring? If so, once a faculty member is appointed, can he or she be bound by any statement of faith, when the main thrust of the 2011 statement would suggest that he or she cannot? It appears that UC is trying to square a circle here, attempting to maintain the language typical of secular universities while trying also to acknowledge differences among some member schools—other examples being schools oriented to francophone or indigenous populations. One might fairly conclude that only a lawsuit will sort this out once for all.[16]

16. There is inescapable ambiguity, if not flat contradiction, in the deliverances of Universities Canada. Its 2011 statement on academic freedom contains this intriguing qualification: "Academic freedom is constrained by the professional standards of the relevant discipline and the responsibility of the institution to organize its academic mission." One might fairly see this as an accommodation of faith-based institutions. Furthermore, its board policy allows for the following: "Having due regard to the fundamental principle of non-discrimination set-out in section 3. (1)(m) of the by-laws, the institution will not impose any occupational requirements in an employment relationship that

Second, in 2018, the Supreme Court of Canada decided (7–2) that ethical codes, sometimes known as "community covenants" or the like, must not restrict the freedom of students according to so-called Charter values, thus setting aside, in particular, requirements that students abide by traditional Christian sexual mores. It remains to be seen, of course, whether such codes will withstand the perhaps inevitable legal challenge in regard to employees.[17]

External issues at stake include at least these three. First, there is the question of support, in general, and funding, in particular, from secular sources: governments, the three scholarly councils (NSERC, CIHR [formerly MRC], and SSHRC), foundations, and so on. Will Christian universities who maintain their distinctive beliefs and practices, as encoded in statements of faith and ethical covenants but in other respects as well, be viewed as fit recipients of tax dollars and other forms of secular support?

Second, there is the question of cooperation. Will Christian universities who maintain their distinctive beliefs and practices be welcome as members of UC, athletic associations, tri-council programs, the Royal Society, and the like?

Third, there is the question of recognition. Will Christian universities who maintain their distinctive beliefs and practices—that is to say, universities who remain substantially and substantively Christian in their outlook

---

would have the effect of discriminating on Prohibited Grounds, *unless such requirements are bona fide occupational requirements that are permitted under applicable human rights law*" (quoted from notice of motion, Universities Canada, 30 September 2016; sent to me via e-mail by Justin Cooper, executive director of CHEC; emphasis added). Three friends who serve as presidents of Canadian universities that belong to UC have privately interpreted to me this package of legislation thus: it will be okay with UC for religious schools to apply bona fide religious tests upon hiring, but not afterward, despite that intriguing clause in the 2011 Statement, which otherwise is typically categorical in its defense of academic freedom. But two others I have interviewed remain unsure about whether religious tests can be applied at all or can be applied throughout the career of a professor. UC may well be leaving it up to the courts to decide. For more on the board policy that is meant to govern application of the bylaws, see Universities Canada, "Statement on Proposed Membership Criterion." And one of the most relevant decisions on such matters will likely be that of the Manitoba Human Rights Commission: *Schroen v. Steinbach Bible College.*

17. Wheaton College's trustees voted during the 2002–2003 school year to lift the ban on dancing, alcohol, and tobacco for employees (and, interestingly, for graduate students) in a significantly less restrictive "Community Covenant," largely because they were concerned that the school not run afoul of a 1991 Illinois law forbidding employers from interfering in the private lives of employees. See Olsen, "Wheaton College Allows Dancing for All, Drinking and Tobacco for Non-Undergraduates."

and operation—have their courses authorized for transfer credit and their degrees acknowledged as preparation for graduate study? Will professional accrediting agencies (such as in education, nursing, and counseling) continue to approve their programs?[18]

Internal issues at stake include two pairs. The first pair consists of integrity and diversity. A Christian university, like any other social organism, must have a mission toward which its energies are directed and constitutive principles by which it operates. Only by some combination of *telos* and *logos* into a defining *ethos* can any organization be organized. Blurring, stretching, eroding, or trading away of this ethos must therefore be guarded against, and leaders do well to take strong measures to improve and ensure the integrity of their institutions.

At the same time, diversity offers a number of goods to a Christian university. Diverse pedagogies can arise from people coming from different experiences who perceive, understand, and communicate different things in different ways, thus providing a much richer education than students would get from the same sorts of teachers teaching the same things in the same ways. Diversity among the faculty and student body provides positive role models for a much wider range of students, many of whom otherwise lack such inspiring Christian figures in their lives and in the mainstream media. Diversity promotes creativity, which emerges only as the conventional is challenged, and challenges to the status quo rarely come from those who are comfortably at its centre. A Christian university that embraces and manages diversity well offers an all-too-rare model of pluralism that is much needed in both the church and the world in these fractious times.

A related, but distinctive, pair of internal issues is that of safety and challenge. Christian parents and students have long looked to Christian schools at every level to provide havens against dangers, both real and imagined. As Canadian culture has become decidedly post-Christian in many respects, and even anti-Christian in some, the desire for—yes, the irony is obvious—"safe spaces" for Christians to study will only increase.

18. There is increasing reason for concern on these fronts. Not only are the afore-mentioned histories of higher education in Canada and the United States disquieting, but so are recent studies by social scientists of how the cultural elites, and educated elites in particular, are biased against evangelical Christians in the United States. I see no reason to hope that the situation is better in Canada (Yancey, *Compromising Scholarship*; and Paul, *From Tolerance to Equality*). When one adds to these broad portraits the following disturbing study of how senior professors blatantly favour grant support for those they like and agree with, one must be careful not to overreact, but also not be blithe about the challenges of the situation (Lamont, *How Professors Think*).

Schools that advertise themselves as such will then have to look hard at their classrooms to make sure that a properly Christian perspective controls the conversation, at dormitories and other parts of student life to make sure that a properly Christian ethic informs each situation, at chapel and other worship situations to make sure that a properly Christian piety is being modelled and commended, and at the work of the board and administration to make sure that a properly Christian ethos governs every policy and procedure. Only a strong sense of teamwork among academic and co-curricular staff, with recognition that everything the university does teaches and trains students, can ensure a consistent Christian environment across campus.

At the same time, the desire for safety against genuine dangers must be complemented by the desire for challenge from authentic alternatives. Individuals and institutions sometimes have difficulty distinguishing threats from opportunities, and frightened individuals and institutions are particularly prone to hypervigilance, rigidity, and intolerance of diversity, let alone dissent. From a Christian perspective, however, everyone and every institution must remain open to challenge, since none of us can claim entire sanctification—except, perhaps, the true Wesleyans. Too heavy a regime of safety threatens to quench the very Spirit of God, who blows where he wills and whose thoughts are not simply our thoughts. We must expect and welcome challenge as a necessary and constant element of the discipline of discipleship as well as of the creativity of our calling.

IN DEFENSE OF CHRISTIAN HIGHER EDUCATION IN CANADA

We must offer an *apologia* for Canadian Christian higher education both to our nation and to our church. To Canada, then, we must make two major claims. First, we must claim freedom of religion for individuals and for groups. The theory of religious freedom for groups in this perhaps hyperliberal age lags well behind the theory of religious freedom for individuals. Many of us, even most of us, including our leading jurists, philosophers, and politicians, seem to have trouble articulating what freedom of religion for groups should be in Canada today. But our Canadian heritage implies religious freedom for groups, most notably perhaps in the provision of religiously different schools in the Constitution.

Even argued from the position of individual religious freedom, however, the case can properly be made for Christian schools and Christian universities in particular. If a certain number of Canadians want to educate themselves, their children, and whoever else wants to enroll in a Christian school, they should be free to do so, short of some overriding concern of the state or some damage done to other people. And there remains some respect for this idea among Canadians today, if only of the "live and let live" variety, even though "Christian schooling" has been badly tarred by the abuses notoriously perpetrated at Mount Cashel, the residential school system, and beyond.

When public support for such education is sought, however—whether in the form of tax revenues, recognition by academic and professional organizations, land use regulations, and the like—the mood in Canada today seems inimical to Christian higher education. When our prime minister can routinely utter phrases about ideas he does not like as having "no place in Canada today," and when the Supreme Court justices can recognize that religious freedom, a clear Constitutional provision, can and should be compromised in the name of "Charter values," a term with no legal standing or even agreed-upon content, appeals for public support of Christian institutions and of universities in particular are bound to come to grief.[19]

Thus the second major claim must be made, namely, that the public good is advanced by Christian institutions, and therefore they deserve public support, not just public toleration. In regard particularly to Christian universities, a coherent and cogent argument must be advanced that certain goods will be gained only if, or at least will be gained best by, Christians who band together to study important problems within a Christian worldview. I have put that argument in public, in the pages of *University Affairs* and *The Globe and Mail*, and it goes like this.[20]

Christian universities pursue truth with a large number of basic questions asked and answered by virtue of common Christian commitment. Those basic questions are not so much ruled out of discussion as simply agreed upon in order to focus on new or perennial questions of common

19. *The Globe and Mail*, [Editorial] "From Trudeau and Scheer, a Lesson in How Not to Treat a Far-Right Protester"; The Supreme Court of Canada, "Summary of Trinity Western University, et al. v. Law Society of Upper Canada." In these fractious times, it might be well for me to note that I have voted for the Blue, Red, and Orange parties in provincial and federal elections depending on what I perceived to be the choice most likely to result in the greatest shalom at that time and in that riding, as well as across the country. I would therefore be misunderstood if my remarks about the current prime minister were interpreted as partisan.

20. Stackhouse, "CAUT versus Trinity Western"; Stackhouse, "Have Some Faith in Christian Law School."

interest. A tremendous synergy can result from such focused inquiry, as it happens, by way of analogy, in natural science when a certain model of astronomy or chemistry or physics is taken for granted, vulnerable as it may remain to challenges from those who do not share it (per Thomas Kuhn). Yes, there is an intellectual loss by not having a more diverse college of scholars working on the problem. To compensate for that loss, researchers at Christian universities must fully engage their respective academic guilds in order to test their work among those with different presuppositions. But there is also great gain to be had by nicely avoiding first- and second-order questions, by not having to argue once more over the ABCs of the discipline in order to work hard and cooperatively on third-order research.[21]

The public good is thus advanced by the research of Christian institutions, as it is by the research of other organizations with homogenous and focused scholars, from think tanks to industries, and even to ideologically homogenous departments in ostensibly pluralistic secular universities. The public good is also advanced, of course, by the donations and tuition fees of Christians willing to pay a considerable share of the costs of Christian higher education, donations and tuition fees that would otherwise likely

21. Some professors and administrators at Christian schools continue to insist that they experience no compromise of academic freedom and that therefore there is no big problem here. I respectfully suggest, however, that they have not fully considered the basic and severe constraints on academic freedom posed by their school's constitutive documents, especially statements of faith and community covenants. Their own work and their own consciences might not (yet) have come up against the fences of their schools' boundaries, but that does not mean those boundaries are not there and making a difference in the life of the institution. See, for example, the recent testimony of a Trinity Western University vice-provost, Stringham, "Academic Freedom and the Faith-Based University." Consider the situation at Wheaton College in Chicago not long ago when a faculty member converted to Roman Catholicism, Golden, "A Test of Faith." For illuminating commentary on this matter (although I conclude differently), see Jacobs, "To Be a Christian College."

For some reflections on these general issues from the American side of things, see Diekema, *Academic Freedom and Christian Scholarship*; and Ringenberg, *The Christian College and the Meaning of Academic Freedom*. Ringenberg describes Christian schools as "coherent intentional communities in which teachers and students can gather together around common ideals, goals, and aspirations" (xii). Ringenberg helpfully draws attention to the important difference between the typical secular university defense of academic freedom couched in terms of the individual professor's freedom to dissent and the typical Christian university defense couched in terms of religious communities' freedom to form educational institutions according to their distinctive values and practices. As Janet Epp Buckingham has recently argued, however, Canadian culture increasingly has difficulty construing religious freedom in anything other than individualistic terms (Buckingham, *Fighting over God*).

be lost to the higher education complex in Canada if Christian universities were to disappear. In a very basic way, Christians are offering "matching donations" for every dollar of tax revenue received by Christian universities, often matching at a greater than 1:1 ratio. It makes sheer economic sense to let those who want to pay so much of the cost of higher education to do so, rather than saddle hard-pressed governments with the whole load, as they did between the end of the first generation of Christian universities and this renaissance of a second one.

There are thus both philosophical and practical reasons to commend Christian higher education to the Canadian public today. They constitute the "carrot" part of a strategy for defending Christian universities. The "stick" part is constituted by two segments: the loss of Christian schools and all of those donation and tuition dollars, and the threat of lawsuits should we not be treated properly. The Trinity Western law school case was long and expensive, as most major lawsuits are. Instead of the Supreme Court's decision being some sort of end, however, it may constitute the beginning of Canadian Christians pushing back in defense of our religious rights and, indeed, on behalf of the public good against overreaching secularists and advocates of non-Christian values. We may—reluctantly and regrettably, to be sure—have to establish a "don't tread on me" stance that keeps anti-Christian sentiments properly at bay by making it more trouble than it is worth to keep encroaching on Christian individuals and institutions.

Other groups—such as Canadian Jews, Muslims, feminists, and LGBTQ+ activists—have developed institutions to respond quickly, clearly, and powerfully to threats upon their dignity and freedom. Without in the least encouraging Christians to become more fearful and defensive than we are already, I suggest it only makes political sense in the post-Christian pluralism of contemporary Canada, dominated as it is by a generally unfriendly outlook and a tendency toward litigation to solve problems, to be wise as serpents as well as being as innocent as doves, and to strategically consider how best to seek shalom for ourselves and our fellow citizens.

As for the internal apologia for Christian higher education, there has literally never been a better time for it. I have written elsewhere about the two main callings upon us: the generic human calling to maximize shalom as we love God, our neighbours, and the rest of creation as best we can each day, and the specifically Christian calling to make disciples as we help people meet Christ, receive him, commit to him, and grow up in him. Christian universities are admirably designed to further both vocations.[22]

As *universities*, our schools advance the mission of cultivating shalom. Indeed, it is the Christian university that best resolves the age-old tensions between pure research versus practical research and between teaching in order to know the truth and teaching in order to make a difference—by embracing them all. Because God has not under-resourced the world and because God has called us to maximize the flourishing of all on this planet, some scholars, both professors and students, will properly pursue the most arcane matters of theory and discovery while others will properly focus on the most pressing matters of problem-solving. In a Christian worldview, it is literally all good. Indeed, many professors and students will alternate between and even sometimes combine these callings.

Moreover, it is increasingly the Christian universities that retain the classical humanism of the university reaching back to the middle ages. Because the expansive Christian outlook refuses to restrict human life to instances of economic struggle, matrices of political power, sites of gender conflict, reiterations of archetypes, or any other reductionism, we welcome what we can learn from these various alternative interpretive foci while placing them in a large framework of complementarity. This is a worldview that expects things to be complex, not simple—indeed, to exceed our capacity while beckoning us onward to further exploration and apprehension. Thus, classes can rejoice in the beauty of a Shakespearean sonnet without neglecting the political, sexual, or economic hints it also contains. Professors and students can reflect upon group dynamics in social science without mistaking human beings for mere molecules in fluid dynamics or as only rational agents maximizing self-interest in economic games. Scholars can even study theology to learn about God, while recognizing that theology also tells us much about the social locations, limitations, and interests of theologians and their audiences. In short, Christian universities are increasingly attractive places of learning precisely because they remain universities, thus avoiding the common complaint that too many schools have become mere training centres turning out components for technopoly.[23]

As *Christian* universities, furthermore, our schools advance the mission of cultivating disciples. By simply being good universities, our schools invite and intrigue non-Christians about the Christian way. Why do these

22 Stackhouse, *Making the Best of It*; Stackhouse, *Why You're Here*.

23. Postman, *Technopoly*; Toulmin, *Cosmopolis*.

curious Christian people maintain these intellectual programs and academic standards? By welcoming, respectfully interrogating, learning from, and critiquing a wide range of views, furthermore, Christian universities say a lot about both the healthy confidence and appropriate humility of Christian faith, while also demonstrating the breadth and vigour of Christian thought. By insisting on high standards applied impartially to everyone, Christian universities declare their seriousness about their calling and their sharing of God's regard for the equality of persons. By connecting each subject and discipline appropriately to the Christian Story in Scripture, Christian universities simultaneously dilate and deepen each student's understanding of the gospel. And by offering rich co-curricula that model and instruct in the fullness of Christian life, Christian universities offer holistic opportunities for discipleship that can complement well whatever the local church provides.

Christian universities therefore act apologetically, evangelistically, and pedagogically, drawing students toward and into Christ, by the power of the Holy Spirit of God working through our feeble, but faithful, enterprise. And as our culture becomes less and less informative about, and supportive of, Christianity, and in some (not all, but some) respects becomes more and more hostile to Christianity, the need for distinctively and thoroughly Christian universities is keener than ever.[24]

COUNSELS AND CHALLENGES

Mission

The evaporation of Christendom in Canada means that Christian institutions cannot take their own existence for granted. In particular, it is no longer just intuitively obvious that there be Christian universities. So Christian universities need a purpose, a *raison d'être*, a *telos*, that will both justify and direct their existence.

I have referred to the twin vocations of our lives as Christians: the universal human calling to make shalom and the specifically Christian calling to make disciples. These callings are advanced significantly by the Christian university as it teaches and researches subjects and skills that are both of universal human interest and of specifically Christian concern.

24. E. J. Thiessen makes the point that while Christian schools teach values that are, because of the lingering effects of Canada's Christian heritage, also taught in "common" or public schools, only the Christian schools teach the *grounds* for such values (Thiessen, *In Defence of Religious Schools and Colleges*, 235–36).

I want to sharpen this rather general point in regard to postsecondary Christian institutions. No other kind of institution can and will do what must be done here. No one else will produce scholarship at this level and offer this level of education in a thoroughly Christian way. Families and churches will not. State institutions will not. Businesses will not. Only Christian universities—and, to be sure, Christian Bible schools and seminaries in their respective fields—offer the world the work of professors steeped in the Christian tradition to both pass along and to increase human knowledge understood Christianly. Because this work is vitally important, therefore, it must be properly protected and directed. A clearly focused and articulated mission is key to protecting and directing our work. Only according to such a sense and statement of mission can we be what we must be: ruthless . . . and humble.

We must be *ruthless* in that the mission must dictate everything we do and how we do it. No longer can initiatives be justified in terms of "It would be good if we . . ." Lots of things a university might do are good in some sense, but not everything is going to advance the mission—and by "mission" I do not mean only the generic mission of all Christian universities, but the particular mission of a particular school. Indeed, schools cannot thrive if they try to be "all things to all people—in order that we might attract some . . . tuition dollars and donations." Instead, each Canadian Christian school has a particular history, identity, location, and calling to do some things and not others, to do things in some ways and not others, and to be and do what it is and does distinctively and excellently.

Excellence is not only a good word; I suggest it is a necessary word for the future of Canadian Christian higher education. What might have been good enough in the days of Christendom, when money and support and students might automatically have flowed to Christian institutions, is now not nearly good enough. Now the requirement is to be so good at what we do that critics cannot gainsay our quality and prospective students cannot dismiss us as second-rate. Excellence is not only honouring to God, in the spirit of the prophet Malachi and in obedience to the command of God to all workers via Paul's letter to the Colossians (3:23–24), but it is a survival strategy. High-quality universities, Christian and secular, are not lacking for funds or applicants these days. My own alumni magazines—from Queen's, Wheaton, and Chicago—brim with news of the latest academic successes of professors and students while trumpeting the results of the latest financial drive.[25]

But, a voice might be heard to say, isn't such an aspiration to excellence *elitist*? Isn't it proud? Isn't it wicked to decide to favour some and ignore others? How can we abandon the lower achievers?

I asked my first dean, Harold Heie, that question some thirty years ago. Harold gave me a twofold answer I have never forgotten: (1) few schools aspire to excellence because it is hard to achieve, so there will always be some school happy to take in whoever will apply; and (2) excellence serves everyone, as the top schools are also characteristically the leading schools who set the pace for everyone else and who bless everyone else through the students and scholarship they produce. If no one sets a better pace, no one gets better. So we must ruthlessly aim at the excellent fulfilment of our mission, pruning away everything that does not advance it and boldly pursuing everything that does. And here is where our not enjoying Harvard-scale endowments helps us, for we cannot afford to do everything, even every "good thing." Lack of endless resources, annoying as it can be, can also compel us to think hard about mission and set priorities accordingly.

At the same time, however, our mission *humbles* us. It keeps us from presuming we can and should do anything we might like to do—such as to open our school to be an all-purpose facility for local Christian organizations and churches, to the compromise of the use of professors and students, or to advance the agenda of a favourite politician or party, to the compromise of our welcome of diverse political views. It keeps us aware that we cannot shape students the way families and churches can, but only in ways appropriate to an educational institution. It keeps us from feathering our own nests and those of our friends. What we pay in salary and benefits for each position in the university should be tied clearly to what will best advance the mission of the university. Particularly those of us with executive rank and power will do well to insist that boards pay us, and everyone else, according to what is required for the university to thrive, and not according to some other, vaguer standard of what someone "deserves."

---

25. Colleagues at Wheaton have whispered to me recently, however, that in order to maintain a roughly 1:1 ratio of men to women at Wheaton, that college has reduced its entrance standards for men. I have no hard data on this report, no idea of whether this trend is long- or short-term, and no sense yet of what this news might mean. I register it here simply in the interest of full disclosure, even as I maintain that excellence is the best survival strategy a serious school can adopt.

We thus are serious about being both *Christian* and a *university*. We offer hospitality to non-Christians (if our school admits them), evangelism to seekers (ditto), and discipleship to believers, and we strive to do an excellent job in each mode, in each course, and in every co-curricular activity. We also guard our metaphors, ensuring that we do not act as anything other than a university, an institution of higher learning. What I mean here is that we beware of referring to our school as a family, a church, or a business, and we are vigilant to make sure—particularly in committee meetings at every level, but also in teaching, coaching, counseling, and otherwise—that decisions are being made not according to familial, ecclesiastical, or commercial values, but according to those of a Christian school. The success of a Christian school will be determined not primarily by whether it has excellent family dynamics, or produces fine piety, or is run with economic efficiency—although each of these values can be useful for a school to bear in mind—but whether it fulfills its mission of producing Christian scholars (by which I mean "educated people," not just professors) and scholarship at a high level. Mission, therefore, is basic. And if the articulation of the mission is poor, or the willingness to adhere to it is weak, all sorts of woolly-minded, sentimental, or vicious results will surely ensue.

Message

Christian universities, having received from the Lord a clear sense of mission, must now send out a strong message, and in at least three respects. First, *apologetic*. Students will not come just because we built it. We evangelicals have learned that about our churches, and we are learning that about our schools. What seems to us to be a luminously obvious idea—sending your child to our school, sending your dollars to our endowment—is a dull nightlight in the flashing kaleidoscope of today's ongoing cultural rave. We must state not only what we are doing but *why*, and that "why" has to be big enough, important enough, and compelling enough for people to change their lives because of it.

I am not nudging us toward cynical alarmism as a marketing theme. But this *is* the end of the world as we know it (!)—the end of the régime of Christendom in Canada—and Christian universities are only going to be increasingly important as bulwarks of treasured tradition, transmitters of core values, producers of new knowledge and wisdom, and trainers of tomorrow's faithful. A lot of good gets done on campus, and that good needs to be articulated cogently, both to those who can benefit by it and to those who can benefit it.[26]

Marketing, then, must be done excellently, starting of course with each school's website. And I will stop there, since for many Canadian institutions to mention the website is embarrassment enough. Yet every other piece of material produced needs to be similarly mission-focused and apologetically powerful, which leads me to the second respect in which our message must be strong.

Comprehensive. To boil it down to an aphorism: Everything messages. Every sign, every label, every webpage, every handbill, every event, every ritual, every classroom, every dorm room, every professor's choice of dress, every student's choice of dress, every building name, every sports team name, every drama production, every concert program, every uniform, every landscape—everything signals something about the school. Good leadership ensures good messaging everywhere and always, realizing that any other message being giving off amounts to static at best and interference at worst.

Here is an exercise I recommend to help institutions understand their messaging. Ask new students, new staff members, and new professors who have been on campus for only one month to complete a survey about everything, no matter how small, that they have noticed that is and is not "on message"—everything that fits what they were told about the school and everything that seems not to fit. Their eyes and ears will never be more sensitive than they are as newcomers. Take advantage of that freshness to see and hear what has been there all along and what needs attention.

It will not do to protect our tender egos by insisting that details do not matter, by assuming a position of intellectual or spiritual loftiness that rises above such petty discussions of how the hall is decorated for this reception or which font is to be used in university communications. It will not do to respond, "Isn't this just another version of arguing about what colour the church's carpeting should be?" First, the university is not a church. Second, carpet colours actually do matter, in churches and in universities,

---

26. I was unable to elicit up-to-date numbers on CHEC schools in this category, but Harry Fernhout published these intriguing statistics a few years ago that give a strong sense that the market for CHEC schools remains largely unreached: "Total university enrollment in Canada (excluding community colleges and technical institutes) stands at about 900,000 students. Total enrollment in CHEC institutions of all types represents only 1.9 percent of this number, while evangelical Christians constitute roughly 12 percent of the general population" (Fernhout, "Quest for Identity and Place," 247).

since environment affects our feelings, thoughts, and actions. Consider the room you are in, and then consider the interior of the most beautiful library you have ever visited, and tell me whether carpet colours, and every other architectural detail, actually do matter to what we do.

Third, younger people have been increasingly well trained by our culture in what Freud called the "narcissism of small differences" to notice what is hot and what is not, what is better and what is worse. The creative power of highly educated and well-funded media experts has trained them to notice what could appear to us to be tiny details in cell phones, footwear, jewelry, tattoos, laptop covers, fingernail polish, and, yes, fonts. We can wish it were not so, and we can pretend it does not matter. But this game is being played, we are in it, and we can play it well or play it poorly. There is no opting out.

The final respect in which we must send out a strong message, after *apologetic* and *comprehensive*, is *strategic*. We need to keep a wide and realistic view of our enterprise. The view must be wide in order for us to set proper priorities and maintain them, refusing to be drawn down into the immediate crisis, reduced to the tunnel vision demanded by the insistently urgent. The view must also be realistic, as we recognize that we cannot do everything, that we certainly cannot do everything perfectly, and that we cannot win every battle, solve every problem, and convince every stakeholder. With such a wide and realistic view, we must resolve to send out messages, in what we say and also in what we do, that maximize the achievement of our mission. We trade small for large and ephemeral for enduring. And we help our colleagues and students and donors and interested others to do the same, reassuring them according to our mission that our choices are strategically derived, aimed at producing the optimal outcome in a complex situation.

It is in the light of our overall mission and our overall message that I finally consider statements of faith (SOFs) and community covenants (CCs). These documents, as well as mission statements themselves, must be formulated to be applied, if they are to exist at all. These summaries of our key values and aspirations must be composed to do certain work that helps to advance the mission and articulate the message of our school.

They need to be at once minimal, complete, and rigorous. By *minimal*, I mean that they must not include any element that is not truly essential to the mission and message of the school. They must be edited down to the bone so that every word tells and every phrase is one that can be lifted up and championed as integral. They also must be minimal in the sense that they do not exclude any element that would, through exclusion, alienate those who should be included.

By *complete* I mean that everything crucial to this aspect of the community and mission is listed. There must be no hidden curricula or agenda, no pull-down menus of extras that "everybody knows" or "we all believe" that lie in wait to perplex and stumble the unacquainted. If someone can sign what you ask them to sign and that should be that, then that should be that. Otherwise, the message being communicated is something quite different—about integrity, if not intelligence.

And by *rigorous* I mean that SOFs, CCs, mission statements, and the like need to be as lucid as possible so that they both inspire and discipline. Every teacher tries to put examination questions as clearly as possible to avoid both good students taking things the wrong way and bad students being afforded grounds for appeal. Lawmakers have similar goals, although usually with higher stakes. So too should it be with our constitutive documents. They should both draw together the members of the authentic community while marking out those who do not belong—again, according to the mission of the university.

It must be said, alas, that these documents cannot advance the mission and message unless they are applied uniformly and univocally. They cannot be qualified with asterisks or parentheses or other dodges connived at, or at least tolerated, by confused or indifferent administrators and disingenuous professors. Any document that cannot be rigorously applied must be sent back to the shop for modification. Any document that comes out of the shop must be rigorously applied, or it does little good and in fact positions the school for scandal.

Moreover, a commitment to due rigor must include firm adherence to due process in resolving concerns. Any administrator, trustee, donor, student, or fellow employee on a vendetta can complain that a faculty member's views hurt the institution in some way and thus compromise its mission. To guard against such abuse—which our doctrine of sin should teach us to *expect* from time to time—Christian universities must protect academic freedom, however appropriately qualified by explicit and commonly agreed commitments. And we must insist on transparent and just policies and procedures for the resolution of such matters.

If Christian universities do not formulate such documents carefully and enforce them uniformly and fairly, how can Christians trust their universities to both provide higher education to vulnerable young people and do some of the hardest and most important thinking on behalf of the church—both critical needs of our time, as in every time? People must be able to rely on us to maintain fidelity to our common faith. And what will happen when an unsympathetic employee, student, or alumnus/alumna finds out about a university's failure to be consistent on either doctrine or process and trumpets the university's hypocrisy to an unsympathetic reporter? What will happen when these matters end up, as they almost certainly will, in court?[27]

Having set out a case for statements of faith and community covenants, I therefore register my dismay at the apparent insistence of Universities Canada on complete academic freedom for professors, at least once they have been hired. It seems nonsensical for Christian institutions not to guard themselves against heresy or apostasy, against changes of professors' minds that result in them working against the fundamental identity and mission of the schools. Doctrine is not everything to Christianity, of course, but it is essential. Too much deviance entails teaching from the perspective of a different religion, thus subverting the very purpose of the institution. Nicholas Wolterstorff has wondered aloud at how much sense it would make for St. John's College, well-known for its Great Books curriculum, to continue to employ a faculty member who became utterly opposed to the teaching of the Great Books. Likewise, it is nonsense for Christian schools to be required to retain faculty who have converted to some other religion.[28]

The so-called Christian colleges affiliated with secular universities who do not have, or who have failed to enforce, such provisions are generally today religious shells housing essentially secular enterprises.[29] And for

27. Malik (*The Two Tasks*) gives a stirring call to Christians to "out-think" the world through the university, and Christian universities ought to provide excellent environments in which this can be done. Ringenberg discusses a daunting array of Christian schools failing to pursue due process (*The Christian College and the Meaning of Academic Freedom*, especially chapter 25, "Theological Nuance" and chapter 29, "Due Process").

28. Ringenberg, *The Christian College and the Meaning of Academic Freedom*, 90. See also the extended defence of theology as key to a Christian university in Glanzer et al., *Restoring the Soul of the University*.

29. I freely confess that this is but an impression, albeit one gained over more than 30 years in Canadian higher education from coast to coast, buttressed by similar views of colleagues across the country—most recently in e-mail correspondence with Robert Derrenbacker, former president of Thornloe (Anglican) University at Laurentian University, and David Seljak, professor at St Jerome's (Catholic) College at the University

UC and its member schools to reply that faculty members who eventually find themselves at odds with the identity and mission of their school can be relied upon to have the integrity to resign is disingenuous, to put it mildly.[30] Who dares abandon an academic job in a market that has been terrible for more than a generation? What ethical bargains and contortions will people undertake to avoid unemployment? Instead of professors nobly renouncing their positions, what likely will happen instead is that either authentic Christianity will erode at that school as people profess beliefs they no longer hold, or insidious pressures will be brought to bear, without due process, on such faculty members to leave, thus corrupting the administration that is trying, ironically, to maintain the school's Christian integrity. I suggest that CHEC needs to ensure that UC will allow member schools to remove professors whose religious commitments no longer line up with their school's, even as I would urge generous severance policies to make such dismissals as respectfully gentle as possible.

As for community covenants, my study of the Bible school movement leads me to see them as useful in that context—in that quasi-monastic, quasi-military mode of training disciplined Christians in every aspect of Christian life. But Christian universities are not merely Bible schools with PhD's. The very nature of university education requires a much larger scope for difference, dissidence, and even deviance. Moreover, many, if not all, Canadian Christian universities today happily admit and graduate non-Christians, students who did not sign up for comprehensive Christian training but who were glad to gain a Christian education. The actual charters of Canadian Christian universities, furthermore, do not always state their mission in such comprehensive life-shaping terms, but instead often in quite minimal intellectual terms, such as Trinity Western's: "The objects of the University shall be to provide for young people of any race, colour, or creed university education in the arts and sciences with an underlying

of Waterloo. Conrad Grebel University College at Waterloo might be something of an exception to the rule as it seems to maintain a distinctive Anabaptist identity. Only a detailed study of its faculty would demonstrate to what extent explicit Christian identity and commitment characterizes each professor versus the general commitment to the school's mission of fostering peace and nonviolence that is all that is required of faculty hires (correspondence with President Marcus Shantz and Prof. Marlene Epp). Conrad Grebel's mission is "to seek wisdom, nurture faith, and pursue justice and peace in service to church and society" (2008)—quoted from Conrad Grebel's Faculty Appointments policy, Policy #333A, page 1 (attached to correspondence from Marlene Epp).

30. Surprisingly, Thiessen also argues this way: *In Defense of Religious Schools and Colleges*, 95–96.

philosophy and viewpoint that is Christian" ("An Act Respecting Trinity Western University," 3:2, 1969).

It would be well, therefore, if Canadian Christian universities looked hard at any behavioural/ethical codes to ensure that they, too, meet the criteria of minimalism, completeness, and rigour, both for staff and, almost certainly differently, for students. How does such a code advance the mission of the university and what message does it send to everyone who reads it?[31]

Mutuality

Having framed a clear mission and articulated a clear message, our universities are then poised for three orders of mutuality. At the least, they ought to *coordinate* their work so as not to uselessly duplicate effort, let alone unintentionally compete and interfere. Matters of common concern, such as relationships with Universities Canada and the Tri-Councils, legal struggles, such as Trinity Western's recent law school case, or the perpetual concerns about enrolment and funding, should be commonly and regularly discussed to observe at least the principle of comity, rather than heedless competition.

Better, in fact, is that such schools *cooperate*. The recent decisions by Universities Canada and the Supreme Court underline the pressing and growing need for CHEC schools to regularly communicate in order to anticipate challenges, not just respond to them, and to strategize about joint actions. It is obvious that a decision affecting one or some would usually have implications for most or all, and it ought to be obvious that working together will normally produce better outcomes than working separately.

Finally, there needs to be some concern for *consolidation*. The great United Church historian John Webster Grant once remarked to me that an awful lot of ecumenical cooperation came as a result of financial pressure, not theological conviction. The theological rationale was often developed after the fact. The same theme—that cooperation and consolidation happened in Canadian Christian higher education generally only under financial duress—is sustained also by Masters in his history.[32] Could the

31. Gidney confirms that *in loco parentis* rules governed university life on secular campuses as well until the 1960s. And for a discussion of ethical rules in American fundamentalist schools—from Moody Bible Institute to Wheaton College—see Laats, *Fundamentalist U*, 87–121.

32. Masters, *Protestant Church Colleges in Canada*.

leaders of Canadian Christian universities demonstrate genuine Christian wisdom and courage by staring hard at the facts on the ground and deciding whether some consolidation of resources would not make more sense than the small multitude of institutions we currently have?

Tiny Bible schools dotting the prairies made a certain sense when educational standards were low, roads were bad, and funds were tight. That sector of education has undergone tremendous attrition, but even still, does having so many still make sense today? I used to think that Ontario, and even just the GTA, surely could sponsor two fine small Christian universities, especially with one arising out of the Christian Reformed network and the other representing transdenominational evangelicalism, a kind of Calvin-plus-Wheaton situation. The jury, however, is still out on that score as Redeemer and Tyndale carry on the best they can. (A similar situation obtains in Alberta, of course, with King's and Ambrose.)

When financial pressures force consolidation, leaders will come up with impressive theological and practical rationales. Why not consider those rationales before matters approach the critical juncture of survival and work constructively instead toward the maximization of shalom? If one focuses intently on mission, are these schools really justified in remaining separate, with all the duplication and competition that result?

Following

I avoided searching for an alliterative title for this fourth and final counsel since it is not on the same plane as the other three. Indeed, it is the concern that governs everything else: *Nachfolge*, our following of Jesus, rather than the expectation that he is supporting us in our projects.[33]

Jesus is Lord, and he is our Lord. He is not our patron, much less the "enabler" of our hopes and dreams. He is not obliged to keep our schools going, however many crosses and fishes show up on our stationery and however many prayer meetings we might hold. We are obliged, instead, to listen to him and to do what he says. And if he tells us to curtail this and stop doing that, we have no choice but to faithfully and thankfully obey. If he gives to us a mission that we do not like, we have no choice but to faithfully and thankfully execute it as well as we possibly can. And if he

---

33. The allusion, of course, is to Bonhoeffer, *Discipleship*. An Anabaptist reader of an earlier draft reminded me that *Nachfolge* is a key term in that tradition stemming from the 1500s.

withdraws his blessing and directs us to close up shop, we have no choice but to faithfully and thankfully comply.

I could have offered this identical challenge decades ago when I started my career. There is nothing conceptually complex about it. It is simply the call to discipleship. It would have been just as true then, but it might be well to confess that I likely would have stated it much more blithely back then than I do now. Every school at which I have held a full-time position since I started at Northwestern College in Iowa in 1987 has been under financial duress. This has not been just financial pressure but actual fear about survival of entire departments, if not of the whole institution itself. I have been on the academic job market several times, and it has been a terrifying experience each time. Be assured that I speak about these matters of following Christ to the full extent of his demands with a keen recognition of the implication for both individuals and institutions. When Christ calls a school, as someone somewhere has almost said, he bids it to be willing to die, or at least to change into something its leaders might currently wish it were not.

The good news, however, is that anything Christ commands of us is for our good and is the path of ultimate life. Jesus does not always give us what we want, as individuals or as institutions. But let us thank God again that he does not. For if we will properly pray, trust, and obey, he will not fail to give us what we and the people we serve most need.

CONCLUSION

I dare not conclude, however, on a note of challenge, but of encouragement, for the times require us to press on with enthusiasm in the work to which we have been called. I continue to champion, then, the great value of Christian higher education in Canada, and particularly the subject of this chapter, Christian universities. As Canadian culture manifestly continues its general divergence from allegiance to the Christian religion while the numbers of evangelical Christians continue to grow, we can hardly worry that the time has passed for what we do. Quite the contrary. The time has never been more fitting for Christian universities in Canada, and for them to be robustly both *Christian* and what we have traditionally called *universities*. Moreover, as we strengthen our commitment to excellence in this worthy pursuit, we can expect God to bless us—and at least many of our neighbours, Christian or otherwise, to recognize, approve of, support, and even join in this crucial enterprise.

Law schools and lawsuits get lots of attention in the media, as perhaps must be. But Christian scholars know that the most important decisions and developments regarding the integrity, mission, and quality of our universities occur in the annual rounds of hiring and promoting staff; recruiting students; supporting research, teaching, and service; raising generous funding; and the many other actions that do not make the news but determine, in fact, the future of Christian higher education in Canada. Only if we undertake such actions with due regard for mission, message, and mutuality in determined and confident discipleship to Jesus Christ will that future be worthy of the words "Christian" and "university."

BIBLIOGRAPHY

Beach, Charles M., et al., eds. *Higher Education in Canada*. Kingston, ON: John Deutsch Institute, 2005.

Bonhoeffer, Dietrich. *Discipleship*. Translated by Barbara Green and Reinhard Krauss. Minneapolis: Fortress, 2001.

Boyer, John W. *The University of Chicago: A History*. Chicago: University of Chicago Press, 2015.

Buckingham, Janet Epp. *Fighting over God: A Legal and Political History of Religious Freedom in Canada*. Montreal: McGill-Queen's University Press, 2014.

Burtchaell, James Tunstead. *The Dying of the Light: The Disengagement of Colleges and Universities from Their Christian Churches*. Grand Rapids: Eerdmans, 1998.

Callaway, Tim W. *Training Disciplined Soldiers for Christ: The Influence of American Fundamentalism on Prairie Bible Institute (1922–1980)*. Bloomington, IN: West Bow, 2013.

Centre for the Study of Canadian Evangelicalism. "Canadian Evangelical Bibliographies Project." No Pages. Online: http://crce.efc-canada.net/index.php?title=Christian_Higher_Education_in_Canada.

Chamorro-Premuzic, Tomas. "Are CEOs Overhyped and Overpaid?" *Harvard Business Review* (1 November 2016). No pages. Online: https://hbr.org/2016/11/are-ceos-overhyped-and-overpaid.

Clarke, Brian, and Stuart Macdonald. *Leaving Christianity: Changing Allegiances in Canada since 1945*. Montreal: McGill-Queen's University Press, 2017.

Diekema, Anthony. *Academic Freedom and Christian Scholarship*. Grand Rapids: Eerdmans, 2000.

Fawcett, Bruce G., and Gilda O. Ryder, eds. *Faith and Education: A History of Crandall University*. Moncton, NB: Crandall University Press, 2014.

Fisher, Donald, et al. *The Development of Postsecondary Education Systems in Canada: A Comparison between British Columbia, Ontario, and Québec, 1980–2010*. Montreal: McGill-Queen's University Press, 2014.

Flatt, Kevin N. *After Evangelicalism: The Sixties and the United Church of Canada*. Montreal: McGill-Queen's University Press, 2013.

Gidney, Catherine. *A Long Eclipse: The Liberal Protestant Establishment and the Canadian University, 1920–1970*. Montreal: McGill-Queen's University Press, 2004.

Glanzer, Perry L., Nathan F. Alleman, and Todd C. Ream. *Restoring the Soul of the University: Unifying Christian Higher Education in a Fragmented Age.* Downers Grove, IL: InterVarsity, 2017.

The Globe and Mail (Editorial). "From Trudeau and Scheer: A Lesson in How Not to Treat a Far-Right Protester." *The Globe and Mail* (21 August 2018). No pages. Online: https://www.theglobeandmail.com/opinion/editorials/article-globe-editorial-from-trudeau-and-scheer-a-lesson-in-how-not-to-treat/.

Golden, Daniel. "A Test of Faith." *The Wall Street Journal* (7 January 2006). No pages. Online: https://www.wsj.com/articles/SB113659805227040466.

Jacobs, Alan. "To Be a Christian College." *First Things* (April 2006). No pages. Online: https://www.firstthings.com/article/2006/04/to-be-a-christian-college.

Jones, Glen A., ed. *Higher Education in Canada: Different Systems, Different Perspectives.* New York: Routledge, 1997.

Hiebert, Al, et al. *Character with Competence Education: The Bible College Movement in Canada.* Steinbach, MB: Association of Canadian Bible Colleges, 2005.

Laats, Adam. *Fundamentalist U: Keeping the Faith in American Higher Education.* Oxford: Oxford University Press, 2018.

Lamont, Michèle. *How Professors Think: Inside the Curious World of Academic Judgment.* Cambridge, MA: Harvard University Press, 2009.

Malik, Charles. *The Two Tasks.* Westchester, IL: Cornerstone Books, 1980.

Manitoba Human Rights Commission: Schroen v. Steinbach Bible College (1999). No pages. Online: http://www.manitobahumanrights.ca/v1/decisions/decisions-%20pages/schroen-v-steinbach-bible-college-july-1999.html.

Marsden, George M. *The Soul of the American University: From Protestant Establishment to Established Nonbelief.* Oxford: Oxford University Press, 1994.

Masters, D. C. *Protestant Church Colleges in Canada: A History.* Toronto: University of Toronto Press, 1966.

Olsen, Ted. "Wheaton College Allows Dancing for All, Drinking and Tobacco for Non-Undergraduates." *Christianity Today* (1 February 2003). No Pages. Online: https://www.christianitytoday.com/ct/2003/februaryweb-only/2-17-32.0.html.

Paul, Darel E. *From Tolerance to Equality: How Elites Brought America to Same-Sex Marriage.* Waco, TX: Baylor University Press, 2018.

Postman, Neil. *Technopoly: The Surrender of Culture to Technology.* New York: Vintage, 1992.

Reimer, Sam, and Michael Wilkinson. *A Culture of Faith: Evangelical Congregations in Canada.* Montreal: McGill-Queen's University Press, 2015.

Ringenberg, William C. *The Christian College: A History of Protestant Higher Education in America.* 2nd ed. Grand Rapids: Baker Academic, 2006.

———. *The Christian College and the Meaning of Academic Freedom: Truth-Seeking in Community.* New York: Palgrave Macmillan, 2016.

Stackhouse, John G., Jr. *Canadian Evangelicalism in the Twentieth Century: An Introduction to Its Character.* Toronto: University of Toronto Press, 1993.

———. "CAUT versus Trinity Western: Academic Freedom or Statement of Faith? They're Both Right." *University Affairs* (January 2010) 16. No pages. Online: https://www.universityaffairs.ca/opinion/in-my-opinion/caut-versus-trinity-western/.

———. "Have Some Faith in Christian Law School." *The Globe and Mail* (3 February 2014). No pages. Online: http://www.theglobeandmail.com/opinion/have-some-faith-in-christian-law-school/article16661053/.

————. *Making the Best of It: Following Christ in the Real World*. Oxford: Oxford University Press, 2008.

————. *Why You're Here: Ethics for the Real World*. Oxford: Oxford University Press, 2018.

Stott, John R. W. *Basic Christianity*. 2nd ed. Downers Grove, IL: InterVarsity, 1971.

Stringham, Eve. "Academic Freedom and the Faith-Based University: Yes, the Two Can Co-exist with a Little Understanding and Goodwill." *University Affairs* (8 May 2018). No pages. Online: https://www.universityaffairs.ca/opinion/in-my-opinion/academic-freedom-and-the-faith-based-university/.

Supreme Court of Canada. "Summary of Trinity Western University, et al. v. Law Society of Upper Canada." No pages. Online: https://www.scc-csc.ca/case-dossier/info/sum-som-eng.aspx?cas=37209.

Thiessen, Elmer John. *In Defence of Religious Schools and Colleges*. Montreal: McGill-Queen's University Press, 2001.

Toulmin, Stephen. *Cosmopolis: The Hidden Agenda of Modernity*. Chicago: University of Chicago Press, 1992.

Universities Canada. "Statement on Academic Freedom" (25 October 2011). No pages. Online: https://www.univcan.ca/media-room/media-releases/statement-on-academic-freedom/.

————. "Statement on Proposed Membership Criterion" (23 September 2016). No pages. Online: https://www.univcan.ca/media-room/media-releases/statement-proposed-membership-criterion/.

Yancey, George. *Compromising Scholarship*. Waco, TX: Baylor University Press, 2011.

7

The Past, Present, and Future of Seminary Education in Canada

STANLEY E. PORTER

INTRODUCTION

AN ASTUTE OBSERVER MIGHT recognize that I am revisiting a topic that I have discussed before. That topic is the past, present, and projected future of seminary education in Canada. I am not sure why it has fallen to me to be the one who has repeatedly investigated this topic. To the best of my knowledge, however, apart from a few incidental references here and there, some of them dependent upon the research that I have done, very few individuals seem to be concerned with the state of seminary education in Canada or at least its numbers—apart of course from the state of their own individual institutions, their current enrolment, and whether they will have enough money to finance another year.

This chapter, however, is the third time that I have examined the numerical condition of theological education in Canada, paying particular attention to the enrolment profiles of the institutions within Canada and in relationship to those in the United States. I made my first survey of the figures in 2006,[1] my second survey in 2011,[2] and I am now making this third survey in 2018—having recently received the figures for 2017. In the

1. Porter, "Theological Education."
2. Porter, "Canadian Theological Education."

183

discussion below, I will review the findings from these first two studies, and then turn to the current figures, before making some comments about the future. My goal in this paper, however, is not simply to recount a bunch of figures, but to attempt to put these figures in an appropriate context that allows us all to learn from what is occurring in seminary education in Canada, including and perhaps especially, institutions that hold membership in Christian Higher Education Canada (CHEC). This will enable us better to approach and address issues that are going to face us in the future.

THE PAST: 2006 AND 2011

I begin with the past, first the more distant past of 2006 and then the more recent past of 2011. In the earlier studies, I did most of my data gathering from the annual reports provided by the major accrediting agency of seminaries in North America, in both the USA and Canada, the Association of Theological Schools in the United States and Canada, or ATS (not to be confused with the American Thoracic Society, which might come up if you Google ATS). Although there are other US Department of Education approved accrediting agencies for seminaries, ATS is the largest and oldest of these groups—celebrating its centennial in 2018, although it was actually founded in a form that is recognizably close to what it is today in 1934. Nevertheless, ATS accredits the largest number of seminaries throughout North America. I will summarize my previous findings first before tracing the trajectory of seminary education over the course of the last seventeen years.[3]

---

3. For each of the first two reports, I used the ATS Bulletins (2007–2008, recounting the 2006 figures; and the 2011–2012 Annual Data Tables), available on their website. At the times, I noted that there are apparent anomalies and/or errors in the figures. For this study, I have used the gross figures provided directly by ATS. ATS apparently corrects their figures as they receive information, so that the figures that they maintain and believe to be accurate are not actually accessible online, as the originally reported figures are maintained on the website. The use of these corrected figures means that I do not have all of the possible figures available. I also have more reliable population figures, relying upon Statistics Canada and a website for the US that has consistent numbers for all of the years concerned. As a result of some variances, I am not always comparing like with like from my previous studies to this one. I wish to thank Chris Meinzer, Senior Director of Administration & CFO of ATS, for providing this recent information. The information I received and have used is in Appendix A at the back of this volume.

Benchmark Figures

Let me begin, however, by noting a number of figures that provide a benchmark for our discussion (Appendix A in the back matter of this volume provides a chart with all of the relevant statistics used in this study).

The high point for student numbers in ATS seminaries in North America cumulatively was in 2004, when ATS reported a total headcount (HC) of 80,250 students, which translated into a full-time equivalent (FTE) of 51,471. Each was the highest figure cumulatively for both Canadian and US institutions. These figures indicate a ratio of headcount to FTE of 1.56 actual bodies for every student taking the equivalent of a full load of courses (however that is calculated by ATS institutions, and it varies, which is an area that ATS has chosen not to address, thus calling their figures into some question). In 2004, there were 249 ATS institutions of varying accreditation status contributing to these figures, with an average ATS institutional size of 322 HC per institution and 207 FTE. This means that, continent-wide, roughly 1 out of every 4,047 North Americans was in seminary in 2004. In the US, this meant roughly 1 out of 3,999, and in Canada, 1 out of 4,539. The average number of people supporting an ATS institution continent wide was 1,304,000 per institution. More particularly, in 2004 there were 73,214 HC and 47,874 FTE in US institutions, a ratio of 1.52 bodies per FTE, and there were 7,036 HC and 3,597 FTE in Canadian institutions, a ratio of 1.96 bodies per FTE. In 2004, the average US seminary (there were 213 of them) had 344 HC, and the average Canadian seminary (there were 36 of them) had 195 HC, while US institutions averaged 225 FTE and Canadian ones 100 FTE. In the US, there was one seminary per 1,375,000 people but, in Canada, one seminary per only 887,000 people. Those cumulative numbers of HC and FTE were the highest that ATS institutions ever reached, and that is now thirteen years ago.

When we mine into the figures a little more, however, there are some further differences between the US and Canada that are important to note in establishing our baseline. 2004 was the high year for total HC and FTE in ATS institutions collectively, but it was not the highest year for headcount in the US. In the US, the highest HC occurred not in 2004 but in 2006, with 73,604 HC. However, with the rise in US population in two years from 2004 to 2006, the increase in HC had lost ground so that now only 1 out of 4,035 Americans was in seminary. For this same year, the FTE was only 46,804 (down from 47,874).[4] For Canada, 2004 was the highest HC, but the high-

---

4. This means that the ratio of HC to FTE was 1.57 in 2006 for US institutions.

est FTE was the previous year, 2003, with 3,654 FTE. By 2004, the Canadian FTE had fallen to 3,597 and by 2006 even further (as we shall see).[5]

With these figures, I think that we get an idea of the overall shape of seminary education in Canada, especially in relation to the US, at the high-point. In Canada, the highest year for cumulative HC was 2004, the highest year for FTE was 2003, and both years had the same number of institutions, 36. However, we were already seeing a drop in the ratio of HC to FTE, in both US and Canadian institutions.

2006

The first systematic study I completed was concerned with seeing where seminary education was in 2006. In 2006, there were a total of 251 ATS institutions, an increase of two from 2004 with its highest cumulative HC and FTE. In 2006, for all ATS institutions, there was now a total of 79,987 HC and 50,003 FTE. The decrease in headcount was marginal (from a high of 80,250), representing only about 263 total students and a percentage decrease of only three tenths of one percent (0.003). The FTE had, however, decreased at a higher rate, to 50,003 (from 51,471), a decrease of 1,468 which represents a decrease of nearly 3 percent (0.028). This means that there were now overall 1.6 students for every full-time load taken in ATS institutions. Again, one might not think that this ratio of HC to FTE is significant, and statistically it probably is not. However, there were other indications of some problematic developments. One is the average size of an ATS institution. The size had decreased to an average 319 HC, an average decrease of 3 HC, and 199 FTE, an average decrease of 8 FTE. However, the population of the US and Canada had now increased so that 1 in 4,138 was in seminary, an increase of 100 from only two years before.

If we examine the statistics for the US alone, we find that 2006 was the highest headcount for the US (as already noted), with 73,604, but a decrease in FTE to 46,804 with a ratio of headcount to FTE of 1.57. This meant that the average US institution, of which there were 215 in 2006, had 342 HC and 218 FTE, but was holding its own, with only slight decreases in either headcount (2 HC) or FTE (7 FTE). The US population growth meant that 1 in 4,053 Americans was in seminary, again a slight decrease. There was also one seminary for every 1,388,000 Americans. So, with the

---

5. This means that the ratio of HC to FTE in Canada in 2003 was 1.90 but then fell the next year to 1.96.

US figures being relatively stable, then the decrease must have occurred in Canadian institutions—and it had.

In 2006, in Canadian seminary education, there were 6,383 HC and 3,198 FTE across 36 institutions. This represented a fall in only two years (from the highest in 2004) of 635 HC, roughly 9% in two years (0.09), and a fall in only three years (from the highest FTE in 2003) of 456 FTE, a decrease of roughly 12% (0.12). The HC to FTE ratio in Canadian institutions was now at 2.0, a serious increase that indicated that two students were needed to take enough courses to create a full-time student load. This meant that the average Canadian seminary had shrunk to 177 HC, down 18 HC average or roughly 10%, and 89 FTE, down 11 FTE or roughly 11%. In 2006, there was one Canadian seminarian for every 5,103 people, and one seminary for every 904,000 Canadians.

The results of only two or three years in seminary education statistics were striking for the Canadian results. Overall, in only two or three years, Canadian seminary numbers of students had fallen by roughly 10%. At the time I wrote my first report, I stated that "Two years are too few to establish a clear trend, but if the downward movement continues at the same rate, in a mere five years there will be fewer than 5,000 students in seminary in Canada, and after ten years less than 4,000."[6] Thankfully, I was wrong.

2011

I was wrong, but I was not entirely wrong. 2011 was five years after 2006, and a number of developments had occurred in seminary education in both the US and Canada. Within the now 258 ATS institutions continent wide— an increase of 7 institutions over 2006 and 9 over 2004 with the highest cumulative numbers—there were only 74,253 HC and 47,545 FTE.[7] This represents a decrease of 5,734 HC or 7% (0.071) over those five years or roughly 1,140 students fewer per year on average. This also represents a decrease of 2,458 FTE or roughly 5% (0.049) over those same five years or roughly 500 FTE fewer per year on average. These are serious accumulating numbers. The result is that the average ATS institution continent-wide was now only 288 HC (down from 319 in 2006) with an average of 184 FTE (down from 199 in 2006). There was now one in 4,660 people continent-wide in seminary education.

6. Porter, "Theological Education," 46.

7. The ratio of HC to FTE is 1.56, a relatively stable ratio.

The situation in the US shared some of the blame for the decline during this time. In 2011 in the US, the number of students was 68,891 HC and 44,776 FTE, in now 219 institutions.[8] These figures represent a decrease of 4,713 HC, or 6% (0.064), from 2006, roughly 800 students per year on average, and a decrease of 2,028 FTE, or 4% (0.043), roughly 400 FTE per year. This means, with the increase in total number of institutions, that the average seminary in the US was now at 314 HC (down from 342 HC in 2006) and 204 FTE (down from 218 FTE in 2006). With the increase in the US population, this means that there was one person out of 4,523 Americans in seminary education and one seminary for every 1,423,000 Americans. There was some decline in the US, but not all of the decline was attributable to declines in the US.

The situation in Canada shouldered its fair share of the burden, in fact probably more of the burden. In 2011, in Canada, the number of seminary students was 5,362 HC and 2,770 FTE, with a ratio of 1.93 students per full time load, in now 39 institutions (this was not yet the highest number!). These figures represented a decrease of 1,021 HC, or a phenomenal 16% decline (0.159) over five years, roughly 200 students per year or one quarter the number per year as in the US with a population of nine times the size, and a decrease of 428 FTE, or an almost as drastic 13% decline (0.133) over five years, roughly 100 FTE per year or again one quarter of the decline in the US. As a result, the average seminary in Canada was now at 137 HC (down from 177 HC in 2006) and 71 FTE (down from 89 FTE in 2006). With the increase in the Canadian population, this meant that there was one person out of 6,404 Canadians in theological education and one seminary for every 880,000 Canadians. In other words, there was a precipitous decline in the seminary student numbers in Canada during this five-year period and an even smaller number of Canadians on average to support them.

The period from 2006 to 2011 marked a serious decline in seminary students in both the US and Canada, but with Canada's losses proportionately larger than those in the US. Although I had predicted a decline in Canadian seminary education to 5,000 HC, the decline had not been as fast as I predicted, even though we had the major economic recession of 2008–2009, which seriously affected institutions continent wide. Nevertheless, if the decline were to have continued over the next five-year period, we would have declined below 5,000 students in only two years.

8. The ratio of HC to FTE is 1.53 students per full course load.

THE PRESENT: 2017

I perhaps should have written this paper in 2017 using the ATS figures for 2016 in order to provide data for another five-year period. I will incidentally describe the results in 2016 as I describe the results throughout the six-year period, but I wish to concentrate upon 2017, the latest available year for ATS statistical student data for theological education in North America.

Before I get to 2017, however, I wish to review the overall trends within the last six years. The total student population for seminaries within ATS, and hence North America generally, continued to decline from 2011, reaching its nadir in 2014, with 71,790 HC. This indicates a decline from the highpoint in 2004, ten years earlier, of roughly a little over 10% decline (0.105) over a decade. The average seminary size in ATS in 2014 was 265 HC. The low point in seminary enrolment throughout ATS in relation to FTE, however, was not reached until 2015, the next year, when the number declined to 44,519 FTE. This represents a decline from the highpoint in 2004, eleven years earlier, of 6,952 FTE or nearly 14% (0.135). I note that the FTE was declining at a faster rate than the overall student headcount. The average size of an ATS seminary in 2014 was 164 FTE (with 271 institutions).

By comparison, for the US, the low point in seminary student enrolment was also reached in 2014, with a student enrolment of 66,690 HC, a decline from the highpoint in 2006, a span of only eight years, of 6,914 HC or roughly 9% (0.093). The situation was arguably as bad if not worse for FTE. The low point in US seminary FTE was in 2015, with the number falling to 41,816 FTE, a decline from the highpoint in 2004 of 6,058 FTE or roughly 13% (0.126). However, one must also note that the number of US seminaries increased during this time from 215 in 2006 and 219 in 2011 to 231 in 2014 and 230 in 2015, an increase of eleven or twelve seminaries over three or four years. This means that the average US seminary had fallen in size in 2014 to 289 HC and in 2015 to 182 FTE, serious declines even from 2011 (314 HC/204 FTE), to say nothing of their high point in 2004 (344 HC/225 FTE).

For Canada, the low point in seminary student enrolment was reached in the same year, 2014, as for the ATS aggregate and for the US. The total enrolment in Canadian seminary institutions reached its nadir of 5,100 HC in 2014. The low point did not reach 5,000 as the numerical trend had once indicated, and it took a further three years to reach its low point than anticipated, but Canadian seminaries nevertheless reached their HC low point in 2014, a period of ten years after their high in 2004, a decline of 1,936 HC or roughly 28% (0.275) over ten years. The low point in FTE also occurred in 2014 for Canadian seminaries, when the FTE fell to 2,683 FTE, a decline from its highpoint in 2003 of 971 FTE or roughly 26% (0.265). In other words, over the course of about ten years, Canadian theological seminaries lost well over one quarter of their total student headcount and over one quarter of their FTE, while also during that time gaining four more seminaries. As a result, in 2014, the average seminary size in Canada had become the relatively minuscule size of 128 HC and 67 FTE (down from their high of 195 HC and 100 FTE).

I am happy to be able to say, however, that those were the low points in enrolment figures in ATS institutions in North America. Since that time, there has been some recovery to report, although not all of it is probably the kind of growth to be welcomed. In 2017, the total number of ATS institutions—remember that this is in an overall period of general decline in student numbers—has now reached 270, although this is not the all-time high number of institutions. In fact, the number of ATS institutions from 2011 to 2017 has generally grown, from 258 in 2011 to 269 in 2012, 266 in 2013, 271 in 2014, 269 in 2015, 273 in 2016 (the highest), and 270 in 2017. In other words, even if 273 was the highest number of institutions, we have now reached 270 as a consistent number of roughly the average number of total seminaries over the last four years. The total headcount for all ATS institutions, since the low point in 2014, has progressively crept up, moving from 71,790 HC in 2014 to 72,080 in 2015, 72,383 in 2016, and 73,175 HC in 2017. This marks an increase of 1,385 headcount over the three-year period or roughly an increase of just short of 2% (0.019)—not per year but over the three years. This is an increase of roughly 450 HC per year on average, or the depressingly small average of only 5 HC per institution over this entire period. Whereas the average size ATS institution in 2014 was 265 HC, in 2017 the average size is now 271 HC. At this rate of growth, it will take roughly fifteen more years of such growth for ATS institutions to regain the headcount they had in 2004. The FTE since the low point in 2015, a year later, has progressively crept up as well, moving from 44,519 FTE in 2015 to 45,836 in 2016 and 46,049 FTE in 2017. This marks an increase of 1,530 FTE over the two-year period or roughly an increase of 3% (0.034). This is an increase of roughly 765 FTE per year or the better, but not overwhelmingly encouraging, average of only 6 FTE per seminary over the two years. At this rate of growth, it will take roughly nine more years of such growth for ATS institutions to regain the FTE they had in 2004. Whereas the average size ATS institution continent-wide in 2015 was 164 FTE, in 2017 the average size is now 170 FTE. In 2014, the number of students per FTE was 1.60, in 2015 it increased to 1.62, and now in 2017 it has declined to 1.59. Thus, there are some signs of recovery within the overall ATS enrolment structure. However, the population in the United States and Canada has grown during this time to a total of 362,427,000 total population. This means that only one in every 4,952 people is enrolled in seminary, and there is one seminary for every 1,342,322 people throughout North America.

These figures merit further refinement in relation to both the US and Canada. I will need to use the figures from 2014 and 2015 for the US just as I did for ATS as a whole, as these were the low years. In the US over this time period, the number of seminaries has remained relatively stable, with 231 in 2014, 230 in 2015, 234 in 2016, and 231 in 2017. The enrolment has also gradually increased from 66,690 HC in 2014, 66,867 in 2015, 67,120 in 2016, and 67,907 HC in 2017. This indicates an overall increase of only 1,217 HC over the three-year period or roughly just under 2% (0.018) growth over that period in the US. This rate of growth would require thirteen or fourteen years of similar growth for US institutions to reach their highpoint in headcount again. The FTE has also gradually increased from 41,816 FTE in 2015 to 43,069 in 2016 to 43,262 FTE in 2017. This indicates an overall increase of 1,446 FTE over only a two-year period or roughly a little over 3% (0.034) growth over that period. This rate of growth would require only six years of similar growth to reach the highpoint in FTE. However, we must also note that the US population continues to grow, so that in 2017 there is roughly only one person in 4,796 in seminary in the US, much less than in 2011 and much, much less than in 2006, and there is one seminary for every 1,410,038 people in the US.

The Canadian figures tell a similar story in most respects, except regarding the increase in numbers of seminaries. There were 39 seminaries in 2011, 40 at the depth of enrolment in 2014, and in the three years since 39 each year. The enrolment figures for Canadian institutions has increased from the low point of 5,100 HC in 2014 to 5,213 in 2015, 5,263 in 2016, to 5,268 HC in 2017. This represents an increase over the three-year period of 168 HC or roughly better than 3% (0.032) growth—interestingly a higher percentage increase than in the US although the numbers are relatively small (an increase of only 5 HC from 2016 to 2017). At this rate of increase, it would take Canadian institutions over thirty years to return to the en-rolment of 2004, a mere thirteen years ago. The FTE figures for Canadian institutions has increased from the low point of 2,683 FTE in 2014 to 2,703 in 2015, 2,768 in 2016, to 2,787 FTE in 2017. This represents an increase over the three-year period of 104 FTE or just short of 4% (0.038) growth—again interestingly a higher percentage increase than in the US although the numbers are very small. At this rate of increase, however, it would take Canadian institutions about twenty-five years to return to the FTE of 2003, a mere fourteen years ago. At this point, the average Canadian theological seminary has 135 HC and 71 FTE. This means that there is roughly one Canadian in 6,968 who is in seminary (down from 5,103 in 2004), and there is one seminary for every 941,230 people (down from 887,000).

We see a slight upturn over the last three or four years in seminary en-rolment throughout the continent and in both the US and Canada. In fact, we see a slightly greater percentage-wise increase in Canadian enrolment, both headcount and especially FTE, over US institutions over this last three or four years. Despite these increases, because of the severe declines in enrolment, again both headcount and FTE, in Canadian institutions from 2006 to 2014, the future is not bright. For the average Canadian institution to regain its average size would require from twenty-five to thirty or more years, depending upon whether we are examining HC or FTE. With the average Canadian theological seminary now at 135 HC and 71 FTE, one must wonder aloud about the future of seminary education in Canada.

I realize that these average figures for Canadian theological institu-tions do not reveal all of the story. Or, to be more accurate, they may reveal the entire story, but they do not reveal the particulars of the story. In par-ticular, what they do not represent is how evangelical, and more particu-larly CHEC, institutions have done in relation to other institutions. As a result, I have mined into these figures in more detail, although admittedly it is difficult in some instances to determine the theological stance of an institution. There is also the problem that some of the figures posted on the ATS website provided by the institutions simply do not make sense or cannot be correct. For example, one institution reports that it has one full time faculty member and twelve part-time faculty members and a total of thirteen full-time faculty members. The math simply does not work (and I wonder why ATS does not query such examples). Of more concern is the fact that two of the accredited institutions listed report 0 students either HC or FTE, although both of these appear to be holding institutions for other constituent institutions apparently reporting their own numbers. This does not appear to be the case for one institution that reports only 7 HC and 1 FTE. There are three institutions within the 39 accredited ATS institutions in Canada with fewer than 10 FTE and five institutions within the same group with fewer than 20 HC. One begins to wonder what constitutes a viable seminary within the ATS framework.

Using the 2017 statistics, I hesitatingly identify 17 of the 39 ATS institutions in Canada as evangelical, or 44% of the total institutions. These institutions range in size from the largest in Canada with 822 HC to the smallest in Canada with 7 HC. These 17 institutions are responsible for 3,099 HC of the 5,268 HC within Canada or 59% of the total headcount of students. These institutions also range in size from the largest in Canada with 410 FTE to the smallest with 1 FTE. These 17 institutions are responsible for 1,596 FTE of the 2,787 FTE within Canada or 57% of the total FTE of students. The average size of an evangelical seminary in Canada is 182 HC and 94 FTE. These figures are reasonable within the larger ATS framework, although this represents a decline from 2006 with 254 HC for the average evangelical seminary in Canada representing 56% of the total student headcount, and in 2011 a 212 HC and 53% of the total HC and 107 FTE and 51% of the total FTE. Much more distressing are the figures for the non-evangelical institutions, which range from the largest of its type with 310 HC to the smallest with two being around 8 FTE. These 22 non-evangelical institutions are responsible for 2,169 HC, or 41% of the total headcount, and 1,191 FTE, or 43% of the total FTE. However, the average size of a non-evangelical seminary in Canada in 2017 is only 98 HC and 54 FTE, a fall from an average in 2006 of 134 HC, and in 2011 a 103 HC and 56 FTE.

These figures indicate that the evangelical institutions are, within a shrinking sector, holding their own against the non-evangelical institutions, even if all of them are generally decreasing from where they were five and ten years ago. The non-evangelical institutions are getting perilously low, to the point where one must examine whether they have sufficient numbers to provide viable theological education. Are we in an educational crisis? If we understand crisis in the sense of immediate peril, we perhaps are not in such a situation. However, if we think of a crisis as longer-term peril, then we are facing such a crisis. The non-evangelical theological institutions in Canada are in the most immediate danger, with numbers that in many cases call into question their ability to continue as educational institutions with sufficient critical mass to create an adequate educational environment. The evangelical theological institutions are overall showing a slow decline, even if the last two or three years have shown an incremental increase. Even if the raw numbers are greater, the larger context within Canada shows continued erosion of the position of evangelical theological education in relation to the general population.

There are many possible explanations of this decline, many of which have been chronicled elsewhere. These include Canadian secularization, reconfiguration of the local church, devaluation of education throughout North America including Canada with replacement by a training-for-jobs mentality, increasing costs of especially undergraduate education that have affected student debt levels and students' desire for further education, perceived unnecessary length and minimal value of seminary degrees especially when compared with the perceived status and financial remuneration of ministry positions within the wider culture, and the perceived prestige and financial reward of almost any other form of employment. I would love to address each of these at more length, but they take me beyond the scope of this paper. I wish to focus on matters closer to the topic at hand. If Canadian seminary education is to survive, much less thrive, seminaries need to find alternatives to convince denominations, individual churches, and potential students of the value of seminary education—to say nothing of the surrounding culture (I will leave that to the die-hard Calvinists to worry about).

THE FUTURE

I turn now to the future of seminary education, in particular the future of theological education in Canada. In previous papers, I addressed a number of issues, besides enrolment figures, such items as curriculum, culture, and finances. I wish to identify four areas here for further consideration.

The Association of Theological Schools Needs to Embrace Canadian Theological Education

In looking to the future, my first observation is that the Association of Theological Schools in the United States and Canada needs to embrace the *second* part of its titular mandate and more fully recognize Canadian institutions. ATS has not, to my knowledge, sufficiently identified the seriousness of the situation in Canadian theological education. As a rough example, I do not know and have not seen any kind of analysis of the enrolment figures in Canadian institutions other than the ones that I have done (or those who have used mine). This is surprising, since the first such analysis appeared in 2009 and the second in 2012. In fact, if one goes to the ATS website and examines the list of member institutions, it is not possible, so far as I can determine, to identify and isolate the Canadian institutions (or the US institutions for that matter) so that one can identify a complete list for aggregating statistics or other purposes. The closest one comes to this capability is a geographical search mechanism that allows one to identify institutions within a certain distance (identified in miles, of course) from one's own institution. That is of minimal help in identifying all of the Canadian theological institutions, as a search of all institutions within three thousand kilometers of Hamilton, Ontario (in order to include British Columbia) encompasses much of the US as well, and even a minimal search to include Ontario also finds Michigan and New York within its scope (in fact, the system does not even work this well, as my first search used an island in the Pacific, apparently called Ontario, as its center point).

All of this is to say that ATS has been notoriously inattentive to Canadian institutions. We Canadian presidents repeatedly hear rumors that ATS is going to pay more attention to us—and there are occasional lunches and fora that occur—but the fact that ATS has not made the Canadian situation more visible is an item of concern. My concerns are in several areas. First, ATS has not shown awareness of the striking decrease in enrolment of Canadian ATS seminaries over the last ten or so years, especially during the period from 2006 to 2011. Second, ATS has not shown awareness of the overall cultural situation in which there is proportionately a greater number of Canadian theological seminaries than in the US. The 39 Canadian seminaries compared to the 231 US seminaries represents a ratio of 1:6, whereas the population ratio between the two countries is 1:9. In other words, if we use the US as a guide, Canada has thirty percent more institutions than it should proportionate to population. If we use Canada as a guide, the US should have fifty percent more institutions than they do for proportionality. In either case, Canada is disproportionately represented within ATS on the basis of the number of institutions. If ATS is an institutionally-based organization, then I would say that Canada is underrepresented within the influence it has had on ATS as an institution, because it is implicitly outvoted by US concerns. However, if we examine the student numbers, Canada has a ratio of 1:13 rather than one of 1:9, indicating that it is underrepresented in terms of student headcount. Canada should have roughly forty percent more students to keep its proportion with the US, or the US 20,000 fewer student headcount to establish parity with Canada. This is all to say that there are some significant disparities, just examining basic institutional numbers, between Canadian and US institutions that, so far as I know, are not regularly taken into account by ATS—whether this is in relationship to analysis, notification, or, and perhaps especially, remedy of the situation.

As the accrediting agency for the vast majority of theological seminaries in North America, ATS needs to take seriously its mandate as the association of theological schools of both the US and Canada, which would entail paying particular attention to the unique characteristics of Canadian institutions—disproportionately over-represented in institutions but under-represented in students—and all that these disproportions entail. This would seem to include, at the least (and there may well be more that can and should be done), analyzing the enrolment trends in more detail to be sure we are constantly apprised of the situation; analyzing these trends in relationship to the larger cultural, ecclesial, and social trends in Canada, which are significantly different from the US in many ways; and suggesting various possible and creative ways forward that allow Canadian ATS seminaries to explore alternatives that may not be appropriate or necessary or desired within the US but that would address the Canadian situation or situations of a diverse body of institutions extending across a large continent from east to west. Nothing less than this reflects a failure of ATS to take seriously its mandate to serve theological education in North America.

Educational Developments

A direct correlative of the first point is that we need to think about educational developments that address Canadian problems with Canadian solutions. There will of course be overlap with problems and solutions within the US as well, but the situation just described merits proposals regarding curriculum, degree programs, and their attendant support structures that address the disproportionate trends within Canadian theological education.

ATS launched a program in 2015 called Educational Models and Practices in Theological Education, sponsored by the Lilly Endowment.[9] This program has several facets to it, including various fora for discussion of models currently in use and potentially to be implemented in theological

9. For a summary of the project and early areas of investigation, see Graham, "ATS Educational Models."

education, the opportunity to propose and receive funding for a variety of types of programs that might have potential for ATS institutions (I hesitate to use the term 'graduate theological education' as some of the ideas being discussed may not merit the term 'graduate'), incremental reporting on advances made by various strands of the program, and culminative events to review and assess the models and practices proposed by various institutions. There have been a number of programs proposed by various institutions. In the interests of full disclosure, I note that McMaster Divinity College received a significant grant to help us develop and implement our recently launched Doctor of Practical Theology program. This is not a PhD or a DMin program. We launched this program—based upon models that have already been implemented in the United Kingdom and Australia—as an alternative to these already established doctoral programs. The educational template is driven by what we call 'practice-led research,' so that students engage in theoretical research, although not to the same degree and not in such a highly theoretical way as in the PhD, and in practice-led thinking, so as to avoid the major problem with many, if not most, DMin programs of their not having any kind of a unified conceptual core. We appreciated the support from the Educational Models initiative that allowed us to undertake a number of activities, including bringing in experts from the UK who were leaders in various dimensions of practice-led research. As a result, all of our faculty—who have PhDs and so know something about how to teach and supervise in research degrees—were given guidance in how to implement this new program. We have been very pleased with the response. We are now in our third year of the program and have 35 students enrolled. We have expanded the originally residential program to it being delivered in a hybrid model so that students can undertake the program from all over Canada and beyond, with their only residential requirement being their coming to Hamilton for one week each semester.

I relate this to show that such an Educational Models initiative has the potential for being a significant innovative factor in theological education in the US and Canada. The several factors that distinguish our DPT program are its uniqueness within English-language North American theological education (the only other institution that offers such a degree does so in French), its attempt to reconceive advanced theological education by introducing a new degree rather than simply trying to tweak an old one, its having a clearly defined and recognizable theoretical orientation upon which to center all of the activities of the program whether in courses or in the research dissertation phase, and, after the first year as we learned more about our constituency, its innovative use of the hybrid format to encourage new ways of achieving its educational aims and objectives. When we designed and launched this program, we undoubtedly had one eye upon the traditional degrees of theological education, especially the MDiv, the MTS, and the DMin, but we strongly believed then, and probably more strongly believe now, that we did not want simply to reinvent these existing degrees—by changing (and lowering) unit requirements, shifting courses around, simply eliminating unwanted courses such as languages, or moving without reflection into various types of mediated learning. Rather, we wanted to fashion something new that fulfilled traditional educational goals in ways that were better able to meet the expectations and demands of theological education and the needs of our students. We believe that we have found such a degree.

I wish I had confidence that others involved in the Educational Models initiative, and by extension ATS, were fulfilling similar goals. However, I do not. The results, so far as I know, have not yet been widely published, but my impression from conversations and presentations at ATS events and reading materials distributed by ATS is that many, if not most (although far from all), of the proposals have revolved around attempts to revitalize old degrees, especially the MDiv degree (and DMin). ATS as an organization has made it clear that the MDiv is dropping in popularity continent wide, and this appears to be the case to an even larger degree in Canada. There have already been many attempts to revitalize the MDiv. These include: the transformation in name but also in curriculum (arguably less stringent in some cases!) of the old BD to the MDiv in the 1970s, the various attempts to diversify the MDiv so that it in effect has become a collection of diverse three-year degrees with the result being divergent degrees often with little in common with each other, various changes in delivery models so that today one can do an entirely online MDiv, and of course the severe decrease in unit requirements to as low as 72, possibly among others. There may have been some local recoveries effected by such alterations but the decrease in salability seems to have continued. I am not arguing against continuing to examine and appropriately modify the MDiv degree. However, I think that we—and ATS along with us—must make two major shifts in perspective. The first is to stop seeing the MDiv degree as *the* degree of seminary education, with the attendant placement of it at the heart of discussions, calculation of statistics, and curricular standards. This simply is not appropriate any longer in an environment where two-year master's degrees are as significant and important in the theological curriculum as three-year master's degrees (i.e., the MDiv, with all of their diversity). The second, and arguably the more important of the two, is to innovate in the area of new degrees, not devoting much or most of our efforts to attempting to revive a dying degree. There will always be some who want and are able to do the three-year master's degree. However, there are numerous temporal, economic, cultural (such as matters of respect), and even ecclesial and theological reasons for demoting the MDiv to one degree among many, rather than being first among others. More important, however, is to develop new degrees to meet the requirements of contemporary theological education. I have seen very few such proposals coming forward, even with the encouragement of the Educational Models project. Some of the ideas that I have in mind are not only observing what is happening in other professions—something we did in developing the DPT degree—but observing what is happening in other academic subjects entirely, development of and endorsement of one-year master's degrees especially for those with previous education in the field, consideration of the role of undergraduate theological education within the seminary milieu, development of a variety of curricular configurations that address varying requirements in regard to the core theological curriculum and areas of specialization, development of new nomenclature to recognize and give status to innovations of merit that move outside and beyond the current strictures, and exploration of alternative means of mediation of theological education rather than simply thinking binarily in terms of traditional residential and distant online—among possibly many others.

The future may be dim for theological education, but with exploratory thinking that draws upon and freely innovates in light of the experience of others, I believe that we can develop new programs of study that will meet both the needs of the contemporary and future church and the needs of contemporary students.

Consolidation and Amalgamation

The statistics that I examined above point to the fact that, at least in Canada and possibly elsewhere in the US, there simply are too many seminaries for the students and resources available. To be proportionate with the US with regard to seminaries in relation to overall population (admittedly only one possible indicator, and perhaps not the best in light of smaller enrolment), Canada should have 30 rather than 39 seminaries.

Thirty seminaries seems like a reasonable number from a statistical standpoint but it raises questions regarding how to achieve such a viable number. If the non-evangelical seminaries continue their death spiral— even with denominational support—there is a chance that these denominations, either because of their own financial problems or because of the application of common sense in realizing the incredible waste of money involved, will choose either to close down some of their institutions or to amalgamate them with other similar seminaries. In a sense, the Toronto School of Theology institutions represent an amalgamation, although they probably have not fully realized necessary economies of scale regarding either faculty or administrative costs. Most of the TST institutions, even if they have smaller than ideal faculties for their size, retain a minimal faculty complement designed to cover the basic areas of theological education. Not only has TST lost out on economies of scale, but they have compounded the difficulty by having zero headcount or FTE, but 1 FTE faculty member, presumably the director. This is clearly not the way to proceed with amalgamation.

When one looks around the expanse we call Canada, one recognizes part of the difficulty. The difficulty is that the territory is so vast that it appears to require institutions all across the country in order to provide at least adequate centers of education throughout. Thus, the distribution of seminaries across Canada is not equal. We have only a few seminaries in the Maritime provinces, along with a disparate number of relatively smaller towns with their own seminaries across the rest of the country.. Nevertheless, there is more than one seminary in a number of major centers throughout Canada. These include the lower mainland of British Columbia, Edmonton, Saskatoon, Montreal, and southern Ontario. No doubt there are the kinds of economies of scale that I was mentioning possible in a number of these places.

I wish, however, to deal with two particular situations, both involving evangelical institutions, as a way of challenging theological education in Canada to address its situation. The first example is the lower mainland in BC. There are at least four evangelical theological seminaries in this area, including ACTS Seminaries at Trinity Western University, Northwest Baptist Seminary, Carey Theological College, and Regent College. Without going into details, several of these institutions have had recent enrolment challenges, and no doubt with it financial stresses. This is not surprising in light of the fact that two of the institutions, Carey and Regent, are located squarely in the middle of some of the most expensive real estate and surrounded by a city with one of the highest costs of living not just in Canada, but in the world. To be honest, I find it hard to fathom how anyone wishing to be a steward of the resources of their own institution, to say nothing of their students, could continue to locate an institution in such an environment. This does not need to be the case. It would seem obvious that the best solution would be for Carey and Regent to join with Northwest and ACTS as a single institution, with a location already purpose built on the campus of TWU, situated in an admittedly still expensive area, but one that is significantly cheaper than downtown Vancouver, where both faculty and students struggle to find affordable housing and some faculty have even been reported to sleep on their office floors as they commute from hours away. The result of such amalgamation would be not only a relocation for some of the institutions into an environment with much lower cost of living for both faculty and staff, but many possibilities of economy of scale with a new theological entity with the potential of 863 HC and 454 FTE. In other words, this seminary could become the largest seminary, in both headcount and FTE, in all of Canada, while saving money and making itself more affordable in the meantime. There is even greater potential to be gained when one realizes the opportunity of this new institution being a part of TWU, and perhaps even bringing a number of Bible colleges in the lower mainland into the university as well.

The second obvious example is in southern Ontario. Disregarding the several non-evangelical institutions—most of them relatively small—the evangelical institutions alone provide a major opportunity for productive amalgamation. The institutions involved include Tyndale Seminary, Wycliffe College, McMaster Divinity College, Heritage Theological Seminary, and possibly even Canadian Reformed Seminary. For the sake of discussion, however, I think that it is also worth considering whether we should bring a number of Bible colleges and universities into this picture, in particular Tyndale University College, Heritage College, Redeemer University College, and Emmanuel Bible College. The potential here is significant. Amalgamating the seminaries alone would result in an institution with the potential size of 1,400 HC and 750 FTE. This would be the largest seminary in Canada by a significant margin. However, while I am dreaming—some might say hallucinating—if we were to include the colleges and universities, we would have the potential of over 2,600 HC and somewhere around 1,700 FTE. Not only this, but such an institution would have the potential to grant degrees from undergraduate to PhD in certain subjects and could well form the critical mass for a Christian university in central Canada only rivaled by TWU in the west. If such an idea were to be pursued, one would need a location. Because of financial constraints of some of the institutions involved, as well as the high cost of living in Toronto for both faculty and students, of the current sites, probably the campus of Redeemer University College would be the best suited to this new institution. If the other properties were sold, their debts paid, and their endowments and other funds amalgamated, such an institution might be able to begin life debt free with invested assets of around 75 million dollars or more.

So what prevents such scenarios from unfolding? I have informally polled several of my colleagues and the major reasons seem to be four: human ego, the curse of the fall; denominations, the curse of the Reformations; the magnification of particular issues, the curse of a dysfunctional Christian church; and self-serving interests, the curse of being human. Ego, the curse of the fall, is probably the biggest barrier to amalgamation and cooperation, especially over who will end up at the top of the heap when the amalgamation is concluded. I have it on good authority that this is also the leading factor in discouraging business amalgamations as well. We are perhaps not too surprised to hear that the business sector has a number of large egos in it, but such egos can be found in seminary education as well. Such egos that demand being the center of what happens no doubt threaten the future of their own seminaries and other educational institutions. Denominationalism is probably the next most important factor in squelching amalgamation. The Reformations, magisterial and otherwise, were necessary in the life of the church, but the curse of continuing division over relatively insignificant—though no doubt seemingly vital—issues continues to haunt us. Denominations also, at least in the past, used to invest heavily in their theological institutions, and the thought of losing absolute control over them as they form partnerships with those from whom they have separated threatens the ability to attempt to overcome such differences and join together in common cause. The magnification of particular issues, whether they are one's view of baptism or of women in ministry or of what it means to be Reformed or Baptist, runs the risk of making it impossible for institutions that otherwise find common cause in a rough alliance called evangelicalism, or even a more particular group called CHEC, to think on a larger or grander scale for the common good of Christendom. Such issues seem to loom ever larger the closer one gets to the possibility of cooperation. Finally, self-serving interests argue against any sort of amalgamation. Institutions with high self-perceptions think it unbecoming of themselves to join with lesser institutions, or institutions of a particular type think it compromising to join with already compromised institutions, and the points of possible avoidance continue.

I realize that there are many reasons, some of them possibly even legitimate, why these institutions may not wish to join together. On the basis of the statistics regarding seminaries, but supported at least anecdotally by information regarding both Bible colleges and university colleges, I think that we need to pay attention to the statement by Benjamin Franklin, "We must, indeed, all hang together, or most assuredly we shall all hang separately."

Recommendation and Support of Others

The final issue is recommendation and support of others, and I need not write on this at length, except to say that I think that we need to ensure that all of the CHEC institutions are aware of the other CHEC institutions and to make every effort to support such institutions where possible.

I am reminded of the time I was consulting with the board of one of our CHEC educational institutions, a board of some size (around 30 members), and I asked how many of the board members had sent their own children to the institution. Only one or two had done so. If we are not willing to recommend our own institutions and send our own children to them, how can we expect others to support the work of Christian higher education in Canada?

Here is what I mean by recommendation and support. I find it unconscionable that any Christian parents with Christian children would think of sending them to anything other than Christian institutions of post-secondary education, whether that means Bible colleges or universities, or both. The reasons that I often hear for not doing so are what I would consider flimsy or tendentious at best. These reasons include such things as cost, perceived prestige, or, the worst reason of all, the possibility of employment after graduation. Parents and students who look at postsecondary education simply as a means of employment already reveal that they view education as pragmatic and instrumental training rather than as genuine education. Gilbert Ryle in his famous essay on the distinction between teaching and training well shows that even our so-called educational institutions run the risk of becoming training colleges.[10] Such institutions emphasize competency-based training, practical instruction, and employability in jobs, without regard for creating educated graduates who are able to adjust to the inevitable changes in society that demand flexible and creative thinking moving into the future. This will happen if we do not pay close attention to our task. I have no doubt in saying that our best CHEC institutions provide better educational opportunities and environments than do provincial universities, with students learning in classes of manageable size rather than in courses with a thousand students taught by graduate assistants. There is no doubt a greater financial commitment to attending CHEC institutions, but making such lifelong and life-changing decisions on the basis of money alone indicates the distorted priorities of our culture, in which there is plenty of money for many things other than education (such as pets, where the US population alone reportedly spends nearly US$ 70 billion per year).

I fear, however, that we do not share this ethos of recommending each other's institutions. My outside perspective is that Bible colleges sometimes discourage Christian university education as perhaps too intellectually risky, while discouraging seminary education because it is seen to be unnecessary or aloof. Christian universities tend to look down on Bible colleges, even as they reduce their own theological curriculum to a bare minimum and are more concerned about placing their graduates in law school and medical school rather than encouraging them to go into various forms of pastoral or academic ministry. And seminaries, again in part because of the past traditions of our own accrediting agency, have discouraged previous theological study, rather than recognizing that the kind of shared Christian cultural tradition that we depended upon as a formative base for further education has seriously eroded. I believe that we who are teaching at seminaries should make every effort to encourage students to study at Bible colleges and Christian universities before coming to seminary, so that their biblical and theological knowledge is secure and can be built upon in their seminary education. Bible colleges and Christian universities should be recommending our CHEC seminaries as the next step in seminary and graduate level education for those who are interested in continuing their educations in various areas of Christian knowledge.

10. Ryle, "Teaching and Training."

In other words, there is much more that we can do for each other, rather than simply looking to our own institutions and building up their success records by placement of students in various secular institutions, as if that and that alone were the standard by which we gauge Christian educational success.

CONCLUSION

I have ranged beyond the simple task of examining seminary education within Canada by placing such discussion within the wider field of theological education within North America. By doing so, I have been able to identify the particular and even perilous situation of seminary education in Canada. I am the first to admit that we are faced with a context that, to a large extent, is beyond our ability to affect significantly or directly, as it involves much larger cultural shifts and transformations, some of them happening at speeds that we could not have anticipated. However, there are a number of factors that are closer to home in which we do have a role to play. I have suggested that there are four considerations that we should address that might help us to effect positive change in seminary education in Canada, and these four considerations are close at hand and should be enthusiastically grasped by all of us.

BIBLIOGRAPHY

Graham, Stephen R. "The ATS Educational Models and Practices Project: Wide-ranging Research to Address Challenges and Embrace Opportunities for Theological Schools in North America." *Theological Education* 50 (2017) 47–77.

Porter, Stanley E. "Canadian Theological Education in the Twenty-First Century—An Update and Evaluation." *McMaster Journal of Theology and Ministry* 14 (2012–2013) 17–41.

———. "Theological Education in the Twenty-First Century." *Toronto Journal of Theology Supplement* 1 (2009) 41–54.

Ryle, Gilbert. "Teaching and Training." In *The Concept of Education*, edited by R. S. Peters, 105–19. London: Routledge & Kegan Paul, 1967.

Part 3

Looking Ahead: Issues and Opportunities

8

Welcoming the Guest

Approach, Design, Procedure
for Hospitable Learning Communities

ELFRIEDA LEPP-KAETHLER AND CATHERINE RUST-AKINBOLAJI

INTRODUCTION

BEGINNING WITH A THEOLOGY of hospitality, this chapter invites faculty and administration to create hospitable learning climates in higher education. Two language teacher educators explore the idea of learning communities within the frame of "welcoming spaces." Hospitality is a central theme in a biblical worldview and in Christian tradition where the relationship between God and humans is frequently presented as a host-guest bond.[1] The Scriptures also call humans to extend God's hospitality towards others. The New Testament begins with stories of Jesus as guest and refugee. Hosting is a recurring theme in Jesus' stories, which revolve around eating, drinking, parties, banquets, and feasts. Since the first centuries, welcoming strangers has been essential to the Christian tradition. Central to the idea of hospitality is Nouwen's notion of converting *hostis* to *hospes*.[2] Hospitality has a sense of "niceness" about it, but feelings towards strangers are at best ambivalent. News headlines are relentless in

1. Janzen, "Biblical Theology of Hospitality," 4.
2. Nouwen, *Reaching Out*, 66.

their display of many forms of hostility rampant in our society. Stories of mass shootings and terror attacks infuse anxiety into daily life and make it easy to rationalize resistance to welcoming strangers into "our" world. Anti-immigration sentiments stoke fears of those who are different, playing into suspicions of people with unfamiliar clothing, religious symbols, and who do not possess "shared Canadian values." Pervasive societal ambiguity towards "strangers" amongst increasingly multicultural student bodies threatens to escalate hostility. This chapter suggests ways of seeing that invite administration, faculty, and students into carefully structured learning relationships. The hospitality metaphor extends to campus and classroom communities that include nurture, warmth, and vulnerability, along with the risks that come with hosting prophets, strangers, and other angels.

APPROACH DESIGN PROCEDURE FRAMEWORK

Learning communities are shaped by the approach, design, and procedure of the educators and administrators responsible for the curriculum and learning environment. In the field of adult language teaching, a commonly held view is that the method of teaching can only be fully understood through an exploration of the approach, design, and procedure of the program or course.[3] This analysis of the learning context may also be applied to the wider sphere of adult education, including Christian higher education.

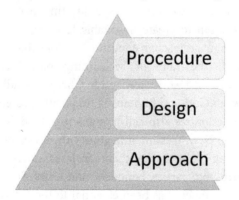

The instructor's approach to content, language, and theology forms the foundation; the design of the course objectives and outcomes, the syllabus, the learning tasks and teaching activities builds on that foundation;

3. Richards and Rodgers, *Approaches and Methods*, 18–32.

and the everyday class procedures are carried out from that design. All three must be understood to fully grasp how teaching and learning occur in a specific learning community. The Christian higher education professional is first and foremost a Christ-follower. Biblical and Christian tradition can be considered the primary approach taken to all aspects of life, including that of the classroom. The course design and procedure will flow out of that Christian worldview; choices made regarding the role of the instructor, the role of the learners, and daily classroom practices and behaviors will all be informed by biblical and Christian principles.

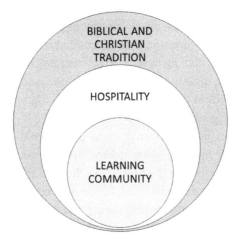

HOSPITALITY

Before we explore the merits of hospitality as a metaphor for our work in Christian higher education, we need to situate our conversation in the context of the world around us. Currently, our world seems to be predominantly marked by exclusion and hostility, specifically hostility towards those outside of our identified tribe. Whether that tribe be familial, ethnic, political, religious, or ideological, protecting the sanctity of the tribe and defending the tribe against outsiders seem to be amongst the most prioritized goals of the world's citizens. Consider the intense and antagonistic oppositional lines drawn by Black Lives Matter and Blue Lives Matter, the Israeli–Palestinian conflict, Indigenous Environmental Network versus Keystone XL, and Pro-life versus Pro-choice, to name but a few. The success of one tribe seems to be possible only through the domination or tearing down of the other.

Yet for many outliers and newcomers, it is the pursuit of a tribe to which they can belong that becomes the ultimate goal. The tribe seems to be the only safe harbor from hostility. Henri Nouwen's description of life as he observes it resonates: "In our world full of strangers, estranged from their own past, culture, and country, from their neighbors, friends, and family, from their deepest self and their God, we witness a painful search for a hospitable place where life can be lived without fear and where community can be found."[4]

On the one hand, we think of higher education as an exciting time for young adults—a time of growth and learning, friendships, and community building. But there is a darker side of this time of life where students experience disorientation, loneliness, and isolation. Christian Smith describes the social and psychological challenges faced by emerging adults in the current context of increasing mass media, consumer culture, and rapid technological change. He describes the moral individualism, relativism, and egotism that launch emerging adults into a moral drift.[5]

At first glance, hospitality may seem like an odd response to this widespread cultural malaise. What does afternoon tea, cake, and polite conversation have to do with the hostility in the world? Andrew Shepherd points to the need for a profound shift in our understanding of hospitality as a cultural concept. He argues that the term "hospitality" suffers from a serious distortion inflicted by ideologies of our time: "To engage in this historical and lifegiving practice faithfully therefore requires a theological rehabilitation of the concept of 'hospitality.'"[6]

Practicing hospitality is a counter-cultural stance that refuses to join the forces of indifference, exploitation, or violence. A hospitable posture does not see others in categories of people who are like us and those who are different than us, who are to be feared, avoided, or ignored. Hospitality cuts through the "us–them" dichotomy that is pervasive in a world filled with territorial turf wars and barbed-wire borders.

Practicing hospitality and creating a welcoming space for learners should be an integral part of the faith-based learning community. As American educator Parker Palmer states,

> Hospitality is a central virtue of the desert teachers and of the monasteries they founded. It is a virtue central to the biblical

4. Nouwen, *Reaching Out*, 65.

5. Smith, *Lost in Transition*, 65.

6. Shepherd, *The Gift of the Other*, ii.

tradition itself, where God is always using the stranger to introduce us to the strangeness of truth. To be inhospitable to strangers
or strange ideas, however unsettling they may be, is to be hostile to
the possibility of truth; hospitality is not only an ethical virtue but
an epistemological one as well.[7]

Christian higher education institutions should be a welcoming space
for all learners to learn about themselves, to explore their own values and
worldviews as well as the viewpoints of others, to learn about biblical and
Christian traditions and worldview, to undertake the "strangeness of truth,"
and to experience the hospitality of a Christ-centred community.

Hospitality in the Old Testament

The Genesis account in the Hebrew Scriptures begins with Yahweh preparing a welcoming world. Five days are spent organizing the chaos, separat-
ing the darks and lights, setting mood lights, landscaping the grounds, and
preparing the wine and the salads. On the sixth day the guests arrive; on the
seventh day the party begins. The theme of God as host and his creatures
as guests runs as an undercurrent through the rest of the Old and New
Testaments. From the beginning, host–guest relationships are life-giving
but complicated. While no doubt lovely, Eden is not an all-inclusive resort.
Humans are expected to pull their weight in tending the gardens and creating taxonomies of animals. Some days are spent in companionable evening
strolls through the gardens; others include awkward conversations about
overstepped boundaries and misconceptions about roles and responsibilities. Things go awry when humans forget they are guests and presume they
own the place. Like European conquerors, humans forget that the earth is
not theirs to usurp. Things go from bad to worse when humans build an
audacious skyline in Babel. Guest privileges are revoked, and the guest list
suddenly becomes very short—just eight people, with Noah in charge of
the cruise ship, the zoo, and the food services.

When Abraham and Sarah arrive on the scene, we see a fresh start
to God's hospitality. For the first time, humans begin to clue in to their
responsibility as co-hosts. They welcome three strangers, serving them with
the best they have at their humble desert inn. Abraham's menu is simple, but
his service is five-star. Unwittingly a role reversal takes place. Theologian
David Smith suggests that Abraham's hospitality is an "act of decentering,

---

7. Palmer, *To Know as We Are Known*, 74.

in which the guest is honored, and the host brings his or her resources to bear in willing service."[8] Humans host the Lord with serendipitous results. As is the custom in many communities, the guests bring a host gift, though in this case, no ordinary one: a promise of new life to a sad, childless, old couple.

Skipping forward a few generations, we find Abraham and Sarah's promised descendants in Egypt, enslaved by hostile hosts. Once freed from oppressive proprietors, the people receive God's hospitality again through the daily desert rations of manna and quail. However, these evoke discontent in the guests, especially when compared with the leek soup and meat stew of slavery. (This unappreciative attitude brings to mind a rude childhood friend, who accepted our family's invitation for lunch only on the condition that chocolate cake and whipped cream be served for dessert.)

God is a relentless and gracious host, offering his people hospitality on the road, where the tabernacle acts as a symbol of hospitality, and in the temple once they arrive in the promised land. The poets of the Psalms often express Israel's status as guest. Psalm 39:12 (NLT) states, "Hear my prayer . . . my cries . . . for I am your guest, a traveler passing through, as my ancestors." Psalm 23:5–6 sets the scene: "you prepare a feast for me . . . surely your goodness and unfailing love will pursue me, and I will live in the house of the Lord forever." Isaiah 25:6 draws a picture of the ultimate banquet table to which God invites all people; he "will spread a wonderful feast for all the people of the world. It will be a delicious banquet with clear, well-aged wine and choice meat."

Yahweh's principles of hospitality find their way into the laws of Moses. These include reminders of Israel's status as long-term guest—perhaps tenant or landed immigrant might better describe the relationship to the land and its maker. "The land must never be sold on a permanent basis, for the land belongs to me. You are only foreigners and tenant farmers working for me" (Lev 25:23 NLT). We find these prompts in the context of laws relating to the Jubilee—a land reform that was to take place every fifty years. This reform was a safeguard against the perennial human tendency to become owners rather than guests and caretakers.

God's hospitality is also a call to human hospitality to one another. Human beings are "fellow guests in the host's house, the created world."[9] Old Testament laws direct Israel to show concern for strangers and aliens.

8. Smith and Felch, *Teaching and Christian Imagination*, 66.

9. Janzen, "Biblical Theology of Hospitality," 9.

"Do not take advantage of foreigners who live among you in your land. Treat them like native-born . . . and love them as you love yourself. Remember that you were once foreigners living in the land of Egypt. I am the Lord your God" (Lev 19:33–34 NLT). Other texts praise hospitality and show that hosts receive more than they give. God, the great host, invites humanity to be his guests in his created world. He expects his guests to follow his example and share the abundance with their fellow guests.

Hospitality in the New Testament

The symbiotic host–guest relationship takes on new flavors in the New Testament. Rather counter-intuitively, the Gospels highlight the Messiah's status as unwelcome guest. The Christ arrives in his own realm, and there is no room in the inn. As an infant, Jesus and his family become political refugees. As an adult, he often appears to be homeless, dependent on the hospitality of his friends. He hosts his last supper in a borrowed hall; his dead body is hosted in a borrowed tomb.[10] Yet those who invite Christ to be their guest find themselves guests at his table. As Zacchaeus hosts Christ, he becomes a guest in the kingdom. The disciples at Emmaus invite the unrecognized Jesus to have supper with them. He enters their home as a guest, yet as he breaks bread they recognize him as their host and Lord.

A recurring theme in Jesus' stories and parables is eating and drinking, parties, banquets, and feasts. The only miracle recorded in all four Gospels is the spontaneous community picnic he hosts. Without a grocery list, this is no Martha-Stewart-style entertaining. All are welcome; his get-togethers seem oddly more in accord with the pulse-beat of a homeless shelter where any ragamuffin can share a meal. The book of Revelation invites us to an image of Christ as both guest and host. Jesus appears as the guest knocking at the door: "Look! I stand at the door and knock. If you hear my voice and open the door, I will come in, and we will share a meal together as friends" (Rev 3:20 NLT). In Rev 19, John sets the scene for the final banquet at the end of the age: "For the time has come for the wedding feast of the lamb" (Rev 19:7 NLT).

The invitation extended to human beings to join in Christ's style of guest/host is articulated more clearly in the New Testament letters. "Always be eager to practice hospitality" (Rom 12:13 NLT). "Offer hospitality to one another without grumbling" (1 Pet 4:9 NLT). "Do not forget to show

---

10. Janzen, "Biblical Theology of Hospitality," 11–12.

hospitality to strangers, for by so doing some people have shown hospitality to angels without knowing it" (Heb 13:2 NLT). Hospitality becomes an indicator of the extent to which believers have truly incorporated their beliefs and have shown them in action.[11]

Donning hospitality lenses while following Paul and Silas into prison adds an interesting layer to the story as it unfolds. The jailor hosts Paul and Silas against their will. This coercive accommodation includes a dungeon equipped with stocks for clamping feet. These are tools in the jailor's craft of fashioning a hostile environment. However, even in these dire circumstances, Paul and Silas embrace the guest/host symbiosis that is available to them. Far from seeing themselves as exclusively victims of an unjust legal system—which they are, without doubt—they choose to become hosts. They offer a midnight worship concert with their fellow prisoners as guests. Paul and Silas's hospitality in these most unconducive conditions creates a dramatic domino effect, pushing back the layers of hostility surrounding them. Who would have thought that hospitality could have the power of an earthquake, breaking the chains not only of Paul and Silas, but also of all the prisoners at the concert? With this seismic shift, the jailor watches in terror as his life work of coercive hostility crumbles. Paul's quick-thinking suicide intervention is yet another counter-intuitive *hospes* move. Not only does he save the jailor's life, but he also empowers him to refashion his bullying craft into a welcoming space for wounds to heal. The astounding end of the story is a dinner party celebrating the family's conversion from hostility to hospitality.

A Theology of Hospitality

Since the first centuries, welcoming strangers has been a hallmark of the Christian tradition. The symbiotic roles of host and guest cannot be separated. God is the ultimate host and we his guests; yet as he becomes our guest and we his hosts, we are the ones blessed and are made capable of hosting others to become guests in his kingdom. In Jesus' day as in our own, hospitality is regulated by social status, wealth, and power. Notice, oddly, that in the "hospitality" industry, only those who can pay are welcome. Most of us share Sunday dinners with those who are similar to us in status and wealth. Jesus broke such rules and dined with sinners and

---

11. Matt 25:35.

prostitutes. Some praised him; others found such behavior offensive.[12] As we open ourselves to his "knock at the door" of our lives, we become hosts and guests. Christ's way of extending hospitality compels us to continue his mission, as we ourselves are sojourners, on our way to that ultimate banquet table.[13]

"*From Hostis to Hospes*"[14]

The learning environment thrives when it is a place of hospitality rather than hostility. The Latin term *hospes* refers to the role of host and guest, while the Latin term *hostis* defines a stranger or enemy. *Hospes* in Latin is uniquely understood to refer to both host and guest, reminiscent of the dual role of Jesus in the New Testament narrative above. The Christian higher education learning community can be a place of true *hospes* where all are free to explore their God-given roles of host and guest. The classroom need not be a gathering place of *hostis* or hostile strangers, but rather a space of *hospes* or hospitality, a welcoming space.

A welcoming space is not simply a safe space. Though the term "safe space" is increasingly used in educational institutions, the classroom is not necessarily best defined as safe. Learners may not always feel safe in the classroom as true learning requires risk. There is a vulnerability and authenticity needed to engage with new ideas and the opinions of others. A welcoming space creates opportunities and boundaries within which risk, vulnerability, and authenticity can be explored.

As mentioned above, an increased need has been perceived for a safe space in institutions of higher learning. The term is often used to refer to a space where the marginalized can be acknowledged and accepted. And it, rightly, assumes a baseline of hostility as the norm in society. A welcoming classroom must also recognize the unique backgrounds and experiences of marginalized learners with openness and respect. The difference is in the way it is addressed in the classroom.

A welcoming space is about more than tolerance or being nice. Tolerance has been a North American ideal in recent decades, but tolerance is often little more than a façade for internally held dislike and hostility. Young learners are often told to "be nice" and to remain silent if they "can't

12. Janzen, "Biblical Theology of Hospitality," 12–13.
13. Rev 19:17.
14. Nouwen, *Reaching Out*, 66.

say something nice" when they dislike or disagree with another instead of being encouraged to observe, engage, ask questions, and listen well to their answers. Rather than teaching tolerance and niceness, a welcoming space encourages vulnerability and relationship. Tolerance requires that a learner *endures* the contributions of others. A welcoming space *engages* learners in open and accepting conversation, with a host that ensures the well-being of all guests.

But what about the guest that threatens the welcoming space for all other guests? Does a host-instructor need to allow any and all comments and behaviors in the classroom? Imagine a potluck where one contributed dish gives off such a putrid smell and unappetizing appearance that the entire potluck is affected. The host does not wish to bring shame on the contributor of the dish but also must address the offensive dish or risk ruining the meal for all present. There are moments in the higher education classroom where the host-instructor is faced with this level of dilemma: the learner who hijacks all class discussions and presentations, the learner who rejects and disrespects the diverse opinions of others, the learner who refuses to engage with anyone but the instructor.

Can and should a hostile guest be removed to ensure the ongoing welcoming space for all others? Just as one would not choose to open their home again to an invited guest that had destroyed the furniture, bullied the other guests, or started a food fight, neither is a class eager to include a learner that brings hostility into a hospitable space. Every effort should be made to privately address disruptive behaviors with confrontational learners, but there is a place and time for respectfully removing the unruly student-guest so as to ensure the well-being of all others in the learning community.

Questions of *hospes* and *hostis* are not limited to the educational institution or classroom. Discussions about hospitality and hostility fill our current airways due to a global debate about immigration and refugee appeals. Rallies around the world have been documented with signs that read both "Refugees not welcome here!" and "Refugees welcome!" In a single evening broadcast, one can hear immigrants referred to as dangerous criminals by one speaker and heralded as trusted friends and neighbors by another. Heads of State have criticized each other publicly for how they handle immigration and are engaging in open discussions of *hospes* versus *hostis*, whether it is wisest and best to keep the stranger outside of the borders or to welcome them within the country as invited and welcome guests.

Consider the graduation address given by Prime Minister Justin Trudeau at New York University on May 16, 2018:

> Whether it's race, gender, language, sexual orientation, religious or ethnic origin, or our beliefs and values themselves—diversity doesn't have to be a weakness. It can be our greatest strength. Now often, people talk about striving for tolerance. Now, don't get me wrong: there are places in this world where a little more tolerance would go a long way, but if we're being honest right here, right now, I think we can aim a little higher than mere tolerance.
>
> Think about it: Saying "I tolerate you" actually means something like, "Ok, I grudgingly admit that you have a right to exist, just don't get in my face about it, and oh, don't date my sister." There's not a religion in the world that asks you to "tolerate thy neighbor." So let's try for something a little more like acceptance, respect, friendship, and yes, even love.[15]

The Christian higher education classroom can be and should be a place of "acceptance, respect, friendship, and . . . even love." It is in the Christian higher education classroom where all viewpoints are to be explored. Students need to feel both empowered and secure to explore and question all viewpoints and this empowerment and safety can be found in a welcoming space. The professor, acting as host, can indeed engage all learners in open and accepting conversation, ensuring the well-being of all student guests. The faith-based classroom should aspire to be, in the words of Orthodox Theologian Georges Florovsky, "a symphony of personalities, in which the mystery of the Holy Trinity is reflected."[16]

The Hospitable Learning Community—A Metaphor

Metaphors for teaching and learning abound, whether we notice this or not. The way we speak of our students and our school betrays our metaphors. When we speak of a "learning journey," we are engaging a travel metaphor; references to a "classroom atmosphere" hint at a weather metaphor. When administrators speak of "credits sold," we have strayed into "education as a commodity to be bought and sold." Smith and Felch suggest that the metaphors we use to speak about teaching and learning have a profound influence on the ways in which we go about these tasks.[17] For the purposes of

---

15. Trudeau, "PM Speaking Notes."
16. Florovsky, "The Church," 67.
17. Smith and Felch, *Teaching and Christian Imagination*, 52.

this chapter, we are using the metaphor of "dinner party" in part because it flows organically out of the larger topic of hospitality. However, we are also aware that the metaphor itself carries meaning. Let the party begin!

COME ON IN! LET ME TAKE YOUR COAT. DO YOU NEED SLIPPERS?

Students come to the classroom as much more than just a mind to be engaged. They arrive as whole persons. Adult learners engaged in higher education arrive as people who likely carry many more roles than that of simply student: they may be parents, employees, spouses, immigrants, children of aging parents, and church or community leaders. Learners arrive wearing coats of many colors and hats of many shapes and sizes. These differences are acknowledged and even celebrated in the welcoming classroom.

Increasingly, Christian higher education classrooms are attracting and accepting students from other faith expressions and worldviews. These learners must be offered an equally hospitable reception to those that share our belief system. In these shared learning communities, the instructor becomes both host-evangelist as well as host-discipler through the living out of authentic Christian faith and hospitality in and out of the classroom.[18]

Students may arrive with physical, mental, and emotional needs, not simply academic ones. And the welcoming instructor recognizes and allows for those needs. Though the school or the professor may lack the resources or skills to address all student needs, they can offer the gift of acknowledging those needs. There are times when a need can be met within the classroom environment, there are times when a referral or support outside of the classroom is required, and there are times when the classroom can offer true support by simply bearing witness to the struggle and walking alongside the learner who is in need. There is immense warmth offered through authentic listening, allowing for needs to be expressed rather than dismissed or ignored.

The welcoming classroom can also offer protection from the cold of research and scholarship. Academia can be a vast expanse of cold facts and hard questions. As Palmer says, "the violence of our knowledge" can lead to "weariness, withdrawal, and cynicism."[19] The host-instructor can offer a personalization of information, making it relevant and applicable to the real life of the learner, creating an emotional and relational climate where knowledge can nurture rather than overwhelm.

18. Dormer, *Teaching English in Missions*, 28–44.
19. Palmer, *To Know as We Are Known*, 1–4.

Research in affective neuroscience increasingly suggests that "learning is dynamic, social and context dependent because *emotions* are, and emotions form a critical piece of how, what, when, and why people think, remember, and learn."[20] In other words, human emotions can accelerate or inhibit learning. A state of "relaxed alertness" can make students thrive, developing and improving their classroom learning.[21] That is to say that when learners feel free from anxiety and fear yet are highly challenged and encouraged to participate, they learn more effectively. When students are overwhelmed by nerves, anxiety, or fear, their amygdala can be overstimulated causing an emotional hijack, which involves rational brain processing being seized by the brain's fight or flight protective mechanism.[22] Thus, a fear-cascade is triggered[23] and students' mental processing can be hijacked. On the other hand, learning can be accelerated when it is connected to the personal lives of the learners[24] in a welcoming space.

FLOWERS FOR THE HOST!

The invited guest often arrives with gifts for the host: flowers, bread, a bottle of wine. Student-guests also arrive with gifts for the host-instructor: curiosity, stories, life experiences, and gratitude. It is the role of the host to graciously accept the gifts that are offered and to honor those gifts by using them. Henri Nouwen observes that "a good host is the one who believes that his guest is carrying a promise he wants to reveal to anyone who shows genuine interest."[25] This includes, first of all, helping students to see that their lives are indeed worthy of serious attention. It is easy to impress students with new scholars and intriguing ideas; however, Nouwen suggests, teachers should let go of their need to impress, and in its place foster a receptiveness to the experiences the students bring with them. It is in this receptivity that students' gifts become visible.[26] The host-instructor shows genuine gratitude and acceptance of their learners' gifts when they receive and make use of them within the learning community. Each adult learner

---

20. Immordino-Yang, *Emotions, Learning, and the Brain*, 17.

21. Caine and Caine, *Human Connections*, 70, 135–54.

22. Goleman, *Emotional Intelligence*, 13–20.

23. Damasio, *Self Comes to Mind*, 119.

24. Immordino-Yang, *Emotions, Learning, and the Brain*, 17.

25. Nouwen, *Reaching Out*, 87.

26. Nouwen, *Reaching Out*, 87.

is indeed a true resource for the higher education classroom, and it is of benefit and blessing to all when this resource is valued and utilized.

There is another resource that the learner provides to the learning community and that is often overlooked as a gift from the guest: money. When it comes to discussions of student fees, the dialogue tends to shift to more commercial or business language. References are made to credits sold or paying for credentials, and it seems the metaphor of host and guest breaks down. But does it need to? Can Christian institutes of higher learning rethink the language used to discuss the money that learners give? If tuition paid was considered an entrusted gift or resource rather than credits sold, perhaps the presence of student-guests would be even more highly valued.

LET US SHOW YOU AROUND

Just as guests are shown around a home they are visiting for the first time, so learners need to be oriented to their new learning environment. Hosts and guests hold different roles and responsibilities, and a welcoming space offers both freedom and boundaries. New students need to be made aware of their various roles and responsibilities, and of the freedom and boundaries that they can expect in the class they have joined. From the first welcome they receive to their first syllabus, from the class rules to the first assignment and grade that is returned, learners should be oriented to their new learning environment.

As guests being welcomed into the new classroom, students take their cues from the host-instructor. It is the responsibility of the professor to clearly communicate expectations to the learners. A student should not have to learn a rule by breaking it and suffering the consequences. Rather, classroom hospitality involves either allowing complete *gastvrijheid*, the Dutch word for freedom of the guest, or clearly specifying how the space is to be used, how conversation and communication will progress, and how the daily class routine will take place.

The host-instructor can offer learners many helpful guides and tools in consistently offering welcome and class orientation:

1. Having an established routine for opening the class and clear policies regarding attendance and late arrivals

2. Offering ongoing opportunities for learners to express their needs, interests and concerns, and ongoing opportunities for open communication within the class

3. Including as much detail as possible in the class syllabus, especially regarding assignments, grading, and policies, also including how learners can and should communicate with the instructor outside of class time

4. Writing the day's agenda on the board

5. Being consistent with the way handouts, lecture notes, slides, and resources are made available to all learners

6. Offering clear instructions for classroom work and asking that students repeat back the steps to ensure understanding

7. Allowing for a variety of learning styles (different modalities and multiple intelligences) and working arrangements (independent, paired, small group, full class)

8. Concluding the class with a clear summary, a chance for reflection, or a preview of next day's class

WHAT CAN I GET YOU TO DRINK?

Metaphors aside, hospitality to our students can begin with something as basic as offering a cup of water, literally. Recently we encountered a former student in the hallway. She spoke effusively of a *revolutionary* idea she had learned in our classroom. We wondered which of our pedagogical innovations may have had such a dramatic effect on her. "Coffee at the start of each class," she said. Yes, that was it. Coffee, tea, and snacks were always available at our "hospitality corner" during our intensive summer courses. She observed that adult learners are more in need of this kind of thing than children. We call it "brain food." Food and drink—central elements in hospitality—tend to change the tone of any meeting and any classroom. It is no accident that the most basic of human needs—the need to eat and drink—becomes the place of the Eucharist, this ultimate food and drink before which we are all equals, all with the same need, before that bread and wine that sustains us all.

JOIN US AT THE TABLE

"Religious as well as secular researchers have recently rediscovered the human need to 'belong' and describe various versions of our longing for community—a place where one is known, or at least a group where everybody knows your name."[27] When invited guests arrive at our homes, we invite them to sit down and, with a larger house party, names need to be connected with faces. So, too, the hospitable classroom has seats for everyone. Even in crowds of thousands, there are ways to let everyone know they are invited to share their "loaves and fishes" in the potluck of learning. Part of this includes acknowledging the empty spots when students are missing. The Jewish Seder tradition includes an empty chair "for Elijah" who can be expected to show up any time to herald the Messiah's arrival. Morning routines can include check-in rituals that invite each person to speak and be heard. "Elijah" may one day arrive in the form of a student with odd habits and strange ideas. Research on group dynamics sheds light on the ingredients of a climate of harmony and cohesiveness. Instructors who see the large mountains of content to be consumed might protest that these "warm fuzzies" are a waste of precious class time. Tim Murphy and Zoltan Dörnyei point out that the field of *group dynamics* is largely ignored by educators[28] for whom teaching content is routinely prioritized over teaching students.[29] Carefully attending to classroom dynamics can have a significant impact on students' effectiveness in ingesting and digesting learning.[30]

As educators we are, of course, concerned with serving our students substantial and nourishing "meals." Susan Felch ponders the metaphor of eating and drinking in relation to university students. Are we truly offering nourishment in our curriculum? How do we decide what to serve? Are we offering the latest trends and fashions in academia? In an age where "research" is expected to materialize in a split second on the screen, we do well to consider the implications of this diet of "fast food." What kind of a party is this? Is it a formal party where the host is responsible for every detail? Is it a potluck where everyone brings a dish? Is it a communal kitchen where we cook the meal together? Given these options, what effect does each type of "menu" have on the learning for the student-guests?[31]

27. Pohl, *Living into Community*, 3.

28. Dörnyei and Murphy, *Group Dynamics*, 5.

29. Dormer, *Teaching English in Missions*, 53–55.

30. Dörnyei and Murphy, *Group Dynamics*, 8.

31. Felch, "Teaching at Table/Learning to Eat."

As parents with families, we adjust our nutritional offerings to our children based on their age, their tastes, and their allergies. We walk a fine line between respecting their preferences and encouraging them to try new flavors. In our school, we have had an increasing number of students whose cultural and religious convictions compel them to eat vegan diets. Our campus food services have had to adjust their buffet options accordingly. What kinds of ingredients do we bring to the "table" of our course of studies? Do our students have allergies to particular "ingredients" in our curriculum? How do we balance validating preferences and values while encouraging students to broaden their palettes and challenge their preconceived notions? Do we adjust our educational "menus" depending on who our students are?

We are fortunate to have a range of options available to our students. Adults generally learn better if they are given choices. English professor Susan Felch ponders the benefits and detractions of the semester system that perhaps encourages a kind of "academic bulimia" where students stuff themselves with knowledge only to regurgitate it at exam time. How do we help our students digest what they have eaten so that they may retain wisdom?[32]

AFTER DINNER CONVERSATIONS

Along with coffee and dessert, relaxed, engaging conversations and storytelling round off a nourishing and satisfying meal. It is probably not new to most of us that stories are among the most profound ways in which we integrate knowledge and ideas. Psychologist Jerome Bruner suggests that narrative is primary in how humans make sense of their lives and shape their identity. Through retelling their experiences, people become the stories they tell about themselves. "In the end, we become the autobiographical narratives we tell about our lives."[33] It seems that we organize and retell our experiences, knowledge, skills, and information in a variety of narrative forms. Dörnyei and Kubanyiova suggest that these autobiographical narratives are so foundational, we in fact, "narrate ourselves into being."[34]

But stories are never told in a vacuum. They only become meaningful if they are told in the context of sympathetic listeners. Expressive Arts

32. Felch, "Teaching at Table/Learning to Eat."

33. Bruner, as quoted in Dörnyei and Kubanyova, *Motivating Learners, Motivating Teachers*, 57.

34. Dörnyei and Kubanyiova, *Motivating Learners, Motivating Teachers*, 57.

therapist Paulo Knill draws attention to the critical role of "witnessing" one another's stories. "Witnessing" entails active listening with our full attention and responding to what has been said that shares how the listener has been affected by the speaker's words or images.[35] In conversation we discover our stories. Russian psychologist Vygotzky elaborates on the dialogic nature of learning. He coined the term "Zone of Proximal Development," which is "an act of negotiated discovery . . . realized through dialogic interaction between learner and expert."[36]

Returning now to the university classroom, we do well to examine the dynamics of story-telling. Who does the talking? Who listens? In the field of language pedagogy, we examine teacher talk time (TTT) and student talk time (STT).[37] We ask questions such as: What is the ratio of teacher and student voices? As teachers we often think we need to be "the sage on the stage."[38] Unfortunately, when we feel compelled to entertain our students, teaching becomes a performance. Notice how this changes the metaphor from hospitality to entertainment. The shift in thinking about our work and our students is profound. There are times and places for our sagacious knowledge, but also times when our students may be in more need of a "guide on the side,"[39] to use a "now-clichéd"[40] term for teacher role. Which stories are told? Who dominates the discussion? Who asks questions? Who gives answers? Are some stories pushed to the margins for fear of the responses their telling might evoke? Are we able to make room in our busy schedules for the silence of listening, being the attentive "witness" to our students' lives, hearing the questions that are accessible only by sensitive perception and literacy between the lines?

AWKWARD CONVERSATIONS AT THE TABLE

At a recent dinner-table conversation in my (Frieda's) home, a discussion emerged about Christ's atonement as a model encouraging child sacrifice. Given that the guests at the table had profound differences in faith commitments, conflicting theological views were not surprising in and of themselves. However, in the companionable flow of conversation, this sharp

35. Paulo Knill, *Principles and Practice*, 89
36. Lantolf, *Sociocultural Theory*, 54.
37. Scrivener, *Teaching Learning*, 14–15.
38. King, "From Sage on the Stage to Guide on the Side," 30.
39. King, "From Sage on the Stage to Guide on the Side," 30.
40. Morrison, "From 'Sage on the Stage' to 'Guide on the Side,'" Abstract.

disparity of worldviews raised its head rather suddenly and unexpectedly, leaving a tension in the air between mashed potatoes and pumpkin pie.

In honest, open conversations, differences in values and worldviews inevitably rise to the surface. Along with knee-jerk defensiveness, many teachers and students have learned how to avoid such conversations, *not* how to enter into them with humility, respect, and honest curiosity.

Psychologist Howard Gardner proposes that one key quality of leadership for the future is the ability to work together with people who are different from oneself. "It is recognizing that the world is composed of people who look different, think differently, have different belief and value systems, and that we can no longer be hermits and live in complete isolation."[41] As with any academic discipline, in the field of Teaching English to Speakers of Other Languages (TESOL) these tensions can become minefields. Several TESOL scholars explore the concept of teaching as reconciliation and peacemaking.[42] Dormer and Woelk expand on the specific tools and strategies for peacebuilding in the classroom to foster a transformative space for teachers and students.[43]

Please take some food with you

"The pilgrim counts on the sustenance provided by inns and hostels along the way, the hope borne of shared eating and singing, the fellowship of traveling companions, and the rhythm of motion and rest that allows God to carry the burden of the world."[44] In many cultures and communities, it is not uncommon to send guests home with a container of food, often a specially selected treat or a portion of a dish that the guest especially enjoyed. Many a North American has returned home from a dinner party or Thanksgiving feast with a container of leftovers or a slice of pie. Filipino hosts often prepare a food gift to be taken home by guests at the end of a visit. Weddings that take place all around the world involve guests taking home cake or sweets to help them remember and cherish the event.

The host-instructor may also wish to present learners with a treat to help them remember and value the learning that has occurred. This may take the form of a thoughtful review or reflection of what has been learned that day. It may include making further resources available, assigning

41. Gardner, *Five Minds for the Future*, 12.

42. Snow, *Teaching English as Christian Mission*, 8.

43. Dormer and Woelk, *Teaching English for Reconciliation*, 16.

44. Smith and Felch, *Teaching and Christian Imagination*, 60.

homework, making the notes or visual presentations available after the lecture concludes. In this way, the learner is encouraged to pack the skills and knowledge they find useful for the future into their metaphoric backpacks to take with them on their journey from the classroom.

Another treat that can be presented to learners as they leave the classroom is a clear sense of connection with the instructor outside of class time. A promise of office hours, email contact, and other forms of availability may be just the thing to hold students over once they return to their homes or dorms.

SEE YOU SOON!

All parties must come to an end; guests and hosts part ways. Dishes must be washed and put away, the floor swept. At the end of a semester, the host-instructor may be left with a sense of exhaustion that can easily slip into restlessness, impatience, and self-doubt. The enthusiasm of the semester's beginning has long waned, and so much ground is left uncovered. Instructors can find themselves questioning their effectiveness, wondering if their efforts have really been well spent and appreciated. Linguist Zoltan Dörnyei tells of traditional Hungarian hosts who endlessly heap more and more food on their guests' plates, urging them to show their appreciation of the hosts' efforts. As the overstuffed guests leave the table, the hosts remark to one another in a quiet voice but just loud enough for the guests to hear, "You see, I told you—they didn't like our food after all. They hardly ate a thing!"[45] Teachers tend to carry with them an unrealistic burden of responsibility that leaves them feeling overwhelmed and inadequate in the face of all they have *not* done. These doubts are often symptoms of a deeper "imposter syndrome" that plagues both teachers and students—the feeling that their lives are a fraud and a façade and sooner or later the school and the world will discover their lack of intelligence and talent. They will be asked to leave, standing naked in a cloud of embarrassment and shame.[46] Nouwen suggests that the hospitality metaphor can help lighten this load. "Students are not just the poor, needy, ignorant beggars who come to the man or woman of knowledge, but . . . they are indeed like guests who honor the house with their visit and will not leave it without having made their

45. Dörnyei, private conversation.
46. Brookfield, *The Skillful Teacher*, 75.

contribution."[47] Our classroom is only one of many our students will visit on their paths.

Exams are not uncommon endings to a semester's work. David Smith questions the tone this pattern sets for departures for hosts and guests in the classroom. He proposes final assignments and exams be completed a week or two earlier, leaving the final class as a time to celebrate and bid farewell. Instead of finishing the semester with judgement and dismissal, he suggests rather culminating it with a blessing and a sending off.[48]

Please come again

As the guests depart the party, the host will often bid them to come again even as they are sent on their way. There is an anticipation of being together again, a promise of an ongoing relationship that will be nurtured in the future. So, the host-instructor welcomes ongoing relationship building and mentoring of the student-guests they host. The welcoming space remains open, encouraging and fostering a longer-term learning relationship. The host-instructor keeps the student-guests in mind even after they are gone, reflecting on the event that was shared and planning for future get-togethers.

What is the cost of this longer-term relationship? While it may be easy to "offer hospitality to one another without grumbling" (1 Pet 4:9 NIV) for one dinner party, hosting an elaborate ongoing dinner club that meets weekly in one's own home can quickly become reason to whine and complain. Hosting and creating a welcoming space consistently for the long term is hard work. It involves self-sacrifice. It requires that the needs of others remain the primary focus and that planning be done for the benefit of the community rather than the convenience of the host. Longer-term relationships also put greater demands on the student-guests. They must extend their commitment to their responsibilities as well. Though *gastvrijheid* or "freedom of the guest" is desirable, the guest is not truly free, especially in an ongoing relationship. They commit to the relationship, they commit to the community, they commit to the welcoming space in very real ways. They are required to remain and even to become increasingly open, vulnerable, accepting, authentic. The student-guest may also need to learn how to host fellow learners along the way.

---

47. Nouwen, *Reaching Out*, 89.

48. Smith, "Extending the Dialogue Across Teachers of Multiple Faiths."

What are the rewards of this longer-term relationship? The relationship that develops between the host and the guests is certainly a reward in and of itself, but there are other benefits as well. Both host-instructor and student-guests are enriched by the gifts of being seen and heard, of knowing and being known in community. We learn richly from each other, from our diverse and shared stories, from our personal and corporate experiences. The welcoming space becomes a place of transformation for host and guest alike. Amongst their student-guests, the host-instructor may be hosting saints, prophets, evangelists, pastors, teachers, and unwittingly angels as well.

CONCLUSION

A Christian higher education approach to teaching is centered in Christ and the Christian tradition and worldview. The design of our program emerges from that approach and, therefore, must embody hospitality in its design. Daily procedures in our learning community must therefore prioritize the relationship of host-instructor and student-guests; we are not just teaching students content but welcoming valued guests to engage in conversation and tell us their stories.

However, embracing hospitality as a metaphor for teaching and learning is no easy task.

It does not make teaching easier; in fact, it demands more of us in and out of class. It requires a level of vulnerability and authenticity that transmitting content or selling credits alone does not ask of us.

True welcoming space is urgently needed in the hostile world that surrounds us. In the current North American context, such life-giving hospitality is vital to our institutions and organizations. We must challenge ourselves and our learners to aspire to be "a blessing as a stranger . . . and to be hospitable to strangers";[49] to transform *hostis* to *hospes*. It is through hospitality that Christian learning communities serve God and serve one another in such a way that nurtures our very own souls.

BIBLIOGRAPHY

Brookfield, S. D. *The Skillful Teacher: On Technique, Trust, and Responsiveness in the Classroom.* San Francisco: Wiley, 2009.

Caine, Renate Nummela, and Geoffrey Caine. *Human Connections: Teaching and the Human Brain.* Menlo Park, CA: Addison-Wesley, 1994.

49. Smith and Carvill, *The Gift of the Stranger*, 58.

Damasio, Antonio. *Self Comes to Mind: Constructing the Conscious Brain*. New York: Vintage, 2012.

Dormer, Jan Edwards. *Teaching English in Missions: Effectiveness and Integrity*. Pasadena: William Carey Library, 2011.

Dormer, Jan Edwards, and Cheryl Woelk. *Teaching English for Reconciliation: Pursuing Peace through Transformed Relationships in Language Learning and Teaching*. Pasadena: William Carey Library, 2018.

Dörnyei, Zoltán, and Magdalena Kubanyiova. *Motivating Learners, Motivating Teachers: Building Vision in the Language Classroom*. Cambridge: Cambridge University Press, 2014.

Dörnyei, Zoltán, and Tim Murphy. *Group Dynamics in the Language Classroom*. Cambridge: Cambridge University Press, 2003.

Felch, Susan. "Teaching at Table, Learning to Eat." Plenary lecture presented for Faith and Teaching: Virtue, Practice, Imagination—sponsored by the Kuyers Institute on Christian Teaching and Learning at Calvin College, Grand Rapids, MI, October 1, 2015. Online: https://www.youtube.com/watch?v=Hrdo5uEV2yg.

Florovsky, Georges. "The Church: Her Nature and Task." In *Bible, Church, Tradition: An Eastern Orthodox View*, edited by Georges Florovsky, 37–48. Belmont, MA: Nordland, 1972.

Gardner, Howard. *Five Minds for the Future: Leadership for the Common Good*. Boston: Harvard Business Press, 2009.

Goleman, Daniel. *Emotional Intelligence: Why It Can Matter More than IQ*. New York: Bantam Dell, 1995.

Immordino-Yang, Mary Helen. *Emotions, Learning, and the Brain: Exploring the Educational Implications of Affective Neuroscience*. New York: Norton, 2016.

Janzen, Waldemar. "A Biblical Theology of Hospitality." *Vision: A Journal for Church and Theology* 3 (Spring 2002) 4–15.

King, Allison. "From Sage on the Stage to Guide on the Side." *College Teaching* 41 (1993) 30–35. Online: http://www.jstor.org/stable/27558571.

Lantolf, James P. *Sociocultural Theory and Second Language Learning*. Oxford: Oxford University Press, 2000.

Morrison, Charles D. "From 'Sage on the Stage' to 'Guide on the Side': A Good Start." *International Journal for the Scholarship of Teaching and Learning* 8 (2014) 15 pp. Online: https://doi.org/10.20429/ijsotl.2014.080104.

Nouwen, Henri J. M. *Reaching Out: The Three Movements of the Spiritual Life*. New York: Image, 1986.

Palmer, Parker J. *To Know as We Are Known: Education as a Spiritual Journey*. San Francisco: HarperCollins, 1993.

Knill, Paolo J., et al. *Principles and Practice of Expressive Arts Therapy: Toward a Therapeutic Aesthetics*. London: Jessica Kingsley, 2005.

Pohl, C. D. *Living into Community: Cultivating Practices that Sustain Us*. Grand Rapids: Eerdmans, 2012.

Richards, Jack C., and Theodore Rodgers. *Approaches and Methods in Language Teaching*. 2nd ed. New York: Cambridge University Press, 2001.

Scrivener, Jim. *Learning Teaching: A Guidebook for English Language Teachers*. Hong Kong: Macmillan Heinemann, 1994.

Shepherd, Andrew. *The Gift of the Other: Levinas, Derrida and a Theology of Hospitality*. PhD diss., University of Otago, Dunedin, NZ, 2010.

Smith, Christian, et al. *Lost in Transition: The Dark Side of Emerging Adulthood.* New York: Oxford University Press, 2011.

Smith, David. "Extending the Dialogue Across Teachers of Multiple Faiths." Paper presented at the TESOL International Convention, Chicago, IL, March 29, 2018.

Smith, David I., and Barbara Carvill. *The Gift of the Stranger: Faith, Hospitality, and Foreign Language Learning.* Grand Rapids: Eerdmans, 2000.

Smith, David I., and Susan M. Felch. *Teaching and Christian Imagination.* Grand Rapids: Eerdmans, 2015.

Trudeau, Justin. "PM Speaking Notes for NYU Commencement Address." Presented at NYU Graduation, May 16, 2018. Online: https://pm.gc.ca/en/news/speeches/2018/05/16/pm-speaking-notes-nyu-commencement-address

9

George Parkin Grant's Advice to Twenty-First-Century Canadian Christian Higher Education

TED NEWELL

INTRODUCTION

GEORGE PARKIN GRANT (1918–1988) traced Canadian higher education's twentieth-century shift away from traditional liberal arts into training for careers in professions or bureaucracies, driven by a growing American influence. Education's philosophical underpinnings moved from idealism toward utilitarian progressivism. A Grant-type analysis indicates that the central problem facing Canadian Christian higher education is the cultural, political, and legal shift that favours increasingly radical forms of individual autonomy.

CHEC'S CHALLENGES

At least since 1976, church educators and school religious educators have been saying that Christian education faces a life-and-death struggle. John Westerhoff's *Will Our Children Have Faith?* was first, followed twenty years later by Marva Dawn's *Is it a Lost Cause?*, Thomas Groome's *Will There Be Faith?*, and Charles Foster's *From Generation to Generation*. Foster sees that church education is up against an adaptive challenge. Solutions to adaptive challenges come not by applying new routines or techniques, but through imaginative leaps. The originators of the adaptive concept explain that such challenges force "organizations to clarify their values, develop new strategies, and learn new ways of operating . . . Adaptive work is required when our deeply held beliefs are challenged, when the values that made us successful become less relevant, and when legitimate yet competing perspectives emerge."[1] Adaptation requires deep systemic change.

Canadian evangelical higher education in those forty years since 1976 seemed not to share church education's trouble. Its institutions grew in enrolment and sophistication. Now, however, its issues amount to an adaptive challenge.

- The Canadian legal system harries evangelical higher education. Some federal and provincial governments, and some professional bodies, perceive that institutions affiliated with Christian Higher Education Canada (CHEC) are not respecting human rights. The Supreme Court of Canada decision of June 15, 2018, may give leeway to government departments, agencies, and professional societies to implement any remedies they think appropriate. Funding a defence may severely test a CHEC institution's financial resources. In time, the state may take a more accommodating stance, but the next decade is likely to be difficult.

- Administrative decisions of governments and agencies trouble CHEC institutions. In 2016, the province of New Brunswick established a free tuition program for students from families of modest income, restricted to those attending publicly-funded institutions. Private and religious colleges, which were put at a comparative disadvantage, protested and initiated a lawsuit. However, the province went on to expand its program to students from middle-income households. In 2017, the federal government's demand that summer jobs sponsors sign an affirmation of progressive principles indicates how it could eventually restrict Canada Student Loans. Charitable status is also vulnerable.

- CHEC's public accreditation is under siege: the Canadian Association of University Teachers established for itself that institutional commitment to Christian beliefs negates academic freedom. After 2020, Universities Canada requires a human rights affirmation that may serve

1. Westerhoff, *Will Our Children Have Faith?*; Dawn, *Is It a Lost Cause?*; Groome, *Will There Be Faith?*; Foster, *From Generation to Generation*; Heifetz and Laurie, "Work of Leadership," 124–34.

to remove accreditation of its four evangelical members. Registrars can disrupt informal accreditation arrangements that benefit CHEC graduates. It is not inconceivable that challenges will arise to provincial charters or other mechanisms that allow CHEC institutions to grant publicly-recognized degrees.

- Challenges come from within its institutions. Students bring unorthodox beliefs about sexuality and gender. The 2012 Hemorrhaging Faith studied nearly 5,000 raised-Christian young adults. Among its Fence Sitter, Wanderer, and Rejecter segments—77% of those surveyed— not less than 88% agreed that "Churches should allow people who are practicing a gay or lesbian lifestyle to participate fully in their ministries."[2] Forty percent of church-engaged young adults agreed. The U.S.-based Pew and Public Religion Research Institute surveys have been reporting liberalizing attitudes to sex by evangelical young adults for at least five years.[3]

- Alongside these challenges are demographics. The churches that supply CHEC institutions with students and money have been declining in members and financial capacity. Whether a constituency will be able to fund its university, and supply sufficient numbers of students, are open questions. Top-rated schools may expect to add 3% more full-time equivalent students every year, but most institutions will maintain their work by programs that cannot fulfil their historic intention of Christian discipleship. Broadening the mission may undermine fundraising and recruiting from the older core constituency.

Canadian Christian higher education faces a litany of issues. The issues indicate an adaptive crisis. Together the issues call for creative and unprecedented solutions. My thesis is that a few big ideas explain Christian higher education's numerous problems. Being clear on the basic issues can help leaders focus on what matters most—a service in an adaptive situation.

GEORGE P. GRANT, ANALYST OF CANADA

My picture of Canadian Christian higher education's environment is from George Parkin Grant. Grant, a professor of philosophy at Dalhousie University and later a professor of religion at McMaster University, died in

2. Penner et al., "Hemorrhaging Faith," 92.

3. Penner et al., "Hemorrhaging Faith"; Diamant, "Though Still Conservative"; Cooperman and Smith, "America's Changing Religious Landscape."

1988. He is not to be confused with a living George Grant, the American pastor, school founder, and writer of biographies. The Canadian Grant gained recognition across the country from a bestselling book published in 1965 entitled *Lament for a Nation*.[4] Grant's bestseller lamented the loss of Canada's independent foreign policy. However, his deeper lament was for the end of a non-revolutionary society that resisted the American empire. Grant said a nation founded to maintain ancient traditions never had a chance against the modern dynamism of its larger southern neighbour. No one since Confederation provoked more discussion about the basic ideas that underwrite a dissenting North American nation.

Many Canadians who came of age in the 1970s saw Grant on television, heard him on public radio, and read him in the national paper of record, the *Toronto Globe and Mail*. Grant talked about something he called technology, though he seemed to mean more than the ordinary meaning of the word. He seemed to mean more than the capacity to make a radio set or to apply physics to make an X-ray machine. I was not sure what he was talking about then, and I have not fully plumbed his depths. Grant himself cautioned humility about more penetrating, more systematic, minds.

Grant was a small-c conservative critic of Canada in the mid-twentieth century. Other mid-century conservative cultural critics included Harold Innis, Donald Creighton, Vincent Massey, Hilda Neatby, W. L. Morton, and possibly Northrop Frye and Marshall McLuhan.[5] The mainstream history of Canada reads like a natural and inevitable liberal triumph. As the maternal connection with Great Britain weakened after 1918 and accelerated by the two world wars, Canada developed institutions such as the National Research Council that sponsored scientific activity. The imperative of progress reshaped Canadian institutions in line with its understanding of the way things should be. Conservatives like Grant, Innis, and Creighton read Canadian history differently and disputed the mainstream narrative.

Canadian conservative critics all saw that the growth in technology led to the substitution of progress for religion as the main spring of society. They did not think this was good. Their historian, Philip Massolin, says that, broadly, the critics accepted the basic Edmund Burke precept that true progress can be only be measured by reference to past accomplishments—physical, moral, philosophical, and intellectual. The critics wanted

---

4. Grant, *Lament for a Nation*.
5. Massolin, *Canadian Intellectuals*, 4, cf. 20–154.

to preserve values and outlooks of former times and ensure the persever-ance of intellectual and social traditions into the future.[6]

Grant goes further than any other conservative critic. To him, the new worldview is far more than technical capacities that can be used for good or ill. The twentieth-century German philosopher Martin Heidegger had used "technique" (*Technik*) to describe an all-encompassing attitude of hu-man mastery.[7] Grant's precise term, "technology," is similar to Heidegger's "technique": "the endeavor which summons forth everything (both human and non-human) to give its reason and through the summoning forth of those reasons turns the world into potential raw material, at the disposal of our recreative wills."[8] Technology in Grant's meaning is not X-rays or circuit boards but the commitment to its circumscription of what humans are able to know. "Technology" for Grant is the compound of *techne*, the ancient Greek term for the activity of making, together with its *logos*, the form or shape or reason behind the visible. Thus, Grant's "techno-logy" is the belief that humans summon the *logos* to control nature and human nature. Technology is not outside us, something we use or disregard. It is a new way of knowing about life and the world, a mindset. Its vision of progress becomes the object of its faith. If religion is any concern that fo-cuses a society toward what is deemed ultimately valuable, then technology working itself out in history is the new religious basis for Western societies. Grant was already saying in 1955 that "[e]conomic expansion through the control of nature by science has become the chief purpose of our existence.[9]

Grant points out that "any set of institutions is finally held together by a general conception of wellbeing which pervades them all."[10] Belief in progress reshaped Canada's institutions over two world wars and a cold war, but it is a different faith than traditional Christian faith. When the necessity of progress is assumed everywhere in every area of life, technol-ogy displaces any tradition that does not comport with it. The change of allegiance reshapes society into a new image with far-reaching and subtle consequences. An individual may be able to go without a car, but mobility altered the city map and city life radically. It is still possible to go without a smartphone. The computer may not exactly impose upon us the way it

6. Massolin, "Context and Content," 82.

7. Heidegger, *Question Concerning Technology*, 32.

8. Grant, *English-Speaking Justice*, 82.

9. Grant, "Minds of Men in the Atomic Age," 52.

10. Grant, "An Ethic of Community," 63.

is used, but who can doubt that the computer altered the way that most people relate to each other most of the time?[11]

Grant continues to inspire academic work. *Lament for a Nation* received a fortieth anniversary edition in 2005.[12] It is on the list of the one hundred most important books of the Literary History of Canada. At least six PhD dissertations since 2004 have his name in their title; others rely on him for a chapter or more. Dozens of articles and essay collections have appeared in the last twenty years.[13] University of Toronto Press published his collected works, the fourth and final volume in 2009.[14] His entry in the *Dictionary of Canadian Biography* states, "interest in his thought is likely to endure because of the gravity of the questions he addresses from a distinctively Canadian perspective."[15]

What would George Grant say to Canadian Christian higher education in 2019? On a review of his writings, he would advise faculty and administrators to keep teaching for a sense of the whole, to debunk historicism, and to grasp the power of lament.

1. Keep Teaching for the Whole

Grant would tell CHEC to keep teaching for the whole. He asked in 1951, "Why do our universities fail in providing a place where young Canadians are encouraged to think about their world in the broadest and deepest way?"[16] The answer was Canada's utilitarian revolution in the twentieth century. The pressure of public opinion brought departments of engineering, commerce, political economy, and medical specialties to universities.[17] Universities came to rely on government funding. The result was the utilitarian university, autonomous in practice from any religious body that founded it. "Since reward in money and power are directed to those concerned with goods . . . (for) a profit . . . all activities tend to become pale shadows of business." Grant said in 1955 that universities have become

11. In "The Computer," 280–98, originally from 1976, Grant analyzed the contention of a computer advocate that the tool is neutral.
12. Grant, *Lament for a Nation*.
13. Forbes, "Grant, George Parkin."
14. Grant, *Collected Works of George Grant*.
15. Forbes, "Grant, George Parkin."
16. Grant, "Philosophy," 173.
17. Massolin, *Canadian Intellectuals*, 75.

"a successful technological venture."[18] Success in most endeavors must be quantitative, so we have the "legal business, the medical business, the newspaper business, the religion business, the education business."[19] Technology sidelined holistic education.

Grant believed in a world higher than the world of human making. He recognized a world beyond time, beyond transitions, beyond change, that possesses a real existence. Grant came to this realization through direct experience. After a time as an air raid warden during the Blitz in London's heavily pounded East End industrial and docking area, Grant convalesced near Oxford. He walked through a gate. As he did so, he became newly aware of a world beyond time. For Grant, as for C. S. Lewis in a famous bus ride, God became real. Grant thus came to university teaching with a special sense of vocation. He believed university education was meant to lead students into a sense of the whole. For his teaching, Grant sought the basic motivations of modern culture. Humans can only know how we should live if we know the kind of universe we find ourselves in, he notes. He saw his task as "enucleating," locating the essence of modern thought intimately from within, laying bare "the animating source from which (its) behaviours come forth."[20] To Grant, his adopted discipline of philosophy was a way to think about life. He engages Heidegger and Ellul on technology, Simone Weil on love, suffering, and knowledge, and Nietzsche and Rousseau on historicism. His intellectual life was a discipleship of peeling the onion.

One might expect that faculties of philosophy would retain an independent assessment of the times, but these have been taken over by the spirit of the age. Grant's battle with his adopted discipline started early in his career with a submission on the subject to Vincent Massey's Royal Commission on National Development in the Arts, Letters and Sciences, whose final report was published in 1951. Grant portrayed Canadian philosophy as a handmaid to universities that trained technicians for the Canadian economy. This is not as it should be. Two decades later his verdict remained: "Analytical logistics plus historicist scholarship plus even rigorous science do not when added up equal philosophy."[21] He contrasted academic technicians with his ideal teachers of philosophy—those "steeped in the wisdom of the past and aware of society as it is . . . they must be aware

18. Grant, "An Ethic of Community," 57, 64.

19. Grant, "An Ethic of Community," 64.

20. Grant, *Time as History*, 14.

21. Grant, *English-Speaking Justice*, 89.

of the meaning of the various other studies in the university."[22] "Philosophy is not ... a technique. Its purpose is to ... see in unity all techniques, so that ... the economist see(s) the productive capacity of his nation in relation to the love of God."[23]

Even humanities departments, shrunken in proportion to science, technology, and professional faculties, adapted themselves to the new idea of research. Grant scoffed:

> The humanities research which is being realized in Canada is not to be identified with the traditional university. It comes forth from intercourse between two very untraditional partners: the post-Nietzschean nineteenth-century German university which mounted American capitalism. The mating of the German model of the university with American capitalism produced in the fifties its Chicagos and Berkeleys and Yales. Now in the 1970s we are producing our imitations of these in English-speaking Canada. Poor old Canada is enthusiastically taking on the American wave in its decadence.[24]

For Grant, it follows that "antiquarianism in the humanities has often been a means to cloak the fact that these studies have nothing significant to say about living in the technological era."[25] Humanities research on the model of physical sciences produces "flies in amber."[26] A quote from one of Grant's students from his two decades at the McMaster University religion department captures his contrasting appeal:

> To him the business of living and the business of philosophy were the same thing. And I think that that was one of the things that made him so attractive to students, because they felt that in a sense he was saying to them that the most important thing you've got is your life and how you live it.[27]

Grant praises faith-based higher learning in his 1951 Royal Commission report. The Catholic church had just founded the Pontifical Institute for Medieval Studies at the University of Toronto. There, Grant said, "Philosophy is not seen as an isolated technique but as something related to the

22. Grant, "Philosophy," 171.

23. Grant, *Collected Works of George Grant Volume 4*, 6.

24. Grant, *Technology and Justice*, 100; cited in Lathangue, "George Grant."

25. Grant, *Technology and Empire*, 81; cited in Lathangue, "George Grant," 50.

26. Grant, "Battle Between Teaching and Research," 201.

27. Grant and David, *George Grant in Conversation*, 8.

other facets of the Catholic life—history and theology, art and liturgy."[28] Arthur Holmes, Wheaton College philosophy professor and author of *The Idea of a Christian College*, writes similarly. The Christian college is not only a nurturing environment, not only for biblical studies per se, and not only for encouragement of commitment. "The Christian college is distinctive in that the Christian faith can touch the entire range of life and learning to which a liberal education exposes students."[29] Grant might encourage Canadian Christian higher education to represent the last holistic education in the country.

Grant made his own attempt at faith-based learning. In 1961, he joined the faculty of McMaster University's recently-formed religion department. Formerly a Baptist college, McMaster University secularized and became a successful research university. It even possessed its own nuclear reactor. Grant hoped for a true university within the McMaster research multiversity. The religion department would provide real education by teaching the insights of Christianity, Judaism, eastern religions, and ancient Greek thought in relation to modernity. After twenty years, Grant resigned. Star scholars who modelled their research on physical sciences battled him over the tenure of candidates who would advance his vision. The stars obtained major funding and came to dominate the department. Grant called their research the output of a museum culture that catalogued and exhibited the past but did not understand it for present-day life. At McMaster University, the American-German research model of education triumphed over the English-classical formation model. Grant called his venture a failure.[30]

Grant's experience at McMaster University shows the need to persist in order to achieve genuinely Christian ways of teaching and institutional policies. As for Grant, teaching for the whole involves a clear contrast with the dominant worldview. Modernity's choices were contingent—they were choices that thought leaders like Machiavelli, Hobbes, Spinoza, Vico, Rousseau, or Hegel consciously made against classical philosophy.[31] Therefore, a university can imagine different choices and a different world. CHEC has a stake in developing a coherent alternative view of politics, economics, social life, epistemology, and ontology. Without a coherent alternative, resistance to the technology juggernaut is unlikely to succeed. Canadian

28. Grant, "Philosophy," 171.

29. Holmes, *Idea of a Christian College*, 45.

30. Christian, "Museum Culture," 302–22.

31. Grant, *Lament for a Nation* (1989), 95.

Christian higher education can differ radically from the mainstream only by exercising discernment.

A CHEC institution's policies must be made to match its aims. Evangelical universities are not research universities with a religious dimension. Grant would urge CHEC to work through the institutional imperatives. CHEC tenure policies should match the aim of the school. Tenure should require integrated Christian scholarship. As difficult as it will be, a tenure application without substantial engagement with the meaning of the whole should be refused. If Christian scholarship is imperative to CHEC schools, their faculty development efforts will be different than secular ones. CHEC's proximate task remains integration of faith and knowledge for Kingdom agents. Grant's own scholarship is a model to emulate, but his struggle with leaders who did not share his concerns means that implementing policies is likely to be hard work.

2. Debunk Historicism

The need to teach for the whole implies Grant's second recommendation. Grant intensified his analysis of technology when he recognized its alliance with historicism. A vivid picture of historicism can be found in Rousseau. Grant recognized him as one of the most important shapers of the modern mind. In his *Émile* (1762), Rousseau runs a thought-experiment on the imaginary education of a boy. His protagonist, Émile, is kept from social contact until maturity. No reactions to unjust authorities including parents will be allowed to deform his innate goodness. Émile's journey to maturity is a simile of the journey needed by a whole society to move progressively toward emancipation. Accepting the institution of property ownership, society took a wrong turn in history and brought on itself unjust relationships that make genuine, that is, autonomous, life impossible. Society will be built on new-model men like Émile. As new-justice institutions eliminate the false motivations spawned by traditionally-unjust ones, humanity's underlying goodness will rise to undreamed-of heights. By changing social institutions, we progressively discover the depths of what it means to be human. Authenticity can take us far. Humanity should make its own destiny in history by willpower.[32]

Historicism is the narrowing of time to history. Transcendent time is not recognized. The meaning of human life is found within the two poles of

32. Bloom, "Introduction," in Rousseau, *Emile*, 3–28.

birth and death. Nothing escapes the historical process. Knowing is relative to its time and place. Consequently, everything humans can know is what we make. Technology is imperative. Everything non-human and human must yield to it. Human control of the future depends on continued summoning of objects to give their reasons. Technology disregards the ancient world's transcendent source of knowledge in favour of knowing-as-making. This world is its only horizon. Historicism and technology are close allies.[33]

Grant noted already in *Lament* that "differences in the technological state are able to exist only in private activities."[34] Liberalism was the perfect political partner for technology: "Tastes are different, and we should have a society that caters to the plurality of tastes. Nobody minds very much if we prefer women, or dogs, or boys, as long as we cause no public inconvenience."[35] Public technology matches well with private heterology. He continued:

> When men are committed to technology, they are also committed to continual change in institutions and customs. Freedom must be the first political principle—the freedom to change any order that stands in the way of technological advance. Such a society cannot take seriously the conception of an eternal order that stands in the way of technological advance.[36]

Grant's most urgent engagement with historicism came after the American Supreme Court decision in 1973 that legalized abortion. As *Lament for a Nation* reacted to Canada's unwillingness to control its territory, Grant's 1974 Wood Lectures at Mount Allison University in New Brunswick reacted to the Supreme Court ruling and John Rawls's democratic contractarian ethics. Grant used the decision to raise a profound problem. Any society revolves around an ultimate good. Its shared life depends on arbitration of the good, that is, justice. Rawls's *A Theory of Justice*, a major work of philosophical ethics, treads lightly around abortion.[37] Academic writing is able to obscure an issue, but judges on the ground are forced to make choices. The Supreme Court decision signaled that the convenience of the articulate strong member overrules justice due to the inarticulate member of the species—that is, the justice due on any traditional view of

33. Grant, *Time as History*.

34. Grant, *Technology and Empire*, 126; cited in Lathangue, "George Grant," 56.

35. Grant, *Lament for a Nation* (1989), 57.

36. Grant, *Lament for a Nation* (2005), 71.

37. Rawls, *Theory of Justice*.

a human being. After the decision, members of the human species may be ruled unworthy of a right to life itself, if unable to defend themselves due to age or intelligence. Thus, the decision made plain the deep injustice that a society organized for progress fosters. Traditional ideas of good and evil have given way to what is pragmatically "good." A progressive society cannot allow any teleological aim—any aim known in advance—to foreclose technology's open future. Since traditional justice can block new possibilities, the state will act to force the future open. Historicism in effect redefines virtue in its own image.

Grant's analysis shows that technology always included implicit ideas of right and wrong. Textbooks for Christian university worldview courses, such as Walsh and Middleton's *Transforming Vision* or James Sire's *The Universe Next Door*, point to the mathematician and philosopher René Descartes as originator of an interior world separated from the public, exterior one.[38] Descartes proposed a subjective starting point for rationality—"I think, therefore I am." He thus inaugurated a dualism of interiority against an exterior world that is measurable, and thus accessible to scientific control. For years, my integration seminar heard about Walsh and Middleton's dual mind. For instance, how scientific thought tends to devalue artistic and religious expression. Or, how the heart of the Romantic rebel opposes the mind of science. That science increasingly pressures human values: as neuroscience and biopsychology press toward scientific understanding of human relationships, biological imperatives rationalize and eliminate love. Cartesian thought oscillates in history between quantities and qualities. On the one hand is artistic and cultural life; on the other hand, objective public facts. So I would say to my seminar students.

Grant showed me that ethics in a technological society is significantly more than an irrational split of human values against scientific facts. Grant's 1965 ideas of technology and liberal public ethics were not a shared system—not yet "thought together," as he would put it. But his 1969 Massey Lectures showed more clearly that Rousseauan and Nietzschean historicism is inseparable from technology.

Technology's ethic was not fully expressed at the beginning of the modern period. The philosopher Friedrich Nietzsche's contribution in the 1870s and 1880s was to show that traditional morality had lost its public foundation. Grant shared with classical philosophy the understanding that ultimate good is real and its derivatives, such as justice and virtue, share

---

38. Walsh and Middleton, *Transforming Vision*; Sire, *Universe Next Door*.

its objective existence. But God died as a factor in public consciousness. Traditional justice died too, said Nietzsche. Modern philosophers who upheld traditional ethics were confused. Nietzsche called Kant's theory of a universal innate ethical imperative a delay tactic. Kant's unfounded theory allowed the traditional content of morality to continue. Technology, however, now drives a replacement ethic better suited to itself—historicist justice. Willful control of nature includes human nature. The fetus is better seen as a biological accident. To Grant, the abortion decision bears out Nietzsche's prescience.[39]

Grant admits that Western societies cannot simply erase scientific knowledge. Modernity brought gifts, including modern medicine and household labour-saving devices. He concluded *English-Speaking Justice* with the challenge to think traditional ideas of good and evil together with technological historicism. Joan O'Donovan suggests this challenge was a false ending. Grant knew that traditional justice is without support after the death of God. A reconciliation of transcendent and purely immanent ideas of justice is a non-starter. The real challenge is not a research project but to restore the possibility of traditional ideas of good and evil.[40] The obstacles faced by religious communities and CHEC are thus systemic. Grant emphasizes that human beings drive their practices based on what they believe is real. They are not occasional differences over public ethics in a normally peaceful, mutual accommodation.

Recent decisions show that the underlying ethic of technological historicism continues to find occasions to express itself. Technology is a view of reliable knowledge that impels courts and governments to act as they do when compromises seem impossible. Since technology is the basic understanding of reality shared by judges, politicians, and most of the public in North America, it is inevitable that law will affirm an open-ended future. As the abortion decision made evident, knowing-as-making will insist on its ethic. When a can-do approach to good and evil prevails, traditional ideas of good and evil appear as premodern choices of individuals. As the sneer goes, if you do not like same-sex marriage, do not choose one. The widespread understanding of marriage that made it a social institution has weakened. Canada's Prime Minister of the time defended the change to marriage law in 2003 by saying, "Society evolves." Grant would tell CHEC that Canadian society's rolling back of Christian marriage is the most recent

---

39. Grant, *Time as History*.

40. O'Donovan, *George Grant*, 152.

frontier in the pursuit of maximum authenticity. Grant makes clear what those who affirm teleological purpose—institutions and individuals—are up against.

The challenge of historicism is within CHEC not outside it. Smith, Denton, Dean, Penner, and other researchers profiled beliefs of young Christians in the past decade. The Hemorrhaging Faith study documented the outright loss of young adults from mainline and evangelical churches. Those still inside the church buy a faith that is "Moralistic Therapeutic Deism."[41] Church and family nurture are not building resistance to a culture carried by peers, social media, and public schools. Student beliefs about marriage and gender bring progressive thinking into CHEC classrooms. Its institutions need to take initiative to counter the trend.[42]

Historicism is an under-appreciated factor in present-day higher education. In the 1940s and 1950s, Christian scholars inspired by the neo-orthodox theology of Karl Barth and Emil Brunner sought to reinstall Christian beliefs as legitimate public beliefs for scholarship. They held con-ferences and maintained a journal on British and American higher educa-tion. The movement collapsed in the early 1960s. Douglas Sloan identifies their Achilles heel as exactly the problem of historicism. Until the reform-ers could articulate a view of Scripture that made it more than another historical-critical artifact, they remained within the modern problematic. Historicism sees a revealed text to be as relative to its own time as any text. Relativism erodes its authority. Thus, no academic needed to pay reform-ing proposals any serious attention.[43] CHEC institutions are less than clear about research that best fits their mission. Lack of clarity on historicism makes some of its research acceptable to the scholarly guild but at the cost of weakening its ability to breed resisters of secularity. Grant would urge CHEC to summon the courage to be different.

Grant would call CHEC to clarity and courage in its mission in Ca-nadian society. Its schools have a stake in promoting an alternative way of understanding the world—a metaphysics—that underwrites God-derived ethics. Any writing that clarifies or extends CHEC's dissent from technol-ogy should be funded and recognized. CHEC's dissent is profound; it be-lieves suffering in life can serve the purpose of the triune God. The modern

41. Smith and Denton, *Soul Searching*, 162.

42. Smith and Denton, *Soul Searching*; Dean, *Almost Christian*; Penner et al., "Hem-orrhaging Faith."

43. Sloan, *Faith and Knowledge*.

period sought to minimize suffering by minimizing chance through control of nature. Openness to God's dealing in history is a key difference—if not *the* key difference—with historicism. Christ embraced the will of God and denied the temptations to any easier path. Thus the central symbol of Christianity—the Cross—reminds its followers of the Christian interpretation of history.

Yet dissent must be incarnated. Formal study of life and family issues would flesh it out. After all, Mennonite schools study peace. A CHEC intellectual *ressourcement* needs to be matched by bold moves to underline Christian commitment to the sanctity of life in all its forms—as Grant said, a truly basic issue for the technological society. An alliance with L'Arche shelters for intellectually challenged persons would be a natural expression of the contrasting worldview—as strange as it might sound at first. Broadly, CHEC urgently needs a Christian social ethic that can incarnate a resistance theology. We need to reimagine holistic education in CHEC institutions. Ultimately, CHEC is not only for student development in all parameters but for the fullest worship of the God of Jesus Christ of the Scriptures—heart, soul, mind, and strength—in a society like ours now.

By contrasting ancient philosophy with Nietzsche, Grant was able to display his major concern, the shift from transcendently-anchored classical to immanent modernity. Critics object that Grant's sources serve his purposes. However, Grant's sustained contrast is between premodern humanity, embedded in its universe and living out beliefs from a religious conception of the whole, and modern buffered humanity, now spectators who seek mastery of the Earth, of its own species, and perhaps even of the universe.[44] Grant discerns a substitution of beliefs, as does Charles Taylor's 2007 *A Secular Age*. As such, Taylor and Grant agree that secularization is not a subtraction narrative, in which superfluous religious belief is progressively stripped away. Taylor takes a finer-grained historical and philosophical approach than Grant by tracing a series of intellectual and social moves in European Christian society and locating the drive toward secularism in Christian civilization's perfectionist pursuit of reforms that would make every Christian a fully practicing Christian.[45] Grant's broad brush predates Taylor's fine detail. Both see substitution not subtraction.

---

44. Planinc, "Paradox," 17–45.

45. Taylor, *A Secular Age*.

3. Harness the Power of Lament

Thirdly, Grant would urge CHEC to harness the power of lament. His 1965 book, *Lament for a Nation*, decried the loss of a way of life to technological imperialism. Lester Pearson's Liberals campaigned in 1963 on accommodating the Americans, who sought to install nuclear warheads on missiles based in Canada. *Lament* said that the election of the Liberals meant that Canada's will to exist was gone. It claimed that the loss of Canada fits a pattern of traditions succumbing to modernity. Like Edmund Burke resisted the French Revolution, the original Canada resisted a revolutionary republic like the United States. Of all societies on the planet, Enlightenment ideas are most fully expressed in American life. Canada's founders were differently minded; they believed that ancient traditions were a good guide to social life and politics. Now the influence of corporations and business thinking in general in politics, the civil service, and higher education doomed Canada, not to mention American cultural influences through print, radio, and film. Formal independence might continue after the warheads, but practical independence was over. Grant famously wrote, "[t]he impossibility of conservatism in our era is the impossibility of Canada. As Canadians we attempted a ridiculous task in trying to build a conservative nation in the age of progress, on a continent we share with the most dynamic nation on earth. The current of modern history was against us."[46] Canada was not a historical accident or merely a nation of losers. If anyone thought so, Grant's work proves otherwise. Definite conceptions had called the nation into being. The conceptions were defunct.

Grant was prophetic about French Canada, in both senses: as one who saw the future and as a truth-teller. Grant said, "Canada originally was put together by two groups of people who didn't have much in common, but did not want to be Americans."[47] The alliance with similarly-minded English Canadians sustained Quebec, alongside its Catholicism. *Lament* saw the Quiet Revolution of the early 1960s as leaving behind the only basis for a distinct linguistic community on the American continent. Quebec young people wished to maintain their traditions, but they also wished for the bounty of technology.[48] The quiet revolutionaries thus failed to disavow the mechanism that drives a single continental culture. Grant was not joking when he pointed to touristy New Orleans as a possible Quebec future.

46. Grant, *Lament for a Nation* (2005), 67.

47. "George Grant," [n.p.].

48. Grant, *Lament for a Nation* (2005), 78.

Creole speech and Cajun cooking notwithstanding, New Orleans is an American city. To Grant, French Canada's demise was inevitable.

Coming when it did, Grant's lament could only be a provocation. The continentalist vision of Canada was birthing initiatives such as the new Canadian flag and Expo '67. Both marked a post-British understanding of the country. Canada could hardly have lost the nationhood it was just gaining. Grant's lament is not conservative in any typical way, however. Part of Grant's appeal is that he transcends the usual categories. The Liberal Party of Canada advanced integration with the USA for most of the twentieth century. But the Progressive Conservatives under Brian Mulroney went further, bringing in North American free trade. Stephen Harper's party abandoned traditional conservatism altogether for pro-market economics. Grant was no Liberal, but he was not a conservative like those conservatives either. For him, only collective national effort and national institutions could maintain independence. *Lament* was an inspiration to far-left thinkers who wished to resist the American empire, but Grant was not on their side either. To Grant, both capitalist and communist systems summon forth reason to turn the world into raw material. Grant was even-handed about the evil empires. Technology spawned both systems.

Grant's lament is not for the weakening of the British connection, either. Critics note his deep family ties to British Canada. Grant's paternal grandfather, George Monro Grant, was a Principal of Queen's College who helped make it one of the country's leading universities and booster of Canada in the British Empire. His maternal grandfather, George Parkin, was a founding secretary of the Rhodes Trust scholarships to Oxford University. Both grandfathers appreciated Great Britain as a cultural and economic counterweight to the giant to the south, but their grandson was not a reflexive Anglophile.

Some who defended the new Canada under-read Grant. Former Liberal leader Michael Ignatieff wrote, "no reasonable person can conclude that the Canadian identity is weaker now (after the new flag and the Charter of Rights, for example) than it was in 1965. Yes, we've gone into free trade with the United States and, as we did so, we feared assimilation, loss of identity and loss of sovereignty. Can we honestly say these fears have been realized?"[49] He seems to prefer the pluralism of technological civilization. Ignatieff dismisses his uncle George Grant as a technological determinist,

---

49. Ignatieff, "George Grant Was 'Wrong, Wrong, Wrong.'"

as do Gad Horowitz, Arthur Kroker, and Andrew Potter.[50] Their objections are shallow. Grant objects to the character of public life. He objects to technology's capacity to narrow a people's range of possibilities to the purely immanent: "the tight circle in which we live sapped the ability to think about objective human excellence, while imposing technological efficiency. Educated in terms of [technology's] curriculum we judge it good."[51] Sheila Grant says the critics miss *Lament*'s closing chapter, where Grant draws his line between classical and modern philosophy.

To lament is to feel profound sorrow for or concerning; to mourn the loss of; bewail.[52] Grant admits that most Canadians could not lament the loss of pre-scientific ideas of being human "because most people think society only moves on to better things . . . how can one lament necessity?"[53] But lament recognizes the good that has passed. A lament does not imply despair. Though a Canadian encyclopedia article on Grant described "a brooding philosopher of apparently implacable pessimism," Grant used to repeat, "It always matters what each one of us does."[54] His writing liberates. Dennis Lee, a poet and Grant's publisher, wrote,

> I recognize all the bleakness for which Grant is often criticised. But only with my head; for months after I read his essays I felt a surge of release and exhilaration. To find one's tongue-tied sense of civil loss and bafflement given words at last, to hear one's own most inarticulate hunches out loud, because most immediate in the bloodstream—and not prettied up, and in prose like a fastidious groundswell—was to stand erect at last in one's own space.[55]

Robin Lathangue compares Grant's prose to Mikhail Bakhtin's publications about carnival in Soviet Russia—ways of busting the pieties. "Grant's very mode of expression constitutes a rejection of what he saw as the sterility of modern academic and political discourse."[56] Grant might frustrate or elate but never falls into sterility. As Lee found, he reorients.

---

50. Potter's introduction to Grant, *Lament for a Nation* (2005), l–lxiii.

51. Grant, "The University Curriculum (1975)," 199.

52. Brown and Trumble, eds., *Shorter Oxford English Dictionary*, s.v. lament.

53. Grant, *Lament for a Nation* (1989), 4–5.

54. Quoted in Westberg, "George Grant."

55. Lee, "Cadence, Country, Silence," 161; Lathangue, "George Grant and the Impulse to Carnival," 48–49.

56. Lathangue, "George Grant and the Impulse to Carnival," 47.

Lament can be culturally productive. Grant ends *Lament* with a line from the Aeneid: "They were stretching out their hands in love to the further shore."[57] The souls awaiting Virgil's selective ferryman ached for something better. Virgil's shades live in the awareness that historical judgment lies beyond this world. All lamenters live in the knowledge of a better way of life. Their longing points to the principle of resistance. Diaspora Jews after 587 BC, their institutions burned to the ground, maintained the faith through lament. They went on to develop durable institutions of resistance, such as the synagogue, and codified their sacred text.

Lament can spur determination. Grant's lament galvanized Canadian politics. Developments of the 1970s including the Committee for an Independent Canada, the Foreign Investment Review Agency, and Petro-Canada may be traced to *Lament*. Grant's influence appears in Canadian political science, literature, communications studies and history, plus religious studies, theological ethics, and education. By lamenting what was lost, Grant stirred a protesting consciousness.

CHEC can no longer succeed by numerical growth. CHEC is losing its immediate horizon. The technological-business pattern of thinking influences its leaders and faculty members too, and disappointment is natural. CHEC must sustain itself against the way most people now think and how they organize themselves. What served to build CHEC institutions when Christianity was borderline—a transformist approach to mainstream culture, often with an open admissions policy—now may work against the ability to educate Christian leaders so the church survives. Moving out of mainstream society may not really be optional.

However, Christianity has done best when not allied with the state. Christianity is a Way. It is initiation into a life. When the church supplied the ideology of the Roman Empire after AD 330, its identity and teaching was distorted. This is the argument of Hauerwas and Willimon in *Resident Aliens*, of Philip Sherrard, and recently of Rod Dreher.[58] CHEC's sponsoring institutions are churches that never were establishment churches. They may accept virtues in marginalization better than a mainline Christian like Grant was able to. Lamenting could spur reorganization.

57. Grant, *Lament for a Nation* (1989), 97.

58. Hauerwas and Willimon, *Resident Aliens*; Sherrard, *The Greek East*; Dreher, *Benedict Option*.

CONCLUSION

Canadian Christian higher education now shares church education's long-time adaptive challenge. That challenge is the pressure of a substitute worldview. Barring unforeseen developments, technology's historicist ethic will drive orthodox Christian faith from the public square. Despair is one reaction. Lament is another. The advantage of lament is its capacity to spur innovative strategies for survival. To borrow from M. C. Hammer—a source Grant would not likely rock to—CHEC is "too legit to quit."

In a widely-reposted article, Carl Trueman predicted that even those Christian universities that refuse government funding are likely to experience state activism. For example, their charitable status can be revoked. Bob Jones University in 1983 lost charitable status for maintaining a racist marriage policy. Now that sexual orientation has joined race as grounds for government intervention, Trueman says that Christian universities should "prepare for winter" by doing two things:

> financial planning for the worst-case scenario, where not only federal money but also tax-exempt status is revoked; and careful reflection on how the curriculum can cultivate accurate and wholesome aesthetic judgment. And, given the very brief time colleges have to shape young people's minds, they need to see their task as adjunct to the greater task of family and, above all, church—the vessels that carry us from the cradle to the grave.[59]

Grant would urge the same.

Occasionally, corporations such as the old IBM perform a startling reorganization. They strip off dead lines of business, set up new structures to advance winners, and preserve their capital. Creative and radical action can preserve the precious seed for the future. In the new cultural climate, churches sell a building to move into a new ministry frontier. CHEC's adaptive challenge can be met by clarified vision, new strategies, and new ways of operating. Grant's exposition of the basic issues helps leaders to avoid making merely technical responses to the adaptive challenge. Grant gives adapters a striking overview of the cultural environment, a system organized for never-ending progress by technological historicism, wielding a sharp anti-tradition ethic. Believers must bear witness for Christ in this time and place. The bedrock of Canadian believers identified by sociologists awaits leadership from CHEC for the next generation.

---

59. Trueman, "Preparing for Winter."

BIBLIOGRAPHY

Bloom, Allan D. "Introduction." In *J.-J. Rousseau, Emile, or On Education*, translated by Allan D. Bloom, 3–28. New York: Basic Books, 1979.

Brown, Lesley, and William R. Trumble, eds. *Shorter Oxford English Dictionary*. 2 vols. Oxford: Oxford University Press, 2002.

Christian, William. *George Grant: A Biography*. Toronto: University of Toronto Press, 1993.

Cooperman, Alan, and Greg Smith. "America's Changing Religious Landscape." Washington, DC: Pew Research Center, 2015.

Dawn, Marva J. *Is It a Lost Cause? Having the Heart of God for the Church's Children*. Grand Rapids: Eerdmans, 1997.

Dean, Kenda Creasy. *Almost Christian: What the Faith of Our Teenagers Is Telling the American Church*. Oxford: Oxford University Press, 2010.

Diamant, Jeff. "Though Still Conservative, Young Evangelicals Are More Liberal Than Their Elders on Some Issues." Pew Research Center (May 4, 2017). No pages. Online: http://www.pewresearch.org/fact-tank/2017/05/04/though-still-conservative-young-evangelicals-are-more-liberal-than-their-elders-on-some-issues/.

Dreher, Rod. *The Benedict Option: A Strategy for Christians in a Post-Christian Nation*. New York: Sentinel, 2017.

Forbes, H. D. "Grant, George Parkin." In *Dictionary of Canadian Biography*. Ottawa: National Archives of Canada and National Library of Canada, 2003. No pages. Online: http://www.biographi.ca/en/bio/grant_george_parkin_21E.html.

Foster, Charles R. *From Generation to Generation: The Adaptive Challenge of Mainline Protestant Education in Forming Faith*. Eugene, OR: Cascade, 2012.

"George Grant." Impressions with Ramsey Cook. Canadian Broadcasting Corp., August 5, 1973.

Grant, George. "The Battle Between Teaching and Research, Globe and Mail, April 28, 1980, 7." In *The George Grant Reader*, edited by William Christian and Sheila Grant, 200–205. Toronto: University of Toronto Press, 2008.

———. *Collected Works of George Grant: Volume 1 (1933–1950)*, edited by Arthur Davis and Peter C. Emberley. Toronto: University of Toronto Press, 2000.

———. *Collected Works of George Grant: Volume 4 (1970–1988)*, edited by Arthur Davis. Toronto: University of Toronto Press, 2016.

———. "The Computer Does Not Impose on Us the Ways It Should Be Used." In *Collected Works of George Grant: Volume 4 (1970–1988)*, edited by Arthur Davis, 280–98. Toronto: University of Toronto Press, 2016.

———. *English Speaking Justice*. Toronto: House of Anansi, 1998.

———. "An Ethic of Community." In *The George Grant Reader*, edited by William Christian and Sheila Grant, 59–75. Toronto: University of Toronto Press, 2008.

———. *Lament for a Nation: The Defeat of Canadian Nationalism*. Toronto: McClelland and Stewart, 1965.

———. *Lament for a Nation: The Defeat of Canadian Nationalism*. Carleton Library Series 50. Ottawa: Carleton University Press, 1989.

———. *Lament for a Nation: The Defeat of Canadian Nationalism*, edited by Andrew Potter. Kingston: McGill-Queen's Press, 2005.

———. "Minds of Men in the Atomic Age." In *The George Grant Reader*, edited by William Christian and Sheila Grant, 51–58. Toronto: University of Toronto Press, 1998.

―――. "Philosophy." In *The George Grant Reader*, edited by William Christian and Sheila Grant, 157–73. Toronto: University of Toronto Press, 1998.

―――. *Technology and Empire*. Toronto: House of Anansi, 1991.

―――. *Technology and Justice*. Toronto: House of Anansi, 1991.

―――. *Time as History*. Toronto: University of Toronto Press, 1995.

―――. "The University Curriculum (1975)." In *The George Grant Reader*, edited by William Christian and Sheila Grant, 191–200. Toronto: University of Toronto Press, 1998.

Grant, George, and David Cayley. *George Grant in Conversation*. Toronto: House of Anansi, 1995.

Groome, Thomas H. *Will There Be Faith? A New Vision for Educating and Growing Disciples*. New York: HarperOne, 2011.

Hauerwas, Stanley, and W. H. Willimon. *Resident Aliens: Life in the Christian Colony*. Nashville, TN: Abingdon, 1989.

Heidegger, Martin. "The Question Concerning Technology." In *The Question Concerning Technology, and Other Essays*, 3–35. Translated by William Lovitt. New York: Harper & Row, 1977.

Heifetz, Ronald A., and Donald L. Laurie. "The Work of Leadership." *Harvard Business Review* 75 (1997) 124–34.

Holmes, Arthur Frank. *The Idea of a Christian College*. Rev. ed. Grand Rapids: Eerdmans, 1987.

Ignatieff, Michael. "George Grant Was 'Wrong, Wrong, Wrong.'" Globe and Mail, April 17, 2009. Online: https://www.theglobeandmail.com/arts/books-and-media/george-grant-was-wrong-wrong-wrong/article4210782/.

Lathangue, Robin. "George Grant and the Impulse to Carnival." *TOPIA: Canadian Journal of Cultural Studies* 20 (2008) 43–64.

Lee, Dennis. "Cadence, Country, Silence: Writing in Colonial Space." *Boundary* 2 (1974) 151–68.

Massolin, Philip A. *Canadian Intellectuals, the Tory Tradition and the Challenge of Modernity, 1939–1970*. Toronto: University of Toronto Press, 2001.

―――. "Context and Content: Harold Innis, Marshall McLuhan, and George Grant and the Role of Technology in Modern Society." *Past Imperfect* 5 (1996) 81–118.

O'Donovan, Joan E. *George Grant and the Twilight of Justice*. Toronto: University of Toronto Press, 1984.

Penner, James, et al. "Hemorrhaging Faith: Why and When Canadian Young Adults Are Leaving, Staying and Returning to Church." Foundational Research Document Commissioned by EFC Youth and Young Adult Ministry Roundtable. Ottawa: Evangelical Fellowship of Canada, 2012.

―――. *Hemorrhaging Faith: Why and When Canadian Young Adults Are Leaving, Staying and Returning to Church*. Richmond Hill, ON: Evangelical Fellowship of Canada, 2012.

Planinc, Zdravko. "Paradox and Polyphony in Grant's Critique of Modernity." In *George Grant and the Future of Canada*, edited by Yusuf K. Umar, 17–45. Calgary: University of Calgary Press, 1992.

Rawls, John. *A Theory of Justice*. Cambridge, MA: Belknap Press of Harvard University Press, 1971.

Sherrard, Philip. *The Greek East and the Latin West: A Study in the Christian Tradition*. Oxford: Oxford University Press, 1959.

Sire, James W. *The Universe Next Door: A Basic Worldview Catalog.* 5th ed. Downers Grove, IL: IVP Academic, 2009.

Sloan, Douglas. *Faith and Knowledge: Mainline Protestantism and American Higher Education.* Louisville: Westminster John Knox, 1994.

Smith, Christian, and Melinda Lundquist Denton. *Soul Searching: The Religious and Spiritual Lives of American Teenagers.* Oxford: Oxford University Press, 2005.

Taylor, Charles. *A Secular Age.* Cambridge, MA: Belknap Press of Harvard University Press, 2007.

Trueman, Carl. "Preparing for Winter." *First Things* (January 2018). No pages. Online: https://www.firstthings.com/web-exclusives/2018/01/preparing-for-winter

Walsh, Brian J., and J. Richard Middleton. *The Transforming Vision: Shaping a Christian World View.* Downers Grove, IL: InterVarsity, 1984.

Westberg, Daniel. "George Grant." *First Things* (November 1994). No pages. Online: https://www.firstthings.com/article/1994/11/george-grant.

Westerhoff, John H. *Will Our Children Have Faith?* New York: Seabury, 1976.

10

How a Common Core Curriculum Serves the Identity and Mission of a Christian Liberal Arts University

Nicki Rehn and Linda Schwartz

BACKGROUND

WHAT WAS THE PROBLEM that this project needed to solve? Initially, the answer seemed clear enough: the need to define institutional distinctiveness as the university we serve grew to include popular professional and science programs, which have heavy credit requirements inside their disciplines, due in no small measure to the prescriptive standards of outside licensing bodies.[1] Conversations to initiate the project soon became fraught and complex because of current parallel challenges with content and delivery of existing core courses. Examples include: (1) major dissatisfaction on the part of students and faculty with the way in which the required introductory English course is taught (literature-based rather than writing-based); (2) the question of where, and to whom, Christian Studies core requirements belong (Faculty of Theology or Faculty of Arts

---

1. This is a longstanding tension in liberal arts and faith-based universities, where the core curriculum is eroded in favor of serving the professional demands of the marketplace. Professional programs may be expedient for institutional recruitment but difficult to reconcile with institutional mission.

and Science); and (3) whether Fine Arts requirements should be dropped from the core curriculum altogether.

Declining enrolments in the humanities threaten the viability of Christian Studies, English, and History as program majors; thus, specific required gateway courses in History, English, Philosophy, Bible, and Theology have become service courses to the rest of the university. This has led to turf wars and siloed disciplines in a small university, an issue that has been identified by V. James Mannoia as "the politics of the core."[2] Furthermore, conversations with students reveal that they are not seeing connections between disciplines in this gateway model and faith and learning.

This is why a discussion about core curriculum is so important at this juncture in the history of our university. Gilbert Meilaender states, "It is foolhardy to suppose that the liberal arts flourish at an academic institution simply because it talks about providing a liberal education."[3] Unpacking what we mean by liberal arts through our programming is important to our integrity. A core should be a statement about what matters to the institution, or put another way, the university's strategic vision should shape its curricula.[4] A common experience revolving around "faith seeking understanding"[5] and what distinguishes a private liberal arts education from other academies of higher learning, despite the fact that students will align with certain programs right from the start, is critical for their unique formation.

Moreover, the embodiment of learning distinctives that align with a stated mission is critical to the survival of liberal arts education and faith-based schooling. If Christian liberal arts education is to be a vital force alongside the current push of public higher education institutions as nothing more than information providers to consumer clients for marketplace-preparedness, it must appeal to and reinforce the stance of the alternative position: a rich, values-based, thoughtful, and transformative experience of undergraduate education.

There were few shared views in the initial stages of the project (2016), but several principles were loosely agreed upon:

2. Mannoia, *Christian Liberal Arts*, 134.

3. Meilaender, "Who Needs a Liberal Education?" 102.

4. McInnes et al., *Handbook for Executive Leadership*, 15.

5. Anselm of Canterbury, *Proslogium*, 178.

- That there be a common core that everyone in an undergraduate program is required to complete. There was strong agreement that this should be set at a minimum of 27 credit hours.
- That our university intentionally sits in the tradition of the Liberal Arts, though the definition of what "liberal arts" means was not shared by all.
- That a university's mission and vision should shape its curricula.

What follows is an examination of literature on liberal arts, core curriculum, and faith-learning integration, a brief overview of the history and context of our process, and the ongoing challenges it has presented for our institution.

POSITIONALITY

This project was led out of the office of the Dean of Arts and Science as part of a larger strategy to break down the program silos in the institution and consider ways in which curriculum (core and interdisciplinary) might better serve the mission. While initiated from above, the intention was always for it to be faculty-led, rather than being driven from the top. Both authors have a strong bias toward interdisciplinary learning, with one of us possessing an interdisciplinary PhD and the other a background as a generalist educator. One of us is situated in the Faculty of Arts and Science, and the other is outside the division (and, therefore, perceived as being more neutral), but with experience in program design facilitation.

LITERATURE REVIEW

Liberal Arts and the Core

What is a liberal arts education and what purpose does it serve? Despite the concept originating long ago in ancient Greece (as an education was seen as essential for a free person to take part in civil society), the answer to this question is still debated in today's context of higher education. A liberal education should free the mind, but what does this look like in reality? At its most basic, a liberal arts education is an undergraduate degree in which students take courses across a broad range of disciplines either to get a general education or to enhance a degree major with courses outside the main field of study. Pragmatically, this is easy to administer with a list of mandatory foundation courses (often called the "core") that all students are required to complete. This ensures that students are exposed to a wide range of information, different ways of thinking, and hopefully, some transferrable skills. An alternative view of liberal arts, and one that is more difficult to enact, downplays breadth and instead emphasizes the connections that students make across disciplines to their prior understandings and to authentic experiences. The liberal arts are often associated with the humanities, which many people claim are essential for the maintenance of a healthy democracy and therefore ultimately a service to society.[6] In contrast, ethicist Meilaender[7] argues that the liberal arts are free, which means they should serve no goal external to themselves. In other words, utility contradicts the essence of liberal arts. In today's marketplace, a degree advertised as such would not survive as more and more students are turning to professional and vocational programs that direct them into work as quickly as possible. Downey and Porter report that in many institutions the rise of the elective system and the rapid growth of specialization and professional programs are causing the notion of a common core of learning or a core set of fundamental disciplines to disappear.[8] Mannoia addresses this issue in depth and offers the notion that a *Christian* liberal arts education, in particular, can be both instrumentally and intrinsically valuable because of its capacity to develop an attitude of humility toward our knowledge of all truth and its ability to direct students to address real-world problems through vocation.[9]

While it is difficult to reach a common understanding of liberal arts in today's higher education, a consistent theme in the conversation is the idea of integration—integration of disciplines, ideas, and in the case of Christian higher education, the integration of faith. Huber et al. propose, in fact, that integrative learning should share equal weight alongside depth and breadth as one of the defining characteristics of a liberal education.[10] However, there is on-going debate about whether integration can happen

---

6. Nussbaum, *Not for Profit*, xvii.

7. Meilaender, "Who Needs a Liberal Education?" 101–8.

8. Downey and Porter, eds., *Christian Worldview*, xxxi, and in particular the opening of the third *Prolegomena* (Part 1) essay by Page, "Developing the Characteristics," 35–37.

9. Mannoia, *Christian Liberal Arts*, 33.

10. Huber et al., "Integrative Learning," 4–7.

and how it should happen, both in the literature and among faculty.[11] Making connections is critical to learning; the question remains whether it is the responsibility of the university to engineer it through core programming and interdisciplinary teaching, or the responsibility of the students to do it naturally themselves. Meilaender, in his examination of liberal arts programming, suggests that one needs to strike a balance between too much interdisciplinary coursework, in which non-specialists are teaching across disciplines on one end of the spectrum, and students running from isolated subject to isolated subject in order to meet requirements on the other. Wherever one falls on this spectrum, it is clear that integration—"the ability for students to connect skills and knowledge from multiple sources and experiences, apply diverse and contradictory points of view, and understand issues and positions contextually"[12]—should not be left up to chance as a hoped-for outcome.

Faith-Integrated Learning

Different Christian traditions view faith-integrated learning differently. As a university that has its roots it one particular tradition, but engages faculty from various Christian traditions, how do we reach a common understanding of the connection between faith and learning? This is not easily done because, as Henry and Agee point out, the nuances of Scripture, the profundity of the faith, the variety of theological traditions, and the complexity of the world mean it is impossible to craft a universally agreed upon way of being responsive as Christian academics to our various disciplines.[13] Perhaps a useful way to approach a common understanding is to use Donald Page's description of a Christian mind—one that is open, focuses on God, learns from history, and is humanistic, ethical, aesthetically sensitive, and truthful.[14] The university is primarily in the business of the mind, after all. If we are to develop and graduate students with a Christian mind, regardless of discipline, how should curriculum be designed to achieve this end?

But Christian scholars do not like to limit their influence to the mind. When discussing how a business degree might integrate faith and learning, Sutherland suggests that one should take a long-range view that

---

11. Meilaender, "Who Needs a Liberal Education?" 101–8.
12. Huber et al., "Integrative Learning," 4–7.
13. Henry and Agree, eds., *Faithful Learning*, x.
14. Page, "Developing the Characteristics," 35–52.

concentrates on the making of whole persons rather than just professionals. For example, he sees a robust Christian business program as including ethics, diversity, global issues, and stewardship.[15]

Agreement on what faith-learning integration looks like is difficult in an institution with theological diversity among faculty and students, but on-going conversation about it is critical. Perhaps stating what it is not is a good place to start. Hasker insists that faith-learning is not a public relations program design to convince constituents of the Christian character of an institution,[16] despite the fact that it is often used in this way as a slogan. Allen and Badley offer seven ways of understanding faith and learning integration, many of which were evident in the thinking of faculty and students[17] in our institution:

1. Fusion—bringing together faith and learning that were otherwise separate things.

2. Incorporation—adding faith elements and components to the curriculum and instruction.

3. Correlational Integration—points of intersection between faith and discipline are noted, but nothing is joined.

4. Dialogical Integration—ongoing conversation between faith and discipline is constructed.

5. Perspectival Integration—making disparate and conflicted elements fit into a larger framework of thought and practice or worldview.

6. Incarnational—Christian academics show forth the life and redemptive work of Christ in their own lives as a witness for students.

7. Appliqué—a cursory mention of faith is applied to the surface but has no transforming power within curriculum, instruction, assessment, or classroom ethos.

Most faculty, when probed, would align with one or another of these ways of understanding faith-learning integration, but rarely are they given the opportunity and encouragement to do so. Faculty, students, and constituents, however, often make assumptions that we are clear and united about what it means. With little attention paid to such an identity-forming

---

15. Sutherland, "A Christian Perspective on Business," 130.
16. Hasker, "Faith Learning Integration," 236.
17. Allen and Badley, *Faith and Learning*, 29.

element of the institution, the cracks of incoherence appear in curriculum, teaching, and student outcomes.

HISTORY AND CONTEXT: CHALLENGES TO THE NOTION OF AN INTEGRATIVE LIBERAL ARTS CORE

The Task Force

From January to December 2016, the Dean of Arts and Science convened a task force consisting of faculty representatives from all Arts and Science programs. They met bi-weekly to consider the current configuration of the Arts and Science core curriculum in light of a new university mission statement, approved in November 2015. The mission states, among other things, that our university prepares women and men for "wise, joyful and redemptive engagement" with society and provides "excellent Christian post-secondary education." The task force members reviewed a number of documents that provided the framework and requirements for our context as an accredited, degree-granting university, such as the Canadian Degree Qualifications Framework.[18] In addition, we did an institutional scan of what other liberal arts programs require of their students in terms of core, in order to provide some alternative perspectives.

1. Trinity Western University: "Our graduates have an education that gives them expertise in their fields, and tools and resources to be thinkers, influencers, and leaders in society. This whole person education comes from our liberal arts core curriculum. All of our students take a core set of courses in history, English, philosophy, religious studies, social sciences, natural sciences and human kinetics. This broad and interdisciplinary exposure helps students develop the critical thinking and adaptation skills that our rapidly changing world requires."[19] Trinity Western students have a robust set of core requirements at a total of 38 semester hours across their four-year degree. There are a large range of courses that students can choose from to meet these

18. The CDQ Framework may be accessed here: http://technicalcouncil.com/files/canadian_qfw.pdf.

19. Accessed from the Trinity Western University website: https://www8.twu.ca/undergraduate/admitted-students/course-registration/university-core-requirements.html.

requirements, but every student, regardless of discipline, has the same guidelines for graduation.

2. Redeemer University College: "The Core curriculum is a set of inter-disciplinary courses that every student takes. It is the foundation for all other courses, complementing your major and ultimately, preparing you for your career and calling. Rooted in the Reformed tradition, the local, global, and non-Western elements of the Core give you the opportunity to think biblically and philosophically about the liberal arts and sciences."[20] Students are required to take 11 core courses across their four-year degree, with the final being an interdisciplinary capstone, for a total of 33 credit hours.

3. Gordon College: "As a Christian liberal arts college, Gordon is dedicated to preparing you for a lifelong journey of Christian faithfulness. The Core Curriculum exists to help us carry out this mission. Taken over your four years at Gordon, the Core Curriculum will ensure that your educational and transformational journey is not one-dimensional, but characterized by both depth and breadth. You will achieve depth by digging deeply into your major area of study, and breadth by exploring a wide range of academic disciplines through the Core Curriculum."[21] Gordon College has divided their core curriculum into two parts: the common core to develop a Christian perspective on life and learning, and an explorational core to explore the breadth of the liberal arts and sciences. Students can choose from a variety of courses (mostly at second- and third-year level across four academic disciplines) to meet the explorational core requirements.

Based on this brief survey, the main differences between our core curriculum and those from similar institutions were identified as follows:

1. Our university only has a set of gateway or foundational courses, rather than a purposeful core. All but one of our required courses are at the 100-level with limited choice for students.

2. There is a lack of rigorous advising. Students will often leave out-of-discipline foundation courses until their final year. For example, it is

20. Accessed from the Redeemer University College website: https://www.redeemer.ca/academics/core-curriculum/.

21. Accessed from the Gordon College website: https://www.gordon.edu/academics/core.

not unusual to find a fourth-year biology student taking a 100-level Introduction to Literature course.

3. There is a disconnect between mission and core. The mission of our institution speaks of transformational learning, but the core requirements have not been intentionally designed around this idea. Other institutions have lower level seminars to prepare students for the notion of liberal learning, upper-level interdisciplinary capstones, and a more robust pathway that scaffolds student thinking through the entirety of their degree.

During our evaluation period, the following questions about our own program were presented for discussion:

- How many credits should make up the core?
- Should the core requirements be uniform or flexible across the programs?
- How does the core shape the kind of student we are aiming to graduate?

Initially, most task force members had a rather simplistic view of the process: they all wanted to see a reduction of core requirements (from ten courses to eight or nine courses). They thought this process might involve some intense discussion and eventual decision about which program areas would have to relinquish core offerings. There was general agreement (although not consensus) to consider a more flexible core, with REL 105 (Introduction to the Bible) and REL 161 (Christian Theology) remaining as requirements for everyone, along with a reworked EN 115 (Introduction to Literature) as a writing course. As the process unfolded, however, there was significant resistance to changing the current configuration of 'core' curriculum and to expand learning outcomes. In addition, faculty disagreed on the degree to which they were responsible for encouraging the connections between faith and learning in their discipline and between the various disciplines. Some thought that the program structure itself, with its broad range of course requirements, would create this condition naturally. Others thought that it was solely the responsibility of the learner to make connections. Even fewer considered that it was their responsibility, citing the challenge of being able to apply a theological lens to their own discipline and the fear of reducing the rigor of their discipline by mixing it with others. A significant nexus of themes underscored the ongoing conversation.

1. Instrumentalism/pragmatics: The current configuration of required first-year, discrete course offerings serves the university well, because every student populates every discipline. It is good for students to experience a wide array of discipline perspectives and to navigate their way through the undergraduate experience, "connecting the dots" for themselves.

2. Fear and vulnerability: Despite stated beliefs in the value of a liberal arts education, the majority of colleagues are not inclined to support the greater goal of undergraduate student formation within a more intentional, liberal arts-focused, and integrative curriculum when confronted with a perceived threat to their disciplinary domain and its place in the institutional hierarchy.

3. Suspicion of interdisciplinary inquiry: Siloed thinking and valuation of disciplinary difference continues to dominate the faculty mindset. There are no curricular openings to enter a conversation with students about big questions that cross disciplinary boundaries, because there are "no faculty members with multiple specializations" to offer this sort of instruction, and there is no will on the part of faculty to model a team approach to teaching and problem-solving that extends beyond traditional disciplinary boundaries to something more transdisciplinary.

4. While there was general acknowledgment of the need for change at the outset of this process (if only at the level of rearrangement that involved getting rid of some of the furniture), it soon became apparent that there were four major obstacles preventing the task force from taking a more comprehensive and learner-centered path to a reinvigorated core curriculum:

   A. *Discipline-specific approach trumps inter- or trans-disciplinarity*: Conversations about the nature of liberal arts learning and examination of numerous integrative or theme-based models of core curriculum from other Christian liberal arts institutions conflicted with many faculty members' experience and preference for discipline-based teaching, which is the established norm in program design and delivery at this university. Introducing students to a broad array of disciplines, represented by introductory or 'gateway' courses across nine discipline areas (30 credits at the 100-level), has constituted the core requirement for Bachelor of

Arts (6 majors/7 concentrations in Humanities and Social Sciences), Bachelor of Science, Bachelor of Business Administration, and Bachelor of Music degrees for more than a decade. Most faculty are suspicious of any faculty who might take an interdisciplinary approach to teaching, because they do not possess a comfort level with methodology outside of their own domain, and they argue that interdisciplinary inquiry requires "way more work" on the part of faculty (either in a team-teaching context or on an individual basis) and would therefore also be more costly to deliver.

B. *Program Breadth vs. Prescriptive Design:* Another challenge in task force discussions was the divide between the Humanities programs (with room for many course electives) and programs such as Science and professional degree programs in Music and Business, whose prescriptive degree requirements limit the number of elective courses that can be taken outside of the primary discipline. Professional undergraduate degree requirements (authorized by national and provincial guidelines, such as the Canadian Degree Qualifications Framework) make it very difficult to balance a liberal arts learning model with the disciplinary demands for theoretical and applied skills mastery. Social Sciences remained a somewhat neutral party in this discussion as the Behavioural Science program offers a balanced set of program requirements that accommodate existing core curriculum elements and program-specific requirements.

Arguably, Science, Business, and Music degree programs have been somewhat 'overbuilt' within a context that self-proclaims as a liberal arts institution, and it is an affront to the champions of these programs to suggest that numerous program streams that have proliferated within these programs over time must be culled in order to streamline and conform to a more general model of degree structure. In the end, it would be the protectionism of small (Humanities) programs, whose faculty desire a greater share of the student population, and the refusal of large programs to yield areas of specialization for a broader curriculum that would be the undoing of the task force process.

C. *Preference for common core over a flexible interdisciplinary core:* Humanities faculty on the task force strongly endorsed a core (of mostly Humanities courses) common to all undergraduate programs, so that programs with smaller enrolments (Christian Studies, English, General Studies, and History) would continue to have the opportunity to offer required "service courses" that bolster their overall numbers. Programs with greater numbers of majors (including Science and Business), because of their more prescriptive curriculum, preferred a more flexible core with course offerings that: a. provide an interdisciplinary, thematic approach to liberal arts inquiry; and b. create liberal arts options from within the home discipline that would do double duty in meeting core requirements and enhancing degree major requirements. (Example: Scientific Writing, a course that teaches writing with clear application to scientific research, is preferred over an across-the-board English course that is focused primarily on literary analysis.)

D. *Foundational learning as opposed to scaffolded learning:* Many task force members preferred the foundational approach, offering an array of first-year or gateway courses as a required core of liberal arts courses. This implies that any opportunity to introduce liberal arts learning is confined to first-year, discipline-specific content rather than introducing students to a broad array of subject content and methodological approaches that has value in establishing a baseline for further critical and reflective thinking.

There is something lacking in an undergraduate context if big questions and ideas are never considered and challenged through wrestling and probing. Self-actualization within one's educational experience is not complete unless there is opportunity to synthesize and articulate complex ideas in an integrative manner. Upper-level interdisciplinary courses provide a platform in which a more rounded sense of knowledge and problem solving can scaffold learning, build aptitude for teamwork and develop competencies required for graduate success.

In the end, the task force was not able to deal with the impasse created by these gaps in perspective and was therefore disbanded after one year. While there was no unanimity on a way forward, these difficult conversations created opportunity for other kinds of inquiry that was crucial in coming to a more collective understanding about institutional and program identity and purpose.

WHAT DID WE LEARN FROM THE TASK FORCE PROCESS?

Contrary to initial conversations, Arts and Science faculty were not convinced that programs should uniformly align with the university mission or carry a singularly defined identity. For some faculty members on the task force, it was unthinkable that we would differentiate from what other (public) universities do in the classroom; there should be no endeavor to distinguish or apply value judgments to the content and theory of a discourse, privileging some perspectives over others. They argued that the students should make these decisions for themselves, based on balanced presentation of the content, and leave the "Christian formation" piece to those who work with students outside the classroom. For others, it was a matter of personal academic freedom to exercise one's own judgment of the content and of its value, a privilege that is accorded to the ranks of the professoriate who have earned the right to opine. These positions are far from unique, as they exist everywhere in academe; but they both display a willful blindness to the reality that they contain strongly rooted biases of their own.

The Arts and Science programs at our university continue to promote and reflect a soft self-definition. This is confusing to potential students and their parents, who are attracted to the university's singular mission statement. The task force could not determine what, if anything, needed to change in the core curriculum (what defined liberal arts and integration of faith and scholarship), nor why change was needed. People do not immediately recognize the value they seek in our programs (as currently defined or delivered), and the value proposition that could be inherent in curricular content does not translate to an institutional brand. University program branding has continued to be non-specific, and enrolments have begun to soften from peak numbers in the 2016–2017 year as the cost of education at a "faith-based" institution is pricing itself out of the local market. In 2019, our university is still not communicating clear distinctives to current and prospective students.

With the task force essentially set aside, the Winter semester of 2017 took on a different focus. We initiated several simultaneous strategies that focused on learning outcomes and learner formation.

COURSE EVALUATIONS AND STUDENT PERSPECTIVE

We decided to tackle the question of how a core curriculum might form our students from a different angle. A sample survey of responses to course evaluations (2015 data) was collected and analyzed. The courses chosen were required core courses, all first-year level, from the Humanities (History, Philosophy, Christian Studies, and English), Social Sciences (Psychology and Sociology), and Science. One hundred and fifty responses in required gateway (core) curriculum were selected at random from each course. We were looking primarily for student feedback to one question that focused specifically on Christian worldview integration and whether this was emphasized and developed through content or instruction in these core courses:

> How did this course help you to think about or expand your understanding of the Christian faith as it relates to this subject?

It was clear from the responses that students had varying expectations and experiences of how Christian faith should intersect or integrate with each of the subject disciplines. Three themes emerged from these student observations. We presented these themes with sample responses to faculty at an Arts and Science Faculty Council meeting:

- Faith was a "topic" to learn about within their discipline, with subjects being either more or less aligned with Christian faith. In fact, some of the comments were explicit about this:

> We didn't really cover this topic;
> It was stuff [sic] I already knew;
> It was touched on;
> This course is not related to the topic of faith;
> Duh, it is a Bible course, it's obvious!

- Christian "touches" were present in the courses (aligned with Allen and Badley's notion of Appliqué):

> The professor prayed before class;
> There were Bible verses on the slides;
> We read Christian poems;
> Some authors inject scripture into their literature.

- The course helped them make connections between faith, disciplinary knowledge, and life:

> I learned the historical significance of our faith;
> The opportunities to discuss how Christian faith relates to society were important;
> It enabled me to look at an issue both spiritually and sociologically;

It challenged my thinking.

In some cases, students in the same class with the same professor had vastly different experiences of faith integration. It was clear that students understood "faith-learning integration" in the context of this Christian liberal arts university very differently from one another. We wondered, then, whether students' prior understanding of faith-learning integration and their expectations of a Christian liberal arts education going into the program affected what they experienced and then noted on the course evaluations. This led to an informal follow-up conversation with two upper level students (from different programs) to gain their perspective on liberal arts and its value to them by asking why they chose a Christian Liberal Arts university and how their coursework was "forming" them toward this end.

Both students came to this university for the liberal arts approach to their respective programs. They understood this to mean a holistic approach to education within a small community that allowed for close intellectual relationships with their professors. When asked about how well their experience thus far matched their expectations, they both offered some astute observations. They acknowledged, first, that they were not a fair representation of their peers. They saw themselves as students with a higher regard for critical thought and difficult inquiry and a willingness to risk being "undone" by their studies. Both were inclined toward the few interdisciplinary courses on offer but also recognized that not everyone was prepared or capable of engaging with the open discourse and integration they sought in these courses. They attributed this in part to the expectations of "safe learning spaces" by many students and in part to inadequate advising. It was noted that many students circumvent advising to leave their out-of-discipline 100-level core course requirements until the end of their degree, preferring instead to take those courses that directly serve their chosen discipline first. They also commented on their experience of faith integration, and both thought that their faith was being strengthened, deepened, and nuanced through their studies. However, they conceded that interdisciplinary connections and faith intersections were rarely made explicit, leaving them to do the wrestling on their own. This was an interesting comment from two of our brightest students considering earlier conversations with faculty about who holds the primary responsibility for engineering interdisciplinary and integrative faith-learning connections.

PROGRAM MISSION AND FACULTY PERSPECTIVES

We also decided to tackle the issue through a focus on program outcomes. Focus groups consisting of program faculty were gathered to discuss each program mission, enduring values, distinctiveness, and the knowledge, skills, and attitudes of the ideal graduate (or the formation of Christian intellect and competencies) within their discipline. Each discipline (Social Sciences, Christian Studies, History, English, Biology, Business, and Music) attempted to identify gaps in graduate competencies/outcomes of their programs and envisage how these gaps might be addressed by a more integrative core curriculum. In addition to creating a set of program outcomes, we were hoping that such discussion would redirect the focus away from the turf protection that had emerged during the taskforce work toward student formation. These discussions also provided faculty a less public, more secluded space to express the challenges they were facing with the current core.

Most programs (but not all) were happy to participate in these sessions because it gave them time to reflect on what was most important. It was clear that faculty had a desire to dedicate time to collaborate on the significance of the Christian faith for their disciplines, a phenomenon that has been identified in the literature.[22] A few interesting observations were made.

- Faculty did not view the mission of the Christian liberal arts university in the same way as each other. In fact, their beliefs about mission and purpose reflected the variety of responses from the students on the faculty evaluations. Some felt that there should be no difference between the education students receive here compared to a large public institution, except that they can study within a familiar, supported, Christian environment—a preference for many of our students. Others felt that a Christian liberal arts education provided the space to engage unsettling and difficult ideas from a Christian perspective.
- Because of the different ideas about the mission of a Christian liberal arts university, advising is inconsistent. The perspective of the advisor directly influences the recommendations made. In one disturbing case, a program Chair was consistently advising students "not to take (a certain core) course" taught by another instructor in another

22. Henry and Agee, eds., *Faithful Learning*, x.

program, or to wait until their last semester to take certain required first-year liberal arts courses.

- Very few program and course outcomes indicate an intention to "unsettle" and then "reorient" student thinking, even in those programs that have a desire for such outcomes.

- There is reluctance from many to challenge the status quo regarding the common core due to cynicism about whether things could really change. We heard more than one person say, "the decision will need to be made above," indicating an unwillingness to innovate and drive the solution themselves. Despite this, there was deep passion and commitment to what they were trying to accomplish that was within their control (i.e., constantly improving curriculum and teaching).

- While there was an acknowledgment that upper level, transdisciplinary capstone-style courses are a nice idea,[23] they struggled to engage the notion of requiring it as part of a common core in such a way that would encourage deep integrative reflection. Barriers were identified such as improper advising that would prepare students for such a course, feeling unqualified to teach in an interdisciplinary way, and a lack of confidence within the institution to adequately resource team-teaching and collaboration.

- Many faculty members wanted to see some of the current core courses redesigned to be more useful for their discipline and for forming students in a purposeful way—Introduction to the Christian Faith and Introduction to Literature, in particular.

Freedom Week

We supported four (senior) students to apply for and attend the Institute of Liberal Studies Freedom Week[24]—two at Simon Fraser University and two at McGill University in the summer of 2017. The students' names were put forth by their respective program chairs as young men and women who

23. There are capstone courses siloed within some of the programs, but these are not interdisciplinary or integrative.

24. Freedom Week is a five-day intellectual adventure that gives participants a chance to explore classical liberal ideas in areas like economics, philosophy, law, and public policy from a faculty of distinguished professors. https://www.liberalstudies.ca/freedom-week/.

had a mature and developed ability to think critically, a strong and articulated sense of faith, and a clear understanding of the essence of a true liberal education. In a way, we believed we were sending them out in the world to test the validity of their undergraduate formation. In the fall of 2017, we followed up with these four students on numerous occasions to debrief their experience. They also agreed to a panel interview in front of all the program chairs about what they learned at Freedom Week and how they felt that their university studies had prepared them to participate there.

While each student accepted to Freedom Week at Simon Fraser and McGill brought different expectations to the experience, all came away with a new appreciation for the kind of liberal arts exposure they had received at our university. But each of them also acknowledged that the university did not prepare them adequately to engage in conversations that would place them at the dangerous intersection of faith and public discourse—*exactly those places for which a Christian liberal arts education should prepare undergraduates*. Our students were stretched enormously by this experience; rather than shrink from it, they discovered, on their own, that they could gain the respect of their compatriots, who represented a wide range of ideologies and perspectives, through their willingness to engage and ardently represent a view that is largely unpopular or ignored by the academy and the public sphere.

OUTCOMES

Predictive Outcomes for the University

1. The brand of our university is not clear and carries no purpose that marks its courses, credentials, or its teaching as distinctive from other institutions of higher learning. And for half the tuition amount, a student would receive the same credential with an institutional brand that has a proven track record.

2. Our university will continue to struggle with marketing its unique mission until a new set of core requirements is established that reflect a common understanding of the university mission, student formation (at multiple levels of learning), and integration of course content with intentional inquiry that seeks to build perspective on critical perspectives *informed by the cultivation of a Christian mind.*

Predictive Outcomes for Learners (that will demonstrate misalignment between the University and its intended Mission)

3. From the vantage point of Fall 2018, it would appear that the potential pool of students in our regional and denominational network who *might* choose a Christian liberal arts institution for their baccalaureate degree will increasingly opt for the more conventional and instrumental route to an education: the public university. Indeed, enrolments at our university and across North American faith-based liberal arts undergraduate schools are shrinking (softening) in those institutions where important questions and values-based curriculum are not clearly identified or addressed as markers of identity.[25] There are students who will seek out this kind of undergraduate education, but they will not consider a school whose missional objectives are not communicated as the "value-added" piece that is embedded in clear sets of learning outcomes.

4. Faith-based liberal arts universities will not be destination schools for students who want a fast-track to employment. The challenge will be to convince prospective students of the value of a liberal arts education that offers tools to navigate the challenging cultural currents that they will encounter during and after undergraduate university education. Without an inquiry-based core that links traditional liberal arts learning with values-based and significant conversations about "big questions" in each discipline, students will not grasp how a Christian university might differentiate from higher education undertaken in the public arena.

Predictive outcomes for the professoriate (aspects of academic culture that negatively impact the sustainability of Christian University education when academic leadership is lacking)

5. A culture of fear and lack of openness to understanding the difference that must mark the Christian liberal arts educational landscape will continue to dominate decision-making about curriculum at our

25. Docking and Curtin, *Crisis in Higher Education*, 1–20. Chapters 1 and 2 ("Why Higher Education Needs This Book" and "A Typical Small Private Baccalaureate Institution") provide many statistics and stories about liberal arts education in America and why these small institutions are in decline.

university, relative to the expressed need for program change and learning outcomes that connect the dots for students in ways that are vital to their success. Turf protection of subject discourses and of program content (perpetrated by faculty as a misguided means of self-preservation) will continue to disadvantage students as faculty retreat to their silos. An increasing number of public university programs are taking on the complex challenges of interdisciplinarity and broad inquiry across domains. These broader conversations are not easy,[26] but they are necessary for relevance and enlargement of the community as a whole.

6. Within the realm of institutional life, it is often observed that a "scholarship of denial" is tied to maintenance of the status quo, *guarding what is familiar or tied to work economics*—keeping things from conflict.[27] The second is a *scholarship of responsibility*—a fidelity to the tradition which practices resistance without reducing the gaps left by the "other." Out of continual exploration and dialogue with the tradition—the *task of inheritance*—comes the possibility (promise) of bringing new voices to utterance. In the day to day life of the university, if the scholarship of denial functions as the modus operandi, academic leaders seldom acknowledge or foresee gaps that would allow creativity and change. Faculty benefit more from a responsible view and positive transformation, and the institution flourishes only as change occurs in disciplinary discourse that is hopeful and lifegiving.

7. The tendency on the part of academic culture is to exercise what Mark Wigley describes as "a form of institutional resistance [denial] that attempts to conceal the convoluted structure of the tradition that makes it."[28] Rather than acknowledge or trace some new thought or idea about learning, additional time and space for these necessary and fraught conversations is excluded or subordinated to produce an "orderly facade, or, rather, the facade of order, to mask an internal disorder."[29]

---

26. Palmer, *The Courage to Teach*, 150–56. Palmer lays out ground rules for academic dialogue and provides a model that he identifies as a "clearness committee" process.

27. Derrida, *Specters of Marx*, 52, 54, 68, 70, 85, 90, 114. These are a few of Derrida's references to a scholarship of "denial."

28. Wigley, *The Architecture of Deconstruction*, 71.

29. Wigley, *The Architecture of Deconstruction*, 71.

Hoped-for Outcomes: Institutional

Our university is undergoing organizational changes that will facilitate more robust discussions about the relationship between university mission and curriculum. A new committee, Academic Policy and Planning, will undertake a discussion of a liberal arts core curriculum in tandem with a number of other key institution-wide conversations about high level learning outcomes that emphasize distinctives in integrative liberal arts education and the strategies that will be required to implement a more interdisciplinary, inquiry-based, and intentionally integrative curriculum across the Arts and Science programs. These conversations will connect to discussions that focus on selective recruitment (differentiated marketing and targeted enrolment strategies) that emphasize the value of the core curriculum.

While this process will take some time (perhaps several more years) to shift us to a more deliberate and shared understanding of how our university self-identifies, these conversations are critical. The irony is that some faculty believe that there is nothing more to be said (when in fact there has never been deep conversation like this about the formation of institutional ethos and identity). These faculty colleagues are impatient with what they see as failure on the part of administrators to impose a curricular process, believing that there is little more to it than to reduce the number of requirements in the current core and to keep the majority of current foundation courses as they are. It is our view that nothing short of a complete shift to a more integrative curriculum that focuses on inquiry-based critical method at multiple levels with a broad array of coursework (culminating with a synthesis of the breadth of that experience in interdisciplinary capstone courses) will truly realize the capacity for differentiated learning possibilities in an undergraduate setting like ours.

Hoped-for Outcomes: Learners

Students for Liberty, formed in 2017, is the largest student club at our university. It is a tangible outcome of the influence of the Freedom Week experiment (involving four students) to manifest on our campus; we have been informed that it is the largest university group in Canada sponsored by the Institute for Liberal Studies (based in Ottawa),[30] sponsors of Free-

---

30. Institute for Liberty (an organization with libertarian leanings that promotes a scholarly foundation in the classical liberal arts) encourages free speech on Canadian

dom Week. Since our students have established Students for Liberty, they have been responsible for co-hosting several events promoting respectful conversations on complex issues with other public universities in our city. Based on the participation of our students in Freedom Week 2017 (at McGill and Simon Fraser), the Institute for Liberal Studies has reached out to other Christian university campuses in Canada to invite them to consider participation in other opportunities for wider engagement, because they recognize that institutions like ours may have something of value to offer to the wider academy.

Students are taking responsibility for their learning, even though the framework in which they study is little more than fuzzy ideology at the moment. We are attracting small but influential numbers of the kind of student who benefits from a liberal arts education and who wants to wrestle with ideas and "big questions" that integrate faith with their disciplinary pursuits. It is our hope that, with more intentional action that aligns mission with curricular content, many more students will be inclined to enroll in our programs.

Hoped-for Outcomes: Curriculum and Teaching

This is the arena that requires the greatest investment of time and resources if transformative change is to be realized in our graduates through a revitalized arts and science curriculum. Prior to 2015, with the convening of the Arts and Science task force on curriculum, any discussion about "worldview" or "integration" was considered the domain of theologians in our academy. Arts and science faculty did not engage that conversation or each other on this issue as they built autonomous frameworks for new degree programs within a relatively new institution (established in 2008 out of the remnants of several denominational Bible colleges who had relocated in order to amalgamate). For the most part, program faculty were left to their own devices to develop academically sound programs that would *meet the standards of public postsecondary quality assurance in our province.* What they developed contains little or no trace of values-driven distinctives or identity because they were never called together to wrestle with

---

university campuses and provides support to institutions that are experiencing challenges navigating the divide between those who promote free speech and those whose rhetoric is dominated largely by an agenda of political correctness. The latter group scrutinizes all conversations on campus for insensitive and marginalizing views that create a power imbalance.

and determine what is critical in the formation of a Christian liberal arts curriculum.

Perhaps most telling is that the University never adopted a mission statement until late 2015 (more than seven years into its formalized constitution), and no individual or faculty cluster could point definitively to markers of identification in laying the groundwork for program and learning outcomes that aligned with an institutional mission. Leadership in the academy, while speaking broadly to institutional distinctives in the formation of that mission statement—in terms of what defines a "Christian liberal arts" university—did not invest any resources or take up any strategic planning process that would result in actions to articulate and embed these values intentionally within the curriculum. We are now only beginning to address program learning outcomes, and that is happening (appropriately) within new academic structures that permit conversations about how to align institutional mission with institutional curriculum design. Faculty in arts and science are now more open to conversations about defining the nature and intention of what they teach. They have a somewhat better understanding of why it is important to distinguish our institutional brand and why the recent decline in numbers will render the institution unsustainable without the *conscious and deliberate working out of distinctives that flow from our institutional mission*. Our survival as a small university depends on conversations that facilitate a focused process, an action plan, and collaborative implementation with respect to re-engineering the curriculum in a way that is "mission-critical" and that is able to assess, gauge, and continually improve learner and graduate outcomes with respect to distinctive markers in our institutional identity.

POSTLUDE: THE PROBLEM THAT CHRISTIAN LIBERAL ARTS EDUCATION HAS THE CAPACITY TO ADDRESS

When we regard higher education settings as communities rather than organizations, space can be made for grand conversations that consider how integrative ideas and institutional mission inform and transform the learning context. Challenges to this notion might well be: *If it is possible for intentional curricular change to occur at all, why does it not happen more frequently in higher education?* The fact is that curricular change does happen all the time in post-secondary education, most often in insidious ways, and without the kind of broad conversations that such change requires to support healthy and vital communities of learning. *What impedes innovation and improvement that drives values-based inquiry in the classroom?* Fear of change. The irony is that, without constant examination of what is informing our current discourses, purposeful change is replaced by curricular and ideological drift. *Is it possible for educational institutions to be a compass for transformational change?* Yes, but those liberal arts, faith-based schools who enjoy a track record of success in embodying their values in curriculum and teaching are able to regularly gather stakeholders around meaningful conversations on issues of vital importance to the ongoing relevancy and identity of the institution.

To change, we have to challenge practices that have always "appeared" sensible, and this is hard to do.

> We need to examine the unstated assumptions behind accepted practices. . . . Change the theory and we will have to learn new habits. If we can get the theory right, the right practices will follow. If we view [universities] as communities rather than organisations, the practices that make sense in [those higher education institutions] understood as organisations just don't fit. In communities, connections are not based on contracts but on commitments.[31]

The love of scholarly work that vigorously pursues wisdom and its application must be central to the enterprise of any Christian higher education institution that wants its graduates to transform the world. If graduates are to engage redemptively[32] with culture, faculty must first be transformed by the "renewing of their minds" in ways that avert scholarly drift and resist the pull toward old systems thinking. Furthermore, the role of curriculum and its responsible transmission as an act of fidelity to the tradition by means of engaging and probing inquiry (not mere repetition or focus on the trivial) will ensure that the narratives, the stories of our discourses—and the particular educational "tattoo" of Christian liberal arts—will live on (*survive*).

Discursive fragmentation contributes to an increasing instability of the academic institution at its core (no pun intended). No longer able to ground itself on common scholarly values or ideals that transcend the material substance of scholarly striving (such as systems, methods, proofs) in order to make meaning, the university and its inhabitants have been set adrift.[33] Scholars and academic leaders alike have lost the ability to inherit

31. Sergiovanni, *Building Community in Schools*, 1–5.

32. "Redemptive engagement" is an expressed goal in our university's mission statement.

33. Schwartz and Belcher, "Scholarly Praxis at the Edges," 46–62. The term

the burden of tradition, to wrestle with its ghosts and gaps, to have grand conversations, and to be challenged by the act of inscribing themselves responsibly into traditional narratives.[34]

This is the task—the scholarly inheritance—of the Christian university. It could be considered a reclamation of an original project, given that all Western universities have inherited the foundational, speculative, classical, and theological study of trivium and quadrivium subjects (the liberal arts) from the earliest ecclesiastical universities by way of Christian thinkers and teachers. Not all Christian institutions have inherited this burden (or gift) of fidelity to the tradition, choosing rather to deny responsibility. Others continue to question, resist, and wrestle. This choice requires courage and love for the work to which we are called. That there is still much to think about and do is the harbinger of hope for the Christian scholar, the student, and for those academies who remain bound to the tradition while seeking to transform it, ensuring the survival of grand narratives and values that are our heritage and that drive our scholarly desire and our deepest confession.

BIBLIOGRAPHY

Allen, Patrick, and Kenneth Badley. *Faith and Learning. A Guide for Faculty*. Abilene, TX: Leafwood Publishers & Abilene Christian University Press, 2014.

Anselm of Canterbury. *Proslogium; Monologium; An Appendix in Behalf of the Fool by Gaunilon; and Cur Deus Homo*. Translated by Sidney Norton Deane. LaSalle, IL: Open Court, 1951.

Derrida, Jacques. *Specters of Marx: The State of the Debt, the Work of Mourning, and the New International*. Translated by P. Kamuf. New York: Routledge, 1994.

Docking, Jeffrey R., and Carman C. Curtin. *Crisis in Higher Education: A Plan to Save Small Liberal Arts Colleges in America*. Transformations in Higher Education: Scholarship of Engagement Series. East Lansing, MI: Michigan State University Press, 2015.

Downey, Deane E. D., and Stanley E. Porter, eds. *Christian Worldview and the Academic Disciplines: Crossing the Academy*. McMaster General Series 1. Eugene, OR: Pickwick, 2009.

Hasker, William. "Faith-Learning Integration: An Overview." *Christian Scholars Review* 21 (1992) 234–48.

Henry, Douglas V., and Bob R. Agee, eds. *Faithful Learning and the Christian Scholarly Vocation*. Grand Rapid: Eerdmans, 2003.

Huber, Mary Taylor, et al. "Integrative Learning for Liberal Education." *Peer Review* 7 (2005) 4–7.

Mannoia, V. James. *Christian Liberal Arts. An Education That Goes Beyond*. Maryland: Rowman & Littlefield, 2000.

"discursive fragmentation" is coined by Schwartz and Belcher.

34. Schwartz and Belcher, "Scholarly Praxis at the Edges," 53.

McInnes, Craig, et al. *A Handbook for Executive Leadership of Teaching and Learning in Higher Education*. NSW: Office for Learning and Teaching, Department of Industry, Innovation, Science, Research and Tertiary Education, 2012.

Meilaender, Gilbert. "Who Needs a Liberal Education?" *The New Atlantis* 41 (Winter 2014) 101–8.

Nussbaum, Martha C. *Not for Profit: Why Democracy Needs the Humanities*. Princeton, NJ: Princeton University Press, 2010.

Page, Donald M. "Developing the Characteristics of a Christian Mind." In *Christian Worldview and the Academic Disciplines*, edited by Deane E. D. Downey and Stanley E. Porter, 35–52. McMaster General Series 1. Eugene, OR: Pickwick, 2009.

Palmer, Parker. *The Courage to Teach: Exploring the Inner Landscape of a Teacher's Life*. San Francisco: Jossey-Bass, 1997.

Schwartz, Linda, and Christina Belcher. "Scholarly Praxis at the Edges: Why Responsible Academic Leadership Matters in Developing Faculty Scholarship." In *Handbook of Research on Administration, Policy and Leadership in Higher Education*, edited by Siran Mukerji and Purnendu Tripathi, 46–62. Educational Marketing, Administration, and Leadership (AEMAL) Book Series. Hershey, PA: IGI Global, 2017.

Sergiovanni, Thomas J. *Building Community in Schools*. San Francisco: Jossey-Bass, 1994.

Sutherland, J. R. "A Christian Perspective on Business." In *Christian Worldview and the Academic Disciplines: Crossing the Academy*, edited by Deane E. D. Downey and Stanley E. Porter, 128–50. McMaster General Series 1. Eugene, OR: Pickwick, 2009.

Wigley, Mark. *The Architecture of Deconstruction: Derrida's Haunt*. Cambridge, MA: MIT, 1997.

11

The 'Charge' We Have to 'Keep'

Enhancing Gospel-Integrity in Christian Higher Education

VICTOR SHEPHERD

"A charge to keep I have,
A God to glorify,
To serve the present age,
My calling to fulfill"

—CHARLES WESLEY[1]

INTRODUCTION

SEVERAL YEARS AGO, TYNDALE University (my current employer) re-joiced that the word 'university' now appeared in its masthead. While the seminary had been a seminary since 1974, the former Bible college was finally elevated to the status of university college. There was exultation throughout the institution.

In the midst of the understandable exuberance, the provost, who had presided over the same sort of transition in academic institutions in Western Canada, took me aside. Without chilling anyone's celebration he

1. Wesley, *Works of John Wesley*, 7:465.

remarked, "The challenge to Tyndale now isn't to increase academic rigour and respectability. In fact, academic rigour and respectability will become its preoccupation. The challenge to Tyndale will be to retain its Christian conviction and identity and mission. I have watched Christian colleges all over North America," he continued, "improve their academic offerings while allowing their Christian character to attenuate."[2]

Decades earlier David D. Lutz, a graduate philosophy student at Notre Dame University, argued that historic Methodist Universities in the USA, including Emory, Duke, Boston, Northwestern, Syracuse, Vanderbilt, and the University of Southern California, may have ongoing ties to the United Methodist Church but have long since forfeited any Christian substance.[3]

I pondered the situation closer to home. From 2002 until 2016 I was an adjunct professor at Trinity College (Anglican), University of Toronto. The faculty of divinity at Trinity is small: four full-time professors. Two of them, however, are self-declared atheists. The provost at Tyndale was correct. Christian educational institutions take pains to ensure their academic integrity. Frequently, however, they appear less concerned about ensuring their Christian identity.

Since such attenuation tempts and threatens Christian institutions of higher education relentlessly, and since there is no shortage of (formerly) Christian institutions who have succumbed, capitulated, and given up their birthright, we should be alert to this development and recognize it.

What are some signs that theological erosion is at the door?

THE SHIFT FROM TRUTH CULTURE TO THERAPY CULTURE

Thomas Oden, a Methodist theologian whose name is still redolent (he died 8 December 2016), has said there are two competing cultures in society and church today: a truth culture and a therapy culture.[4]

A truth culture, Oden maintains, asks two questions: "What *is*" and "What is *right*?" A therapy culture asks but one question: "How does it *feel*?"

It can be maintained that Christian higher education (or at least seminary education) in North America prior to World War II largely presupposed a truth culture; but after World War II, a therapy culture. In the wake of World War II, North Americans felt jarred and jolted if not wounded

---

2. Provost Earl Davey, in a private conversation with Prof. Victor Shepherd.

3. Lutz, "Can Notre Dame Be Saved?"

4. Oden, *Care of the Soul in the Classic Tradition*, 28–30.

(even though they had suffered far less than the European and Slavic people in whose front yards the war had been fought, and whose wartime civilian deaths outnumbered combatants' deaths for the first time in military history). In light of the North American people's conviction that they were suffering extraordinarily, they introduced pastoral theology and pastoral psychology to the seminary curriculum. At first it was merely one more subject in the curriculum, an addition to, but not a rival of, the traditional disciplines of Scripture, theology, history, liturgy, and homiletics. Little by little, however, it came to dominate the curriculum. It came to dominate not by crowding out formally the place of other disciplines, but rather by intruding itself into the substance of these disciplines, with the result that theology, for instance, gradually became less the articulation of the catholic substance of the faith "once for all delivered to the saints" (Jude 3) in the thought-forms and language of contemporaneity, less a mandate to "guard the truth that has been entrusted to you [Timothy] by the Holy Spirit who dwells within us" (2 Tim 1:14). Incrementally theology became the religious legitimization of a psychological preoccupation whose agenda derived largely from the social sciences and the prioritizing of intra-psychic contentment and self-fulfillment.

In my own seminary, Tyndale (in Toronto), the single largest major by far is counselling. And whereas in my seminary days (1967–1970) everyone in the seminary was pursuing ordination to the ministry of Word, Sacrament, and Pastoral Care, today (at Tyndale, at least), only 11% of students plan to enter the pulpit/pastoral ministry. Most graduates of the counselling programme will seek counselling positions outside the institutional church. In order to be employed in secular venues they will have to minimize their identity as Christians and maximize their identification with the psycho-social *Zeitgeist*. As a professor of theology and philosophy, I have observed the shift in seminary students' concerns from truth culture to therapy culture.

Let's examine briefly the distinction between truth and therapy cultures respectively. The truth culture asks first, "What is?"—that is, "What is real? What is real rather than merely apparent? What is real rather than merely actual? What is *ultimately* real?" In relation to this question, the truth culture also asks, "What is right? What ought we to do? How is what we ought to do constrained by what is? In short, how does the real constrain the righteous?" If our ability to discern reality is diminished, is our ability to exemplify righteousness comparably threatened?

When Jesus says, "I am the way, the truth and the life" (John 14:6), the Greek word John uses for truth is *aletheia*. Today we regularly use 'truth' as a predicate of statements. The statement "The sun is 93 million miles from the earth" is adjudged truth. In the Greek of antiquity, however, *aletheia*, truth, was 'reality disclosing itself.' Not only did ancient Greek philosophy understand 'truth' to be 'reality disclosing itself'; so does a modern philosopher (Martin Heidegger, we might note), even if what he means by 'reality disclosing itself' is certainly something other than 'Jesus Christ in the power of the Spirit.'[5]

The therapy culture, on the other hand, asks one question only: "How does it feel?" The concern here is the adjusting of feeling. Overlooked here is whether the feeling is appropriate, inappropriate, or out-and-out neurotic. The therapy culture aims at reducing intrapsychic discomfort (which aim, we should note, is not to be slighted or trivialized). The question of whether the person who feels guilty, for instance, *ought* to feel guilty; this question isn't paramount, if it is raised at all.

In my work as pastor (I was a pastor with denominational appointment from 1970 to 2006) I frequently had congregants in my study telling me, for instance, that one had to be wary of extra-marital affairs just because such liaisons might 'get you hurt.' Not merely the predominant issue here but the only issue was whether and how one might be hurt. Not even to be considered was the 'truth' issue of what is real and right; namely, the holy God's engagement with a people he is fixed upon rendering holy. Holiness happens to be Scripture's preoccupation, or in the words of John Wesley, its "general tenor," one ingredient of this being our recognition of God's righteous claim upon our obedience and God's blessing promised to it.[6]

What are the signs that such a shift is underway?

Signs of the Shift

FIRST SIGN: SHIFTS IN MEANINGS

One sign of such a shift in the church and its related institutions is the retention of Christian vocabulary while importing non-Christian meanings.

---

5. Heidegger, *Being and Time*, 219–23.

6. Wesley uses this expression throughout his *Works*. See *Works of John Wesley*, 26:158–60.

Consider the word 'guilt.' At one time 'guilt' described one's situation before God. As sinners, we are guilty inasmuch as we have violated God-in-person (not inasmuch as we have violated a moral code, it must be noted). Having violated God-in-person we have broken God's heart, provoked God's anger, and aroused God's disgust.[7] Our guilty condition, guilty state, imperils us before God. Be sure to notice that as sinners we *are* guilty before God regardless of how we *feel*. We may feel blissfully happy (because living in the spiritual equivalent of a fool's paradise), unaware of our perilous predicament before God, as happy as party-goers on a boat-outing who are unaware that the boat is about to capsize.

In this regard C. S. Lewis has pointed out that the language of the Anglican *Book of Common Prayer* is realistic at all points. When worshippers confess, week by week, that they are 'miserable offenders,' their misery pertains not to how they happen to feel but to their predicament before God.[8]

Another instance of retaining Christian words while importing non-Christian meanings pertains to forgiveness. The word 'forgive' has been retained although the meaning now is 'excuse.' "I forgive you" now has the force of "I understand the extenuating circumstances that explain, in part or in whole, why you did what you did. I see now what factors precipitated what you did, and therefore I recognize that you can't finally be held accountable for it. Therefore, I can excuse it." Lost here is the crucial distinction between forgiving and excusing; namely, we excuse what is excusable, whereas we forgive precisely what is inexcusable. The day you tell me you have forgiven me is the day you have judged me wholly inexcusable. In the same vein, to say with the Apostles' Creed, "I believe in the forgiveness of sins," is to say that God, the Holy One, has pronounced us utterly without excuse; and God, the just judge, has condemned us. His forgiveness, in other words, is a reprieve that spares us ultimate loss.

Related to the shift we are illustrating is the vocabulary of sin. Whereas sin is a violation of God born of our disobedience, ingratitude, rebellion, defiance, and disdain; in short, the 'unbelief' of the heart (not merely or chiefly of the head), 'sin' has come to mean immorality. Overlooked here is the scriptural insistence that moral people sin as much in their morality as

---

7. Martin Luther frequently reminds readers that sin provokes God's disgust. No less frequently Luther uses his characteristically earthy language to speak of it. See Oberman, "Teufelsdreck: Eschatology and Scatology in the 'Old' Luther," 51–68. Concerning fallen humans, Calvin (*Sermons on the Epistle to the Ephesians*, 129) says as much: "There is nothing but rottenness and infection in us. God loathes us . . . "

8. Lewis, *Miserable Offenders*.

immoral people sin in their immorality. The apostle Paul, we should note, never says that Jesus died for the immoral; he insists that Jesus died for the ungodly (Rom 5:6). Moral people and immoral are alike ungodly, alike equidistant from the Kingdom of God. Did Jesus ever suggest anything else? Did our Lord ever receive better treatment at the hands of the moral than at the hands of the immoral? Among whom were his friends found? And who found him insufferable? Were not the most moral people those who hated him most thoroughly? Was he not faulted for the welcome he accorded moral failures and rejects? Let me say it again: according to Scripture's understanding of sin, moral and immoral persons alike are equidistant from the Kingdom.

While the Apostles' Creed gathers up the whole of the Christian life in the expression, "I believe in the forgiveness of sins"—meaning, "I believe that in Jesus Christ, God's only Son, and in that Spirit the Son bears and bestows, the entire cosmos is renewed and me with it"—today we are told in many areas of the church, with increasing frequency, that the church should jettison a liturgical confession of sin because such confession is 'too negative'; people go to church, we are told, 'to hear something positive'; any mention of sin is deemed at best counterproductive turnoff, and at worst a pathological diminution of ego-strength.

I am dismayed as I come upon more and more congregations whose service of public worship no longer includes a corporate prayer of confession and declaration of absolution. Plainly all such services assume that worshippers are not sinners. They may be anxious, unfulfilled, fretful, frustrated, nervous; they may be ardent, ambitious, zealous, or eager. But they are not sinners.

Scripture contradicts such self-deception and folly. Together with Luther, all the Protestant Reformers insist that Christians remain under two determinations: the righteousness of Christ, and the 'old' man/woman of sin. Admittedly, these determinations are not weighted equally: the determination of Christ's righteousness is definitive and characterizes the Christian; the determination of sin, however, remains operative, and for this reason the 'old' man/woman, slain at the cross but refusing to die quietly, says Luther, paradoxically must be slain anew every day. For this reason Luther has as the first of his Ninety-Five Theses, "When Our Lord and Master Jesus Christ said, 'Repent,' he willed the *entire* life of believers to be one of repentance."[9] Luther never moved away from his insistence that Christians

---

9. Luther, *Luther's Works*, 31:25. Emphasis added.

remain *simul totus iustus et simul totus peccator*: we are simultaneously both wholly justified in Christ and wholly sinful in ourselves.[10] Calvin concurs: concerning Christians he insists, "For what have we but infection and filthiness? . . . We are loathsome in his sight, yet in spite of this, it is his [i.e., God's] will to have us joined to him [i.e., Jesus Christ]."[11]

"The contemporary declension and concomitant shallowness are grievous, for if people aren't sinners, then Jesus Christ may be a good example but he certainly isn't Saviour. If we aren't sinners, then the cross may be an instance of martyrdom (neither more nor less significant than the martyrdom of John the Baptist or Dietrich Bonhoeffer), but the cross certainly isn't atonement wherein the Holy God and unholy creatures are made 'at-one,' reconciled. If we aren't sinners, then Good Friday may be 'good' in the sense that it's psychologically good for us to "pour contempt on all our pride" (please note that Isaac Watts' hymn *When I Survey the Wondrous Cross* says nothing, utterly nothing, about the cross and what God achieved there), but Good Friday isn't 'Good' in the sense of 'God's Friday' (as our mediaeval Christian foreparents called it). Good Friday, we ought to acknowledge, is good since God the just judge judged sin in the cross of his Son, and simultaneously God the just judge *absorbed in himself* his own judgment on sin, thereby allowing sinners a future they could never merit. Apart from 'God's Friday,' the predicament of sinners is hopeless.

Retaining biblical words while simultaneously importing non-biblical meanings is a clear sign that the shift from truth culture to therapy culture is underway in the church.

SECOND SIGN: SHIFT IN IDEOLOGIES

Related to the above and no less ominous is the replacement of biblical categories with non-biblical ideologies. Consider the word 'mutuality.' It appears innocuous. In fact, it points to a tectonic shift in our understanding of human sexuality.

Scripture insists that humanity is co-humanity. The text of Gen 1 reads, "Let us make man (*adam*, humankind) in our image . . . Male and female (*ish* and *ishah*) he created them" (Gen 1:26–27). According to the text, the definition of the human always entails gender correlation. It is male and female *together* who are made in the image of God.[12]

10. For a discussion of this point, see Shepherd, *Interpreting Martin Luther*, 145–68.

11. Calvin, *Sermons on the Epistle to the Ephesians*, 123.

12. While Karl Barth has highlighted gender-complementarity with respect to the

Am not I, Victor, an individual agent, possessed of my own identity, and the subject of my own existence; am I not made in the image of God? Indeed, I am—as long as it is remembered that I am what I am only in the context of what I am not: woman. This truth is operative whether I am married or not, sexually active or not.

It should be noted here that our Lord tacitly endorses this truth repeatedly. Luke tells us, for instance, that Jesus, an unmarried male, included in his expanded band of disciples both married and unmarried women (Luke 8:1–3). His encounter with the Samaritan woman at the well was nothing less than scandalous, in view of the strictures of his era (John 4:1–26). He received the affection of a woman who unpinned her hair in public (no less), and then proceeded to wipe his bare feet with her hair—an act, most any psychiatrist will admit, that is unambiguously erotic (Luke 7:36–50). Not to be overlooked is the fact that Luke, in his written Gospel, mentions thirteen encounters with women that are mentioned nowhere else.

According to Scripture, male-female complementarity is just that: a complementarity that is unsubstitutable. This complementarity entails correlation: male and female are correlates, not correspondents. If man and woman merely corresponded to each other in some sense, then the disappearance of one would permit the survival of the other. Since, however, they are correlates, the disappearance of one entails the disappearance of both.

Three decades ago The United Church of Canada, the first major Protestant denomination to normalize homosexual behaviour and the ordination of persons involved in same-gender genital intimacy, began using 'mutuality' intentionally as a protest against and alternative to 'complementarity.' Male/male mutuality; female/female mutuality; this notion replaced male/female complementarity. The replacement, with its attendant codeword, was a major item in the elevation and implementation of the homosexual agenda.

At a recent meeting of the Board of Trustees of a Christian university, a speaker invoked the 'God of mutuality.' Immediately I recognized a code word; immediately I knew what was presupposed is divine legitimization for something that Scripture everywhere rejects.

---

image of God in *Church Dogmatics* III/2: 45, it should be noted that Calvin anticipated Barth on this point in the former's *Commentary on Genesis* (addressing 1:26). Calvin reinforces this point in *Commentary on Genesis*, 132–33 (addressing Gen 2:21) and in *Sermons on 1 Timothy*, 295–310 (Sermon #20).

It must be noted that according to Scripture, the distinction between male and female is the one distinction built into the creation rather than arising from the Fall. Other distinctions—between rich and poor, for instance; between learned and ignorant, between healthy and ill—are all concomitants of the Fall. They can be overcome and should be since they contradict God's intention concerning the human good. The distinction (and human alienation arising therefrom) between rich and poor is reduced through graduated income tax and social assistance. That between learned and ignorant we aspire to reduce through government-funded public education; that between healthy and ill through medical insurance and health care plans and tax-supported access to medical services. In other words, we recognize all such distinctions to violate what God wills for our blessing.

The distinction between male and female, however, is unique. It isn't a concomitant of the Fall but is rather an ingredient of the creation. Any attempt to deny it and overcome it is sin. For this reason, for instance, the Torah is horrified at cross-dressing: "A woman shall not wear anything that pertains to a man, nor shall a man put on a woman's garment; for it is an abomination to the Lord your God" (Deut 22:5). It isn't a matter of cultural stereotyping. It isn't a matter of whether a man wears a skirt (as kilted men do in Scotland), or whether a woman wears trousers (as Western women do more often than not). Cross-dressing is forbidden in Scripture, rather, in that Scripture forbids the attempt at eliminating the *one* distinction God has ordained for the human creation. The denial of this distinction God deems to be sheer defiance born of ingratitude and disobedience.

While the shift from the category of complementarity to the category of mutuality betokens a major departure from the catholic substance of the faith, it is, needless to say, not the only shift. Discerning Christians (discernment is the major activity of the Holy Spirit within the Christian community, according to Acts) should be alert to such shifts and render explicit what they entail.

THIRD SIGN: SHIFT IN VIEWS OF GOD

In light of needed discernment, consider substitutions concerning the Trinity. In Scripture, God names himself Father, Son and Spirit. In some circles today it is fashionable to rename God creator, liberator, and sustainer—or any other threefold description that the neologist deems to represent the deity. Again, such a substitution may appear harmless, even helpful; I submit, however, it is not.

Why is there a substitution at all? What drives it? I think there are two motivators at work.

One is the feminist objection to the putative maleness of Father and Son.[13] Another objection pertains to the salvific uniqueness of Christ, and to the historical specificity of Jesus of Nazareth.

With respect to the first objection, it should be recalled that the church catholic has *never* said that God is gender-specific. Any such sexualizing of God would have horrified the covenant people, Israel, and would have provoked the protest of the prophets that Yahweh had become no more than a Canaanite fertility force. If, on the other hand, some uninformed Christians have read (misread) the language of Father and Son as ascribing maleness to God, I can only reiterate that such misreading the church catholic has never endorsed. Gender-specificity, we must always be aware, pertains only to the creation; never to God. Then if 'Father' and 'Son' don't betoken maleness, can't the male-sounding vocabulary be dropped and something else replace it? (I shall return to this point shortly.)

In our discussion of the Trinity and the suitability of language for it, the substitution 'creator, liberator, sustainer' might appear to be an improvement. In truth, danger lurks.

(1) First, 'creator, liberator, sustainer' doesn't reflect the personhood of 'Father and Son.' Instead it reflects a function, what is done rather than who someone is, rather than the identity of a person. Substitute-trinities speak of *what* is *done* in time, not of *who* someone *is* eternally. Right here, it should be noted, the personhood of God is receding (and with it the personhood of humans, since we are persons, according to Scripture, only as we are 'personned' by the Person of God).

(2) In the second place, the use of such expressions as 'liberator' is a substitution deployed largely by those who do not uphold Jesus Christ as sole saviour but who rather want to attribute salvific efficacy to other individuals and movements. Liberation theology, for instance, claims not merely to liberate economically or socially; it claims to liberate the human most profoundly; it claims to liberate from the root human bondage. In a word, it claims to fashion the new creature. The vehicle of all such liberation and re-creation is Marxist philosophy.

Coincident with this shift is the shift from 'Jesus Christ' to 'Christ figure.' The question then posed today is "Who is the Christ figure for us?"

---

13. It should be noted that the eternal Son is not male; Jesus of Nazareth, the Son incarnate, is.

"Who has messianic force for us?" Or in the words of a former moderator of The United Church of Canada, "Who rings the bell for us?" Whoever "rings the bell for us" is the Christ figure, the liberator.

More pointedly, many feminists, unable to call God 'Father' for any number of reasons, object to the maleness of Jesus of Nazareth. While God the eternal Son indisputably isn't male, the Son-incarnate indisputably is ("circumcised on the eighth day," in case anyone is in doubt). Theologian Catherine LaCugna asks, "Can a male saviour save women?" As her theology unfolds through several steps she finally pronounces God not to be self-existent; God's existence is no more than God's existence *for us*. Answering her own question, "Can a male saviour save women?" she concludes that human loving communion with each other *replaces* the redemptive achievement of Jesus Christ in the power of the Holy Spirit.[14] Our salvation doesn't hinge upon what has been done for us and in us by a saviour given to us; our salvation hinges on what we do for each other. We may be 'Christ figures' for each other, but Jesus of Nazareth cannot be sole, sufficient saviour.

Catherine LaCugna maintains that Christian theology shouldn't commence with revelation whose content is redemption (the logic of Scripture in both older and newer testaments, recognized and recovered by the Protestant Reformers, we should note); instead, she insists, Christian theology should start with the "experience of being saved."[15]

What LaCugna means by 'saved,' however, isn't what Scripture means; namely, relief from sin's condemnation (under God) and release from sin's grip.[16] In addition, to begin theology with an experience of being saved (especially where 'saved' has been secularized) can only mean that theology is no more than an articulation of experience, experience of life, experience of one's intra-psychic history, indistinguishable from an experience of God—which experience is self-referential in any case, since 'God' no longer transcends world occurrence and human history. As soon as substitutions are made with respect to the Triune God, the unsubstitutability of Jesus Christ is forfeited.

14. See LaCugna, *God for Us*, 223–28.

15. LaCugna, *God for Us*, 223–28.

16. LaCugna is unable to distinguish God from creatures, with the result that the God she depicts is unable to act upon creatures so as to save them. LaCugna, *God for Us*, 304.

(3) In the third place, all such substitutions deny the immanent Trinity, or at least collapse the immanent Trinity into the economic Trinity.

The economic Trinity is God in his action upon us and within us. The one and only God who is eternally transcendent simultaneously comes among us in Jesus of Nazareth. Unlike John the Baptist who was "sent from God" to be a "witness to the light" (John 1:6–7), Jesus isn't sent from God: he *is* God. Neither is he a witness to the light; he *is* the light. We must always remember that the first people to recognize and insist that a hayseed from a one-horse backwoods village is God-with-us, Emmanuel; the first people to acknowledge and celebrate such were Jews for whom the identification of God with anything creaturely was blasphemous and therefore anathema.

Yet there's more to the economic Trinity. The God who comes to dwell among us, who comes into our midst, is also the God who comes within us. Were God only to come into our midst, we'd be left inert, no more than a spiritual corpse unable to profit from a visitor. As God comes within us, according to the apostles, dry bones live; the new creature comes forth; fruits of the Spirit appear and gifts of the Spirit operate.

The next question must be asked: Is what God does among and within us *merely what God does*, or *is it one with who God is*? If it is merely what God does, then plainly God could as readily do something else and might at any time. If, on the other hand, what God does is who God is, then God himself can be known and trusted.

Think of what God does as the face he displays before us; think of who God is as God's heart. The inescapable question then is: Are God's face and God's heart the same? Or might God's face be a false face?—not necessarily a malicious face, but a false face in any case? A Hallowe'en mask, after all, need not be frightening; nonetheless, it remains a mask hiding the identity of the person behind it. For if God's face turned toward us is not or even might not be who God is in himself, then in submitting ourselves to Jesus Christ and the Spirit-power in which he acts we still don't have to do with God himself, only with an activity of God unrelated to God himself—as surely as human beings frequently wear a 'false face,' as it were, their action contradicting who they regard themselves to be.

If God himself is to be known and trusted, the face of God and the heart of God must be one. *What God does* is *who God is*; and *who God is* is neither more nor less than *what God does*. In other words, the economic Trinity must be grounded in the immanent Trinity.

The doctrine of the Trinity witnesses to God's *identity*: what we see in Jesus of Nazareth is what we get: God himself and nothing other than God himself. In addition, the doctrine of the Trinity witnesses to God's *unity*: what is done *for us* in Jesus Christ and *in us* through the Holy Spirit is an act of the one God. These two acts are not the activities of two different deities or two lesser deities or two non-deities.

The oft-voiced question 'Who is God?' is a question Scripture never answers directly. Scripture answers this question indirectly by posing two other questions: 'What does God do on our behalf?' and 'What does God effect within us?' The answers to these two questions add up to the question 'Who is God?' Christology plus pneumatology equals theology. God is Father, Son, and Holy Spirit. This God is one. The doctrine of the Trinity attests the unity of God, the singularity of God, and the identity of God. Any substitution here imperils the unity of God, the uniqueness of God, and the identity of God.

Let me say it for the last time. If God is what God does, then in Jesus Christ (the face of God) we have to do with God himself, not merely with an activity unrelated to God's nature. On the other hand, if what God does is who God is and all God is, then there doesn't lurk behind the face we see in Jesus Christ an aspect of God that might victimize us. It is essential that the immanent Trinity and the economic Trinity presuppose and imply each other.

CATHOLICITY

To this point it may have appeared that I regard the church, and church-related institutions, to be chiefly on the defensive in our era, preoccupied with fending off frontal threats and subtle erosions. This is not the case. I continue to insist on the catholicity of the church and the catholicity of church-related institutions.

Catholicity consists of identity plus universality. Identity is given by gospel-uniqueness that distinguishes the church from the world. Identity is given by the effectual presence of Jesus Christ, who in his singularity cannot be replaced or substituted or modified.

Universality is that which impels the church to embrace the world. Only that which is different from the world can exist for the world.

When we confess with the creed, "I believe in God the Father almighty, maker of heaven and earth, the entire cosmos seen and unseen," we are upholding universality. When we confess, "I believe in Jesus Christ his only Son our Lord, crucified under Pontius Pilate," we are upholding identity.

The missionary enterprise of the early church gave rise to catholicity, particularly the church's outreach to the Gentiles. Since Jesus had said he was "sent only to the lost sheep of the house of Israel" (Matt 15:24), were the apostles disobedient when they announced the gospel beyond the precincts of the sheepfold of Israel? Did the apostles prosecute a mission that Jesus, at least, never foresaw, and at most, would never have countenanced?

On the contrary, the seeds of the Gentile mission are found in the ministry of Jesus. Here we need only think of the reception he accorded Gentiles who came to him; the centurion for instance who wanted his servant healed, who trusted unreservedly our Lord's Kingdom-manifestation, and whose faith elicited our Lord's marvel just because it was greater than anything Jesus had found in Israel (Luke 8:5–13). On a larger scale, we need only recall his parable of the mustard seed (Luke 13:18–19). From the tiniest seed, says Jesus, there comes forth a shrub, a tree in whose branches perch all the birds of the air. 'Birds of the air' is a rabbinic circumlocution meaning 'all the Gentile nations of the world.' Jesus is telling unimaginative, skeptical disciples that from their small numbers (twelve at first, one of whom proved unhelpful), from such a pathetically small number, from their supposedly simplistic message, from their apparently insignificant mission there will come—what? There will come that kingdom-attestation which gathers in people of every nation and language and outlook, as Gentiles of every description will one day owe everything that is their glory to this handful of nondescript Jews who are already wondering if they shouldn't go back to their fishing (John 21:3).

And of course, the trajectory that the risen Jesus mandates for the apostles during the post-Easter Forty Days; the Lord's engagement with them during the forty days determines the trajectory that he wills the church to have forever, which trajectory indisputably includes the Gentile world.

We know that Peter opposed such universality; all Gentile Christians, he maintained, were to become Jews first as part of a two-step conversion (Gal 1–2). Peter, correct with respect to identity, was clueless as to universality. So very grievous was Peter's error that Luke devoted two entire chapters in Acts (the incident of Peter and Cornelius) to render unambiguous God's will concerning universality (Acts 10–11).

The unique message *of* the church guarantees its identity. The varied converts *to* the church guarantee its universality. By extension, a Christian university must preserve its identity by never surrendering the gospel, never compromising "the faith once for all delivered to the saints" (Jude 3), never hiding its light under a basket but always aspiring to remain a city set on a hill. At the same time, varied students enrolling in the college, and varied academic disciplines studied at the university (don't "all things hold together in Christ"? Col 1:17), preserve its universality. In a Christian university identity is defined by exalting Jesus as Lord; in a Christian university universality is defended by articulating Christ's lordship over every aspect of the creation.

In the church of the Patristic era the bishops or presbyters were responsible for ensuring catholicity. (In the New Testament *episkopos* and *presbuteros* mean the same.) In the Reformation era, scholarly pastors were responsible for ensuring it. (It must always be remembered that all the outstanding Protestant thinkers were preachers and pastors first, exegetes second, theologians third, and guardians of the public good fourth.) For the Christian liberal arts and science university, it is the Board of Trustees who are charged with ensuring the institution's catholicity. The trustees must see to it that the college doesn't forfeit its gospel-identity (whether through inadvertence or perfidy) and at the same time doesn't endeavour to preserve its identity self-protectively by forgetting its universality (therein rendering itself sectarian). If the Christian college surrenders its identity, the college ceases to be Christian; if it loses sight of universality, it denies that "the earth is the Lord's" (Ps 24:1).

I have extolled the church's mission to the world, one aspect of which is the Christian university's engagement with the totality of the creation. In order to engage the world, we must adapt ourselves and our language to modernity. If we don't adapt, then however much we may have to say, no one will be able to hear us—and for this predicament we have only ourselves to blame.

I am a student of seventeenth-century Puritan thought. (By the way, are you aware that of the 50 books John Wesley included in his *Christian Library*, which collection Wesley expected Methodists to read, 32 are authored by Puritans?) As much as I cherish Puritan thought (they are the master-diagnosticians of the human heart), next Sunday morning I can't read a Puritan sermon to a congregation. 'I adjure you, by the bowels of mercy, that forsooth you forswear . . . '; no one would profit. We must *adapt* to the world if we are going to be heard.

On the other hand, if we *adopt* the world's mindset and its anti-gospel *Tendenz*, then we may be heard but now we have nothing to say. We shall find ourselves doing no more than repeating the world back to itself. If we adopt the world's outlook, the world's agenda, and the world's schemes, we shall have performed the grand counter-miracle: we shall have turned wine into water.

I admire the effort Friedrich Schleiermacher, the progenitor of liberal theology, made to adapt the Christian message to its "cultured despisers."[17] Schleiermacher maintained that many people of his era rejected the gospel not out of extraordinary hardness of heart but out of their bewilderment at a gospel-presentation that wasn't remotely connected to their daily existence. Surely Schleiermacher can only be commended here. Alas, however, in attempting to adapt he uncritically adopted; the gospel was denatured.

If we think that it all sounds as if the line between adapting and adopting is an exquisitely fine line, I must agree. The line in question happens to be finer than a hair and harder than diamond. Yet this is no reason to be discouraged. I maintain that preachers, teachers, congregations, and Christian universities, all of whom aspire to tiptoe down the line, in truth are rarely exactly on the line but rather are divagating back and forth, first on one side then on the other, always endeavouring to come out on the line at the end of the day as we exercise our God-given vocation.

Once again, discerning the crucial line between adapting and adopting is just that: discernment.

A CONSEQUENCE OF THE SHIFT

Several times to this point it has been emphasized that our naming God as God reveals and names himself (Father, Son, Spirit) doesn't mean God discloses himself as gender-specific; nor does it mean that we are projecting human gender-specificity onto God. At the same time, it has been stressed that substitutes of the sort advanced by Catherine LaCugna (for her, God must be feminized to be credible) entail forfeiting the gospel.[18]

---

17. Schleiermacher, *On Religion*.

18. LaCugna, *God for Us*, 18.

Let me say it again: to speak of God as Father, Son, and Spirit is *not* to render God masculine. On the other hand, to reject God's self-naming here and endorse an explicitly feminization of God is to render God female.

What happens, what *has* happened, in history when such a move has been made? In the history of religions, John Oswalt points out, wherever the deity is feminized, several accompaniments appear.[19]

(1) The radical transcendence of God is lost. In this regard, it ought always to be remembered that the being of God and the being of the creation are utterly discontinuous. The being of God is infinite and eternal; the being of the creation is finite (even if immeasurably large) and contingent. A creation that was brought forth *ex nihilo*, from nothing, can as readily be returned *ad nihilum*, to nothing. (We might as well note in passing that for every time Scripture speaks of God as creator, it speaks fifty times of God as destroyer—an insistence, a caution, a sobering check on all human presumptuousness that the church appears completely to overlook.) At all times, it must be kept in mind that while the universe is made *by* God it isn't made *from* God. It is made by God, and made from—nothing. If the universe and God are regarded as on a continuum of any sort, the radical transcendence of God is forfeited, and with it the notion that God ever remains *Lord* of his creation however intimately he may choose to relate to it. When God is regarded as continuous with the universe, God has become finitized, and God's being rendered contingent. At this point God and world are regarded as belonging to the same order, or God and world are regarded as needing each other, neither one yet of a conclusive nature, the matter still undecided as to what either one will turn out to be.

(2) When God's lordship over the universe is compromised, the forces of nature are elevated and worshipped. Specifically, life-forces or fertility are upheld for veneration. This in turn means that sexual activity is viewed as religiously significant; sexual activity is inherently salvific. Related to this notion is the phenomenon of sacral prostitution, a religious/psychological insistence reflecting the logic of 'sympathetic magic'; namely, sexual congress with a prostitute representing the deity renders the worshipper one with that deity.

Sacral prostitution occurred everywhere in the eastern religions surrounding Israel. More than surrounded Israel; it lapped at Israel, and lapped so very persistently as to gain entry repeatedly. No less frequently

19. Oswalt, *Called to Be Holy*, 11–17.

Israel's prophets had to denounce it in the name of Yahweh who is holy (Deut 23:17–18).

Lest the point I am making be dismissed as irrelevant, I should like to bring forward here a line from the second-last hymn book The United Church of Canada and the Anglican Church of Canada developed jointly in 1971.[20] The line spoke of "The sacrament of sex." Now sex is a gift of God, to be received with thanksgiving and, like any gift from God, not to be warped to purposes other than he intends and blesses. Sex, however, is not a sacrament. If sex were a sacrament, then sexual congress of any sort would intensify one's intimacy with Jesus Christ. What is this except sacral prostitution all over?

The people of God in the era of the Older Testament weren't the only ones threatened. The church in Corinth lived in closest geographic proximity to the fertility cult and temple of Aphrodite. Religious prostitutes from the temple plied their trade among the inhabitants of Corinth. (Corinth, a seaport, never lacked sailors looking for something to do.) Sexual promiscuity was so very notorious that the city's 'red light' business gave rise to a neologism, 'corinthianize.' In the ancient Near East, to 'corinthianize' was to engage in any and all abject expressions of sexual malfeasance.

To his horror, sorrow, and anger, the apostle Paul found Gentile Christians in Corinth evincing more than a little of a Corinthian mindset. In the midst of this ungodliness, he never told the Corinthians that they weren't Christians; he never refused to address them as 'saints.' He did, however, tell them they were a disgrace (1 Cor 5:1).

We live in a highly sexualized culture. The secularization of sexuality in our culture has rendered sexual congress of any sort the occasion of intensifying one's intimacy with the deities of secularization. Since the church, and church-related institutions, are faced with unrelenting pressure, not to say financial sanctions, concerning the secularization of sexuality, vigilance (not grimness, not paranoia, not non-biblical asceticism); good-natured vigilance and cheerful discernment are essential if capitulation is to be avoided and the gospel given up. Church-related schools are charged with prizing the gospel and the implicates of the gospel, especially where young people are concerned for whom the school acts *in loco parentibus*.

(3) If the above two points are considered together—the loss of God's transcendence and with it the loss of God's lordship—what's left, religiously,

---

20. The Anglican Church of Canada and The United Church of Canada, *The Hymn Book of The Anglican Church of Canada and The United Church of Canada*.

is the notion that there is nothing that isn't God. If all that is *is* God (pantheism); or if all that is *of* God (pan*en*theism), then there's nothing that isn't God or of God. And if there's nothing that isn't God or of God, then by definition there is no evil and no sin. No sin: how convenient for our New Age suburbanite 'yuppie' friends who find that New Ageism fits like a glove. Everything they do is itself of god, regardless of who or what that deity might be.

TRADITION

As we reflect upon the challenges we must meet we shouldn't overlook the help we can find in the catholic Christian tradition.

Different metaphors are ready-to-hand in a consideration of tradition, one of which pertains to sailing. Sailboats are constructed with a leaden keel deep below the water line. At the end of the keel there is a torpedo-shaped lead weight. Keel and torpedo-shaped attachment are known as ballast. Ballast acts as a counterpoise whenever the ship heels over in high winds. The counterweight in the ballast rights the boat whenever a squall howls down upon it; it keeps the boat from capsizing. Even if a squall knocks the boat flat, the ballast returns the boat to an upright position.

In addition, the boat's keel keeps the boat on course when the direction of the boat and the direction of the wind are not the same. If the wind is blowing immediately behind the boat in its intended course, no keel is necessary. However, as soon as the wind is blowing from another direction, across the boat or from in front of the boat, the keel allows the boat to sail across the wind or even against the wind. In other words, the keel allows the boat to use wind from any direction as the boat endeavours to stay on course.

Think of tradition, or Christian memory, as the ballast and keel of that boat known as 'church.' Tradition as ballast renders the boat able to survive sudden, unforeseen squalls. Even a flash knockdown finds the boat righting itself, thanks to the counterweight below the waterline. Tradition as keel allows us to stay on course regardless of the direction of the winds that come upon us.

Admittedly, when keel and ballast have been immersed in the water for a protracted period, marine growths attach themselves. These growths are unsightly, yet are rarely seen since they are below the waterline. On the other hand, as these growths proliferate they impede the boat. For this reason, the boat has to go into dry-dock occasionally to have such impediments removed.

In other words, not everything in the church's tradition is good. More than a little is deplorable, anti-gospel beyond doubt. No Christian, therefore, should embrace tradition uncritically. At the same time, only a fool would sever ballast and keel from a boat because of unsightly marine growths attaching themselves to it. If we are so foolish as to disown tradition, we can only be blown off course by current wind and capsized by unforeseen squall.

The rule of thumb in sailing is this: the greater the sail area above the waterline, the greater the ballast needed below the waterline. Methodists, for instance, speak much of the wind of the Spirit. Good. Unless sail is hoisted the wind of the Spirit can't be caught, and the boat goes nowhere. At the same time, the keener we are to catch the wind of the Holy Spirit, the more eager we should be to attend to keel and ballast, tradition.

Reference has been made several times already to multi-directional winds. The wind isn't always blowing in the direction the boater prefers. By extension, there is only one wind the Christian prefers: the wind of the Spirit. Spirits abound, but only one Spirit is holy. Therefore, it is essential that keel and ballast be attended to, for only then will the boat move ahead, on course, regardless of what wind, from whatever direction, the hoisted sail catches.

Let's change the metaphor. Let's think of tradition as memory, Christian memory, the church's memory. To lose one's memory is to suffer from amnesia, a terrible affliction. It isn't terrible because amnesiac persons can't remember where they left their umbrella. (They can always buy another one.) Amnesia is tragic, rather, in that amnesiacs can't remember who they are; not aware of who they are, they lack identity; lacking identity, they can't be trusted.

It isn't the case that amnesiac persons can't be trusted because they are uncommonly wicked or uncommonly stupid. They can't be trusted simply because they don't know who they are, and therefore don't know how they should act in conformity with who they are. Amnesia always means someone is untrustworthy.

Tradition, Christian memory, means we know who we are; we have an identity; and we can be trusted.

A preacher, a congregation, a denomination, an educational institution that allows its tradition to attenuate has rendered itself untrustworthy.

No doubt someone wishes to object that tradition can be a tyrant. Yes, it can. But in our era, with its superficial disavowal of history, the greater danger is that we shall forfeit tradition as our teacher.

G. K. Chesterton wisely reminds us that tradition is "democracy of the dead"; tradition means the dead are allowed to vote.[21] Why shouldn't the dead should be allowed to vote? Tradition*ism*, on the other hand, could mean that only the dead are allowed to veto. Or to put it differently, tradition is the living faith of the dead, while traditionalism is the dead faith of the living.[22]

Owning our tradition, owning it critically yet appreciatively, means we aren't pretending we are the first Christians, and we aren't so naïve as to think that generations of Christians haven't faced the challenges confronting us. It means we know who we are; we have an identity; we can be trusted.

Institutions of Christian higher education will have a future as long as they have a past. They will thrive in fair winds and survive in foul as long as they are unashamed of their Christian heritage, which heritage is a crucial ingredient in the tradition of the church of Jesus Christ and in any educational institution that aspires to exemplify Christ's lordship over the entire creation.

Always aware of the responsibility parents bear concerning the spiritual and intellectual formation of their children; and aware as well of the responsibility academic institutions bear to facilitate the same, Charles Wesley summarizes the aspiration of families, congregations, and Christian universities:

> Unite the pair so long disjoined,
> Knowledge and vital piety;
> Learning and holiness combined,
> And truth and love, let all men see
> In those whom up to thee we give,
> Thine, wholly thine, to die and live.[23]

21. Chesterton, *Orthodoxy*, 29–44.

22. Pelikan, *The Vindication of Tradition*, 65.

23. Wesley, *Works of John Wesley*, 7:644.

BIBLIOGRAPHY

Anglican Church of Canada and United Church of Canada. *The Hymn Book of The Anglican Church of Canada and The United Church of Canada.* Toronto: The Anglican Church of Canada and The United Church of Canada, 1971.

Barth, Karl. *Church Dogmatics.* Volume III, Part 2. Translated by H. Knight, G. W. Bromiley, J. K. S. Reid, and R. H. Fuller. Edinburgh: T. & T. Clark, 1960.

Calvin, John. *A Commentary on Genesis.* Translated and edited by John King. London: Banner of Truth Trust, 1965.

———. *Sermons on the Epistle to the Ephesians.* Translated by Banner of Truth Trust. London: Banner of Truth Trust, 1973.

———. *Sermons on 1 Timothy.* Volume 1. Edited by Ray Van Neste and Brian Denker. Charleston: CreateSpace Independent Publishing Platform, 2016.

Heidegger, Martin. *Being and Time.* Translated by Joan Stambaugh. Albany: State University of New York Press, 2010.

LaCugna, Catherine M. *God for Us: The Trinity and the Christian Life.* San Francisco: HarperSanFranciso, 1991.

Lewis, C. S. *Miserable Offenders.* Cincinnati: Forward Movement Publications, 1954.

Luther, Martin. *Luther's Works.* Volume 31. Translated and edited by Harold J. Grimm. Philadelphia: Fortress, 1957.

Lutz, David W. "Can Notre Dame Be Saved?" *First Things* 1 (January 1992) 35–42.

Oberman, Heiko A. *The Impact of the Reformation.* Grand Rapids: Eerdmans, 1994.

———. "Teufelsdreck: Eschatology and Scatology in the 'Old' Luther." *Sixteenth Century Journal* 19 (1988) 435–50.

Oden, Thomas C. *Care of Souls in the Classic Tradition.* Philadelphia: Fortress, 1984.

Oswalt, John. *Called to Be Holy.* Nappanee, IN: Evangel, 1999.

Pelikan, Jaroslav. *The Vindication of Tradition.* New Haven, CT: Yale University Press, 1986.

Schleiermacher, Friedrich. *On Religion: Speeches to Its Cultured Despisers.* Translated by John Oman. New York: Harper & Brothers, 1958.

Shepherd, Victor A. *Interpreting Martin Luther.* Toronto: BPS Books, 2016.

Wesley, Charles. *Works of John Wesley,* Volume 7. *A Collection of Hymns for the Use of the People Called Methodists,* edited by Franz Hildebrandt and Oliver A. Beckerlegge. Nashville: Abingdon, 1983.

Wesley, John. *Works of John Wesley.* Volume 26. Edited by Frank Baker. Oxford: Clarendon, 1982.

1 2

Working in Tandem

Toward an Ecology of Denomination and Seminary

PHIL C. ZYLLA

INTRODUCTION

MY FIRST EXPOSURE TO the politic between denomination and seminary came when I went to a denominational orientation for new pastors at the North American Baptist Conference office in Chicago. I was a young pastor in my first charge and, while I had attended both the denominational Bible college and its seminary, there was clearly an interest within the denominational leadership in ensuring that I understood what it meant to be a North American Baptist pastor. I was particularly interested in the historical presentation which, to my surprise, left out many of the elements of Baptist history that I had studied deeply in seminary. In my naiveté I called my former professor of Church History to ask him why it was that the denominational office did not rely on him for a more comprehensive and erudite session on the history of the denomination. I don't recall his answer, but it quickly became clear that there were different expectations and understandings of what it meant to think theologically about ministry in the seminary as opposed to the denominational office. I was puzzled about the lack of integration between the academic institution that had trained me for Christian ministry and the institution that was responsible for the shepherding of the congregations for whom I was providing leadership and pastoral care.

A second incident that has shaped my thinking about this topic is an experience I had teaching a third-year Master of Divinity class at one of the institutions affiliated with Christian Higher Education Canada (CHEC). A student approached me one day after class to ask a question that I had not given much thought to before: "How do you choose a denomination to belong to when you want to apply for a pastoral position?" This third-year student was in the dark about how to affiliate with a denomination. As a person who had always linked myself with the ministry of a specific family of churches, I did not have much advice for this student. I probably suggested that they look for congruity between their own operative theology and that of denominations that they would like to see themselves serving. I suggested that they begin attending a church in one of those denominations and that they should identify persons that they knew in such denominations to align themselves with. This would allow them to seek out support and counsel as they worked toward a more formal affiliation.

Another marker that gave rise to this paper is my own career trajectory. I served four churches over a total of seventeen years as a pastor in a single denomination, the North American Baptist Conference. I was then thrust into denominationalism in a big way when I became the Principal of ACTS Seminaries of Trinity Western University—a consortium of (at that time) six denominationally affiliated seminaries. ACTS had an orientation to the believer's church tradition shared in common by all six of these denominations but allowed for denominational loyalty to develop and grow through specialized courses, individual mentoring, and the financial and placement support of the regional denominational offices. For the past eleven years I have served as Academic Dean at McMaster Divinity College. The College is historically affiliated with the Canadian Baptists of Ontario and Quebec. However, like most seminaries, we have reached out to other like-minded denominations and networks to create strategic partnerships. Like many theological schools in Canada, our student body now consists of over forty denominational backgrounds and we welcome women and men from all of these churches to study with us. My experiences as a pastor and as a theological educator have shaped my perspective, and this paper is an attempt to reflect on what I have observed. My aim is to offer some fresh thinking on how the ecology of churches, their sponsoring denominational offices, and the affiliated seminaries work. I believe that we can work creatively, collaboratively, and efficiently towards a new future together, but this will take fresh effort and initiative on the part of all concerned.

This chapter seeks to explore the 'ecologies' of churches, their supporting denomination, and the affiliated theological institution related to those churches and that denomination. In the early 2000's the *Lilly Endowment* foundation launched a project to support what they termed the 'ecology' of seminary, congregations, and denominations. The links are obvious, as most theological institutions were founded by their sponsoring denomination. However, the "ties that bind" have lost their efficacy and the situation has become complicated.

WHAT IS THE ECOLOGY OF THE CHURCHES, A SEMINARY, AND A SPONSORING DENOMINATION?

A denomination is a unique ecclesial family of churches that historically have shared a common mission, vision, and theological orientation. The churches that affiliate with this denomination share in common a theological orientation (usually in a formal statement of beliefs) and have shared values and goals that tap into the larger mission of the ecclesial family. The affiliated seminary was founded to be a trusted educational institution that inhabits the common mission, theology, and values of the denomination. Its mandate is to partner in the formation of professional ministry leaders that will, in turn, serve the churches and strengthen the larger mission of the denomination. Ecology language assumes symmetry and symbiosis. Ecosystems describe the network of relations among organisms at different scales of organization. Symbiosis literally means, "living together." However, there are different modes of symbiosis that are instructive for our purposes in understanding the ecology we are talking about here. These five types of symbiosis[1] are:

   a. *parasitism*: a symbiotic relationship where one organism is harmed, and the other is helped

   b. *competition*: the use of the same limited resources by two or more species at the same time and in the same place

   c. *commensalism*: a symbiotic relationship where one organism benefits and the second is neither harmed nor helped

---

1. https://www.slideshare.net/emneistadt/ecology-symbiotic-relationships

d. *cooperation*: a type of symbiosis that promotes a beneficial interaction with the same kind of organism

e. *mutualism*: a symbiotic relationship where both organisms are helped in some ways

Our goal will be to overcome parasitism and competition in improving our ecologies of mission between seminary and churches. Furthermore, commensalism may not be an ideal state as one of the two primary institutions does not benefit. Therefore, it will be beneficial to understand and support processes that will facilitate authentic *cooperation* and *mutualism* in the ecology of church, denomination, and seminary.

IDENTIFYING THE SITUATION

The majority of theological seminaries affiliated with CHEC[2] have a sponsoring denomination and are seeking ways to strengthen the bonds of their base while at the same time expanding to serve a much wider swath of students from various theological positions and backgrounds. This paper seeks a greater understanding of the pitfalls and problems of denominationally-affiliated seminaries and to identify ways to strengthen the common aims of leadership formation and development. Of the twenty-one graduate theological institutions affiliated with CHEC, fourteen have particular denominational ties:

Acadia Divinity College: affiliated with the *Canadian Baptists of Atlantic Canada.*

McMaster Divinity College: affiliated with the *Canadian Baptists of Ontario and Quebec.*

Northwest Baptist Seminary: affiliated with the *Fellowship of Evangelical Baptist Churches of British Columbia, Alberta, Saskatchewan, the Yukon, and the Territories;* member school of the *Associated Canadian Theological Schools (ACTS).*

Canadian Baptist Seminary: affiliated with the *Baptist General Conference of Canada;* member school of the *Associated Canadian Theological Schools (ACTS).*

2. This chapter is focused on member schools of Christian Higher Education Canada (CHEC) that have graduate programs of theological study related to Christian leadership development. There are many other seminaries and theological schools that are not members of CHEC, and there are many undergraduate institutions that are both denominationally affiliated and that have programs for Christian leadership development.

Canadian Southern Baptist Seminary: affiliated with the *Canadian National Baptist Convention.*

Taylor Seminary: affiliated with the *North American Baptist Conference* and a partner with *North American Baptist Seminary.*

Heritage Seminary: affiliated with *The Fellowship of Evangelical Baptist Churches (Central Region).*

Ambrose Seminary: affiliated with the *Christian and Missionary Alliance of Canada* and *Church of the Nazarene Canada.*

Masters Seminary: affiliated with the *Western Ontario, Eastern Ontario, Quebec and Maritime Districts of the Pentecostal Assemblies of Canada*; partner with *Tyndale Seminary.*

Horizon Seminary: affiliated with the *Pentecostal Assemblies of Canada*; partner with *Providence Seminary, Lutheran Theological Seminary,* and *Saskatoon Theological Union.*

Canadian Mennonite University: affiliated with the *Mennonite Church Canada* and the *Mennonite Brethren Church of Manitoba.*

Mennonite Brethren Biblical Seminary: affiliated with the *Canadian Conference of Mennonite Brethren Churches*; member school of the *Associated Canadian Theological Schools (ACTS)* and partner with *Canadian Mennonite University.*

Trinity Western Seminary: affiliated with the *Evangelical Free Church of Canada*; member school of the *Associated Canadian Theological Schools (ACTS).*

Canadian Reformed Theological Seminary: affiliated with the *Federation of Canadian Reformed Churches.*

There are four seminaries that do not specifically identify with a particular denomination within the CHEC affiliated schools, though they may have active elements of denominational alignment:

Regent College: statement from website, "Regent is truly transdenominational—welcoming students from all ends of the theological spectrum. As an institution, Regent is both evangelical and orthodox, but our first priority is to remain true to orthodox faith as recorded in the Scriptures."[3]

Briercrest Seminary: statement from website, "Briercrest is a Christ-centred, Bible-anchored, and ministry-focused community that includes a high school, college and seminary."[4]

---

3. https://www.regent-college.edu/about-us.

4. https://www.briercrest.ca.

Providence Seminary: statement from website, "rooted in the Protestant evangelical faith, that celebrates international and ecumenical diversity."[5]

Tyndale Seminary: statement from website, "Tyndale University College & Seminary is a Christian institution of higher education standing in the Protestant Evangelical tradition."[6]

There are two schools affiliated with CHEC that are not seminaries but offer graduate programs that are theological or ministry related:

Institute for Christian Studies: "The Institute for Christian Studies is a community-supported graduate school in the Kuyperian stream of the Reformed tradition"[7] and is affiliated with the Toronto School of Theology.

Kingswood University: affiliated with *The Wesleyan Church*; offers the Master of Arts in Pastoral Theology.

While all of these schools are affiliated with a denomination or a "family of churches," they all relate to churches in a variety of ways and those relationships are changing. Timothy Weber suggests in his study of denominations and seminaries that "merely labeling a school as denominational or inter/nondenominational does not explain very much about that institution's actual relationship to churches."[8] Factors that weigh heavily on the relative ecology of denomination and seminary include: governance/ trustee structures (how much is the denomination involved in the governance of the institution and the election of trustees?); hiring of faculty and key administrators (what level of involvement does the denomination play in the hiring of the senior administrators or faculty members?); financial support (to what extent does the denomination offer financial support to the school or supply the school with candidates for theological education?). There are many variables at play here; however, the trend appears to be toward multiple denominationalism with some denominational schools receiving "unofficial recognition." Because of this, Weber notes, "the lines that separate denominational and inter/nondenominational schools have become quite blurry."[9]

---

5. https://www.prov.ca/why-providence/who-we-are/.

6. https://www.tyndale.ca/about/mission-statement-of-faith.

7. http://www.icscanada.edu/about/story.

8. Weber, "The Seminaries," 67.

9. Weber, "The Seminaries," 71.

REORIENTATION OF CHRISTIAN HIGHER EDUCATION

In his essay on the future of Christian higher education, David Dockery invites us to consider "a future for Christian higher education that seeks more intentionally to connect teaching, learning, research, and scholarship with the church's heritage and tradition."[10] He continues by stating, "at the heart of this calling is the need to prepare a generation of Christians to think Christianly, to engage the academy and the culture, to serve society, and to renew the connection with the church and its mission."[11] In their study of church related schools Glanzer et. al. offer this insight: "a common evangelical tendency [is] the propensity to focus on certain common Christian beliefs about the Bible, Christ, salvation, and activism that cross denominational boundaries as a source for common partnerships."[12] More and more the trend seems to be away from a specific denominational loyalty to a 'kind' of church and the interactive engagement of a network that is loosely affiliated by theological themes and missional activities.

Ron Benefiel notes a significant shift away from denominational loyalty in evangelicalism. He states, "Denominations have declined as the primary way of organizing North American religious life. In many circles, brand-name loyalty has given way to 'switching,' by which people choose to attend local churches for reasons other than their denominational connections. Nondenominational, independent, and denominational congregations that never mention their pedigree are all on the rise."[13] There is an inherent tension here. While valuing and appreciating the significant support and allegiance that a sponsoring denomination has of its graduate theological institution, most seminaries and graduate schools in Canada welcome students of every denomination to their programs of study. Very few are exclusively operating within the sphere of a denominational context.

My two case studies have something to offer about this situation. There is a need for an intentional cooperation between the denominational churches and the seminary *and* there is a need for wider affiliation agreements for nondenominational/transdenominational theological education. It was a good instinct, I think, when I was a young pastor to want the rich resources of the theological seminary to come to bear on my orientation to the history and context of the work of a pastor in that denomination. It

10. Dockery, "Toward a Future," 115.

11. Dockery, "Toward a Future," 116.

12. Glanzer et al., "Assessing the Denominational Identity," 182.

13. Benefiel, "The Ecology," 22.

was a fair expectation that the leadership responsible for shaping the discourse about 'who we are as a denomination' would have the expert input of church historians and theologians affiliated with the denomination.

It was also imperative that my former student, who was training for Christian ministry in a nondenominational context, be more aware of the importance of aligning with and actively serving within a particular network of churches. My student was receiving a quality theological education. However, there was a practical need to engage in a particular ministry context, to become familiar with the ebb and flow of denominational ties, and to orient oneself to doing ministry with the wider support and guidance of a family of churches. The expectation of both seminary, churches/denominations, and individual seminarians is that all of these will be fully interactive, engaged, and thoughtful about their common mission.

THE SITUATION OF THE CHURCHES IN CONTEXT

In his Schaff Lectures at Pittsburgh Theological Seminary, Dan Aleshire offered an optimistic perspective on the situation of the church, stating, "much has changed; more will change. Some structures, congregations, and patterns of churchly connectional life will not make it into the future, but the Christian project—with faithful adherents, lively congregations, and viable structures that support and extend ministry—will be around."[14] This statement appears to have support from the evidence in the Canadian context provided by sociologist of religion Reginald Bibby, who states, "the Christian faith is anything but passé in Canada."[15] Bibby's research predicts that while religious life in Canada is polarizing between the secular and religiously affiliated, more than 60% of the population will continue to identify with Christian groups in 2050.[16] This more optimistic way of viewing things, however, must take seriously the importance of the kinds of changes that are occurring.

There are some signs of renewal and strengthening and there are serious signs of decline, diminishment, and strain on the same churches and their supporting denominations. In a study of American congregations from 2000–2010 David Roozen acknowledges some areas of strength that account for the heightened vitality of churches in North America. First,

14. Aleshire, "Wilderness," 1.

15. Bibby, "Post-Christendom," 126.

16. Bibby, "Post-Christendom," 136.

they have seen a dramatic increase in the use of contemporary worship, which has had a renewing effect on the spiritual vitality of the churches (Evangelical Protestant churches increased their involvement in contemporary worship styles from 38% in 2000 to 50% in 2010; mainline Protestants increased from 12.6% in 2000 to 25.2% in 2010).[17] There has also been an increase of racial/ethnic minority congregations as a result of both higher birth rates in minority communities and greater immigration.[18]

Bibby notes that the landscape of Canadian churches in the last two decades also reflects significant immigration but this is primarily in the Catholic tradition.[19] However, the trend to ethnic diversity in congregations is also impacting evangelical churches in Canada. The third area of strengthening the churches noted by Roozen is the trend of an increase in mission-oriented programs in local churches which is up about 7% overall from 2000–2010.

Despite these small gains, the overall trends for changes in the churches in North America indicate significant stress. In particular, there are three areas of strain identified by Roozen in his decade-long study. The first of these has a major impact on this study and demonstrates a "steep drop in financial health."[20] In this decade, churches dropped from 31% who reported a healthy financial situation to just 14%. Year over year financial strength and vitality dropped by 4%–9% per year. This steep decline took place in a relatively short period of time which changed the dynamics of ecclesial activity dramatically. A second concern is the rise in corrosive church conflict. Roozen's study identified four key areas of congregational planning: worship, finances, leadership, and the establishing of priorities. The study concluded that "almost two of every three congregations in 2010 had experienced conflict in at least one of the four key areas in the past five years. In a third of the congregations the conflict was serious enough that members left or withdrew contributions, or a pastoral leader left."[21] The third area impacting the erosion of congregational vitality identified by Roozen is the aging demographic of the congregations. Congregations

17. Roozen, "A Decade of Change." This trend has also been matched by a significant use of technology in churches. The churches that use technology heavily are no more spiritually vital but tend to attract younger adherents which accounts for a strength not present in low technology using churches.

18. Roozen, "A Decade of Change."

19. Bibby, "Post-Christendom," 131.

20. Roozen, "A Decade of Change,"

21. Roozen, "A Decade of Change."

are getting older and are proportionately less populated by young adults. From 2000–2005 that average percentage of Sunday worship participants over 60 years old increased, while the percentage of young adults in that same period decreased. From 2008–2010 the same trend appears. The average percentage of participants over 65 increased slightly, and the average percentage of 18–34 year olds continued to decline. How do these three issues play into the ecology of churches, denominational offices, and the seminaries?

Declining Financial Support

The impact of declining denominational support for affiliated educational institutions is directly linked to the steep decline in financial strength of their affiliated local churches as a whole. Funding the enterprise has become a primary concern of administrators in theological education. It is also a primary concern of denominational leaders and executives. The funding patterns of the past are not compatible with the current situation. Declining resources means a primary shift in the way that institutions are operated. There has been a sea change in the ability of denominations to support their affiliated institutions. This has resulted in weaker direct ties between the institution and the denomination. However, it has also resulted in new opportunities for schools to broaden their constituencies by creating new partnerships that are less exclusive and less directly dependent.

There are questions about whether the denominational system is still viable. As Weber comments, ". . . many have questioned the viability of the denominational system itself. Fewer members mean fewer dollars to finance denominational programs. As a result, many denominations are a shadow of their former selves. A strong trend in the broader culture . . . is the shift to decentralized power and the preference for local networks where accountability is high, and involvement is more hands-on."[22]

On the other hand, congregational studies expert Nancy Ammerman suggests that there are ways in which the renewal of denominational distinctives and ties is being preserved. This is particularly in areas of shared liturgy, shared mission activity (because there is strength in numbers when it comes to large missional projects), and denominational orientations/ preferences. She states,

22. Weber, "The Seminaries," 75.

These [denominationally oriented] congregations see their theological heritage as a gift, intentionally teach newcomers about the faith, and celebrate their own unique worship traditions. They may, in fact, assert their own retrieval of the denominational tradition over the versions represented in national denominational offices. Still, most choose to use their own denomination's educational curriculum, and many cherish the national and international denominational connections that enable them to do good work in the world.[23]

The reality is that there are trends in the financial support of denominations that require major adjustment in our expectations about the future economic viability of the denominational structures, and the parallel institutions related to it. As one writer on denominational decline states it, "when trends don't change, institutions must."[24]

Conflict in the Churches

The problem of local church conflict is something that preoccupies many denominational leaders. A lot of the energy and time commitments of denominational leaders is wrapped up in addressing the fractures that happen in congregations over issues of worship, finances, leadership, and divided visions over the priorities of the congregations. This demonstrates one of the more complex aspects of the ecology of church and seminary. Who is responsible for the cultivation of leaders? What are the requirements for ordination? Who decides what a theologically responsible plan for the priorities of the congregation should be? What input processes are there for the practical, theological, and ecclesial problems being faced by the churches?

The challenges that seminaries face and that denominations face are not as similar as one might think. The seminary context is preparing people for future ministries while the church context is embedded in complex current situations. There are many times that the pressing needs of denominational offices are aligned with those of the educational institutions preparing women and men for various vocations in ministry. However, there are also many times when these realities do not share the same urgency, priority, and financial commitments. They are pulling in different directions.

I would also argue that there are significant opportunities embedded in this complex situation. Such issues require further reflection and

23. Ammerman, "New Life for Denominationalism," 5.
24. Coffman, "Are We Entering?"

intentional collaboration between seminary leaders/faculty and the ecclesial leaders/denominational staff. I think that a more nuanced understanding of the issues faced by seminary faculty and denominational leaders
would bring about a fruitful path for strengthening the ecology of these
institutions.

Changing Demographics

If young adult participation in most churches is down significantly, what is
the impact on the prospects of young adults going into Christian ministry
and theological education? Statistics from seminaries affiliated with the Association of Theological Schools in the United States and Canada (ATS)
indicate a shifting demographic in seminary enrolment. In 2016, enrolment for all ATS schools leveled off at 72,372. However, a deeper analysis
according to Meinzer and Brown, "reveals significant shifts in the make-up
of the student population and its academic interests."[25] Shifts taking place
over the last two decades show the over-50 cohort as the fastest-growing
(up 16% in absolute numbers over the past 10 years alone). The under-30
crowd "still makes up the largest cohort of students (30% of those reporting
age). The over-50 cohort had climbed to 22% of all ATS students in 2015,
the second highest age-grouping. The 30–39 age group of ATS students
increased from 2% since 2009 to 27%, but still quite short of its high point
of 33% in 1995. The 40–49 age group declined to 20% of enrolment from
its peak of 25% in 2005.[26] See Appendix B for enrolment in ATS schools in
Canada by denomination for 2017.

EMERGING TRENDS IN SEMINARY EDUCATION

Weber notes, "today's theological schools are more complex than they used
to be, offer more degrees than ever, often feel stretched to the limit by their
expanding programs, wonder where their future students and funding will
come from, and are searching for ways to cope with the changes that are
occurring in their supporting churches and in the broader culture."[27] Some
of these emerging educational trends include localization, increasing cost
of education, the pressures of ministry, and new pathways of credentialing.

---

25. Meinzer and Brown, "New Data," 1.

26. Brown, "Did you Know."

27. Weber, "The Seminaries," 72.

Localization

"Prospective students whose denominational/theological dispositions are more open and flexible may be more likely to consider studying in schools that offer greater prestige, lower tuition, or proximity to home regardless of the theological orientation of the schools. As a result, many denominational seminaries are finding it more difficult to recruit students from their denominational/theological traditions, especially those who live at a distance."[28]

The problem is exacerbated by the fact that, even with a denominational context, a seminary may not be well known or understood. A key Auburn Center study concluded that seminaries are largely invisible in their supporting churches by stating, "most of the seminaries we studied are known to only a fairly small circle of insiders of their own religious tradition—denominational executives, clergy, and the members of some congregations that are either large or located close to the seminary's campus."[29]

Whereas previously theological education was full-time and on site, the delivery model for theological education has drastically changed. Weber notes, "to attract additional students, schools also employed new delivery systems: block scheduling; evening, weekend, and intensive courses; extension sites; online classes; continuing education for clergy; and non-degree certificate programs for clergy and lay people."[30]

Increasing Cost of Education

The financial pressures of Christian higher education play into the ongoing situation of theological education. In the past, seminaries would receive substantial financial support from their sponsoring denominations and key donors. However, the situation has shifted as a result of declining memberships in most denominations in Canada. The flow of income from sponsoring denominations has slowed considerably, forcing schools to move to more tuition-driven models of education. Seminaries are at risk with the high fixed costs of education. Most seminaries have relatively small endowments, making the benefits of a seminary education for students much less tenable.

---

28. Wyatt, "The Canadian Ecology," 22.
29. Lynn and Wheeler, "Missing Connections," 4–5.
30. Weber, "The Seminaries," 72.

Ron Benefiel cautions, "it is apparent that most seminaries cannot continue business as usual in this environment. It will be necessary for most of them to find new ways to fund and deliver theological education if they are to continue to effectively carry out their missions."[31]

The trends indicate that students are starting seminary later; have more accumulated educational debt, and therefore, have shorter careers in ministry as a result.[32] Tony Ruger advises, " . . . leaders of denominational seminaries must engage their sponsoring church bodies in serious conversations about the shape of a mission partnership in which financial support will play a smaller role."[33] These conversations will not be easy. They inevitably require a change in priorities, in expectations, and in the overall symbiosis of denomination and school.

The Pressures of Ministry

Observers to the scene of Canadian ecclesial life have recognized the increasing complexity of ministry formation. As Peter Wyatt notes, "Church life tends to 'grind people down.'"[34] This situation heightens both the fragility of recruiting the best and brightest persons to pursue Christian ministry and the sense of obligation that all participants have to pay attention to the rising complexity of ministry in the increasingly secular environment of Canadian society. While some researchers, like Bibby, do not see the rise of post-Christendom as an immediate concern, many others are concerned about the erosion of religious freedom and the reduced influence of the church in culture. Those who are involved in Christian ministry are already underpaid and overworked. These other cultural pressures can only increase the uncertainty about the future patterns of Christian ministry. Such pressures both create strain on the leader development patterns within the denomination (resisting erosion of theological commitments) but also create educational challenges within theological institutions. The pressures heighten the complexity of the ecology of church, seminary, and ministry agent.

---

31. Benefiel, "The Ecology," 24.

32. Weber, "The Seminaries," 72.

33. Ruger, "Lean Years Fat Years," 3.

34. Wyatt, "The Canadian Ecology," 19.

New Pathways of Credentialing

At one time the seminary had a corner on the market of theological education. However, new paths of preparation for credentialed ministry have emerged, particularly in the evangelical churches. Weber comments, "for a number of reasons, many of the same churches that insisted on an educated and ordered ministry have recently developed alternate paths to ordination that do not require a seminary degree."[35] This has had a dramatic effect on enrolment in professional degrees in many theological schools. There are many reasons for this changing pattern, but it no doubt has affected the ecology of sponsoring denomination and seminary.

This is coupled with other sea changes that are happening in the formation of ministering persons. No longer are the educational pathways provided by seminaries the required or even the preferred path to ministry training. As Benefiel states,

> The view of the ministry and how people become ministers is changing. Competition from non-seminary sources weighs heavily on everyone's table. In many circles, theological schools at one time cornered the market on training ministers. But that is no longer the case, thanks to the Internet, the rise of 'virtual seminaries' and online courses, and the proliferation of popular conferences, workshops, and the like, often under the auspices of [a] so-called teaching church. Choices abound, and increasing numbers of leaders no longer look to theological schools as the primary source for the latest information on best practices, new ministry models, or developing strategic plans for reaching the culture.[36]

The rise of church-based educational programs, denominational credentialing paths, and other educational options in Bible colleges and other educational institutions dilutes the range of educational programs that seminaries and graduate schools can mount. Even if these programs were supported by the denominations, the enrolment would be insufficient for a sustainable future. Therefore, the whole pattern of how one trains for Christian ministry must be examined, discussed, and renegotiated. How this reassessment of educational pathways is conducted will determine much of the future of the ecology of seminary and denomination when it comes to leadership development.

35. Weber, "The Seminaries and the Churches," 79.
36. Benefiel, "The Ecology," 23.

NAMING THE CHALLENGES

This chapter is not meant to be exhaustive but rather suggestive in terms of concrete issues that might help to synchronize the efforts of the denominational office, the seminaries and graduate schools that are engaged in theological education, and the individuals who themselves have a vocation to Christian ministry.

Competing Educational Visions

Every year in the Canadian context millions of dollars are spent by the church in educational endeavors that are intended to strengthen the church. Very few people would question the importance of this effort but there is an inherent tension between the educational mission of the church as conceived by faculty in seminaries and as constructed by denominational offices. At the root of such reflections are competing expectations about what an 'educated clergy' looks like. The schools tend toward an intellectual integration while the churches prefer a pragmatic orientation to a kind of ministerial effectiveness. The differing measuring sticks used for 'excellence' often lead to an educational impasse—the seminary does not want to relinquish its aims of a well-rounded theologically educated clergy and the churches will continue to complain "that seminaries are not producing such well-balanced and multitasked ministers because their faculties are more interested in scholarship than in matters of faith or practical ministry."[37]

In an interview on the subject of Christian higher education, experienced statesman of theological education Ted Ward had this to say about the expectations of churches for theological training of the clergy:

> More and more churches are asking questions related to the non-formal paradigm which leads me to believe that church are going to be less and less interested in simply copying the values, habits, and the ideals of a schooling model. Churches, today, are coming to reject a curriculum that looks like a seminary curriculum, especially in those areas where they feel that the pastors they have hired from seminary have not been able to make any effective use of a major portion of that curriculum. They will reject that which may be deemed important for some theoretical reason, but has

---

37. Weber, "The Seminaries," 82.

not contributed to the pastor's effectiveness—as they understand effectiveness.[38]

There is an evident tension in the portrayal of educational pathways, whether formal or informal, when it comes to measures of success. One might well agree with the perspective of Weber when he says,

> Now more than ever, ministerial students need the time and guided reflection to acquire the knowledge and discernment to become effective leaders of religious communities. One simply cannot attain such things in short spurts or weekend exposures. Face-to-face encounters in ongoing scholarly communities are still the best way to prepare leaders in changing and difficult times.[39]

Competition for Resources

However much funding we do have for leadership development in the ecology of church and seminary, it will always fall short of what we need. This indicates that, for the immediate future, there will be strong competition for the same resources. In the competitive version of symbiosis there is a winner and a loser. The ecology is not sustainable if this competitive approach becomes rooted. What are alternatives? Working in tandem, as the title of this paper suggests, requires more than goodwill and optimism. Three things are required to facilitate meaningful collaboration. First, there must be mutual participation in decision-making. How can the boards of our denominations and our seminaries be linked in their decision-making processes? The more meaningful engagement that takes place at this level; the more likely there will be positive mutual influence that one has on the other. Second, cooperation requires meaningful goals that are mutually beneficial to both the founding denomination and the affiliated school. Often such goals are not meaningful and fail to inspire commitment to the mutual benefit of both institutions. This requires correction by establishing a meaningful framework for decision-making and goal-setting. Third, the leadership style of seminary and denominational executives will have to become more cooperative not only in terms of mutual goals but in the allocation of staff resources that support the mutually sustained organizational directions. Subordinates take their cues from the leadership about

38. Ward and Cannell, "Theological Education," 33.
39. Weber, "The Seminaries," 82.

whether they should have a competitive or a collaborative stance toward other institutions.

Changing Patterns of Professional Ministry

In a large 2015 study, *The National Congregations Study*, Mark Chaves of Duke University discovered a significant shift in secondary ministerial staff. The study notes, "across religious traditions, 49% of full-time and 55% of part-time secondary ministerial staff in 2012 were drawn from the congregations in which they currently work."[40] This shift has created a division in the pathways to full-time church ministry. The study concludes, "in general . . . there seems to be two different models of ministerial work operating within [American] congregations, one that emphasizes formal education and one that emphasizes personal connection to the congregation and on-the-job training, and different religious groups lean towards one or the other of these models." Seminaries have been "slow to adapt and develop new models that take into account the disruptive forces acting in congregations and the culture . . . Seminaries still tend to offer curricula rooted in assumptions of cultural and denominational stability."[41]

The ecology of both denomination and seminary is threatened if we do not change course on some of the traditional approaches that have become embedded in our recruitment and training of emerging leaders. Kenneth Carter Jr. states,

> . . . rather than creatively discerning the church's leadership needs, challenges and opportunities and then finding candidates to address them, denominational and seminary leaders have relied primarily on potential candidates working through their own sense of call to ministry. The result has been weak talent pools, poorly defined roles, narrow descriptions of essential clergy skills, and ineffective and underfinanced systems of leadership development.[42]

Preoccupied with 'Many Things'

Many articles relating the concerns of this paper pit the denominational office against the seminary. The pragmatic, church-based training program of the denomination against the intellectual, ivory-tower version

40. Chaves and Eagle, "Religious Congregations," 19.
41. Carter, "Disruption and Leadership."
42. Carter, "Disruption and Leadership."

critical-thinking version of theological formation in the seminary. While these caricatures may carry vestiges of the past situation, they do not really tell the story. I would want to offer that the intensity and demand of institutions to make ends meet, to accomplish many things with fewer and fewer resources, and the correlate preoccupation that comes with such burdens is at the root of the impasse. We need to free up our thinking and make room for the serious attention that these matters require of us. The denomination needs time to think and reflect. The seminary needs time to measure and sift and discern. These actions of a carefully measured response call for a new paradigm for cooperation and mutuality—one in which our minds can gather and collect the best thinking for the way forward. We need a theology of time that allows deep consideration and reflection to be part of the primary work that we are engaged in. Without such attention, our busyness and the strains of 'many things' will disrupt our creativity and the path forward will be remarkably similar to the pathways of the past which haven't worked for a long time. To see this change, we [all of us] need to take responsibility for the kind of deep, forward-thinking reflection that is required. Ward recounts a lesson he learned from Edmund Clowney, a former president of Westminster Theological Seminary. Ward tried to get out of a key question by stating that he was a social scientist and not a theologian. Clowney replied, "No, Ted, you're a Christian. I'm a Christian . . . therefore it's *our* question." Ward remarks on the indelible impression this discussion had on him:

> That probably did more to change me as an intellectual person than any other moment that I can put a finger on in my whole life, because it was then that I said, 'Okay, I cannot speak to theological education as it exists without accepting a share of the responsibility for why it is the way it is. Not just in terms of its structure and curriculum, but in terms of its substantive, theological character and its relationship to the church. I think it is part of any pilgrimage to recognize that the whole question of the development of leadership for the church is an everybody question within the community of Christ.[43]

SOLUTIONS AND THE WAY FORWARD

This chapter is not calling for a renewed denominational loyalty that rewinds to a period in Canadian church history where the ecclesial context

43. Ward and Cannell, "Theological Education," 46.

was closely aligned with the mission of the established (and sanctioned) theological institution that was tasked with the education of its clergy. Nor is this an effort to strengthen the hand of one or the other institutional partner in the ecclesial/seminary context. Rather, the solutions that are proposed have to do with *how* we relate to each other with respectful, creative, and aligned purposes.

Develop Deliberate Dialogue Patterns that Focus on the Future

It seems obvious from all that has been said that relationships between denominational executives, regional judicatories, and seminaries need to have a proper and regular forum for deep conversation about matters of importance to all. In his article on the ecology of church and seminaries in Canada, Wyatt notes that, "many schools are learning to 'listen to the church' by involving judicatory committees and congregational leaders in the discovery stage of curriculum revision."[44] This conversation, however, will only be helpful if it is oriented toward the future and not the past. Here is how the task force on seminaries and churches posed the way forward for deep conversations:

> Life as we knew it has changed, our world is different, and the pace of change in our North American culture is constantly accelerating. For the church to be a vital part of these changing communities, the church will have to be attentive. Too often our dialogue continues on outmoded assumptions about the needs of pastoral leadership in the church and how to prepare it. Yet just being attentive to the present is not enough. For that will leave us constantly beyond, always just missing the next era of young Christians. Thus, careful analysis of present needs as well as the attempt to predict future needs is called for.[45]

None of us have all the answers about the future of Christian leadership. However, the critical engagement of thoughtful leaders about trends, patterns, and mission-critical observations may indeed account for the kind of thinking that is required for both an effective ministerial formation and the adjustments to curricular offerings in the formal setting of theological

44. Wyatt, "The Canadian Ecology," 18. Wyatt notes the improvement and greater focus in curricular planning from seminaries on items of importance to the churches including leadership capacity, spirituality of the ministering person, and conflict management.

45. Rohrbough and Mendenhall, "Recommendations," 93–94.

education. These conversations can shape the future of both institutions giving fresh impetus to an educated and effective Christian leadership.

A significant study of the relation of churches to their sponsoring or founding denomination was conducted over the period of 2004–2008. One of the most fundamental findings of that study, though not a surprize to the researchers, "was that theological schools and congregations need to communicate more effectively with one another."[46] This is not simply highlighting the importance of better communication, but the need to "find new and creative ways . . . to work together to prepare leaders."[47] In his address to the ATS biennial gathering in 2008, Dan Aleshire called for a deep, intellectually engaged listening by seminaries to their ecclesial family of churches. Such listening moves beyond the practice of talking *past* each other to talking *with* those who have a vested interest in theological education and the training of ministry persons. "Pastors, lay persons, judicatory officers, seminary faculty, denominational leaders, and members of pastoral search committees [all have a stake in this]. People in all of these roles know part of the story, and it takes all of them together, in conversation over time, to get the full picture."[48] This creative work takes time and effort. The essential listening should be scheduled over a period of years with regular intervals of engagement, reflection, and mutual decision-making. The investment of personnel in the task of conversation will require a commitment to move out of our silos of activity to create room for honest dialogue and to create pathways for new ways of relating between denomination and seminary.

Collaborate with All Stakeholders in the Formation of Leaders for the Church

Isolationist strategies that seek to control or monopolize the 'corner on leadership development' for the church will falter. The costs are too high, and the resources are too thin to sustain such an approach. Seminaries will need to learn to take seriously the needs of the churches to which they are both formally and informally connected. The need for consultation with pastors and with denominational (both regional and national) offices, and a truly collaborative structure for curricular design are required in every

46. Graham, "Theological Schools," iv.
47. Graham, "Theological Schools," iv.
48. Aleshire, "Making Haste," 3.

sphere of Christian higher education. This will involve at least three key changes in the ways that such enterprises are currently operating:

1. We will need to set aside specific and regular time for deep conversation. Busyness is a major factor in contemporary organizations. While goodwill and mutual concern are present, it takes time to invest in conversations that will facilitate understanding and growth.

2. We will have to invent meaningful, collaborative programs for the education of Christian leaders. However, in order for the collaborative efforts to be meaningful they will have to be: (a) significant enough to justify the commitment of resources to these initiatives and (b) they will have to be mutually beneficial for both organizations.[49]

3. We will need to innovate around the changing situation of the church in culture. Our discussion strategies will have to be more sophisticated if we are going to get past the common impasses. Several scenarios are possible here. One scenario is that those involved fail to anticipate the problem. Or, it may be that the problem is noticed but not diagnosed properly. A third scenario fails to even try to solve the problem because of internal conflict of ideological interests. Finally, the organizations involved may see the problems involved but not have adequate resources to manage or alleviate them.

Intractable problems have many pitfalls. Our efforts to reimagine pastoral leadership training that benefits from both the support of a larger family of churches and the education resources entrusted to a seminary will require that we anticipate approaching problems, diagnose them correctly, overcome our prevailing ideologies that are getting in the way and share the resources at our disposal to overcome these challenges. Such effort will require new patterns of leadership at both the seminary and the denominational offices. It is important, if such talks are to succeed, that "process losses"[50] be considered and that meaningful and mutually enriching goals are established.

49. Tjosvod, "Cooperation Theory," 758. Tjosvod suggests that the terms 'collaboration' and 'competition' are charged with idealist connotations. He argues that both competition and collaboration may have benefits to organizations, but that the key to effective collaboration is that the ideas ventured are significant enough to benefit both organizations. Often collaboration fails because modest goals can be achieved more efficiently.

50. Tjosvold, "Cooperation Theory," 758. 'Process losses' include both efficiencies and quality of the ideas produced. 'Groupthink' can result in poor choices and, if the

Cultivate New Models of Theological Education and Leadership Formation

Arguing that contemporary theological schools must move beyond the 'school' paradigm, Theodore Brelsford of Emory University asks some probing questions:

> Might new models of religious education soon emerge for both clergy and laity? What kinds of formal or informal structures might develop for non-seminary or non-schooling clergy education? How might such structures impact models of education in congregations, and models of education in our seminaries and theological schools? How might our scholarship inform or be informed by such developments? How might these developments relate with curricular and pedagogical and structural challenges in seminaries and theology schools? In what ways and to what extent can scholars of religious education embrace and advocate (or even 'objectively' analyze) alternatives to the schooling model, given our dependence on that model?[51]

It behooves the twenty-something theological schools in Christian Higher Education Canada to consult with its direct constituency on matters that are of deep importance to the training and formation of ministry leaders. Weber advises, "Most faculties and administrators in theological schools would profit greatly by regularly listening to pastors talk about their work. If seminaries are really interested in discovering what transformational leadership means in local congregations, all they have to do is ask the men and women who have demonstrated such giftedness."[52]

Don't Buy into the Scarcity Paradigm

Parker Palmer invites us to move past the scarcity paradigm and to have a deep conviction about God's provision and abundance in the enterprise of theological education in the church. Palmer states,

> Daily I am astonished at how readily I believe that something I need is in short supply. If I hoard possessions, it is because I believe that there are not enough to go around. If I struggle with

---

goals are not significant or meaningful, they can result in the costly dedication of personnel and financial resources that might have been used more efficiently.

51. Brelsford, "Religious Education," 360.

52. Weber, "The Seminaries," 84.

others over power, it is because I believe that power is limited. If I become jealous in relationships, it is because I believe that when you get too much love, I will be short-changed. Even in writing this essay, I have had to struggle with the scarcity assumption. It is easy to stare at the blank page and despair of ever having another idea, another image, another illustration . . . The irony, often tragic, is that by embracing the scarcity assumption, we create the very scarcities we fear.[53]

Our efforts to establish God's rule and reign are not detached feats that erode our diminishing resources until they disappear. Rather our efforts unite among all those who are carried along by God's Spirit to establish God's kingdom and righteousness. It is a community effort of pastors and leaders, of denominational executives and seminary faculty, and of all believers who enact their contribution to an "incredibly complex ecology in which each part functions on behalf of the whole and, in return, is sustained by the whole. Community doesn't just create abundance—community is abundance."[54]

CONCLUSION

I happen to like denominations very much. They can form a creative cluster of like-minded congregations who have a deep sense of journeying together towards something greater than a local church. The importance of belonging, of having a sense of home, and deliberately aligning one's ministry with something larger is critical in a world of lost connections, aimlessness, and truncated missions. At the same time, denominations can become very clingy, separate, and isolated. There can be a false sense of completeness that fails to take seriously the other ways that God is at work through the church to accomplish His purposes. Aleshire offers a prediction that has impact on the way we might conceive of the future of Christian higher education:

> Most theological schools will still have more mission than money, will have more tasks to do than can be done, and will do most of them better than anyone thinks that they can be done. They will accomplish their missions by the dedication and competence of faculty and staff. They will have re-defined their missions to fit their work effectively in a culture in which religion does not

53. Palmer, *Let Your Life Speak*, 107.
54. Palmer, *Let Your Life Speak*, 108.

enjoy much cultural privilege. The most robust forms of theological education will be deeply missional and entrepreneurial which
is the very way that theological education has been conducted in
cultures that have been less friendly to Christianity.[55]

Pastors and those who are ably ministering on the ground have much to
teach us. We need to be good listeners and create regular forums for the
engagement of real problems, life-on-the-ground-scenarios, and the establishment of new markers for ministry in an increasingly complex cultural
context. Ministry is exacting and demanding. It requires our full attention
and all of the resources that have been gathered and accumulated in the
storehouses of the church need to be called forth to serve the needs of the
actual situation of the churches that are within our sphere. The ecology of
church, seminary, and denomination is vital. It is changing, but it is still
vital. I hope that this chapter will stimulate fresh imagination for the future
of such important and missional enterprises.

BIBLIOGRAPHY

Aleshire, Daniel O. "Making Haste Slowly: Celebrating the Future of Theological Schools."
Theological Education 44 (2008) 1–9.
———. "The Future of Theological Education: A Speculative Glimpse at 2032." *Dialog: A
Journal of Theology* 50 (Winter 2011) 380–85.
———. "Wilderness: The Changing Seminary and Church." *Schaff Lecture* 2, Pittsburgh
Theological Seminary, March 2010. Online: https://www.ats.edu/uploads/resources/
publications-presentations/documents/aleshire-schaff-lecture-2-wilderness.pdf
Ammerman, Nancy T. "New Life for Denominationalism." *Christian Century* 117.9
(March 2000) 1–5.
Beardsall, Sandra. "The Church/Theological School Relationship in Canada: A Reflection
on Historical and Recent Trends." *Theological Education* 44 (2008) 43–64.
Benefiel, Ron. "The Ecology of Evangelical Seminaries." *Theological Education* 44 (2008)
21–28.
Bibby, Reginald W. "Post-Christendom in Canada? Not So Fast." *Journal for Post-
Christendom Studies* 1 (2016) 125–41.
Brelsford, Theodore. "Religious Education Beyond the Schooling Model." *Religious
Education* 100 (2005) 357–61.
Brown, Eliza Smith. "Did you Know . . . " No pages. https://www.ats.edu/uploads/
resources/publications-presentations/documents/seminary-students-over-50.pdf
Brown, Eliza Smith, and Chris Meinzer. "New Data Reveal Stable Enrolment but Shifting
Trends at ATS Member Schools." *Association of Theological Schools, The Commission
on Accrediting* (2016) 1–2. Online: https://www.ats.edu/uploads/resources/
publications-presentations/colloquy-online/new-data-reveal-stable-enrollment.pdf

55. Aleshire, "The Future of Theological Education," 384.

Cannell, Linda, and Ted Ward. "Theological Education and the Church." *Christian Education Journal* 3 (1999) 29–47.

Carter, Kenneth, Jr., et al. "Disruption and Leadership Development in Mainline Protestantism." *Faith and Leadership* (March 2014). No Pages. Online: https://www.faithandleadership.com/disruption-and-leadership-development-mainline-protestantism.

Chaves, Mark, and Alison Eagle. *Religious Congregations in 21st Century America: National Congregations Study* (2015) 1–2. Online: http://www.soc.duke.edu/natcong/Docs/NCSIII_report_final.pdf.

Coffman, Elesha. "Are We Entering the End Times for Mainline Seminaries?" *Religion Dispatches* (August 2016). No Pages. Online: http://religiondispatches.org/are-we-entering-the-end-time-for-mainline-seminaries/

Dockery, David S. "Toward a Future for Christian Higher Education: Learning from the Past, Looking to the Future." *Christian Higher Education* 15 (2016) 115–19.

Glanzer, Perry L., et al. "Assessing the Denominational Identity of American Evangelical Colleges and Universities, Part I: Denominational Patronage and Institutional Policy." *Christian Higher Education* 12 (2013) 181–202.

———. "Assessing the Denominational Identity of American Evangelical Colleges and Universities, Part II: Faculty Perspectives and Practices." *Christian Higher Education* 12 (2013) 243–65.

———. "Assessing the Denominational Identity of American Evangelical Colleges and Universities, Part III: The Student Experience." *Christian Higher Education* 12 (2013) 315–30.

Kinney, John W. "Theological Education and the Needs of Students and the Church." *Faith and Leadership* (October 2017). No Pages. Online: https://www.faithandleadership.com/john-w-kinney-theological-education-and-needs-students-and-church.

Leath, Jeffrey. "The Craving for Truth." *Faith and Leadership* (April 2010). No Pages. Online: https://www.faithandleadership.com/jeffrey-leath-craving-truth.

Lynn, Elizabeth, and Barbara G. Wheeler. "Missing Connections: Public Perceptions of Theological Education and Religious Leadership." *Auburn Studies* 6 (1999) 4–5.

Odom, David L. "Cultivating a Denomi-network." *Faith and Leadership* (July 2014). No Pages. Online: https://www.faithandleadership.com/cultivating-denomi-network.

Pacaia, Leon. "The Presidential Experience in Theological Education: A Study of Executive Leadership." *Theological Education* 29 (1992) 11–38.

Palmer, Parker. *Let Your Life Speak: Listening for the Voice of Vocation.* San Francisco: Jossey-Bass, 2000.

Rohrbough, Faith E., and Laura Mendenhall. "Recommendations of the Task Force of the Theological Schools and the Church Project." *Theological Education* 44 (2008) 93–96.

Roozen, David A. *A Decade of Change in American Congregations 2000–2010.* No Pages. Online: http://faithcommunitiestoday.org/sites/default/files/Decade of Change Final_0.pdf.

Ruger, Anthony. "Lean Years Fat Years: Changes in the Financial Support of Protestant Theological Education." *Auburn Studies* 2 (1994) 1–5.

Ruger, Anthony T., and Barbara G. Wheeler. "The Big Picture: Strategic Choices for Theological Schools." *Auburn Studies* 7 (2000) 1–28.

Scharen, Christian. "Vocational Formation for Ministry: The Need for Contextual Reflection." *Bread* 33 (2013) 406–8.

Tjosvold, Dean. "Cooperation Theory and Organizations." *Human Relations* 37 (1984) 743–67.
Weber, Timothy P. "The Seminaries and the Churches: Looking for New Relationships." *Theological Education* 44 (2008) 65–91.
Wyatt, Peter. "The Canadian Ecology." *Theological Education* 44 (2008) 15–20.

Appendix A

ATS Statistics

Fall	CANADA Schools	CANADA HC	CANADA FTE	USA Schools	USA HC	USA FTE	Total Schools	Total HC	Total FTE
2001	38	6,254	3,343	200	67,293	44,904	238	73,547	48,247
2002	37	6,643	3,512	204	69,376	44,395	241	76,019	47,907
2003	36	6,925	3,654	205	71,284	46,285	241	78,209	49,938
2004	36	7,036	3,597	213	73,214	47,874	249	80,250	51,471
2005	36	6,939	3,518	217	73,135	47,873	253	80,074	51,392
2006	36	6,383	3,198	215	73,604	46,804	251	79,987	50,003
2007	35	5,893	3,063	214	72,989	46,686	249	78,882	49,748
2008	36	5,814	3,079	212	70,531	44,058	248	76,345	47,137
2009	36	5,719	3,023	212	69,377	44,501	248	75,096	47,524
2010	39	5,466	2,969	219	70,285	44,745	258	75,751	47,714
2011	39	5,362	2,770	219	68,891	44,776	258	74,253	47,545
2012	39	5,122	2,663	230	68,960	43,756	269	74,082	46,419
2013	40	5,231	2,827	226	67,427	42,548	266	72,658	45,374
2014	40	5,100	2,683	231	66,690	41,961	271	71,790	44,644
2015	39	5,213	2,703	230	66,867	41,816	269	72,080	44,519
2016	39	5,263	2,768	234	67,120	43,069	273	72,383	45,836
2017	39	5,268	2,787	231	67,907	43,262	270	73,175	46,049

Appendix B

Enrolment in ATS Schools in Canada
by Denomination (2017)

Denominational Enrollment, Canada, Fall 2017 Statistics provided by the Association of Theological Schools of the United States and Canada	
	Enrollments
African Methodist Episcopal	3
American Baptist Churches USA	3
Anglican Church of Canada	218
Anglican, Other	167
Assemblies of God	31
Associate Reformed Presbyterian Church	1
Associated Gospel Churches of Canada	40
Baptist	182
Baptist Missionary Association of America	1
Brethren in Christ Church	40
Buddhist	24
Byzantine Catholic	15
Canadian Baptists of Ontario and Quebec	51
Canadian Baptist of Western Canada	45
Canadian Baptists of Atlantic Canada	112
Canadian National Baptist Convention	27
Canadian Reformed Churches	28

Christian and Missionary Alliance	258
Christian Brethren (Plymouth Brethren)	8
Christian Church (Disciples of Christ)	5
Christian Churches and Churches of Christ	19
Christian Reformed Church	49
Church of God (Anderson, Indiana)	3
Church of God in Christ	2
Church of the Brethren	4
Church of the Nazarene	12
Churches of Christ	12
Churches of God, General Conference	6
Conference of Mennonites	5
Converge Worldwide	6
Episcopal Church	22
Evangelical Church in Canada	35
Evangelical Congregational Church	5
Evangelical Covenant Church	9
Evangelical Formosan Church	3
Evangelical Free Church of America	6
Evangelical Free Church of Canada	78
Evangelical Lutheran Church in America	2
Evangelical Lutheran Church in Canada	26
Evangelical Presbyterian Church	5
Fellowship of Evangelical Baptist Churches in Canada	178
Foursquare Gospel Church	2
Free Methodist Church	27
Friends, Quaker	1
General Association of General Baptists	4
General Association of Regular Baptist Churches	3
Independent Baptist	4
Independent Methodist	3
Inter/Multidenominational	21
Jewish	4
Korean American Presbyterian Church	78
Korean Evangelical Holiness Church	2

Lutheran Church-Canada	36
Lutheran Church-Missouri Synod	3
Lutheran, Other	18
Mennonite Brethren Church in North America	87
Mennonite Church Canada	33
Mennonite, Other	19
Missionary Church in Canada	26
Moravian Church in North America	1
Muslim	30
National Baptist Convention	1
Nondenominational	263
North American Baptist Conference	37
Orthodox Church in America	4
Orthodox, Other	15
Other	1259
Pentecostal Assemblies of Canada	239
Presbyterian Church (U.S.A.)	9
Presbyterian Church in America	11
Presbyterian Church in Canada	156
Presbyterian Church International	17
Reformed Church in America	2
Reformed Church in Canada	5
Reformed Episcopal Church	2
Reformed Presbyterian	2
Roman Catholic	655
Salvation Army	37
Seventh Day Baptist General Conference	1
Seventh-day Adventist	14
Southern Baptist Convention	14
Unitarian Universalist	11
United Church of Canada	203
United Church of Christ	49
United Methodist Church	11
United Pentecostal Church International	7
Wesleyan Church	14

Modern Authors Index